Intelligent Systems and Industrial Internet of Things for Sustainable Development

The book studies emerging and sustaining technologies for applications of Industry 5.0 to develop technological solutions to address numerous real-life challenges to solve sustainable development-related issues. It identifies limitations, pitfalls, and open research questions in Industry 5.0, discusses real-time problems, and challenges with equivalent solutions with a focus on sustainable growth to develop, humanization and environmentally friendly intelligent system applications. It analyzes applications enabled by Industry 5.0 such as healthcare, supply chain, smart framing, remote sensing, production in manufacturing, and cloud manufacturing. It also includes the difficulties and problems posed by the organization between robots and humans on the assembly line to maintain sustainability.

- Addresses key challenges in implementing intelligent systems in IoT-based applications, including issues ranging from cost and energy efficiency to availability and quality of service
- Explores the technologies to allow human–machine association and its impact on consumption and sustainability
- Provides sustainable solutions to emerging industrial problems, especially in healthcare, manufacturing, remote sensing, environmental engineering
- Examines the need for data pre-processing, classification and prediction, cluster analysis, mining multimedia, text, and web data, and advanced machine learning techniques for scientific programming in Industry
- Presents success stories in the form of case studies of IIoT, IIoRT, Big Data, Intelligent Systems, and Deep Learning in the Industry 5.0 era.

The text is for postgraduate students, professionals, and academic researchers working in the fields of computer science and information technology, especially for professionals and researchers interested in the technological side of sustainable development.

Digital Technologies and Innovative Solutions for Sustainable Development Series

Intelligent Systems and Industrial Internet of Things for Sustainable Development
C. Kishor Kumar Reddy, P. R. Anisha, Marlia Mohd. Hanafiah, Srinath Doss, Kari Lippert

For more information on this series please visit: https://www.routledge.com/Digital-Technologies
-and-Innovative-Solutions-for-Sustainable-Development/book-series/DTISSD

Intelligent Systems and Industrial Internet of Things for Sustainable Development

Edited by
C. Kishor Kumar Reddy,
P. R. Anisha,
Marlia Mohd Hanafiah,
Srinath Doss,
Kari Lippert

CRC Press
Taylor & Francis Group
Boca Raton London New York

CRC Press is an imprint of the
Taylor & Francis Group, an **informa** business

A CHAPMAN & HALL BOOK

Designed cover image: ©ShutterStock Images

First edition published 2024
by CRC Press
2385 NW Executive Center Drive, Suite 320, Boca Raton FL 33431

and by CRC Press
4 Park Square, Milton Park, Abingdon, Oxon, OX14 4RN

CRC Press is an imprint of Taylor & Francis Group, LLC

© 2024 selection and editorial matter, C. Kishor Kumar Reddy, P. R. Anisha, Marlia Mohd. Hanafiah, Srinath Doss, Kari Lippert; individual chapters, the contributors

ISBN: 9781032640914 (hbk)
ISBN: 9781032642772 (pbk)
ISBN: 9781032642789 (ebk)

DOI: 10.1201/9781032642789

Typeset in Times
by Deanta Global Publishing Services, Chennai, India

Contents

Editors

C. Kishor Kumar Reddy is currently working as Associate Professor in the Department of Computer Science and Engineering, Stanley College of Engineering and Technology for Women, Hyderabad, India. He has research and teaching experience of more than ten years. He has published more than 50 research papers in national and international conferences, book chapters, and journals indexed by SCIE, Scopus, and others. He is the author of two textbooks and two co-edited books. He acted as the special session chair for Springer FICTA 2020, 2022, SCI 2021, INDIA 2022, and IEEE ICCSEA 2020 conferences. He is the corresponding editor of the AMSE 2021 conferences, published by IoP Science JPCS. He is a member of ISTE, CSI, IAENG, UACEE, and IACSIT.

P. R. Anisha, TEDx Speaker, is currently working as Associate Professor in the Deptartment of Computer Science and Engineering, Stanley College of Engineering and Technology for Women, Hyderabad, India. She holds a teaching experience of more than nine years. She received her Doctoral Degree from K. L. University, Guntur, India. Her areas of interest includes artificial intelligence, machine learning, and image processing. She has had 35+ research articles published in international conferences and journals. She has co-authored two books named *Introduction to C and C++ Programming*. She has acted as the special session chair for International Conferences for Springer—INDIA 2019, 2022, SCI 2021, and FICTA 2020, 2022, and for the IEEE conference ICCSEA 2020. She is a member of ACM and IAENG professional bodies.

Marlia Mohd Hanafiah is Professor and Head of the Centre for Tropical Climate Change System, Institute of Climate Change, The National University of Malaysia, Malaysia. Areas of research expertise include life cycle impact assessment (LCA) and environmental foot printing of green materials and energy, environmental engineering, wastewater treatment and water management, green technology, and sustainability. She has a total academic teaching experience of 15+ years with more than 170 publications in reputed journals and online book chapter contributions (indexed by: SCI, SCIE, SSCI, Scopus, DBLP). She received a research grant and consultation (as project leader and team member) of more than RM 7 million.

Srinath Doss is Professor and Dean in the Faculty of Engineering and Technology, Botho University, responsible for Botswana, Lesotho, Eswatini, Namibia, and Ghana campuses. He has previously worked with various reputed engineering colleges in India, and with Garyounis University, Libya. He has written a number of books and more than 80 papers in international journals and attended several prestigious conferences. His research interests include MANET, information security, network security and cryptography, artificial intelligence, cloud computing and wireless and sensor networks. He serves as an editorial member and reviewer for reputed international journals, and an advisory member for various prestigious conferences. Srinath is a member of IAENG and an associate member of UACEE.

Kari Lippert is Assistant Professor at the University of South Alabama, USA. Kari received her D.Sc. from the University of South Alabama in 2018, her Ph.D. in 2012, and MS from Johns Hopkins University in 2002. She is an instructor and subject matter expert bringing deep expertise in systems engineering, data science, and cyber analysis and significant experience teaching undergraduate and graduate students. She has a diverse industry background across analytical science, digital network exploitation, programming, systems architecture and design, mathematics, medicinal chemistry, protein folding, big data analysis, and research for well-known organizations and agencies.

Contributors

Nedumaran A
Kombolcha Institute of Technology,
    Wollo University
Ethiopia

Saleem Raja A
University of Technology and Applied
    Sciences
Oman

Ramesh Kumar Ayyasamy
Universiti Tunku Abdul Rahman
Malaysia

Santosh Kumar B
New Horizon College of Engineering
India

Shaik Mohammad Rafi B
Rajiv Gandhi University of Knowledge
    Technologies—R K Valley Campus
India

Sundaravadivazhagan B
University of Technology and Applied
    Sciences
Sultanate of Oman

Rithika Badam
Stanley College of Engineering &
    Technology for Women
India

Mohamed Imran Kareem Basha
Merit Haji Ismail Sahib, Arts and
    Science College
India

Swathi Baswaraju
New Horizon College of Engineering
India

Almas Begum
Saveetha School of Engineering,
    Saveetha Institute of Medical and
    Technical Sciences
India

Ramana Murthy B V
Stanley College of Engineering and
    Technology for Women
India

Nisarga Chand
Adamas University
India

Hemalatha D
Vel Tech Rangarajan Dr Sagunthala
    R&D Institute of Science and
    Technology
India

Ayontika Das
Adamas University
India

Srinath Doss
Botho University
Botswana

Elakkiya Elango
Government Arts college for Women
India

Aravind G
Rajiv Gandhi University of Knowledge
    Technologies—R K Valley Campus
India

Ayyappan G
Saveetha School of Engineering,
    Saveetha Institute of Medical and
    Technical Sciences
India

Ramesh G
Rajiv Gandhi University of Knowledge
    Technologies—R K Valley Campus
India

Madhuri Atmaram Gurale
Dr. D. Y. Patil College of Engineering
India

Vijay Arputharaj J
CHRIST (Deemed to be University)
India

Senthil K
Saveetha School of Engineering,
    Saveetha Institute of Medical and
    Technical Sciences
India

Arijit Karati
National Yat-Sen University
Taiwan

Balasubramanian Prabhu Kavin
SRM Institute of Science and
    Technology
India

Vijaya Sindhoori Kaza
Stanley College of Engineering &
    Technology for Women
India

Carmel Mary Belinda M J
Saveetha School of Engineering,
    Saveetha Institute of Medical and
    Technical Sciences
India

Anindya Nag
Khulna University
Bangladesh

Anisha P R
Stanley College of Engineering &
    Technology for Women
India

Rachana Yogesh Patil
Pimpri Chinchwad College of
    Engineering
India

Yogesh H. Patil
Dr. D. Y. Patil College of
    Engineering
India

Nilanjana Roy
Adamas University
India

Althaf S
Rajiv Gandhi University of
    Knowledge Technologies—
    R K Valley Campus
India

Ramesh Kumar S
SASTRA University
India

Santhosh Kumar S
SASTRA University
India

Sivagami S
Saveetha School of Engineering,
    Saveetha Institute of Medical and
    Technical Sciences
India

Anwesa Sarkar
Adamas University
India

Moyuri Sen
Adamas University
India

Gan Hong Seng
XJTLU Entrepreneur College
    (Taicang), Xi'an Jiaotong—
    Liverpool University
China

Balasubramanian Shanmuganathan
Alagappa University
India

Tarunika Sharma
New Horizon College of Engineering
India

Arunadevi Thirumalraj
K.Ramakrishnan College of Technology
India

Vinay U
Rajiv Gandhi University of Knowledge
    Technologies—R K Valley Campus
India

Anusuya Devi V S
New Horizon College of Engineering
India

Rishi S Vagadia
CHRIST (Deemed to be University)
India

Joanna Mariam Varkey
CHRIST (Deemed to be University)
India

1 Industry 5.0
Empowering Collaboration through Advanced Technological Approaches

Yogesh H. Patil, Rachana Yogesh Patil,
Madhuri Atmaram Gurale, and Arijit Karati

1.1 INTRODUCTION

Industry 4.0 has significantly transformed the digital infrastructure, which is characterized by the integration of the Internet of Things (IoT), cyber-physical systems, and advanced data analytics [1]. The innovative practices of Industry 4.0 have led to substantial improvements in manufacturing efficiency and product quality [2]. Emphasizing techno-economic development, Industry 4.0 drove the implementation of emerging technologies at an industrial scale, facilitating agile value chains and adaptive responses to evolving market demands [3–6].

The advent of Industry 5.0, introduces a paradigm shift, integrating autonomous manufacturing with human intelligence [7, 8]. This technological progression poses challenges to businesses and industries, even as global deployment and integration of Industry 4.0 continue. The inception of Industry 5.0 emerges concurrently with the adoption of Industry 4.0, resulting in a seamless continuum of industrial advancement [9]. Industry 5.0 represents an era of collaborative man–machine production, where human ingenuity harmoniously combines with automated systems. Despite the transformative potential of Industry 4.0, certain concerns have arisen regarding its environmental impact and social implications in the workplace [10].

As the landscape transitions toward Industry 5.0, the convergence of cutting-edge technologies and human intelligence necessitates strategic considerations. Addressing technological challenges, ensuring seamless human–machine collaboration, and optimizing systems for productivity, reliability, and safety will be pivotal in harnessing the complete perspective of Industry 5.0 in driving technological, economic, and societal advancements. Embracing Industry 5.0 requires a comprehensive approach that balances technical prowess with ethical and sustainable practices, thereby shaping a future of enhanced industrial capabilities and positive societal impact.

DOI: 10.1201/9781032642789-1

Industry 5.0 represents a huge move toward a human-centric approach, addressing the challenges and limitations of Industry 4.0 through the collaboration of workers at the core of the production process [11]. The formal introduction of Industry 5.0 occurred through a document released by the European Commission (EC) in January 2021, following comprehensive online brainstorming sessions held in 2020. The primary objective of the EC's initiative is to catalyze sustainable and human-centered transformations in the business and industrial sectors, in alignment with European societal goals, including environmental protection, worker safety, job creation, and resilient economic growth [12–14].

Distinct from the digitalization focus of Industry 4.0, Industry 5.0 stands on three foundational pillars: resilience, sustainability, and human centricity [15]. It aims to fully exploit the potential of human–machine collaboration, where operators collaboratively work alongside and receive support from advanced digital technology. In intelligent manufacturing environments, Industry 5.0 fosters interactive cooperation between human operators and machinery, optimizing productivity while ensuring equitable and sustainable workspaces. The widespread implementation of Industry 5.0 across industries is projected to drive positive transformations and promote the overall well-being of workers in the dynamic production landscape.

In this chapter, we conducted an in-depth study of the pivotal role played by various technologies in Industry 5.0. In essence, Industry 5.0 represents a transformative set of technological practices that foster seamless cooperation between humans and machines, resulting in an advanced and highly efficient production environment.

1.1.1 Advancement from Industry 1.0 to Industry 5.0

The evolution of industrial revolutions has been a transformative journey for mankind, spanning over 200 years and reshaping the world's economic and societal landscape. The journey began with Industry 1.0, the "Steam Age," where water steam-powered equipment ushered in the first wave of industrialization, accompanied by the introduction of market dynamics and significant social and economic changes [16].

Industry 2.0, often referred to as the "Electric Age," emerged as a transitional phase driven by the pivotal role of energy in generating electric power. This phase brought about clear divisions of labor and laid the foundation for the production assembly line [17].

Industry 3.0 emerged with mass customization at the IT level, enabling more personalized production approaches [18]. Subsequently, Industry 4.0 marked the convergence of IT and OT in a cyber-physical system.

Now, Industry 5.0 represents the pinnacle of this evolutionary journey, symbolizing the fusion of human intelligence and subjectivity with artificial intelligence (AI), efficiency, and precision of machines [19]. This remarkable integration reflects the essence of humanistic care and signifies the evolution toward human–machine collaboration.

The entire journey of industrial revolutions has been fueled by science and technological innovations, replacing ignorance with progress and opening new possibilities. Capital surged forward, unleashing waves of revolutionary industrialization.

1.2 THE ROLE OF ADVANCED TECHNOLOGIES IN INDUSTRY 5.0

Industry 5.0 is predicated upon a wide range of sophisticated technologies that fundamentally transform the manufacturing domain [20]. This chapter explores the significant role that these technologies play in facilitating the transition toward a collaborative and intelligent manufacturing environment.

1.2.1 ADVANCED ROBOTICS AND AUTOMATION

Advanced robotics and automation have emerged as crucial components in the context of Industry 5.0, exerting a significant influence on the transformation of production processes and the enhancement of operational efficiency. This chapter delves into the significant influence exerted by these technologies and their capacity to affect the trajectory of industrial output in the future, as shown in Figure 1.1.

In recent times, there has been notable progress in the domain of automation and robotics, resulting in a heightened concentration on the relationship between humans and robots [21]. Collaborative robots, also referred to as cobots, have arisen as a revolutionary technological advancement aimed at operating in conjunction with human operators, hence augmenting production efficiency and capacity. These collaborative robots utilize sophisticated AI and intelligent technologies, allowing for

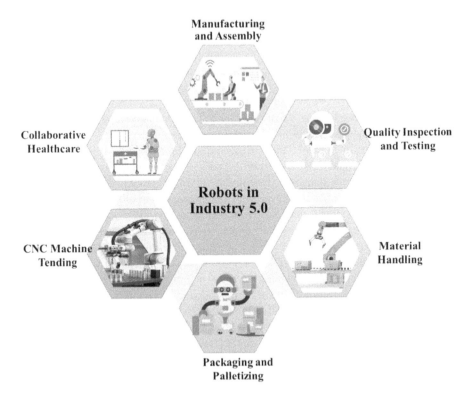

FIGURE 1.1 Role of robotics and automation in Industry 5.0

flexibility and continuous learning, hence enabling them to effectively respond in dynamic settings. Cobots, characterized by their user-friendly interfaces and simplified programmability, serve to democratize the field of automation, hence increasing their accessibility to individuals and small organizations. The inherent adaptability of these entities enables them to effectively manage intricate assignments, therefore liberating human laborers to concentrate on higher-level facets of the manufacturing process. Collaborative robots possess considerable potential for utilization across several industries, facilitating enhanced operational efficiency and promoting a safer working environment [22].

Nevertheless, despite the considerable potential of the partnership between people and cobots, there are still enduring obstacles in ensuring safety in human–robot contact, safeguarding data privacy, and achieving seamless integration. Continual research and development endeavors play a crucial role in maximizing the capabilities of cobots and effectively addressing the aforementioned problems [23]. As technology continues to evolve, collaborative robots are poised to revolutionize industries, paving the way for a future of innovative human–robot cooperation and redefining the landscape of work.

The inception of cobots can be traced back to 1996 when Northwestern University developed the first prototypes. These early cobots lacked motors, were operated passively, and incorporated brakes during operation. However, the evolution of cobots has been remarkable, setting them apart from traditional industrial robots by enabling direct collaboration with humans without the need for safety enclosures [24]. Modern cobots are equipped with embedded sensors that make them highly responsive to unforeseen impacts. This responsiveness allows them to spontaneously halt their movements when they detect any dropped objects along their path. Consequently, cobots have earned a reputation for exceptional reliability and safety in the workplace, surpassing standard industrial robots [25]. Their ability to detect and respond to unpredictable situations makes them valuable allies in ensuring a secure and harmonious human–robot working environment.

Robots have proven highly efficient in the manufacturing of high-volume products, surpassing human capabilities in certain aspects. However, they lack critical thinking abilities, posing challenges in customization and personalization of products, where human guidance becomes essential. The management of human connections within production processes becomes crucial in achieving success in Industry 5.0.

Cobots have emerged as valuable assets in Industry 5.0. Their collaboration enables the delivery of mass personalized and customized products with remarkable accuracy and speed. In the medical field, cobots play a transformative role, providing medical treatments, summarizing patients' health data, and creating fully customized health fitness routines. In surgical applications, cobots, exemplified by the Davinci surgical system, work hand in hand with highly skilled doctors, enhancing surgical capabilities and benefiting medical centers in urology, gynecology, etc. [25].

The role of cobots fosters a new connection between machines and humans, improving safety, performance, and providing more engaging responsibilities for human workers. Embracing cobot technology represents a significant step toward shaping a more productive and efficient future in Industry 5.0.

1.2.2 THE IoT AND CONNECTIVITY

In Industry 5.0, the IoT and connectivity play integral roles in driving transformative changes and enhancing industrial processes. The IoT refers to a network of networked devices, sensors, and systems that are capable of collecting and exchanging data [26]. This connection enables smooth and continuous communication between these many components.

Industry 5.0's IoT integration ushers in a new era of intelligent production where machines, equipment, and even goods can communicate and collaborate in real time. Predictive maintenance, optimization, and resource allocation are possible due to system interconnectivity [27]. The IoT helps create a flexible, responsive production environment. Intelligent sensors in machinery can detect deviations from expected patterns, monitor operational efficiency, and automate actions to ensure smooth operation. The described connectedness helps create a dynamic and adaptable production environment that can adapt to changing market needs and customer preferences. The applications of the IoT in Industry 5.0 are represented in Figure 1.2.

In the context of Industry 5.0, the IoT enables continuous and uninterrupted connection that surpasses the boundaries of the production environment. The integration of the complete supply chain is achieved, encompassing the many stages from the acquisition of raw materials to the final delivery of the product. This integration facilitates comprehensive visibility and traceability throughout the entire process.

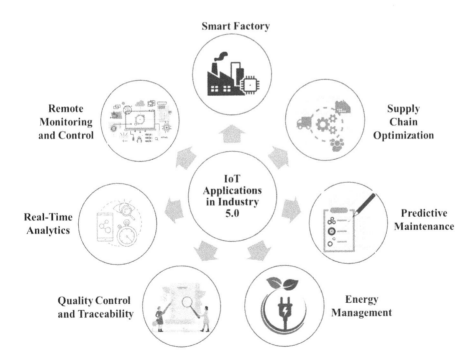

FIGURE 1.2 Applications of the IoT in Industry 5.0

The integration of various components improves the efficiency of the supply chain, resulting in reduced lead times and less wastage [28]. Consequently, this integration contributes to the establishment of a more sustainable and economically viable process.

The implementation of mass customization on a broad scale can be facilitated by the integration of the IoT and connectivity in the context of Industry 5.0. The capacity to collect up-to-date data regarding client preferences and behavior facilitates the provision of individualized products and customized services, hence augmenting customer pleasure and fostering loyalty [29].

The preservation of security and data privacy has the utmost importance within the interconnected realm of Industry 5.0. It is imperative to establish robust cybersecurity protocols in order to ensure the protection of sensitive data and mitigate potential cyber threats. Manufacturers must prioritize data integrity and implement encryption and authentication protocols to ensure a secure IoT ecosystem.

Efficiency in the supply chain is a key challenge in Industry 5.0, and the IoT provides a powerful solution. Leveraging IoT technologies enables industries to optimize production processes, and achieve greater operational efficiency.

The rapid development of the IoT has facilitated wireless information sharing between individuals through the utilization of wireless sensors. For instance, in the domain of the Internet of Medical Things, sensors attached to patients detect abnormalities and transmit real-time data to healthcare professionals. This enables prompt and well-informed actions based on the received information.

1.2.3 Artificial Intelligence and Machine Learning

AI and machine learning (ML) are the fundamental drivers of Industry 5.0, revolutionizing industrial processes with intelligent and data-centric approaches, as shown in Figure 1.3. In this industrial paradigm, AI-driven decision-making and predictive maintenance form the bedrock of operational excellence. By analyzing real-time data from diverse sources, including sensors and IoT devices, AI algorithms make informed decisions and optimize resource allocation. Predictive maintenance, enabled by ML models, anticipates equipment failures, reducing downtime and enhancing reliability [30].

Industry 5.0 embraces autonomous systems and self-optimizing processes, powered by AI and ML. Autonomous robots and machines operate without constant human intervention, adapting to real-time data and environmental changes. These systems optimize tasks like material handling, assembly, and quality control, boosting efficiency and precision. Additionally, self-optimizing processes continually analyze data with AI algorithms, identifying areas for improvement and adjusting parameters in real time [31]. This self-optimization maximizes productivity, reduces waste, and optimizes resource usage.

AI also thrives in collaborative workflows within Industry 5.0, where humans and machines work synergistically. Collaborative robots exemplify this application. Cobots collaborate safely with human workers, complementing their skills. AI empowers cobots to adapt actions based on human inputs and safety considerations,

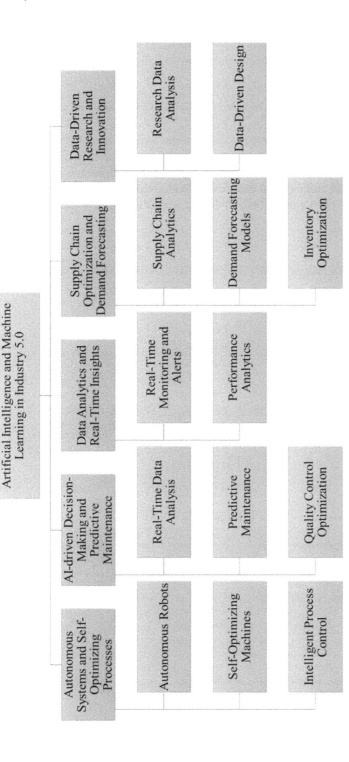

FIGURE 1.3 Artificial intelligence and machine learning in Industry 5.0

ensuring efficiency and safety [32, 33]. Moreover, AI optimizes workflows by analyzing data on worker performance, preferences, and expertise. Intelligent task allocation and resource management streamline collaborative workflows, increasing
productivity.

1.2.4 BIG DATA ANALYTICS

Big Data Analytics has emerged as a prominent topic of interest in both industry
and academia, encompassing a vast and diverse collection of data from various
sources [34]. Its analysis involves cutting-edge technologies such as ML, AI, social
networking, data mining, and data fusion. Within the context of Industry 5.0, Big
Data Analytics plays a pivotal role in driving innovation and efficiency, as shown in
Figure 1.4.

FIGURE 1.4   Role of Big Data Analytics in Industry 5.0

Companies in Industry 5.0 employ Big Data Analytics to reduce costs across the board by optimizing product prices, production efficiencies, and administrative expenses. to learn about their customers' habits [35]. Challenges arise, however, when trying to make sense of user behavior, social interactions, and human behavior patterns in this setting. To gain actionable insights from the mountains of data available in the Industry 5.0 era, the ability to untangle these interdependencies is crucial.

Industry 5.0 companies can fully capitalize on data-driven decision-making when they apply cutting-edge Big Data Analytics techniques. Predictive modeling, real-time data processing, and anomaly detection are all made possible through the combination of ML and AI technologies; these allow for preventive maintenance and quick reactions to shifting market conditions. When multiple data sets are combined through data fusion, a more complete picture of the industrial ecosystem can be gleaned.

Industry 5.0's emphasis on connectivity, automation, and collaboration further amplifies the significance of Big Data Analytics. Extracting actionable insights from massive datasets facilitates process optimization, resource allocation, and personalized customer experiences. Moreover, as Industry 5.0 drives the convergence of physical and digital realms, Big Data Analytics becomes a driving force for unlocking the potential of intelligent manufacturing and industrial systems

Certain companies like Facebook, Twitter, and LinkedIn utilize Big Data Analytics to leverage consumer satisfaction data for product promotion and increased sales. In the Industry 5.0 ecosystem, data infusion, customized manufacturing, and smart automation are pivotal for seamless operations. Big Data Analytics plays a crucial role in making real-time decisions, providing predictive insights for major events, and enhancing industries' competitive edge in Industry 5.0 applications.

The collaboration between smart systems and real-time analytical data empowers manufacturers to handle and process large volumes of data efficiently. To meet the constant process upgrade demands of Industry 5.0, detailed information from throughout the manufacturing cycle must be collected. By employing Big Data Analytics techniques, manufacturers can identify and eliminate non-essential elements, maximizing predictability and exploring new opportunities for innovation. By harnessing the power of Big Data Analytics, Industry 5.0 enterprises can drive agility, productivity, and predictive capabilities, transforming the industrial landscape for a data-driven future.

1.2.5   DIGITAL TWIN

A Digital Twin (DT) refers to a digital replication of a physical system or object. This concept, proposed as early as 2002, has materialized in recent years, pushed by the proliferation of the IoT [36]. Various real-world entities as shown in Figure 1.5, ranging from wind farms, factories, and jet engines to entire smart cities, can now be digitally characterized through DTs [37]. The rise of the IoT has made DTs cost-effective and accessible to many industries, as data from physical objects are collected through IoT devices and served to their digital counterparts for simulation and analysis.

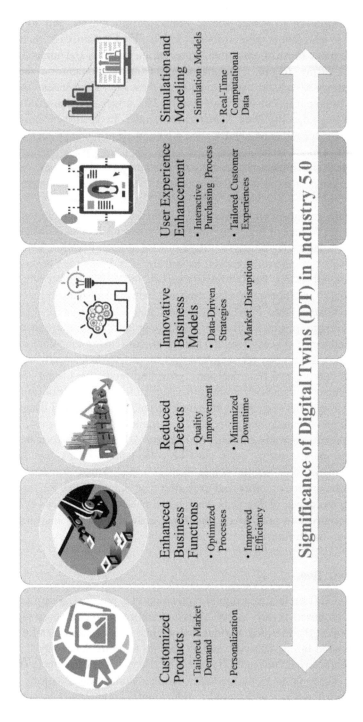

FIGURE 1.5   Significance of Digital Twins in Industry 5.0

The ability to examine and monitor digital representations of real-time objects and systems allows for the detection and prevention of problems before they manifest in the physical world. In order to successfully lower maintenance costs and maximize system performance, DTs have been further enhanced by the rapid development of AI, ML, and Big Data Analytics [38]. By fusing these technologies, DTs equip businesses with actionable intelligence, boosting operational efficiency and propelling proactive decision-making. Digital twins play a crucial role in the realization of intelligent and networked industrial systems within the framework of Industry 5.0. Industrial processes are enhanced by the implementation of technologies that enable data-driven strategies, predictive maintenance, process optimization, and seamless communication between physical and digital environments. DTs enable the creation of market-specific goods in Industry 5.0. These technologies can optimize corporate operations, reduce errors, and integrate new business frameworks, improving financial performance. DTs help Industry 5.0 quickly identify and resolve technical issues. They also help identify productive components for replacement or modification, optimizing operations and reducing downtime.

DTs also improve the ability to predict errors and failures, reducing the risk of major financial losses. The intelligent architectural design of the system enables enterprises to attain economic benefits at an accelerated pace compared to previous methods. In the context of Industry 5.0, the utilization of DTs allows for the creation of simulation models and the retrieval of real-time computational data. This capability empowers organizations to remotely make modifications and updates to physical things. The degree of flexibility and adaptation exhibited by industries enables them to remain at the forefront of technological breakthroughs.

In the realm of customization, DTs play a critical role in improving user experiences by tailoring products to individual needs. Clients can engage in a purchasing process that allows them to build virtual environments and visualize the end results before finalizing their choices. This level of interactivity and personalization fosters strong customer engagement and satisfaction, ultimately driving brand loyalty and business growth [39].

Digital Twins hold immense potential in Industry 5.0, revolutionizing product development, manufacturing processes, and customer experiences. Their integration into smart architecture and real-time data access opens up new horizons for industries to achieve greater efficiency, agility, and success in the rapidly evolving industrial landscape.

1.2.6 BLOCKCHAIN

Blockchain technology holds immense potential to revolutionize Industry 5.0, addressing critical challenges related to the centralized management of diverse connected devices. The role of blockchain in Industry 5.0 is illustrated in Figure 1.6. By leveraging blockchain, decentralized and distributed management platforms can be designed, establishing trust across the network [40]. This technology utilizes an immutable ledger to maintain records. The resulting transparency and accountability

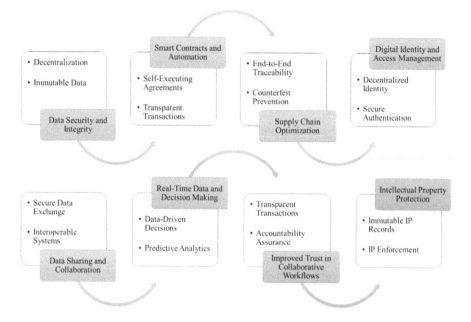

FIGURE 1.6   Role of blockchain in Industry 5.0

in Industry 5.0 applications prove instrumental, particularly for dispute resolution within the ecosystem [41].

Smart contracts play a pivotal role in Industry 5.0's security enforcement, ensuring authentication and automating service-oriented actions. Security is also improved because blockchain uses a compartmentalized and distributed approach to protecting data and transactions. In addition, blockchain makes it easier to receive and collect data [42], which improves data integration and collaboration on the network.

Blockchain technology is positioned to become a fundamental component in future Industry 5.0 applications due to its decentralized nature and robust security features. Its potential to establish a trustless setting, increase visibility, and mandate secure protocols is a major boon to the development of Industry 5.0's production processes and infrastructure.

To optimize subscriber management, blockchain technology is a potent tool in the context of Industry 5.0, where it is used to create and manage digital identities for individuals and organizations. By leveraging blockchain, access control and authentication of stakeholders in industrial activities can be seamlessly executed above a public network [43]. These digital IDs can be expanded more to encompass the management of properties, possessions, objects, and services, providing a comprehensive and secure framework.

Furthermore, blockchain technology finds application in the registration of intellectual property (IP) rights, enabling the cataloging and secure storage of original works. The integration of blockchain and smart contracts also streamlines the contracting between diverse stakeholders, enhancing efficiency and reducing manual intervention.

By leveraging blockchain for cloud manufacturing, industries can achieve enhanced interoperability and secure data sharing, fostering a connected and efficient ecosystem.

1.3   EMPOWERING COLLABORATION THROUGH INDUSTRY 5.0

The promotion of collaborative efforts facilitated by Industry 5.0 is a crucial element of the ongoing industrial revolution. This paradigm places emphasis on leveraging cutting-edge technologies to cultivate cooperation and generate mutually beneficial outcomes among diverse participants. The objective of this collaborative method is to establish a connection between humans and machines, fostering a symbiotic environment in which both entities collaborate to accomplish shared objectives [44]. The essential elements for fostering collaborative empowerment in the context of Industry 5.0 encompass:

1.3.1   ENHANCING HUMAN–MACHINE COLLABORATION

1.3.1.1   Reskilling and Upskilling the Workforce
- *Identification of Critical Skills:* The process of conducting skill gap assessments is utilized to determine the specific skills necessary for Industry 5.0, encompassing areas such as data analytics, AI, and automation.
- Implementation of comprehensive training programs is recommended to provide the workforce with the requisite skills and knowledge required for optimal performance in a technology-driven setting.
- The promotion of lifelong learning is advocated as a means to foster a culture that embraces ongoing education in order to effectively navigate the ever-changing technology environment.

1.3.1.2   Redefining Roles and Responsibilities in Collaborative Environments
- *Role Evaluation:* The process of assessing and redefining the respective roles of humans and robots in order to optimize their individual strengths and enhance their mutual capabilities.
- *Task Allocation:* Developing explicit protocols for the distribution of tasks, facilitating a smooth and efficient collaboration between human workers and automated systems across different phases of the production workflow.

The objective of this research is to establish collaboration protocols and frameworks that enhance the efficiency of communication and coordination between human workers and intelligent machines.

1.3.1.3   Fostering a Culture of Collaboration and Trust
- *Fostering Open Communication:* Cultivating a work environment that embraces inclusivity and encourages people to openly express their ideas, concerns, and comments.
- The focus of this study is on human–machine interaction, specifically on the establishment of confidence in autonomous systems. This is achieved by

improving transparency and explainability in processes powered by artificial intelligence.

- *Training and Familiarization:* Offering comprehensive training and familiarization sessions to employees on the use of intelligent equipment, hence cultivating a sense of confidence and reliance on their functionalities.
- To optimize human–machine collaboration in the context of Industry 5.0, it is imperative to adopt a proactive stance in terms of workforce development, role delineation, and fostering an atmosphere that facilitates seamless partnership between humans and machines. This strategy is essential for achieving heightened levels of productivity and efficiency in industrial operations.

1.3.2 CROSS-SECTOR COLLABORATION AND ECOSYSTEMS

The success of Industry 5.0 hinges on the essential role of cross-sector collaboration and ecosystems, which facilitate the convergence of many industries, the exchange of knowledge, and the collective advancement of innovation.

The fundamental elements of cross-sector collaboration and ecosystems in Industry 5.0 encompass:

1.3.2.1 Building Collaborative Ecosystems for Innovation

- *Developing Collaborative Platforms:* Constructing inclusive platforms that facilitate the convergence of stakeholders from diverse sectors, including industry, academia, research institutions, and startups.
- Knowledge exchange is the facilitation of the transfer of ideas, technology, and best practices in order to cultivate a culture of innovation and ongoing enhancement.
- Co-creation spaces refer to the provision of either physical or virtual environments that facilitate the collaboration and joint creation of innovative initiatives among a broad group of stakeholders.

1.3.2.2 Public–Private Partnerships for Sustainable Development

- *Fostering Collaborative Objectives:* Facilitating alliances among governmental bodies, private enterprises, and non-governmental organizations (NGOs) to tackle collective social, environmental, and economic predicaments.
- *Sustainable Solutions:* Engaging in collaborative endeavors centered around sustainable development, the promotion of renewable energy sources, the mitigation of waste generation, and the adoption of environmentally conscious habits.
- *Policy Advocacy:* Collaboratively engaging in advocacy efforts aimed at advancing policies and regulations that foster sustainable behaviors and facilitate the development and adoption of environmentally friendly technologies.

1.3.2.3   Leveraging Open Innovation Platforms

- *Fostering Collaboration with External Innovators:* Adopting an open innovation approach that incorporates the active participation of external innovators, entrepreneurs, and startups in developmental endeavors.
- *Utilizing Open Innovation Platforms for Enhanced Idea Access:* Employing open innovation platforms as a means to access a wider array of ideas, technology, and skills from varied sources.
- *Enhancing Innovation Velocity:* Facilitating the expeditious progression of the innovation process through collaborative engagements with external partners, thereby incorporating unique views and novel ideas.

Industry 5.0 derives advantages from the amalgamation of talent, resources, and viewpoints through cross-sector collaboration and ecosystems. The utilization of a collaborative approach fosters expeditious innovation, effective problem-solving, and the promotion of sustainable growth. Consequently, this engenders a more robust and adaptive industrial landscape, capable of effectively addressing intricate global concerns.

1.3.3   Collaborative Product Development and Design

Collaborative product development and design are integral components of Industry 5.0, a paradigm in which a multitude of stakeholders converge to generate inventive and customer-centric goods. The essential elements of collaborative product development and design in Industry 5.0 encompass:

1.3.3.1   Co-Creation and Participatory Design Approaches

- *User-Centric Design:* The practice of actively engaging end-users, customers, and stakeholders in the design process to ensure that products are tailored to their specific needs and preferences.
- *Co-Creation Workshops:* Facilitating collaborative workshops and brainstorming sessions among interdisciplinary teams to foster the generation of novel ideas and concepts.
- Iterative feedback involves the integration of input from users and stakeholders at various stages of the design process in order to enhance and optimize the product.

1.3.3.2   Virtual Collaboration Tools and Technologies

- AR and VR technologies are employed to facilitate virtual product development and immersive design assessments.
- Digital Twins involve the creation of digital clones of physical objects, which are utilized to imitate and enhance performance. This technology facilitates real-time cooperation and problem-solving.
- Cloud-based collaboration refers to the utilization of cloud-based platforms in order to promote efficient and smooth collaboration among teams that are located in different geographical locations.

1.3.3.3   Accelerating Product Development Cycles Through Collaboration

- *Agile Development:* The adoption of agile approaches to improve coopera-tion, flexibility, and reactivity in the process of product development.
- Concurrent Engineering refers to the integration of many facets of product design, encompassing engineering, production, and marketing, in order to oper-ate simultaneously, hence diminishing the duration of the development process.
- Rapid prototyping involves the utilization of 3D printing and other approaches to swiftly iterate and evaluate design concepts.

Through collaborative product development and design, Industry 5.0 achieves faster innovation, higher product quality, and greater customer satisfaction. The integration of diverse perspectives and the utilization of advanced collaboration tools ensure that products are not only technologically advanced but also meet the ever-evolving needs and expectations of consumers in the dynamic market landscape.

1.4   CHALLENGES AND FUTURE DIRECTIONS

Industry 5.0 holds the promise of providing highly customized services to customers through cognitive-enabled manufacturing processes. However, to ensure seamless implementation of such services, certain potential challenges need to be addressed. As industrial processes become more digitized, it is crucial to address security vul-nerabilities [45] in handling heterogeneous data and using cloud services for diverse users. Measures like maintaining privacy data sharing and ethical considerations must also be taken into account when offering personalized and predictive services to customers.

Integrating human intelligence with machines can be effective, but compliance and practical issues must be carefully managed. This involves providing effective training to both human workers and intelligent machines to foster harmonious col-laboration. Scaling up the user base and manufacturing processes should be care-fully planned to ensure efficient customer support with human–robot partnership. Moreover, the adoption of AI should be approached with ethical considerations to avoid potential drawbacks and negative societal impacts.

By addressing these challenges, Industry 5.0 can unlock its full potential in deliv-ering customized services and driving innovation across various industries. It is essential to proactively address these issues to create a sustainable and responsible Industry 5.0 ecosystem that benefits both businesses and society at large.

1.4.1   Addressing the Ethical and Societal Implications of Industry 5.0

Addressing the ethical and societal implications of Industry 5.0 [46] is of utmost importance to ensure the responsible and sustainable implementation of advanced technologies. Several key aspects need to be considered:

- The advent of Industry 5.0 is characterized by a significant dependence on the collection and analysis of data, thereby giving rise to apprehensions regarding the safeguarding of data privacy and security. It is imperative for companies to adopt stringent data protection protocols in order to safeguard sensitive information and guarantee responsible and transparent utilization of user data.

- The emergence of AI and automation in the context of Industry 5.0 necessitates the establishment of ethical frameworks to govern decision-making processes and autonomous systems. It is imperative to prioritize the establishment of fairness, impartiality, and accountability in AI algorithms in order to mitigate the risk of discrimination and adverse societal consequences.
- The proliferation of automation and AI has the potential to result in job displacement within specific industries. Investing in reskilling and upskilling programs is of utmost importance in order to provide the workforce with the essential skills required to effectively adapt to evolving job roles and sustain employability.
- The social impact of Industry 5.0 should be a central consideration in its design. It is imperative to ensure that technology is inclusive and equitable, benefiting all segments of society, particularly marginalized communities, while also avoiding the amplification of pre-existing disparities.
- Transparency and accountability are essential components for fostering trust among stakeholders. It is imperative for companies to prioritize transparency regarding the utilization of data and actively engage users in decision-making procedures.
- *Human–Machine Interaction:* As humans collaborate with intelligent machines in Industry 5.0, the design of human-machine interfaces and interactions should prioritize safety, user-friendliness, and accessibility.
- *Environmental Sustainability:* Industry 5.0 should be aligned with sustainable practices to minimize its environmental footprint. Embracing green technologies and eco-friendly production processes can contribute to a more sustainable future.
- *Regulation and Policy:* Policymakers and regulatory bodies should work collaboratively with industry stakeholders to develop appropriate regulations that address the ethical and societal challenges of Industry 5.0 while fostering innovation and economic growth.

By actively addressing these ethical and societal implications, Industry 5.0 can pave the way for a technology-driven future that is not only technologically advanced but also socially responsible and beneficial for all.

1.4.2 Overcoming Barriers to Widespread Adoption of Collaborative Technologies

Overcoming barriers to the widespread adoption of collaborative technologies is essential to fully realize the potential [47] of Industry 5.0. Several key barriers need to be addressed:

- The establishment of interoperability is of paramount importance as it guarantees the seamless integration and compatibility of diverse collaborative technologies. The implementation of standardized and openly accessible communication protocols can effectively support and enhance cross-platform collaboration and facilitate the exchange of data.

- The cost and complexity associated with the implementation of collaborative technologies can pose a substantial obstacle for numerous organizations, particularly those of smaller scale. It is imperative to prioritize endeavors aimed at enhancing the affordability and user-friendliness of these technologies.
- Cultural resistance poses a significant obstacle to the implementation of new technologies within organizations, as it is characterized by a reluctance to embrace change and a deficiency in fostering a collaborative culture. The implementation of awareness campaigns and training programs for employees has the potential to cultivate a corporate environment that promotes collaboration and innovation.
- The sharing and processing of sensitive data in collaborative technologies give rise to significant cybersecurity concerns. The implementation of robust cybersecurity measures and the assurance of data protection can foster trust and instill confidence in these technologies.
- The attainment of proficiency in collaborative technologies necessitates a workforce that possesses the requisite skills. It is imperative to offer upskilling and reskilling initiatives to ensure that employees are equipped with the requisite skills to proficiently leverage these technologies.
- The process of integrating collaborative technologies with pre-existing legacy systems can present significant challenges. It is imperative for companies to formulate strategic approaches that facilitate the seamless integration of these technologies into their existing operational procedures.
- The implementation of collaborative technologies may give rise to legal and regulatory considerations, specifically pertaining to data privacy and the protection of intellectual property rights. It is imperative to establish explicit guidelines and regulations in order to effectively address these issues.
- *Uncertainty Surrounding Return on Investment (ROI) in Collaborative Technologies:* Certain organizations may exhibit reluctance in allocating resources toward collaborative technologies owing to the ambiguity surrounding the potential return on investment. Illustrating the concrete advantages and worth of these technologies can aid in surmounting this obstacle.
- *Scalability:* Ensuring that collaborative technologies can scale up to meet the demands of growing businesses is essential. Scalability considerations should be built into the implementation strategy.

By proactively addressing these barriers, organizations can unlock the full potential of collaborative technologies and drive innovation and productivity in the Industry 5.0 ecosystem. Collaboration between industry stakeholders, policymakers, and technology providers is crucial in overcoming these challenges and creating an enabling environment for the widespread adoption of collaborative technologies.

1.4.1.3 Future Trends and Potential Advancements in Industry 5.0

The future of Industry 5.0 holds several exciting trends and potential advancements that are likely to shape the industrial landscape:

- *Edge Computing and AI:* Advancements in edge computing, where data is processed closer to the source, combined with AI capabilities, will enable real-time decision-making and reduced latency. This will enhance the responsiveness and efficiency of Industry 5.0 processes.
- *Swarm Robotics:* Collaborative networks of robots that work together autonomously, known as swarm robotics, will gain prominence. Swarm robotics will enhance flexibility, adaptability, and scalability in various industrial settings, leading to improved productivity and resource utilization.
- *6G Connectivity:* The emergence of 6G technology will bring ultra-high-speed and low-latency communication, enabling more advanced and complex Industry 5.0 applications. This will facilitate seamless data exchange and enhance the performance of connected devices.
- *Quantum Computing:* The potential of quantum computing will be harnessed to address complex optimization and simulation challenges, transforming Industry 5.0 processes. Quantum computing will significantly enhance processing capabilities and enable innovative solutions in various industries.
- *Digital Twins at Scale:* Digital Twins, which are digital replicas of physical systems or objects, will be deployed on a larger scale. Advanced digital twin technologies will enable real-time simulation and reduced downtime.
- *Human–Machine Collaboration:* The seamless collaboration between humans and intelligent machines will evolve further, leading to more sophisticated and productive co-working environments. Robots and AI will increasingly complement human skills, leading to higher productivity and efficiency.
- *Sustainable Manufacturing:* Industry 5.0 will witness a greater emphasis on sustainability and eco-friendly practices. Sustainable manufacturing processes, green technologies, and circular economy principles will gain traction to reduce environmental impact.
- *Smart Factories and IoT Integration:* IoT integration with smart factories will lead to smarter, interconnected production environments. Real-time data analytics and predictive maintenance will optimize manufacturing processes and reduce operational costs.
- *Personalized Customer Experiences:* Industry 5.0 will focus on delivering highly personalized and tailored customer experiences through the use of advanced analytics and AI-driven insights. Customer-centric approaches will drive product innovation and market responsiveness.

As technology continues to advance, these future trends and advancements will drive Industry 5.0 toward a more efficient, connected, and sustainable future. Embracing these innovations will enable industries to stay competitive, enhance productivity, and create new possibilities for economic growth and societal development

1.5 CONCLUSION

Industry 5.0 is a revolutionary step forward in manufacturing that places a premium on human–machine cooperation enabled by cutting-edge technologies. Applications of key technologies, such as robotics, AI, the IoT, Big Data Analytics, Digital Twins, and blockchain, are explored in depth in this chapter. Productivity and innovation are encouraged by the emphasis on collaborative empowerment, which leverages the strengths of both human and machine intelligence to solve problems.

Connectivity and systemic integration are cornerstones of Industry 5.0. Manufacturing processes can be monitored, controlled, and optimized in real time thanks to the IoT, which improves the quality of decisions and the effectiveness of operations. In addition, this chapter provides empirical examples to show how these technologies promote complementary interactions between human agents and automated systems, which in turn leads to higher productivity and creativity.

The chapter stresses the significance of a skilled and adaptable workforce, effective lines of communication, and a culture that encourages continuous learning and the exchange of knowledge in order to achieve successful integration. Industry 5.0 envisions a future industrial framework that is characterized by increased efficiency and sustainability in the context of anticipating forthcoming patterns and obstacles. The overarching goal of this structure is to foster a harmonious and mutually beneficial dynamic between human and mechanical laborers. Industry 5.0's emphasis on collective agency promises a brighter, more interconnected future for smart manufacturing and beyond.

REFERENCES

1. Jazdi, N., 2014, May. Cyber physical systems in the context of industry 4.0. In *2014 IEEE International Conference on Automation, Quality and Testing, Robotics* (pp. 1–4). IEEE.
2. Jayakumar, D. and Kumar, K.S., 2021. Internet of Things (IoT)-Cyber Physical Systems (CPS)-An exploratory survey on the security of IoT-CPS framework using blockchain technologies. *Turkish Online Journal of Qualitative Inquiry, 12*(5), pp. 4992–5009.
3. Pivoto, D.G., de Almeida, L.F., da Rosa Righi, R., Rodrigues, J.J., Lugli, A.B. and Alberti, A.M., 2021. Cyber-physical systems architectures for industrial internet of things applications in Industry 4.0: A literature review. *Journal of Manufacturing Systems, 58*, pp. 176–192.
4. Mosterman, P.J. and Zander, J., 2016. Industry 4.0 as a cyber-physical system study. *Software & Systems Modeling, 15*(1), pp. 17–29.
5. Krugh, M. and Mears, L., 2018. A complementary cyber-human systems framework for industry 4.0 cyber-physical systems. *Manufacturing Letters, 15*, pp. 89–92.
6. Lu, Y., 2017. Cyber physical system (CPS)-based industry 4.0: A survey. *Journal of Industrial Integration and Management, 2*(03), p. 1750014.
7. Zizic, M.C., Mladineo, M., Gjeldum, N. and Celent, L., 2022. From industry 4.0 towards industry 5.0: A review and analysis of paradigm shift for the people, organization and technology. *Energies, 15*(14), p. 5221.

8. Xu, X., Lu, Y., Vogel-Heuser, B. and Wang, L., 2021. Industry 4.0 and Industry 5.0—Inception, conception and perception. *Journal of Manufacturing Systems*, *61*, pp. 530–535.

9. Frick, J. and Grudowski, P., 2023. Quality 5.0: A paradigm shift towards proactive quality control in Industry 5.0. *Asia-Pacific Journal of Business Administration*, *14*(2), pp. 51–56.

10. Zizic, M.C., Mladineo, M., Gjeldum, N. and Celent, L., 2022. From industry 4.0 towards Industry 5.0: A review and analysis of paradigm shift for the people, organization and technology. *Energies*, *15*(14), p. 5221. *Industry 4.0—from Smart Factory to Cognitive Cyberphysical Production System and Cloud Manufacturing*, p. 1.

11. Doyle-Kent, M. and Kopacek, P., 2020. Industry 5.0: Is the manufacturing industry on the cusp of a new revolution? In *Proceedings of the International Symposium for Production Research 2019* (pp. 432–441). Springer International Publishing.

12. Huang, S., Wang, B., Li, X., Zheng, P., Mourtzis, D. and Wang, L., 2022. Industry 5.0 and society 5.0—Comparison, complementation and co-evolution. *Journal of Manufacturing Systems*, *64*, pp. 424–428.

13. Hein-Pensel, F., Winkler, H., Brückner, A., Wölke, M., Jabs, I., Mayan, I.J., Kirschenbaum, A., Friedrich, J. and Zinke-Wehlmann, C., 2023. Maturity assessment for Industry 5.0: A review of existing maturity models. *Journal of Manufacturing Systems*, *66*, pp. 200–210.

14. Coronado, E., Kiyokawa, T., Ricardez, G.A.G., Ramirez-Alpizar, I.G., Venture, G. and Yamanobe, N., 2022. Evaluating quality in human-robot interaction: A systematic search and classification of performance and human-centered factors, measures and metrics towards an industry 5.0. *Journal of Manufacturing Systems*, *63*, pp. 392–410.

15. Brückner, A., Hein, P., Hein-Pensel, F., Mayan, J. and Wölke, M., 2023, July. Human-centered HCI practices leading the path to Industry 5.0: A systematic literature review. In *International Conference on Human-Computer Interaction* (pp. 3–15). Cham: Springer Nature Switzerland.

16. Yavari, F. and Pilevari, N., 2020. Industry revolutions development from industry 1.0 to Industry 5.0 in manufacturing. *Journal of Industrial Strategic Management*, *5*(2), pp. 44–63.

17. Xu, X., Lu, Y., Vogel-Heuser, B. and Wang, L., 2021. Industry 4.0 and industry 5.0—Inception, conception and perception. *Journal of Manufacturing Systems*, *61*, pp. 530–535.

18. Huang, S., Wang, B., Li, X., Zheng, P., Mourtzis, D. and Wang, L., 2022. Industry 5.0 and society 5.0—Comparison, complementation and co-evolution. *Journal of Manufacturing Systems*, *64*, pp. 424–428.

19. Leng, J., Sha, W., Wang, B., Zheng, P., Zhuang, C., Liu, Q., Wuest, T., Mourtzis, D. and Wang, L., 2022. Industry 5.0: Prospect and retrospect. *Journal of Manufacturing Systems*, *65*, pp. 279–295.

20. Iyengar, K.P., Pe, E.Z., Jalli, J., Shashidhara, M.K., Jain, V.K., Vaish, A. and Vaishya, R., 2022. Industry 5.0 technology capabilities in Trauma and orthopaedics. *Journal of Orthopaedics*, *32*, pp. 125–132.

21. Fazal, N., Haleem, A., Bahl, S., Javaid, M. and Nandan, D., 2022. Digital management systems in manufacturing using industry 5.0 technologies. In *Advancement in Materials, Manufacturing and Energy Engineering, Vol. II: Select Proceedings of ICAMME 2021* (pp. 221–234). Singapore: Springer Nature Singapore.

22. Massaro, A., 2021. *Electronics in Advanced Research Industries: Industry 4.0 to Industry 5.0 Advances*. John Wiley & Sons.

23. Nahavandi, S., 2019. Industry 5.0—A human-centric solution. *Sustainability*, *11*(16), p. 4371.

24. Pizoń, J., Cioch, M., Kański, Ł. and Sánchez-García, E., 2022. Cobots implementation in the era of Industry 5.0 using modern business and management solutions. *Advances in Science and Technology Research Journal*, 16(6), pp. 166–178.

25. Alojaiman, B., 2023. Technological modernizations in the industry 5.0 era: A descriptive analysis and future research directions. *Processes*, *11*(5), p. 1318.

26. Aslam, F., Aimin, W., Li, M. and Ur Rehman, K., 2020. Innovation in the era of IoT and industry 5.0: Absolute innovation management (AIM) framework. *Information*, *11*(2), p. 124.

27. Özdemir, V. and Hekim, N., 2018. Birth of industry 5.0: Making sense of big data with artificial intelligence, "the internet of things" and next-generation technology policy. *OMICS: A Journal of Integrative Biology*, 22(1), pp. 65–76.

28. Chi, H.R., Wu, C.K., Huang, N.F., Tsang, K.F. and Radwan, A., 2022. A survey of network automation for industrial Internet-of-things towards Industry 5.0. *IEEE Transactions on Industrial Informatics*, 19(2), pp. 2065–2077.

29. Patil, R.Y. and Patil, Y.H., 2023. A proxy signcryption scheme for secure sharing of industrial IoT data in fog environment. *International Journal of Computational Science and Engineering*, 26(2), pp. 118–128.

30. Anisha, P.R., Reddy, C.K.K., Nguyen, N.G., Bhushan, M., Kumar, A. and Hanafiah, M.M. eds., 2022. *Intelligent Systems and Machine Learning for Industry: Advancements, Challenges, and Practices*. CRC Press.

31. Pant, P., Rajawat, A.S., Goyal, S.B., Singh, D., Constantin, N.B., Raboaca, M.S. and Verma, C., 2022, December. Using machine learning for Industry 5.0 efficiency prediction based on security and proposing models to enhance efficiency. In *2022 11th International Conference on System Modeling & Advancement in Research Trends (SMART)* (pp. 909–914). IEEE.

32. Chander, B., Pal, S. De, D. and Buyya, R., 2022. Artificial intelligence-based internet of things for industry 5.0 In: Pal, S., De, D., Buyya, R. (eds) *Artificial Intelligence-Based Internet of Things Systems* (pp. 3–45). Springer, Cham. https://doi.org/10.1007/978-3-030-87059-1_1

33. Vermesan, O. ed., 2022. *Artificial Intelligence for Digitising Industry–Applications*. CRC Press.

34. Skobelev, P.O. and Borovik, S.Y., 2017. On the way from industry 4.0 to Industry 5.0: From digital manufacturing to digital society. *Industry 4.0*, 2(6), pp. 307–311.

35. Sachsenmeier, P., 2016. Industry 5.0—The relevance and implications of bionics and synthetic biology. *Engineering*, 2(2), pp. 225–229.

36. Wang, W., Guo, H., Li, X., Tang, S., Li, Y., Xie, L. and Lv, Z., 2022. BIM information integration based VR modeling in digital twins in industry 5.0. *Journal of Industrial Information Integration*, 28, p. 100351.

37. Wang, B., Zhou, H., Li, X., Yang, G., Zheng, P., Song, C., Yuan, Y., Wuest, T., Yang, H. and Wang, L., 2024. Human digital twin in the context of industry 5.0. *Robotics and Computer-Integrated Manufacturing*, 85, p. 102626.

38. Wang, H., Lv, L., Li, X., Li, H., Leng, J., Zhang, Y., Thomson, V., Liu, G., Wen, X., Sun, C. and Luo, G., 2023. A safety management approach for Industry 5.0′s human-centered manufacturing based on digital twin. *Journal of Manufacturing Systems*, 66, pp. 1–12.

39. Mincă, E., Filipescu, A., Cernega, D., Șrne, R., Filipescu, A., Ionescu, D. and Simion, G., 2022. Digital twin for a multifunctional technology of flexible assembly on a mechatronics line with integrated robotic systems and mobile visual sensor—Challenges towards Industry 5.0. *Sensors*, 22(21), p. 8153.

40. Verma, A., Bhattacharya, P., Madhani, N., Trivedi, C., Bhushan, B., Tanwar, S., Sharma, G., Bokoro, P.N. and Sharma, R., 2022. Blockchain for industry 5.0: Vision, opportunities, key enablers, and future directions. *IEEE Access*, 10, pp. 69160–69199.

41. Rupa, C., Midhunchakkaravarthy, D., Hasan, M.K., Alhumyani, H. and Saeed, R.A., 2021. Industry 5.0: Ethereum blockchain technology based DApp smart contract. *Mathematical Biosciences and Engineering, 18*(5), pp. 7010–7027.
42. Singh, S.K., Yang, L.T. and Park, J.H., 2023. FusionFedBlock: Fusion of blockchain and federated learning to preserve privacy in industry 5.0. *Information Fusion, 90*, pp. 233–240.
43. De, D., Karmakar, A., Banerjee, P.S., Bhattacharyya, S. and Rodrigues, J.J., 2022. BCoT: Introduction to blockchain-based internet of things for Industry 5.0. In *Blockchain Based Internet of Things* (pp. 1–22). Singapore: Springer Singapore.
44. Xian, W., Yu, K., Han, F., Fang, L., He, D. and Han, Q.L., 2023. Advanced manufacturing in industry 5.0: A survey of key enabling technologies and future trends. In *IEEE Transactions on Industrial Informatics* (pp. 1–15).
45. Akundi, A., Euresti, D., Luna, S., Ankobiah, W., Lopes, A. and Edinbarough, I., 2022. State of industry 5.0—Analysis and identification of current research trends. *Applied System Innovation, 5*(1), p. 27.
46. George, A.S. and George, A.H., 2023. Revolutionizing manufacturing: Exploring the promises and challenges of industry 5.0. *Partners Universal International Innovation Journal, 1*(2), pp. 22–38.
47. Gagnidze, I., 2023. Industry 4.0 and industry 5.0: Can clusters deal with the challenges? (A systemic approach). *Kybernetes, 52*(7), pp. 2270–2287.

2 From Industry 4.0 to 5.0
Enriching Manufacturing Excellence through Human–Robot Interaction and Technological Empowerment

S. Santhosh Kumar, S. Ramesh Kumar, G. Ramesh

2.1 INTRODUCTION

The Industrial Revolution, propelled by technological advancements, originated in Great Britain. It all started in the late 1700s with the textile business, where groundbreaking inventions transformed how cloth was produced. The population explosion in Britain, brought about by the agricultural revolution, led to an increased demand for clothing. This, in turn, spurred further developments in the textile industry, which paved the way for growth in other sectors. The Industrial Revolution brought numerous benefits, such as creating job opportunities and increasing the nation's wealth. It also fostered technological advancements, resulting in a significant boost in goods production and living standards. Also, the Industrial Revolution brought about better living conditions, a healthier diet, and mass-produced clothing. The demand for engineers, clerical and professional employees was high during this period, leading to educational opportunities for many. As a result, the impact of these developments was felt globally.

The Sustainable Development Goals (SDGs) are pivotal for enhancing global productivity, competitiveness, and job creation through technological advancements. By promoting sustainable practices and innovations, the SDGs drive increased efficiency and long-term competitive advantages in industries and economies. These goals also encourage the adoption of advanced manufacturing technologies, fostering new job opportunities and economic growth. Particularly in developing countries, the embrace of technical advancements in manufacturing serves as a crucial avenue for economic development and global market participation, enabling these countries to navigate the challenges and prospects of the evolving industrial landscape [1–5]. The emergence of Industry 4.0 sparked rapid advancements across high-performance domains, including cloud computing, Big Data analytics, advanced robotics, augmented reality, smart sensors, artificial intelligence (AI), the Internet of

DOI: 10.1201/9781032642789-2

Things (IoT), nanotechnology, human–machine interfaces, 3D printing, and cyber-physical systems (CPSs). These transformative technologies have revolutionized industries, enabling scalable data management, informed decision-making, autonomous robotics, immersive experiences, real-time monitoring, adaptive AI, interconnected devices, innovative materials, intuitive interfaces, customizable production, and intelligent systems. This collective progress has ushered in an era of interconnectedness, efficiency, and innovation with far-reaching implications for industries and societies. These technologies converge in the vision of a "smart factory," where products, humans, and machines seamlessly communicate physically and virtually, leading to heightened sustainability. This technological synergy optimizes resource utilization, reduces waste, and enhances energy efficiency, underscoring the transformative potential of Industry 4.0 in harmonizing innovation and human ingenuity for a more sustainable industrial future [6–13].

Industry 5.0 marks a transformative phase in manufacturing, emphasizing the harmonious partnership between humans and advanced technologies. Unlike its predecessors, Industry 5.0 envisions a cooperative relationship where human creativity, problem-solving, and emotional intelligence complement the strengths of automation, AI, and robotics. This approach seeks to create workplaces that prioritize employee well-being, foster innovation, and combine human expertise with technological innovation for holistic growth and sustainable development. Industry 5.0 aims to forge a more inclusive, forward-looking industrial future that leverages human potential and technological progress by nurturing a synergy of human-centered values and cutting-edge advancements. Collaborative robots (cobots) are essential in Industry 5.0, where humans and technology work together smoothly. Cobots act as helpers, working alongside humans to handle tasks. Humans focus on important jobs, while cobots handle repetitive or tough work. This partnership allows quick changes, keeps things safe, and prevents strain. Cobots also help experts from different fields work together and improve product quality. They are smart and can learn, making work more efficient and better. In Industry 5.0, cobots fit perfectly as helpful, smart assistants that work well with humans. Therefore, Industry 5.0 marks a transformative shift in personalizing products and services by seamlessly integrating technical and social systems. This entails evolving human roles within industries to encompass socio-technical understanding and recognizing the importance of human behavior alongside technological advancements. The entire value chain can be optimized by leveraging smart techniques, advanced manufacturing, and communication technologies, allowing businesses to customize offerings and meet customer needs. This convergence of human expertise and cutting-edge tools fosters collaboration, innovation, and efficiency, ultimately shaping a future where products are efficiently produced and deeply attuned to individual preferences and market trends. Cobots stand out as a promising advancement in the evolution of more intelligent manufacturing systems under the umbrella of Industry 5.0. These innovative robotic entities hold the potential to bring about a revolution in industrial operations, streamlining procedures and enhancing overall productivity. By deploying cobots, tasks with minimal value addition are efficiently delegated, freeing human workers to channel their expertise into intricate, high-value undertakings that call for creativity, problem-solving, and emotional understanding. A unique strength of cobots lies in their seamless ability to function alongside human counterparts within intricate and dynamic work environments. This exceptional attribute presents a range of benefits that could substantially reshape the manufacturing landscape, ranging from heightened efficiency and precision to enhancing workplace ergonomics and reducing physical strain on human laborers [14–17]. Notwithstanding these promising prospects, accepting cobots in workplace settings poses a significant challenge. The successful integration of cobots hinges on a delicate equilibrium between technological implementation and human adaptability. Since cobots operate closely with human personnel, cultivating a sense of acceptability and harmonious coexistence within the manufacturing milieu becomes paramount. This process encompasses more than addressing technical and safety-related concerns; it necessitates nurturing a synergistic rapport between cobots and human workers, ensuring that their roles complement each other rather than compete. A noticeable void in current research is the absence of a comprehensive organizational-centric framework that comprehensively addresses the intricate subtleties of cobot acceptability in manufacturing contexts. Consequently, a critical avenue for research emerges in exploring and establishing exhaustive guidelines, strategies, and practices centered around optimizing cobot integration, all while fostering a constructive, collaborative work culture that effectively harnesses the collective potential of both human and robotic elements. Existing studies have provided limited insights into the objectives and performance criteria guiding the implementation of cobots in manufacturing settings. Furthermore, the crucial aspect of how cobots effectively communicate within a smart, collaborative environment designed for human interaction remains underexplored, presenting a vital consideration for ensuring seamless workflow. Establishing a shared workspace becomes paramount to breaking away from the conventional practice of segregating workplaces into distinct human and robotic domains. This dynamic workspace holds far-reaching implications for the manufacturing landscape, fundamentally influencing the allocation of tasks between human workers and cobots. Remarkably, a noteworthy gap exists in the current body of research, as no prior study has presented a comprehensive framework highlighting the intricate interdependence between cobots and human workers in manufacturing. Consequently, leveraging a socio-technical perspective within the Industry 5.0 paradigm, the present study aims to deepen our understanding of the mutually beneficial collaboration between human workers and cobots.

2.2   INDUSTRY 4.0

The First Industrial Revolution of 1780 marked the beginning of a transformative era, utilizing mechanical power from diverse sources and later incorporating electrical energy into assembly lines, revolutionizing production. Subsequent advancements in information technology ushered in automation, fundamentally altering manufacturing processes by harnessing digital systems and algorithms to replace manual tasks, resulting in increased efficiency and innovation across successive industrial revolutions. "Industry 4.0" originated in Germany in 2011 as part of its "High-Tech Strategy 2020." It signifies the Fourth Industrial Revolution, involving integrating digital technologies like IoT, AI, and cloud computing into manufacturing. Industry 4.0 envisions smart factories where machines, systems, and people are interconnected, enhancing efficiency and customization. This concept builds upon earlier industrial revolutions, representing a digital transformation of manufacturing with global influence. The Industry 4.0 paradigm signifies a revolutionary transformation in manufacturing, uniting physical and digital technologies within an interconnected framework where components communicate effortlessly, facilitating real-time data exchange and decision-making. This fusion enhances efficiency, flexibility, and responsiveness across machinery, materials, and human labor. Industry 4.0 promotes agile manufacturing capable of rapid adjustments by enabling instantaneous data analysis and adaptable processes. This interconnectivity extends throughout the value chain, encompassing suppliers, logistics, and customers, ultimately reshaping industries, stimulating innovation, boosting productivity, and fostering economic advancement [18, 19]. Integrating sensors, actuators, and autonomous systems under the Industry 4.0 framework presents a transformative shift in manufacturing. This convergence empowers factories with heightened intelligence, adaptability, and efficiency, enabling real-time data capture, precise control, and AI-driven decision-making. This leads to improved operational effectiveness, customized, high-quality products, enhanced sustainability, open innovation, and the emergence of innovative business models. Ultimately, Industry 4.0 reshapes manufacturing by creating intelligent, collaborative, and agile factories, driving efficiency, sustainability, innovation, and new revenue avenues [18–21]. The essence of Industry 4.0 lies in its design principles and defining attributes, which collectively shape its fundamental framework. These encompass crucial concepts like vertical and horizontal integration within the supply chain, guaranteeing seamless collaboration and information flow across production stages. Interoperability facilitates effective communication and synergy among diverse systems and elements. The concept of decentralization empowers decentralized decision-making, fostering agility and adaptability. Modularity, a core tenet, enhances flexibility by facilitating the easy replacement or upgrade of components, thereby promoting scalability. Customer personalization underscores tailoring products and experiences to individual preferences. Automation optimizes operations, enhancing efficiency while minimizing human intervention. Lastly, traceability ensures transparency and accountability by meticulously tracking and documenting product and process details. These principles and attributes collectively embody the essence of Industry 4.0, propelling innovation and revolutionizing contemporary manufacturing practices [22]. The central innovation of Industry 4.0 is the merging of physical and virtual domains, facilitated by advanced technologies like IoT, AI, AR, and VR. This integration enables real-time communication between physical objects and digital platforms, enhancing decision-making and optimizing processes. Smart factories exemplify this convergence, with machines monitored and controlled remotely, ensuring efficiency and predictive maintenance. The fusion of virtual and physical worlds also revolutionizes training through immersive experiences, from medical simulations to retail showrooms, offering safe and personalized interactions. This transformative shift redefines industries, driving innovation, efficiency, and customized experiences that were previously unimaginable [9, 23]. Industry 4.0, characterized by cyber-physical systems, capitalizes on IoT and cloud technology to bridge the gap between virtual and physical domains. IoT-equipped objects communicate through data-sharing sensors, while the cloud provides a robust data storage and analysis infrastructure. This interconnected ecosystem extends to manufacturing, healthcare, and urban environments, enabling remote monitoring, predictive maintenance, personalized healthcare, and efficient urban living. Ultimately, Industry 4.0's fusion of IoT and the cloud promises a future where diverse industries reap the benefits of real-time connectivity and data-driven insights, reshaping processes and enhancing overall experiences [12, 19, 24–28]. Industry 4.0 comprises a transformative landscape with key components driving its evolution: the Internet of Things enables real-time data exchange; cyber-physical systems merge digital and physical realms; additive manufacturing revolutionizes production with 3D printing; artificial intelligence empowers machines to learn and decide; cloud computing offers scalable data processing; Big Data analytics extracts insights for optimization; augmented and virtual reality enhance interactions; digital twins simulate and monitor real-world assets; decentralized decision-making enables agile autonomy; interoperability fosters seamless collaboration; cognitive computing enhances human–machine engagement; and robotics and automation streamline tasks. These interconnected components redefine industries, fostering innovation, efficiency, and competitiveness in a data-driven era [29–32]. Industry 4.0 aims to forge intelligent production systems by seamlessly integrating machines and equipment into a cohesive network that communicates and collaborates. This envisions smart manufacturing, where machines gather and share real-time data, enabling autonomous decision-making and adaptive processes. Complemented by the Smart Products dimension, this concept extends beyond the factory to incorporate customer data. Smart manufacturing encompasses diverse technologies, including vertical integration, digitalization, automation, traceability, flexibility, and energy management. These technologies enable real-time data exchange and decision-making, simulating and optimizing processes, enhancing automation, and utilizing artificial intelligence for predictive maintenance and quality control. Internal traceability ensures efficient inventory control, while additive manufacturing offers customization and sustainability. Energy management enhances efficiency through intelligent scheduling. Collectively, these elements drive the evolution of manufacturing into a more responsive, efficient, and adaptable ecosystem [33–37].

Figure 2.1 illustrates the comprehensive scope of Industry 4.0, showcasing the integration of pivotal concepts like artificial intelligence, cloud computing, the Internet of Things, Big Data analytics, robotics, cyber-physical systems, edge computing, and virtual reality. These interconnected elements collectively converge to realize the core principle of Industry 4.0: smart manufacturing [38–41]. Table 2.1 presents each Industry 4.0 technology with its corresponding key components, key characteristics, and impacts on manufacturing and operations. Industry 4.0, a transformative concept underscored by Dalenogare et al., constitutes a paradigm shift emphasizing process automation within the manufacturing landscape [62]. This emphasis aims to curtail human involvement in routine manufacturing tasks, enabling a shift toward more efficient and streamlined operations. This drive for automation is intertwined with a

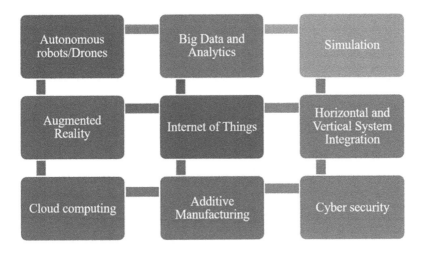

FIGURE 2.1   Core technologies of Industry 4.0 for smart manufacturing

broader objective: creating unique and tailored products that resonate with customer preferences, thus enhancing overall customer satisfaction. Moreover, the seamless incorporation of advanced machine learning techniques, as underscored by the research of [63–65], constitutes a pivotal facet of Industry 4.0's strategic approach. This integration stands as a transformative cornerstone, endowing Industry 4.0 with the capability to imbue intelligence across an extensive network of interconnected devices and applications. This infusion of intelligence catalyzes a dual optimization of mass production and overall performance within manufacturing. As a result, Industry 4.0 fosters a manufacturing landscape characterized by remarkable efficiency and an inherent ability to seamlessly adapt to the ever-shifting contours of the market. At the heart of Industry 4.0's architecture lies the strategic deployment of cyber-physical systems to orchestrate a seamless and fluid exchange of information between commodities and the intricate web of manufacturing processes. Stock et al. emphasize that this foundational concept is underscored by the interconnectivity of the Internet of Things network [18]. This symbiotic integration forms a dynamic ecosystem where real-time data exchange and synchronized coordination serve as catalysts for elevated levels of operational efficiency, setting the stage for a manufacturing landscape that operates with precision and agility. In the wake of Industry 4.0's transformative influence on manufacturing, a digital renaissance unfolds, with data taking the stage as a paramount asset. The substantial influx of data, a product of the intricate interplay between interconnected devices and processes, is harnessed to fuel streamlined processing and meticulous analysis.

Frequently finding its abode within cloud-based platforms, this approach, as examined by Ivanov et al. and Maddikunta et al., serves as a dual-edged sword [12, 66]. Not only does it fine-tune data management with unparalleled precision, it also emerges as a potent catalyst for informed decision-making and the strategic formulation of plans, encapsulating the essence of Industry 4.0's data-driven ethos.

TABLE 2.1

Significance of Industry 4.0 Technologies for Smart Manufacturing and Operations

Technology	Description	Components	Characteristics	Advantages	Challenges	References
Cybersecurity	Ensures safe, attentive, and adaptive cyber security strategies to manage risk in interconnected systems.	Encryption, authentication, monitoring	Safe, attentive, adaptive cyber strategies	Data protection reduced cyber risks and privacy assurance.	Rapidly evolving threats and complex technological landscape.	[30], [42], [43]
Additive Manufacturing	Integrates AI to enhance design accuracy and create custom prototypes, reducing supply chain costs.	3D Printing, AI algorithms, optimization	Design precision, cost efficiency	Improved design accuracy, rapid prototyping, and cost reduction.	Limited material options and scalability concerns.	[34, 42, 44, 45]
Cloud Computing	Utilizes cloud platform for data management, enabling CPS and IoT to reach their full data potential.	Scalability, data storage, processing	Real-time data handling, scalability	Enhanced scalability, cost savings, and real-time data processing.	Data privacy concerns, latency in remote data access.	[12, 42]
Internet of Things	Enables devices to communicate and share data, offering remote accessibility and new market insights.	Sensor networks, data exchange, monitoring	Remote access, new insights	Remote monitoring, data-driven insights, and improved decision-making.	Security vulnerabilities, data overload.	[34, 42, 46, 47]

(Continued)

TABLE 2.1 (CONTINUED)
Significance of Industry 4.0 Technologies for Smart Manufacturing and Operations

Technology	Description	Components	Characteristics	Advantages	Challenges	References
Augmented Reality	Enhances maintenance and shop floor tasks, allowing visualization of complex processes.	AR devices, data overlay, simulations	Real-time visualization, task enhancement	Simplified maintenance, improved training, and better decision-making.	Technical challenges, adoption barriers.	[42, 48]
Simulation	Integration of simulation in production processes enhances design and efficiency.	Digital twins, virtual prototypes, optimization	Process simulation, design enhancement	Improved design validation, reduced time-to-market, and cost savings.	Model accuracy and data availability.	[42]
Big Data	Utilization of large volumes of data improves customer service and personalization.	Data analytics, mining, predictive modeling	Customer insights, personalization	Better customer service, targeted marketing, and data-driven insights.	Data quality, privacy concerns.	[42, 49]
Horizontal System Integration	Collaboration among organizations in the value chain enhances product offerings and success.	Supply chain integration, collaborative networks	Collaborative environments, extended value	Enhanced collaboration and improved product offerings.	Integration complexity, partner alignment.	[50]

(Continued)

TABLE 2.1 (CONTINUED)

Significance of Industry 4.0 Technologies for Smart Manufacturing and Operations

Technology	Description	Components	Characteristics	Advantages	Challenges	References
Vertical System Integration	Hierarchical subsystem integration enhances flexibility and production efficiency.	ERP integration, data sharing, protocols	Streamlined information flow, adaptability	Efficient data flow and enhanced production flexibility.	Organizational silos, system complexity.	[50–52]
Autonomous Robots	AI-driven robots (cobots) collaborate with humans, enhancing productivity and skills automation.	Cobots, AI algorithms, human–robot interaction	Productivity, agility, accuracy	Increased productivity, reduced human effort, and safety improvement.	Integration challenges, retraining needs.	[34, 42, 53, 54]
Cyber-Physical Systems	Integrates physical operations with computing, enabling automation and human–machine interaction.	Sensors, actuators, human–machine interfaces	Complete automation, robustness, flexibility	Full automation, improved reliability, enhanced production flexibility.	Technical complexity, interoperability issues.	[9, 24, 34, 42]
Cognitive Computing	Cognitive computing systems mimic human intelligence to process complex data and provide insights.	Machine learning, natural language processing	Data interpretation, pattern recognition	Enhanced decision-making and efficient data analysis.	Data bias, interpretability challenges.	[55–57]
Edge Computing	Edge computing enables real-time data processing and analysis at the network's edge.	Edge devices, data processing	Low latency, local data processing	Faster data processing and reduced network latency.	Infrastructure constraints, security concerns.	[58–60]

Moreover, the far-reaching implications of Industry 4.0's revolution become apparent through its profound effect on the intricacies of cost dynamics and the fabric of production capabilities. A testament to this transformation, the works of Calış Duman and Akdemir and Meyer substantiate how integrating Industry 4.0 principles has yielded tangible outcomes [10, 67]. Notably, adopting Industry 4.0 practices has led to a discernible reduction in costs across the manufacturing, logistics, and quality control spectrum. Industry 4.0 has engendered an environment conducive to heightened mass production, representing a marked departure from the conventional norms of manufacturing methodologies. This paradigm shift underscores the magnitude of Industry 4.0's impact, ushering in a new era of operational efficiency and production scalability. In essence, the convergence of process automation, machine learning, cyber-physical systems, data-driven insights, and cost optimization under the umbrella of Industry 4.0 presents a comprehensive and forward-looking approach to manufacturing. This multifaceted paradigm not only redefines operational efficiency but also sets the stage for a customer-centric, adaptable, and technologically empowered future of manufacturing.

2.3 INDUSTRY 5.0

Industry 4.0 has significantly reduced production costs but has somewhat overlooked the potential for minimizing human-related expenses through thorough process optimization. This oversight could inadvertently hinder employment reduction and amplify labor union influence, potentially impeding the full adoption of Industry 4.0. To address this, Industry 5.0 has emerged as a solution, envisioning a harmonious integration of human creativity and technological prowess. Industry 5.0 seeks to capitalize on human ingenuity alongside advanced machines, striking a balance between the distinct strengths of both. This shift acknowledges the need to optimize efficiency while recognizing the critical role of human expertise in fostering innovation and driving sustainable growth in the evolving industrial landscape [68]. Industry 5.0, as envisioned by numerous technical visionaries, is poised to reintroduce a distinct human element into the industrial landscape. This concept rekindles the human element within manufacturing processes, juxtaposing human intuition and creativity with advanced technologies for a more holistic approach. Notably, Industry 5.0 empowers consumers with personalized and customized products, aligning with contemporary preferences for individualized goods. This shift heralds a new era of productivity and adaptability through seamless cooperation between traditional machinery and collaborative robots (cobots), promising direct accountability and continuous monitoring. By synergizing human ingenuity and technological efficiency, Industry 5.0 aims to reshape industries, inspire innovation, and create a manufacturing ecosystem catering to individualized preferences and overarching production goals [69, 70].

Figure 2.2 illustrates the progression of industrial revolutions in a chronological timeline. The initial three industrial revolutions ushered in a concerning rise in environmental pollution, prompting the manufacturing sector to take collective action to mitigate the negative ramifications of waste management and its detrimental effects

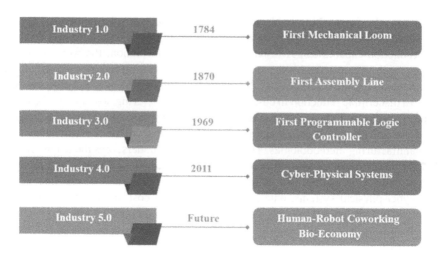

FIGURE 2.2   A timeline of the industrial revolutions

on the fragile ecosystem. Despite the progress of Industry 4.0, it has not inherently integrated environmental safeguards into its fundamental framework. This has led to a pivotal juncture wherein the subsequent Industrial Revolution, Industry 5.0, has arisen as a response to the imperative of devising technological interventions that facilitate pollution-free manufacturing processes. The ethos of Industry 5.0 is rooted in securing the long-term sustainability of human civilization, achieved through a strategic reduction in waste output by embracing the principles of the bio-economy. This transformative approach promises to cultivate a world devoid of pollution, ushering in a paradigm where waste is minimized, and resources are judiciously managed.

Compared to the ongoing industrial transformations, Industry 5.0 provides cleaner options, none promoting the environmental conservation proposed by M. Tabaa et al. [71]. Industry 5.0 encapsulates a dynamic framework built upon a synergistic trio of core values: human-centricity, sustainability, and resilience. In the realm of Industry 5.0, a transformative ethos emerges, placing human needs at the forefront of production dynamics and veering away from a technology-centered approach toward a more human-centric and society-oriented perspective. This recalibration redefines the valuation of workers, nurturing adaptability and inclusiveness within the manufacturing domain. Establishing a secure workplace environment accentuates the significance of physical and mental well-being. At the same time, the strategic pursuit of upskilling amplifies individual expertise and paves the way for enriched career prospects and harmonized work–life equilibrium. This comprehensive shift underscores the profound influence of humanity on the industrial landscape, ushering in a more all-encompassing, agile, and ecologically sustainable manufacturing milieu. Sustainability takes the stage within the ethos of Industry 5.0, assuming a pivotal role in driving the adoption of circular processes that intricately reconfigure resource utilization. The objective is to minimize waste, mitigate environmental impact, and propel the realization of a circular economy characterized by heightened levels of resource efficiency. This commitment to responsible resource management underscores Industry 5.0's dedication to immediate operational considerations and the enduring and conscientious utilization of valuable resources. Embedded within the very essence of Industry 5.0, the principle of resilience emerges as a formidable shield safeguarding against potential disruptions. By fortifying industrial production's robustness, Industry 5.0 establishes a fortified foundation to confront the turbulent tides of change, skillfully navigating geopolitical shifts and environmental challenges. This steadfast resilience and a keen aptitude for navigating intricate circumstances impart a lasting equilibrium to Industry 5.0. As a result, Industry 5.0 thrives as a dynamic force in the industrial landscape and serves as a catalyst, nurturing societal well-being and prosperity to new heights.

Envisioned as a fusion of cutting-edge machinery's precision and speed with the intricate cognitive capabilities of humans, Industry 5.0 embodies a paradigm shift toward personalized mass production that caters to individual preferences and necessities. This forthcoming industrial era is poised to significantly amplify manufacturing efficiency, nurturing a harmonious partnership between humans and machines characterized by interactive involvement and continual monitoring. The collaborative synergy aims to accelerate production rates, bolstering product excellence by delegating routine tasks to machines while reserving critical-thinking tasks for human expertise [66, 72]. Industry 5.0 brings more skilled jobs than Industry 4.0 by teaming up smart professionals with machines. It's all about personalizing things with human guidance for robots. While Industry 4.0 focuses on connecting machines, Industry 5.0 links with Industry 4.0 and collaborative robots. It uses predictive analytics and operating intelligence to make better decisions. Most of the work is done by machines in Industry 5.0, using real-time data and skilled experts to improve things. Smart manufacturing is at the core of the Fifth Industrial Revolution, allowing robots to work alongside humans and reintroducing human thought to the factory floor. It will result in value-added services and secure jobs [66, 72–74].

In recent years, there has been a remarkable and rapid expansion in the adoption and utilization of collaborative robots, commonly known as cobots. These machines, designed to work alongside humans, have witnessed a substantial increase in their application across various industries and sectors. This surge in cobot usage can be attributed to several factors, including advancements in robotics technology, increased affordability, improved safety features, and a growing recognition of their potential to enhance productivity and efficiency in various work environments. As a result, more and more businesses and organizations are incorporating cobots into their operations, capitalizing on their ability to perform repetitive and labor-intensive tasks in collaboration with human workers. This trend underscores cobots' significant impact and potential on modern industries, reshaping work dynamics and contributing to the evolution of efficient and harmonious human–robot collaboration [75]. Cobots had a market value of $649 million in 2019, with a 45 percent increase expected between 2019 and 2025. Manufacturing companies began using cobots to improve productivity, accessibility, and flexibility in the workplace, including in the automotive and electronic industries [76]. Compared to a human worker, cobots can reduce the chance of error in operations, and specific individuals are required for supervision in each step of the manufacturing process. Cobots work in the same environment as humans but do separate tasks [71]. As a result, integrating cobots into workplaces encourages employees to focus on generating innovative solutions and decision-making. Cobots surpass traditional industrial robots in terms of their capabilities and adaptability. They exhibit versatility by efficiently performing both routine tasks and challenging ergonomic responsibilities. Equipped with built-in sensors, cobots can discern intentional interactions with their surroundings from unintentional ones. Consequently, the interactions between cobots and human workers are underpinned by priorities such as safety, effective operation, and user-friendliness, thus enhancing their coexistence and collaborative potential [77–79].

2.4 HUMAN–ROBOT INTERACTION FOR MANUFACTURING

While Industry 4.0 primarily aims to optimize factory operations by promoting autonomy using cyber-physical systems, the Internet of Things, and related technologies, Industry 5.0 takes a different approach by refining the interaction between humans and machines, placing a renewed emphasis on the role of humans. In this context, Industry 5.0 complements these initiatives by leveraging the creative abilities of human specialists in collaboration with intelligent and precise machines and robots. This highlights the critical need to establish effective, efficient, and well-optimized human–robot interactions (HRI) to successfully realize the goals of Industry 5.0. Human–robot interaction in manufacturing refers to the collaboration and communication between humans and robots within a production environment. This interaction involves various levels of cooperation, coordination, and integration between human workers and robotic systems to perform tasks, optimize processes, and enhance manufacturing efficiency [80]. In 2012, a new generation of collaborative robots called cobots was introduced. These robots were explicitly designed to work alongside humans, prioritizing safety by incorporating sensors, force limitations, and more ergonomic and rounded designs. Unlike conventional robots, cobots are engineered to ensure a higher level of safety when interacting with human workers in various settings [81, 82]. Cobots are lightweight and can be easily moved between different tasks. Their setup is straightforward; engineers and workers can operate them with the proper training. Importantly, cobots are designed to avoid causing harm or injury to humans if they come into contact with them. These technological advancements open new possibilities for factory workers and cobots to collaborate in manufacturing. The collaboration of humans and cobots can drastically minimize human idle time. It improves the health and safety of humans by taking more dangerous tasks. Cobots are simple to set up, run, and maintain and don't need an on-site robotic specialist. The cobot operator, also known as a coboter, primarily works alongside the cobots and collaborates with them. Maintenance technicians also perform tasks such as maintenance, repairs, and interventions.

Bender et al. have outlined five distinct levels of interaction between humans and robots in manufacturing [83]. These levels provide a structured hierarchy that characterizes the extent of cooperation and collaboration between these entities:

Cell: This initial level of interaction involves a relatively limited form of cooperation, where the robot operates within a designated enclosure or cage. While it may perform tasks, there is a clear physical separation between the robot and human workers, ensuring safety but limiting direct collaboration.

Coexistence: The workspace is shared between humans and robots at the coexistence level. However, interactions are primarily indirect, with minimal or no direct cooperation. This level allows for the simultaneous presence of both entities within the same physical space but lacks substantial engagement.

Synchronized: Moving up the hierarchy, the synchronized level entails a scenario where either the human or the robot occupies the workspace at a given time, but not both simultaneously. They take turns performing tasks, effectively sharing the workspace in a coordinated manner.

Cooperation: At this level, genuine cooperation between humans and robots emerges. Both entities share the workspace, engaging in tasks. However, their actions are non-simultaneous and work on separate objects or components. This level allows for coordinated efforts without direct interference.

Collaboration: The highest interaction tier signifies the most advanced cooperation between humans and robots. Both entities work concurrently on the same product or task, exhibiting a seamless and synchronized effort. This level embodies the pinnacle of synergy and coordination, where the strengths of both humans and robots are harnessed to achieve optimal outcomes.

Human–robot interaction in manufacturing involves several crucial factors and components to ensure effective collaboration between humans and robots. These include designing robots with ergonomic features, advanced sensors for perception, safety measures, intuitive programming interfaces, optimal task planning, and communication mechanisms. Integrating human skills, data sharing, training, and continuous improvement is vital. Key considerations include ethics, trust, maintenance, adaptability, data security, and privacy. Combining these elements enhances productivity, safety, and overall manufacturing performance in HRI systems [84–90].

2.5   CASE STUDY—ENGINE BLOCK MACHINING PROGRESSION IN DIFFERENT INDUSTRIAL EPOCHS

An engine block, commonly known as a cylinder block, constitutes a sturdy metallic framework central to the functionality of an internal combustion engine. It establishes the groundwork that accommodates vital constituents like cylinder bores, which accommodate piston motion, guide pistons through combustion cycles, facilitate the flow of coolant and oil, and furnish anchoring locations for imperative engine components. The block's inherent strength enables it to endure the rigors of combustion, contributing to effective heat regulation and power generation. Its precision, durability, and serviceability are pivotal in enhancing engine efficiency, longevity, and overall performance. Therefore, the fabrication of an engine block holds significant importance. Fabricating an engine block involves a structured series of steps to create a functional and precise component for internal combustion engines. Suitable materials like cast iron or aluminum alloys are chosen and refined, starting with material selection and preparation. Pattern making and mold preparation lead to casting molten metal into sand molds, shaping the initial block structure. Machining refines the block's shape through roughing and finishing operations, while core creation shapes internal passages. Surface treatments enhance aesthetics and durability. Quality control ensures dimensional accuracy, and assembly integrates key components. Testing validates performance, followed by surface coating and a final quality check. The block is then securely packaged for transportation to its destination. This intricate process ensures the creation of a high-quality engine block.

The evolution of cylinder block machining techniques across different industrial transformations, from Industry 3.0 to Industry 5.0, has been studied and compared. This study summarizes and compares how manufacturing has evolved from Industry 3.0 to Industry 5.0, specifically in cylinder block machining. The goal is to examine and highlight the critical aspects and changes that have taken place in each phase of industry development. The engine block machining process comprises multiple stages, as outlined below:

Loading Components: At the start of the engine block machining process, raw engine block castings or partially finished blocks were meticulously positioned onto a conveyor or dedicated fixture. Ensuring proper alignment and secure clamping was paramount to guarantee precise and accurate subsequent machining operations. This loading phase established the groundwork for the entire machining process.

Leak Test: Manufacturers conducted a leak test on the engine block casting before machining. This procedure involved pressurizing the block's cooling and lubrication passages to identify potential cracks, voids, or imperfections. Detecting these flaws at this stage prevented the production of faulty engine blocks and ensured the structural integrity of the final product.

Machining: In this step, specialized machinery, frequently controlled by Computer Numerical Control (CNC), was utilized to execute intricate operations. Engine block machining encompassed various crucial tasks: cylinder boring was adjusted for new pistons, honing enhanced cylinder wall qualities, deck surfacing ensured effective gasket sealing, line boring precisely aligned main bearings, and crankshaft/camshaft grinding and polishing enhanced functionality. Additionally, thread repair was conducted to maintain integrity. Skilled experts meticulously carried out these processes, restoring the engine block to optimal condition and promoting efficient and dependable engine performance.

Washing: After machining, the engine block could have been contaminated with residual coolant, lubricants, metal chips, and other debris. It underwent a thorough washing process to prepare the block for further processing or assembly. This step guaranteed the block was clean and devoid of contaminants that could compromise the engine's performance or longevity.

Marking and Grading: Engine blocks were frequently marked with vital information during this phase. Part numbers, manufacturing dates, and quality control indicators were engraved or marked onto the block's surface. Some engine blocks might have undergone a grading process to assess their dimensional accuracy and overall quality. This process categorized the blocks based on performance characteristics, ensuring that only blocks meeting desired specifications progressed to subsequent production stages.

Unloading Component: Following the completion of the machining, washing, marking, and grading processes, the finished engine block was cautiously unloaded from the machining fixture or conveyor. Proper handling at this stage was crucial to prevent damage to the freshly machined surfaces. The engine block was prepared for further assembly, testing, or other downstream processes.

Each step is crucial in converting raw engine block castings into high-quality, precision-engineered components. The entire process requires a combination of advanced machinery, skilled operators, and stringent quality control measures to produce reliable and efficient engine blocks. Figure 2.3 illustrates a schematic representation of the engine block machining process across different industrial revolutions, featuring sequentially numbered operations.

In the Industry 3.0 model for engine block machining (Figure 2.3a), human operators actively participate in all stages of the machining process and can interface with machinery, including handling component loading and unloading tasks. Specifically, Person 1 is responsible for loading the casting component of the cylinder block into the machines once the previous operation is completed. Notably, the honing machine, which requires a longer duration for cylinder bore finishing, determines the overall cycle time. Subsequently, a washing machine cleanses the component and removes oil residue from the honing process. Following this cleansing process, the component undergoes marking, after which either Person 1 or Person 2 inspects

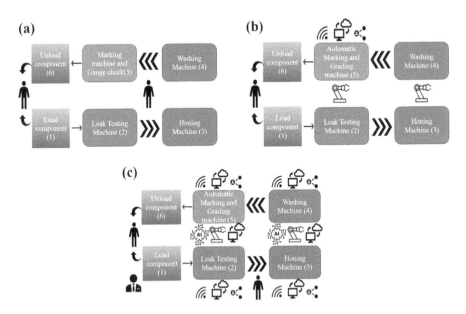

FIGURE 2.3 Engine block machining progression in different industrial epochs (a) Industry 3.0, (b) Industry 4.0, and (c) Industry 5.0

using a pressure gauge. Notably, any available individual can execute this gauge assessment with a machining or component handling scheduling window. However, this approach can lead to fatigue among human operators and does not contribute to enhancing the overall productivity of manufacturing companies.

Industries tried to enhance productivity by changing their process through adding robots and technologies. Robots are vital in managing heavy and intricate tasks, especially within sectors like the electrical and automotive industries [91]. Cyber-Physical Systems, a blend of digital and physical elements, seamlessly integrate into the manufacturing process to optimize efficiency and precision. These systems facilitate real-time data exchange between the physical production environment and the digital world, enabling intelligent decision-making and responsive adjustments [92]. Figure 2.3b illustrates a model for engine block machining within the context of Industry 4.0. Robots are integrated into the machining process, guided by teaching pendants to minimize unintended arm movements and enhance precision. In contrast to Industry 3.0's manual marking and gauge checks for components, Industry 4.0 adopts automatic grading and marking machines supported by IoT integration. The automatic marking and grading machine labels the component grade and records manufacturing date and time details. The Industrial Internet of Things (IIoT) encompasses machine-to-machine (M2M) communication, industrial communication technologies (ICT), and automation applications [93]. This integration of IoT technologies provides real-time insights into critical process information and individual worker details. Combining process data and worker engagement improves efficiency, productivity, and overall performance. However, the manufacturing industry confronts a growing threat of cyber-attacks focused explicitly on exploiting vulnerabilities in IoT connections within machining areas. As a result, regular assessments become imperative to address these cybersecurity risks effectively [94]. The machine is interconnected with computers, underscoring the need to secure and safeguard its software. Digital twins have found widespread application, with approximately 85 percent of global IoT systems utilizing them for security monitoring and process simulation tasks [95]. The Fourth Industrial Revolution is replacing humans in the workplace to enhance safety and production. However, this shift poses a challenge for the human workforce, potentially leading to job displacement [96]. In the Industry 3.0 model for engine block machining (Figure 2.3a), human operators actively participate in all stages of the machining process and can interface with machinery, including handling component loading and unloading tasks. Specifically, Person 1 is responsible for loading the casting component of the cylinder block into the machines once the previous operation is completed. Notably, the honing machine, which requires a longer duration for cylinder bore finishing, determines the overall cycle time. Subsequently, a washing machine cleanses the component and removes oil residue from the honing process. Following this cleansing process, the component undergoes marking, after which either Person 1 or Person 2 inspects it using a pressure gauge. Notably, any available individual can execute this gauge assessment with a machining or component handling scheduling window. However, this approach can lead to fatigue among human operators and does not contribute to enhancing the overall productivity of manufacturing companies.

Industries tried to enhance productivity by changing their process by adding robots and technologies. Robots are vital in managing heavy and intricate tasks, especially within sectors like the electrical and automotive industries [91]. Cyber-Physical Systems, a blend of digital and physical elements, seamlessly integrate into the manufacturing process to optimize efficiency and precision. These systems facilitate real-time data exchange between the physical production environment and the digital world, enabling intelligent decision-making and responsive adjustments [92]. Figure 2.3b illustrates a model for engine block machining within the context of Industry 4.0. Robots are integrated into the machining process, guided by teaching pendants to minimize unintended arm movements and enhance precision. In contrast to Industry 3.0's manual marking and gauge checks for components, Industry 4.0 adopts automatic grading and marking machines supported by IoT integration. The automatic marking and grading machine labels the component grade and records manufacturing date and time details. The Industrial Internet of Things encompasses machine-to-machine (M2M) communication, industrial communication technologies, and automation applications [93]. This integration of IoT technologies provides real-time insights into critical process information and individual worker details. Combining process data and worker engagement promotes improved efficiency, productivity, and overall performance. However, the manufacturing industry confronts a growing threat of cyber-attacks focused explicitly on exploiting vulnerabilities in IoT connections within machining areas. As a result, regular assessments become imperative to address these cybersecurity risks effectively [94]. The machine is interconnected with computers, underscoring the need to secure and safeguard its software. Digital twins have found widespread application, with approximately 85 percent of global IoT systems utilizing them for security monitoring and process simulation tasks [95]. The Fourth Industrial Revolution is replacing humans in the workplace to enhance safety and production. However, this shift poses a challenge for the human workforce, potentially leading to job displacement [96].

Industry 5.0 promotes collaboration between humans and robots to address unemployment while enhancing product value. Figure 2.3c illustrates the Industry 5.0 model for cylinder block machining. Robots can use AI, enabling IoT integration across all machines [97]. Cobots will support robots within the workspace, while skilled laborers will monitor machines and cobots. Industry 5.0 synergizes human intelligence with cognitive computing to generate value-added products [98]. Representing a new evolutionary stage, Industry 5.0 embodies a harmonious partnership between humans and machines, significantly reshaping tasks and manufacturing processes. Human workers will receive training in cognitive tasks for value-added activities, focusing on supervisory and decision-making roles [77]. This paradigm will create employment opportunities and enhance economic behavior by providing appropriate training to workers [54]. In a shared workspace, cobots specialize in tasks to assist human workers [99, 100]. As people concentrate on jobs demanding intelligence and creativity, cobots must collaborate with humans to enhance process efficiency and productivity. The Fifth Industrial Revolution introduces challenges for humans collaborating with smart working systems within organizations, reaffirming the pivotal role of human workers on manufacturing floors. Effectively addressing these challenges requires socio-technical approaches.

Table 2.2 summarizes the key characteristics of engine block machining across different industrial revolutions. The study conclusively illustrates that the progression from manual procedures to advanced automation methodologies, spanning the transition from Industry 3.0 to Industry 5.0, entails a focus on enhancing efficiency, ensuring precise data handling, and redefining job roles. Industry 4.0 and Industry 5.0 introduce advanced technologies like IoT, AI, and cobots to enhance productivity and create higher value-added products. It also emphasizes the need to tackle challenges and establish a smooth working relationship between humans and machines as manufacturing continues to evolve.

TABLE 2.2
Engine Block Machining Progression

	Industry 3.0	Industry 4.0	Industry 5.0
Process	Humans actively participate in all stages, with manual loading, unloading, and inspection.	Human–robot partnership. Robots handle repetitive tasks, while humans oversee and guide operations.	Symbiotic collaboration. Humans, robots, and cobots work harmoniously, combining their strengths for optimized efficiency.
Technological Integration	Limited technological integration. Manual operations and occasional use of CNC.	Increased technological integration. CNC-controlled robots enhance precision and efficiency. IoT integration for marking, grading, and data collection.	Advanced technological integration. AI-driven robots and cobots perform tasks linked to IoT for real-time process insights.
Key Components	Human operators, CNC machines, manual loading and unloading.	Robots, CNC-controlled machinery, IoT-enabled systems.	Robots, cobots, AI algorithms, IoT-integrated processes.
Advantages	Human expertise and flexibility in manual operations.	Enhanced precision, reduced human error, consistent quality, and data-driven decision-making.	Optimal efficiency, higher productivity, seamless human–robot collaboration, and real-time insights for process optimization.
Challenges	Limited precision, potential human error, variable quality control.	Initial implementation costs, maintenance of complex robotic systems, and cybersecurity vulnerabilities.	Human–machine collaboration complexities, potential job displacement, ethical considerations.

2.6 CHALLENGES TOWARD INDUSTRY 5.0

Industry 5.0 could give customers personalized services through a cognitive-enabled manufacturing process. Some potential implementation problems in this section must be addressed for seamless services. Additionally, while providing clients with personalized and more predictive services, privacy-preserving data transfers, data collecting, and ethical aspects must be considered. Bringing human resources and access to the factory floor may be helpful. Still, adequate training for both parties should address practical difficulties, such as cooperation between machines and humans. Customized customer service with human–robot collaboration must account for challenges with increasing customers and the manufacturing process [101]. Furthermore, AI adoption's ethical problems must be considered to minimize significant drawbacks.

Laws and Regulations: Laws and regulations are required for any Industrial Revolution to be fully implemented [102]. Although there are basic standards for automation, such as innovation policy and norms, the more particular norms for this new age must be implemented. As part of Industry 5.0, various human and cobot policies must be developed, as the goal is to reintroduce humans to collaborate and share with cobots and cognitive technologies. In this co-production environment, several challenges may occur if suitable norms and legal procedures are not in place. Controlling AI and other industrial devices should be created to improve co-production forecasts. Adoption will be faster, more complete, and more managed with improved rules, regulations, and standards. As a result, a robust Industry 5.0 framework must contain blockchain for data protection and preservation and the cognitive edge for quick information analysis.

Trained employees: A skilled worker is required in Industry 5.0 to complete a high-value manufacturing task. Standardization and regulatory standards must be introduced to solve technological or management challenges. Management, personnel, corporate culture, management infrastructure, and standard rules all play a part in developing a skilled employee. The main issue in the skill sector is a lack of qualified trainers and cost limits in providing suitable training to humans who collaborate with robots. When Industry 5.0 is implemented, the demand for skilled workers will increase, as will the need for new technologies, necessitating proper training for trainees and future trainers. It has the potential to promote public-private collaboration. Reforming regulations will also be required.

Furthermore, a well-trained workforce can aid organizational performance. Many sectors would adapt to the rapidly developed technology to keep up with digital competency, but management may not understand it. The culture and skilled employees may take advantage of the management's ignorance. If the workers are not forward thinkers, the company will have to spend a lot of money on training, and reengineering will take time. Some industries may lack the infrastructure required to accommodate the new technologies. As a result, these obstacles should be considered while building an innovative corporate structure and long-term recruiting qualified personnel. Providing continuous and practical training for humans and cobots can avoid most co-working concerns. Ongoing training for operational staff will also contribute to skilled labor.

Privacy and Security: Industry 5.0 must meet specific standards because it depends on intellectual property, privacy and organizational materials. Data is exchanged via the internet in Industry 5.0 to link machines to humans, and designers between other users, and process and reporting data is displayed. To retain the security of the cloud manufacturing environment, such data must not be available to hostile internet users [103]. Human workers generally believe that AI will result in job losses, whereas Industry 5.0 will offer jobs for people. Its influence on humans should be addressed for seamless collaboration between people and cobots for co-production [53]. Cobots must incorporate social decisions, ethical principles, relationships, and cultural traditions. The Industrial Revolution's policymakers must consider the ethical implications of human–machine collaboration [104, 105]. Human data protection rights, or the rights of individuals to govern their data, are one of the privacy concerns. They have the right to bring a claim if their personal or confidential information is stolen. As a result, while using user data for cognitive analysis, data security must be ensured. Explainable AI should increase trust in AI systems by making them more transparent. As a result, privacy should be incorporated as a development idea to confirm that AI-based systems evolve smoothly and generate correct predictions. While many businesses are still figuring out how to adopt Industry 4.0, transitioning to Industry 5.0 will be far more difficult. By integrating AI and automation, Industry 5.0 will develop a new threat. For security, AI/ML functions require trustworthy execution. The data set security utilized for AL and ML model training should be secured for maintaining the Industry 5.0 applications. New security requirements are obtained in Industry 5.0 applications, which depend on ICT systems. Quantum computing can potentially move Industry 5.0 into the quantum computing era. A quantum computer will significantly simplify the safeguarding of legacy security systems. Industry 5.0 should use encryption techniques such as post-quantum or quantum-resistant to attain the maximum level of security.

Human–Robot Collaboration in Industry: Industry 5.0 places humans on the manufacturing floor, where they will collaborate with cobots. Though it appears to be a cost-effective method of developing customized products, unique difficulties with human–robot collaboration must be explored. Humans will also have less fear of losing their jobs if robots and humans work together. The cobots will do the repetitive tasks, allowing humans to focus entirely on creativity and invention. The human–robot collaboration will be more productive but can affect the corporate culture and the organization. Also, humans who work with cobots are highly trained and can expect more than a standard work environment.

2.7 SUMMARY

Manufacturing companies have consistently adapted their production strategies by embracing innovative technologies to meet the rapidly evolving demands of the modern market. As technology advances rapidly, manufacturers must proactively prepare for the transition to Industry 5.0, positioning themselves to capitalize on market expansion opportunities. The advent of Industry 5.0 will usher in transformative changes to manufacturing systems, leading to heightened levels of productivity and efficiency. Within the realm of Industry 5.0, interventions are strategically oriented toward fostering long-term growth and sustainability. The integration of emerging technologies inherent to Industry 5.0 promises to substantially enhance the production of customized products, thereby engendering heightened customer satisfaction. It's noteworthy that human involvement remains pivotal in overseeing and managing manufacturing processes in the Industry 5.0 era.

Human adaptability has played a pivotal role in generating novel ideas and facilitating collaboration with collaborative robots or cobots in response to technological shifts. This symbiotic partnership between humans and cobots has emerged as a key enabler, offering many advantages. Cobot integration within manufacturing domains allows these autonomous robotic assistants to collaboratively complete designated tasks, leading to optimized and more efficient production workflows. The significance of Industry 5.0 is underscored by this study, which employs a sociotechnical approach to illustrate the profound relationship between cobots and human operatives within the manufacturing industry. This approach holds the potential to foster economic growth, elevate living standards, and promote environmental sustainability. In the future, researchers will explore further to expand the scope and implementation of cobots across diverse applications.

REFERENCES

1. M. Krzywdzinski, "Automation, skill requirements and labour-use strategies: Highwage and low-wage approaches to high-tech manufacturing in the automotive industry," *New Technol. Work Employ.*, vol. 32, no. 3, pp. 247–267, 2017, doi: 10.1111/ntwe.12100.
2. J. D. Sachs, G. Schmidt-Traub, M. Mazzucato, D. Messner, N. Nakicenovic, and J. Rockström, "Six Transformations to achieve the Sustainable Development Goals," *Nat. Sustain.*, vol. 2, no. 9, pp. 805–814, 2019, doi: 10.1038/s41893-019-0352-9.
3. T. Salimova, N. Guskova, I. Krakovskaya, and E. Sirota, "From industry 4.0 to Society 5.0: Challenges for sustainable competitiveness of Russian industry," *IOP Conf. Ser. Mater. Sci. Eng.*, vol. 497, no. 1, pp. 0–7, 2019, doi: 10.1088/1757-899X/497/1/012090.
4. R. Brozzi, D. Forti, E. Rauch, and D. T. Matt, "The advantages of industry 4.0 applications for sustainability: Results from a sample of manufacturing companies," *Sustain.*, vol. 12, no. 9, 2020, doi: 10.3390/su12093647.
5. I. S. Khan, M. O. Ahmad, and J. Majava, "Industry 4.0 and sustainable development: A systematic mapping of triple bottom line, circular economy and sustainable business models perspectives," *J. Clean. Prod.*, vol. 297, p. 126655, 2021, doi: 10.1016/j. jclepro.2021.126655.
6. R. Davies, T. Coole, and A. Smith, "Review of socio-technical considerations to ensure successful implementation of industry 4.0," *Procedia Manuf.*, vol. 11, no. June, pp. 1288–1295, 2017, doi: 10.1016/j.promfg.2017.07.256.
7. A. Grybauskas, A. Stefanini, and M. Ghobakhloo, "Social sustainability in the age of digitalization: A systematic literature Review on the social implications of industry 4.0," *Technol. Soc.*, vol. 70, no. May, p. 101997, 2022, doi: 10.1016/j.techsoc.2022.101997.
8. M. Hermann, T. Pentek, and B. Otto, "Design principles for industrie 4.0 scenarios," *Proc. Annu. Hawaii Int. Conf. Syst. Sci.*, vol. 2016-March, pp. 3928–3937, 2016, doi: 10.1109/HICSS.2016.488.

9. M. Javaid, A. Haleem, R. P. Singh, R. Suman, and E. S. Gonzalez, "Understanding the adoption of Industry 4.0 technologies in improving environmental sustainability," *Sustain. Oper. Comput.*, vol. 3, no. May 2021, pp. 203–217, 2022, doi: 10.1016/j. susoc.2022.01.008.

10. U. Meyer, "The emergence of an envisioned future: Sensemaking in the case of 'Industrie 4.0' in Germany," *Futures*, vol. 109, no. January 2018, pp. 130–141, 2019, doi: 10.1016/j.futures.2019.03.001.

11. X. Wang, S. K. Ong, and A. Y. C. Nee, "A comprehensive survey of augmented reality assembly research," *Adv. Manuf.*, vol. 4, no. 1, pp. 1–22, Mar. 2016, doi: 10.1007/s40436-015-0131-4.

12. D. Ivanov, A. Dolgui, and B. Sokolov, "Cloud supply chain: Integrating Industry 4.0 and digital platforms in the 'supply chain-as-a-service'," *Transp. Res. Part E Logist. Transp. Rev.*, vol. 160, no. February, p. 102676, 2022, doi: 10.1016/j.tre.2022.102676.

13. W. P. Neumann, S. Winkelhaus, E. H. Grosse, and C. H. Glock, "Industry 4.0 and the human factor – A systems framework and analysis methodology for successful development," *Int. J. Prod. Econ.*, vol. 233, no. May 2020, p. 107992, 2021, doi: 10.1016/j. ijpe.2020.107992.

14. Y. E. Spanos and I. Voudouris, "Antecedents and trajectories of AMT adoption: The case of Greek manufacturing SMEs," *Res. Policy*, vol. 38, no. 1, pp. 144–155, 2009, doi: 10.1016/j.respol.2008.09.006.

15. T. W. Campbell, "Technologies, potential, and implications of additive manufacturing," Cbpp.Uaa.Alaska.Edu, 2012, [Online]. Available: http://www.cbpp.uaa.alaska.edu/afef/ AdditiveMFG.pdf

16. B. Berman, "3-D printing: The new industrial revolution," *Bus. Horiz.*, vol. 55, no. 2, pp. 155–162, March 2012, doi: 10.1016/j.bushor.2011.11.003.

17. L. Gerlitz, "Design management as a domain of smart and sustainable enterprise: Business modelling for innovation and smart growth in Industry 4.0," *Entrep. Sustain. Issues*, vol. 3, no. 3, pp. 244–268, 2016, doi: 10.9770/jesi.2016.3.3(3).

18. T. Stock, M. Obenaus, S. Kunz, and H. Kohl, "Industry 4.0 as enabler for a sustainable development: A qualitative assessment of its ecological and social potential," *Process Saf. Environ. Prot.*, vol. 118, pp. 254–267, 2018, doi: 10.1016/j.psep.2018.06.026.

19. S. Bartoloni et al., "Towards designing society 5.0 solutions: The new Quintuple Helix - Design thinking approach to technology," *Technovation*, vol. 113, no. November 2021, 2022, doi: 10.1016/j.technovation.2021.102413.

20. J. M. Müller, O. Buliga, and K. I. Voigt, "Fortune favors the prepared: How SMEs approach business model innovations in industry 4.0," *Technol. Forecast. Soc. Change*, vol. 132, no. January, pp. 2–17, 2018, doi: 10.1016/j.techfore.2017.12.019.

21. S. S. Kamble, A. Gunasekaran, and R. Sharma, "Analysis of the driving and dependence power of barriers to adopt industry 4.0 in Indian manufacturing industry," *Comput. Ind.*, vol. 101, no. March, pp. 107–119, 2018, doi: 10.1016/j.compind.2018.06.004.

22. A. G. Frank, L. S. Dalenogare, and N. F. Ayala, "Industry 4.0 technologies: Implementation patterns in manufacturing companies," *Int. J. Prod. Econ.*, vol. 210, no. January, pp. 15–26, 2019, doi: 10.1016/j.ijpe.2019.01.004.

23. F. E. García-Muiña, M. S. Medina-Salgado, A. M. Ferrari, and M. Cucchi, "Sustainability transition in industry 4.0 and smart manufacturing with the triple-layered business model canvas," *Sustain.*, vol. 12, no. 6, 2020, doi: 10.3390/su12062364.

24. G. Bitsch, "Conceptions of man in human-centric cyber-physical production systems," *Procedia CIRP*, vol. 107, no. 2021, pp. 1439–1443, 2022, doi: 10.1016/j. procir.2022.05.171.

25. F. Lima et al., "Digital manufacturing tools in the simulation of collaborative robots: Towards industry 4.0," *Brazilian J. Oper. Prod. Manag.*, vol. 16, no. 2, pp. 261–280, 2019, doi: 10.14488/bjopm.2019.v16.n2.a8.

26. A. Korodi, R. Crisan, A. Nicolae, and I. Silea, "Industrial internet of things and fog computing to reduce energy consumption in drinking water facilities," *Processes*, vol. 8, no. 3, 2020, doi: 10.3390/pr8030282.

27. O. Rholam, M. Tabaa, F. Monteiro, and A. Dandache, "Smart device for multi-band industrial IoT communications," *Procedia Comput. Sci.*, vol. 155, pp. 660–665, 2019, doi: 10.1016/j.procs.2019.08.094.

28. C. Zhu, J. J. P. C. Rodrigues, V. C. M. Leung, L. Shu, and L. T. Yang, "Trust-based communication for the industrial internet of things," *IEEE Commun. Mag.*, vol. 56, no. 2, pp. 16–22, 2018, doi: 10.1109/MCOM.2018.1700592.

29. B. Bigliardi, S. Filippelli, and L. Tagliente, "Industry 4.0 and open innovation: Evidence from a case study," *Procedia Comput. Sci.*, vol. 200, no. 2019, pp. 1796–1805, 2022, doi: 10.1016/j.procs.2022.01.380.

30. N. Kumar and S. C. Lee, "Human-machine interface in smart factory: A systematic literature review," *Technol. Forecast. Soc. Change*, vol. 174, no. October 2021, p. 121284, 2022, doi: 10.1016/j.techfore.2021.121284.

31. K. E. Kushida, J. Murray, and J. Zysman, "Diffusing the cloud: Cloud computing and implications for public policy," *J. Ind. Compet. Trade*, vol. 11, no. 3, pp. 209–237, 2011, doi: 10.1007/s10842-011-0106-5.

32. A. O. Laplume, B. Petersen, and J. M. Pearce, "Global value chains from a 3D printing perspective," *J. Int. Bus. Stud.*, vol. 47, no. 5, pp. 595–609, 2016, doi: 10.1057/jibs.2015.47.

33. D. K. Singh and R. Sobti, "Long-range real-time monitoring strategy for Precision Irrigation in urban and rural farming in society 5.0," *Comput. Ind. Eng.*, vol. 167, no. February, p. 107997, 2022, doi: 10.1016/j.cie.2022.107997.

34. J.-P. Bootz, S. Michel, J. Pallud, and R. Monti, "Possible changes of Industry 4.0 in 2030 in the face of uberization: Results of a participatory and systemic foresight study," *Technol. Forecast. Soc. Change*, vol. 184, no. October 2021, p. 121962, 2022, doi: 10.1016/j.techfore.2022.121962.

35. S. Jayashree, M. N. H. Reza, C. A. N. Malarvizhi, A. Gunasekaran, and M. A. Rauf, "Testing an adoption model for Industry 4.0 and sustainability: A Malaysian scenario," *Sustain. Prod. Consum.*, vol. 31, pp. 313–330, 2022, doi: 10.1016/j.spc.2022.02.015.

36. G. Reischauer, "Industry 4.0 as policy-driven discourse to institutionalize innovation systems in manufacturing," *Technol. Forecast. Soc. Change*, vol. 132, no. February, pp. 26–33, 2018, doi: 10.1016/j.techfore.2018.02.012.

37. F. Zantalis, G. Koulouras, S. Karabetsos, and D. Kandris, "A review of machine learning and IoT in smart transportation," *Futur. Internet*, vol. 11, no. 4, pp. 1–23, 2019, doi: 10.3390/FI11040094.

38. R. Ashima, A. Haleem, S. Bahl, M. Javaid, S. K. Mahla, and S. Singh, "Automation and manufacturing of smart materials in additive manufacturing technologies using Internet of Things towards the adoption of industry 4.0," *Mater. Today Proc.*, vol. 45, pp. 5081–5088, 2021, doi: 10.1016/j.matpr.2021.01.583.

39. G. Büchi, M. Cugno, and R. Castagnoli, "Smart factory performance and industry 4.0," *Technol. Forecast. Soc. Change*, vol. 150, no. June 2019, p. 119790, 2020, doi: 10.1016/j.techfore.2019.119790.

40. F. Longo, A. Padovano, and S. Umbrello, "Value-oriented and ethical technology engineering in industry 5.0: A human-centric perspective for the design of the factory of the future," *Appl. Sci.*, vol. 10, no. 12, pp. 1–25, 2020, doi: 10.3390/APP10124182.

41. F. Tao, J. Cheng, Q. Qi, M. Zhang, H. Zhang, and F. Sui, "Digital twin-driven product design, manufacturing and service with big data," *Int. J. Adv. Manuf. Technol.*, vol. 94, no. 9–12, pp. 3563–3576, 2018, doi: 10.1007/s00170-017-0233-1.

42. R. Sindhwani, S. Afridi, A. Kumar, A. Banaitis, S. Luthra, and P. L. Singh, "Can industry 5.0 revolutionize the wave of resilience and social value creation? A multi-criteria framework to analyze enablers," *Technol. Soc.*, vol. 68, no. November 2021, p. 101887, 2022, doi: 10.1016/j.techsoc.2022.101887.

43. G. Westerman, D. B. Onnet, and A. N. Mca, *Digital Into Business Transformation.* 2014. Harvard Business Review Press.

44. M. Attaran, "The rise of 3-D printing: The advantages of additive manufacturing over traditional manufacturing," *Bus. Horiz.*, vol. 60, no. 5, pp. 677–688, 2017, doi: 10.1016/j.bushor.2017.05.011.

45. M. Bogers, R. Hadar, and A. Bilberg, "Additive manufacturing for consumer-centric business models: Implications for supply chains in consumer goods manufacturing," *Technol. Forecast. Soc. Change*, vol. 102, pp. 225–239, 2016, doi: 10.1016/j.techfore.2015.07.024.

46. M. S. Hossain and G. Muhammad, "Cloud-assisted Industrial Internet of Things (IIoT) - Enabled framework for health monitoring," *Comput. Networks*, vol. 101, pp. 192–202, 2016, doi: 10.1016/j.comnet.2016.01.009.

47. I. C. L. Ng and S. Y. L. Wakenshaw, "The Internet-of-Things: Review and research directions," *Int. J. Res. Mark.*, vol. 34, no. 1, pp. 3–21, 2017, doi: 10.1016/j.ijresmar.2016.11.003.

48. M. J. Kim, X. Wang, S. Han, and Y. Wang, "Implementing an augmented reality-enabled wayfinding system through studying user experience and requirements in complex environments," *Vis. Eng.*, vol. 3, no. 1, 2015, doi: 10.1186/s40327-015-0026-2.

49. M. Ghobakhloo, "The future of manufacturing industry: A strategic roadmap toward Industry 4.0," *J. Manuf. Technol. Manag.*, vol. 29, no. 6, pp. 910–936, 2018, doi: 10.1108/JMTM-02-2018-0057.

50. J. M. Müller, D. Kiel, and K. I. Voigt, "What drives the implementation of Industry 4.0? The role of opportunities and challenges in the context of sustainability," *Sustain.*, vol. 10, no. 1, 2018, doi: 10.3390/su10010247.

51. E. Hofmann and M. Rüsch, "Industry 4.0 and the current status as well as future prospects on logistics," *Comput. Ind.*, vol. 89, pp. 23–34, 2017, doi: 10.1016/j.compind.2017.04.002.

52. D. Kiel, C. Arnold, and K. I. Voigt, "The influence of the Industrial Internet of Things on business models of established manufacturing companies – A business level perspective," *Technovation*, vol. 68, no. September 2016, pp. 4–19, 2017, doi: 10.1016/j.technovation.2017.09.003.

53. N. Barker and C. Jewitt, "Future touch in industry: Exploring socio-technical imaginaries of tactile (tele)robots," *Futures*, vol. 136, no. November 2021, p. 102885, 2022, doi: 10.1016/j.futures.2021.102885.

54. O. Kolade and A. Owoseni, "Employment 5.0: The work of the future and the future of work," *Technol. Soc.*, vol. 71, no. August, p. 102086, 2022, doi: 10.1016/j.techsoc.2022.102086.

55. Y. Qu, S. R. Pokhrel, S. Garg, L. Gao, and Y. Xiang, "A blockchained federated learning framework for cognitive computing in industry 4.0 networks," *IEEE Trans. Ind. Informatics*, vol. 17, no. 4, pp. 2964–2973, 2021, doi: 10.1109/TII.2020.3007817.

56. S. R. Pokhrel and S. Singh, "Compound TCP performance for industry 4.0 WiFi: A cognitive federated learning approach," *IEEE Trans. Ind. Informatics*, vol. 17, no. 3, pp. 2143–2151, 2021, doi: 10.1109/TII.2020.2985033.

57. P. Thorvald, J. Lindblom, and R. Andreasson, "On the development of a method for cognitive load assessment in manufacturing," *Robot. Comput. Integr. Manuf.*, vol. 59, no. April, pp. 252–266, 2019, doi: 10.1016/j.rcim.2019.04.012.

58. B. Bajic, I. Cosic, B. Katalinic, S. Moraca, M. Lazarevic, and A. Rikalovic, "Edge computing vs. Cloud computing: Challenges and opportunities in industry 4.0," *Ann. DAAAM Proc. Int. DAAAM Symp.*, vol. 30, no. 1, pp. 864–871, 2019, doi: 10.2507/30th.daaam.proceedings.120.

59. I. Sittón-Candanedo, R. S. Alonso, S. Rodríguez-González, J. A. García Coria, and F. De La Prieta, "Edge computing architectures in industry 4.0: A general survey and comparison," 2020, pp. 121–131. doi: 10.1007/978-3-030-20055-8_12.

60. C. Zhang, G. Zhou, J. Li, F. Chang, K. Ding, and D. Ma, "A multi-access edge computing enabled framework for the construction of a knowledge-sharing intelligent machine tool swarm in Industry 4.0," *J. Manuf. Syst.*, vol. 66, no. November 2022, pp. 56–70, 2023, doi: 10.1016/j.jmsy.2022.11.015.

61. L. S. Dalenogare, G. B. Benitez, N. F. Ayala, and A. G. Frank, "The expected contribution of Industry 4.0 technologies for industrial performance," *Int. J. Prod. Econ.*, vol. 204, no. December 2017, pp. 383–394, 2018, doi: 10.1016/j.ijpe.2018.08.019.

62. L. S. Dalenogare, G. B. Benitez, N. F. Ayala, and A. G. Frank, "The expected contribution of Industry 4.0 technologies for industrial performance," *Int. J. Prod. Econ.*, vol. 204, no. July, pp. 383–394, 2018, doi: 10.1016/j.ijpe.2018.08.019.

63. M. Ammar, A. Haleem, M. Javaid, S. Bahl, and A. S. Verma, "Implementing industry 4.0 technologies in self-healing materials and digitally managing the quality of manufacturing," *Mater. Today Proc.*, vol. 52, pp. 2285–2294, 2021, doi: 10.1016/j.matpr.2021.09.248.

64. E. Coronado, T. Kiyokawa, G. A. G. Ricardez, I. G. Ramirez-Alpizar, G. Venture, and N. Yamanobe, "Evaluating quality in human-robot interaction: A systematic search and classification of performance and human-centered factors, measures and metrics towards an industry 5.0," *J. Manuf. Syst.*, vol. 63, no. April, pp. 392–410, 2022, doi: 10.1016/j.jmsy.2022.04.007.

65. P. Osterrieder, L. Budde, and T. Friedli, "The smart factory as a key construct of industry 4.0: A systematic literature review," *Int. J. Prod. Econ.*, vol. 221, no. November 2017, p. 107476, 2020, doi: 10.1016/j.ijpe.2019.08.011.

66. P. K. R. Maddikunta et al., "Industry 5.0: A survey on enabling technologies and potential applications," *J. Ind. Inf. Integr.*, vol. 26, no. July 2021, p. 100257, 2022, doi: 10.1016/j.jii.2021.100257.

67. M. Calış Duman and B. Akdemir, "A study to determine the effects of industry 4.0 technology components on organizational performance," *Technol. Forecast. Soc. Change*, vol. 167, no. January, pp. 0–3, 2021, doi: 10.1016/j.techfore.2021.120615.

68. F. Aslam, W. Aimin, M. Li, and K. U. Rehman, "Innovation in the era of IoT and industry 5.0: Absolute innovation management (AIM) framework," *Inf.*, vol. 11, no. 2, 2020, doi: 10.3390/info11020124.

69. Y. Lu et al., "Outlook on human-centric manufacturing towards Industry 5.0," *J. Manuf. Syst.*, vol. 62, no. November 2021, pp. 612–627, 2022, doi: 10.1016/j.jmsy.2022.02.001.

70. J. Leng et al., "Industry 5.0: Prospect and retrospect," *J. Manuf. Syst.*, vol. 65, no. August, pp. 279–295, 2022, doi: 10.1016/j.jmsy.2022.09.017.

71. M. Tabaa, F. Monteiro, H. Bensag, and A. Dandache, "Green industrial internet of things from a smart industry perspectives," *Energy Reports*, vol. 6, no. June, pp. 430–446, 2020, doi: 10.1016/j.egyr.2020.09.022.

72. S. Grabowska, S. Saniuk, and B. Gajdzik, "Industry 5.0: Improving humanization and sustainability of Industry 4.0," *Scientometrics*, vol. 127, no. 6, pp. 3117–3144, 2022, doi: 10.1007/s11192-022-04370-1.

73. A. Adel, "Future of industry 5.0 in society: Human-centric solutions, challenges and prospective research areas," *J. Cloud Comput.*, vol. 11, no. 1, 2022, doi: 10.1186/s13677-022-00314-5.

74. Z. Saadati and R. V. Barenji, "Toward industry 5.0: Cognitive cyber-physical system," 2023, pp. 257–268. doi: 10.1007/978-981-19-2012-7_12.

75. M. Doyle-Kent and P. Kopacek, "Adoption of collaborative robotics in industry 5.0. An Irish industry case study," *IFAC-PapersOnLine*, vol. 54, no. 13, pp. 413–418, 2021, doi: 10.1016/j.ifacol.2021.10.483.

76. C. Bai, P. Dallasega, G. Orzes, and J. Sarkis, "Industry 4.0 technologies assessment: A sustainability perspective," *Int. J. Prod. Econ.*, vol. 229, p. 107776, 2020, doi: 10.1016/j.ijpe.2020.107776.

77. G. F. Prassida and U. Asfari, "A conceptual model for the acceptance of collaborative robots in industry 5.0," *Procedia Comput. Sci.*, vol. 197, pp. 61–67, 2021, doi: 10.1016/j.procs.2021.12.118.

78. M. Peshkin and J. E. Colgate, "Feature cobots," *Ind. Rob.*, vol. 26, no. 5, pp. 335–341, 1999.

79. A. Weiss, A. K. Wortmeier, and B. Kubicek, "Cobots in industry 4.0: A roadmap for future practice studies on human-robot collaboration," *IEEE Trans. Human-Machine Syst.*, vol. 51, no. 4, pp. 335–345, 2021, doi: 10.1109/THMS.2021.3092684.

80. R. Jahanmahin, S. Masoud, J. Rickli, and A. Djuric, "Human-robot interactions in manufacturing: A survey of human behavior modeling," *Robot. Comput. Integr. Manuf.*, vol. 78, p. 102404, 2022, doi: 10.1016/j.rcim.2022.102404.

81. T. B. Sheridan, "Human–robot interaction: Status and challenges," *Hum. Factors J. Hum. Factors Ergon. Soc.*, vol. 58, no. 4, pp. 525–532, Jun. 2016, doi: 10.1177/0018720816644364.

82. O. Maksimchuk and T. Pershina, "A new paradigm of industrial system optimization based on the conception 'industry 4.0'," *MATEC Web Conf.*, vol. 129, 2017, doi: 10.1051/matecconf/201712904006.

83. W. Bauer, M. Bender, P. Rally, and O. Scholtz, *Lightweight robots in manual assembly – Best to start simply! Examining Companies' Initial Experiences with Lightweight Robots*, 2016. Fraunhofer Institute for Industrial Engineering IAO, Stuttgart.

84. L. Gualtieri, E. Rauch, R. Vidoni, and D. T. Matt, "Safety, ergonomics and efficiency in human-robot collaborative assembly: Design guidelines and requirements," *Procedia CIRP*, vol. 91, no. March, pp. 367–372, 2020, doi: 10.1016/j.procir.2020.02.188.

85. F. M. Amin, M. Rezayati, H. W. van de Venn, and H. Karimpour, "A mixed-perception approach for safe human–robot collaboration in industrial automation," *Sensors (Switzerland)*, vol. 20, no. 21, pp. 1–20, 2020, doi: 10.3390/s20216347.

86. J. Berg and S. Lu, "Review of interfaces for industrial human-robot interaction," *Curr. Robot. Reports*, vol. 1, no. 2, pp. 27–34, 2020, doi: 10.1007/s43154-020-00005-6.

87. A. Bonarini, "Communication in human-robot interaction," *Curr. Robot. Reports*, vol. 1, no. 4, pp. 279–285, 2020, doi: 10.1007/s43154-020-00026-1.

88. G. A. Odesanmi, Q. Wang, and J. Mai, "Skill learning framework for human–robot interaction and manipulation tasks," *Robot. Comput. Integr. Manuf.*, vol. 79, no. August 2022, p. 102444, 2023, doi: 10.1016/j.rcim.2022.102444.

89. R. Etemad-Sajadi, A. Soussan, and T. Schöpfer, "How ethical issues raised by human–robot interaction can impact the intention to use the robot?," *Int. J. Soc. Robot.*, vol. 14, no. 4, pp. 1103–1115, 2022, doi: 10.1007/s12369-021-00857-8.

90. N. Emaminejad and R. Akhavian, "Trustworthy AI and robotics: Implications for the AEC industry," *Autom. Constr.*, vol. 139, no. October 2021, p. 104298, 2022, doi: 10.1016/j.autcon.2022.104298.

91. M. T. Ballestar, Á. Díaz-Chao, J. Sainz, and J. Torrent-Sellens, "Impact of robotics on manufacturing: A longitudinal machine learning perspective," *Technol. Forecast. Soc. Change*, vol. 162, no. September 2020, p. 120348, 2021, doi: 10.1016/j.techfore.2020.120348.

92. J. Lee, B. Bagheri, and H. A. Kao, "A cyber-physical systems architecture for Industry 4.0-based manufacturing systems," *Manuf. Lett.*, vol. 3, pp. 18–23, 2015, doi: 10.1016/j.mfglet.2014.12.001.

93. E. Sisinni, A. Saifullah, S. Han, U. Jennehag, and M. Gidlund, "Industrial internet of things: Challenges, opportunities, and directions," *IEEE Trans. Ind. Informatics*, vol. 14, no. 11, pp. 4724–4734, 2018, doi: 10.1109/TII.2018.2852491.

94. L. J. Wells, J. A. Camelio, C. B. Williams, and J. White, "Cyber-physical security challenges in manufacturing systems," *Manuf. Lett.*, vol. 2, no. 2, pp. 74–77, 2014, doi: 10.1016/j.mfglet.2014.01.005.

95. W. Wang et al., "BIM information integration based VR modeling in digital twins in industry 5.0," *J. Ind. Inf. Integr.*, vol. 28, no. April, p. 100351, 2022, doi: 10.1016/j.jii.2022.100351.

96. E. G. Margherita and A. M. Braccini, "Managing industry 4.0 automation for fair ethical business development: A single case study," *Technol. Forecast. Soc. Change*, vol. 172, no. July, p. 121048, 2021, doi: 10.1016/j.techfore.2021.121048.

97. D. Avishay, V. Pavlov, G. Pavlova, B. Petrov, and N. Dimitrov, "Industry 4.0 – Robots with distributed mobility and elements of AI," *Glob. J. Comput. Sci. Technol. D Neural Artif. Intell.*, vol. 19, no. 1, pp. 1–19, 2019.

98. X. Xu, Y. Lu, B. Vogel-Heuser, and L. Wang, "Industry 4.0 and industry 5.0—Inception, conception and perception," *J. Manuf. Syst.*, vol. 61, no. September, pp. 530–535, 2021, doi: 10.1016/j.jmsy.2021.10.006.

99. J. Reis, N. Melão, J. Salvadorinho, B. Soares, and A. Rosete, "Service robots in the hospitality industry: The case of Henn-na hotel, Japan," *Technol. Soc.*, vol. 63, no. September, 2020, doi: 10.1016/j.techsoc.2020.101423.

100. F. Seyitoğlu, S. Ivanov, O. Atsız, and İ. Çifçi, "Robots as restaurant employees - A double-barrelled detective story," *Technol. Soc.*, vol. 67, no. October, 2021, doi: 10.1016/j.techsoc.2021.101779.

101. D. Guo, S. Ling, Y. Rong, and G. Q. Huang, "Towards synchronization-oriented manufacturing planning and control for Industry 4.0 and beyond," *IFAC-PapersOnLine*, vol. 55, no. 2, pp. 163–168, 2022, doi: 10.1016/j.ifacol.2022.04.187.

102. K. A. Demir, G. Döven, and B. Sezen, "Industry 5.0 and human-robot co-working," *Procedia Comput. Sci.*, vol. 158, pp. 688–695, 2019, doi: 10.1016/j.procs.2019.09.104.

103. A. Basaure, A. Vesselkov, and J. Töyli, "Internet of things (IoT) platform competition: Consumer switching versus provider multihoming," *Technovation*, vol. 90–91, no. July 2018, p. 102101, 2020, doi: 10.1016/j.technovation.2019.102101.

104. M. Conti and A. Passarella, "The internet of people: A human and data-centric paradigm for the next generation internet," *Comput. Commun.*, vol. 131, pp. 51–65, 2018, doi: 10.1016/j.comcom.2018.07.034.

105. G. Beier, A. Ullrich, S. Niehoff, M. Reißig, and M. Habich, "Industry 4.0: How it is defined from a socio-technical perspective and how much sustainability it includes – A literature review," *J. Clean. Prod.*, vol. 259, 2020, doi: 10.1016/j.jclepro.2020.120856.

3 Exploring the Feasibility of Internet of Things in the Context of Intelligent Healthcare Solutions
A Review

Anwesa Sarkar, Anindya Nag, Moyuri Sen, and Nisarga Chand

3.1 INTRODUCTION

The IoT is experiencing significant growth in multiple industries, including the healthcare sector. This trend offers a promising prospect for transforming healthcare delivery by enabling instantaneous connectivity and communication between devices and sensors. The integration of IoT technology in the healthcare sector, sometimes referred to as "smart healthcare" holds significant promise in enhancing patient outcomes, reducing costs, and enhancing overall efficiency [1]. The IoT has emerged as a revolutionary technology that plays a crucial role in the advancement of remote and intelligent healthcare systems. It achieves this by enabling the networking and communication of various devices. The convergence of Big Data and the IoT in healthcare unlocks innovative avenues for managing healthcare processes, including remote patient monitoring, early disease detection, and disease prevention, particularly for chronic illnesses like diabetes, obstructive pulmonary disease, cancer, arthritis, and heart disease. The IoT, as a network of interconnected devices, is essential for enabling automation in various industries, including the establishment of remote and intelligent healthcare systems [2]. Technologies such as wireless sensor networks (WSNs), radiofrequency identification (RFID) and wireless body area networks (WBANs) contribute to individualized, proactive, and cost-effective healthcare solutions, facilitating tasks like tracking people and objects, authentication and identification, as well as automated data collection and sensing. The Healthcare IoT (HIoT) or Internet of Medical Things (IoMT) is used in healthcare systems to facilitate telemonitoring, teleconsultation, computer-assisted therapy, and elderly supervision. The convergence of big data and IoT presents a unique paradigm for smart healthcare management, empowering remote patient monitoring,

DOI: 10.1201/9781032642789-3

early disease detection, and disease prevention for chronic illnesses. It is noteworthy that conducting a systematic literature review that specifically emphasizes research challenges, trends, and future directions for HIoT is a rarity. This study explores the possibilities of IoT for smart healthcare solutions while identifying key challenges that must be resolved to fully fulfill their potential [3].

Figure 3.1 illustrates a theoretical scenario in which IoT technology is utilized in the healthcare sector. The IoT offers a diverse array of applications within the realm of medical care, encompassing remote monitoring, intelligent sensors, and integration of medical devices. The use of this practice serves to guarantee the security and welfare of patients, simultaneously augmenting the perception of the physician's attentiveness toward their requirements. Healthcare devices gather a wide range of information from many real-world scenarios, hence improving the accuracy and breadth of medical data [4]. Table 3.1 presents statistical data related to the field of smart healthcare, accompanied by the respective sources and the extent of the data coverage.

3.1.1 Healthcare IoT

In order to optimize the healthcare system, it is imperative to incorporate Information and Communication Technology (ICT) inside the realm of medicine. The need to

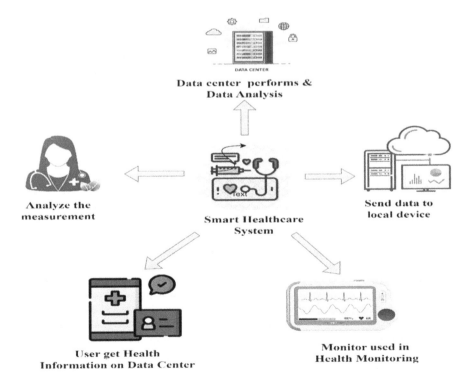

FIGURE 3.1 A hypothetical situation involving IoT technology and healthcare.

TABLE 3.1

Sources and Scope of Statistical Data Relating to Smart Healthcare

Statistical Data	Price (In USD) For Market	Percentage (% Of Market)	Source	Year	Scope
Expected percentage of medical devices connected to the internet by 2025	$262.4 billion	50% (of medical devices)	Deloitte	2025	Worldwide
Compound Annual Growth Rate (CAGR) of the smart healthcare market from 2021 to 2026	$173.45 billion	23.5% (annual growth rate)	Markets and Markets	2021	Worldwide
Potential reduction in hospital stays through smart healthcare technologies	$18.6 billion	Up to 40% (reduction in hospital stay)	HP	2021	Worldwide
Global smart healthcare market size by 2026	$220 billion	—	Markets and Markets	2021	Worldwide
Potential reduction in hospital admissions through smart healthcare technologies	$26 billion	Up to 70% (reduction in hospital admissions)	HP	2020	United States
Remote patient monitoring (RPM) market size in 2020	$17.4 billion	—	Fortune Business Insights	2020	Worldwide
Percentage of medical devices connected to the internet in 2020	$25.4 billion	25% (of medical devices)	Deloitte	2020	United States
CAGR of the global telehealth market from 2020 to 2027	—	25.2% (annual growth rate)	Grand View Research	2020	Worldwide
Global telehealth market size projected by 2027	$559.52 billion	—	Grand View Research	2020	Worldwide
Potential reduction in hospital readmissions through smart healthcare technologies	$13.4 billion	Up to 50% (reduction in hospital readmissions)	HP	2020	Worldwide

enhance the healthcare system to enhance its reliability, manageability, and convenience has been underscored by the recent global pandemic. This chapter centers around the development of a patient health monitoring system utilizing IoT and 6G technology, with the aim of providing advantages to a specific cohort of patients necessitating uninterrupted health monitoring. Approximately 30–35% of annual deaths are attributed to delayed treatment or inadequate medical resources in rural regions, according to estimates. The issue of disparate allocation of healthcare services around the nation presents a substantial obstacle. In order to address these obstacles, a new paradigm for remote health monitoring is introduced, which enables treatment to be administered from any geographical location, hence eliminating the constraints imposed by physical distance or network limitations [5]. IoT technology is assuming a prominent position in diverse domains, encompassing healthcare and systems for managing diseases. In contrast, 6G technology represents a recent advancement in the realm of wireless cellular communication, offering the potential to establish a sustainable healthcare system and enhance the suitability of wireless devices in remote regions. The objective of this chapter is to integrate these two sophisticated technologies in order to establish an enhanced health monitoring system that contributes to the attainment of a sustainable future. The text also examines the difficulties associated with establishing a healthcare system and proposes alternative ways to enhance health management and support. The primary contribution of this research is in the use of two sophisticated technologies inside the healthcare industry. This integration has the potential to enhance automation, decrease operational expenses, and expedite decision-making procedures [6]. Figure 3.2 depicts a Healthcare IoT system that has been purposefully developed for the purpose of monitoring the health of patients.

The healthcare industry has experienced substantial effects due to the implementation of various services and concepts aimed at addressing a diverse array of healthcare challenges. The growing demand for healthcare services and the rapid progress of technology have resulted in a constant expansion of service offerings on a daily basis. The incorporation of these components has become more imperative in the architecture of a HIoT framework. Within the framework of the HIoT, each service provides a diverse array of healthcare solutions. The exact demarcation of these concepts/services is subject to a lack of consensus in terms of a widely accepted definition. The salient feature of HIoT systems is in their wide array of applications [7]. Hence, it presents a formidable task to furnish an all-encompassing definition for every concept. However, in order to enhance comprehension of the topic, this section will expound upon a number of the often-employed IoT healthcare services, as depicted in Figure 3.3.

3.1.2 Challenges of HIoT

The HIoT is a dynamic technology that connects devices, sensors, and objects to the internet, enabling seamless communication and data exchange. While the IoT holds tremendous potential for transforming our lives, it also presents several challenges. Security is a major concern due to the vulnerability of IoT devices to hacking, which

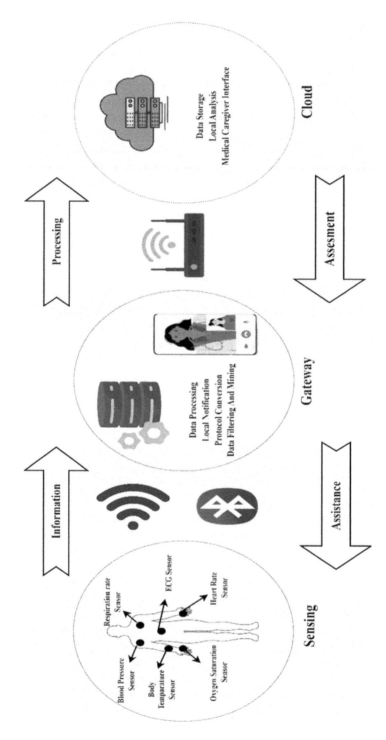

FIGURE 3.2 The IoT in healthcare—patient health monitoring system

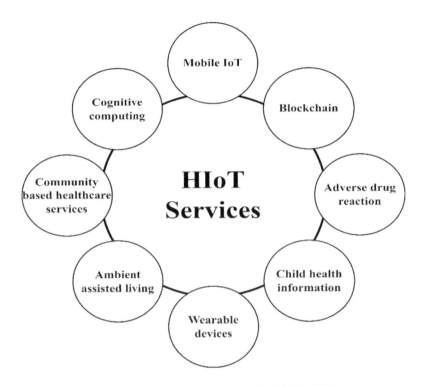

FIGURE 3.3 The use of widely available services in the field of HIoT.

can lead to the misuse of compromised devices. Privacy is another challenge as IoT devices collect vast amounts of data without always informing users, raising ethical and responsible data usage concerns. Standardization is crucial as various companies manufacture IoT devices using different protocols, making interoperability a challenge. Scalability becomes increasingly difficult as the number of IoT devices continues to grow, requiring efficient infrastructure management. Energy consumption is also a concern as many IoT devices rely on batteries, limiting functionality and lifespan. Developing energy-efficient devices with extended operation periods is an ongoing challenge.

Furthermore, effectively managing and processing the vast amounts of data generated by IoT devices is critical for accurate insights and decision-making [8]. Addressing these challenges necessitates interdisciplinary collaboration, encompassing engineering, computer science, security, privacy, and data management. Ongoing investment in research and development is crucial to drive the evolution of the IoT and ensure it meets the needs of individuals and businesses.

This chapter results in the investigation of the transformative potential of HIoT in creating smart healthcare solutions. It carries out a thorough, review to examine the methods, tools, and strategies used in HIoT areas. Finding, categorizing, and systematically contrasting current research that investigates the use of IoT in healthcare are the main goals of this review. The outcomes of this review offer an in-depth comparison, revealing both the shortcomings and opportunities found in the available literature on this topic. This article also covers the benefits of federated learning in relation to the HIoT.

Section 3.2 provides a concise overview of the pertinent literature that has been published in this area up to the present time. Section 3.3 delves into the application of the HIoT. Section 3.4 provides an in-depth analysis of federated learning as it pertains to the MIoT. Section 3.5 discusses the advantages of implementing IoT technology in the healthcare industry. Section 3.6 delineates the features of HIoT, while Section 3.7 provides an overview of the study's findings.

3.2 LITERATURE SURVEY

This section presents a summary of the relevant literature that has been published in this field to date. Table 3.2 presents the comprehensive compilation of the existing literature review that has been published in this particular field up until now.

3.3 APPLICATION OF THE HIOT

IoT applications' transdisciplinary uses have completely changed our way of life. IoT applications like smart healthcare use sensors to link intelligent machines, patients, medical professionals, and sensors to the internet. Intelligent health applications have revolutionized the conventional healthcare system by improving health management through the use of their applications. The Healthcare IoT system is examined in terms of its applicability for resolving various healthcare problems as well as its enabling technologies, healthcare services, and applications [8].

3.3.1 REMOTE HEALTHCARE MONITORING APPLICATIONS

The ability to maintain remote connectivity with patients allows physicians to deliver healthcare services promptly and efficiently in response to patient needs. Doctors and other carers can give patients timely and effective medications by having sensing devices implanted inside of them or by using internet-connected sensors that are placed nearby. Patients are no longer required to travel to a medical facility in order to have their temperature, blood pressure, and other vital signs taken. Every time an IoT gadget gathers patient data, it sends the information to a software programmer that patients and/or healthcare providers can view. Algorithms can analyze data in order to create alerts or treatment recommendations [9–10].

3.3.2 DIABETES MONITORING

Diabetes monitoring results in the glucose level for each patient only being recorded at the exact time the test is done, which is not only cumbersome to check glucose levels and record findings manually. Testing on an ongoing basis may not be able to catch issues with levels that vary greatly [11]. IoT devices can automatically and continuously monitor patients' glucose levels. Using glucose monitoring devices,

TABLE 3.2

Synopsis of Existing Studies

Authors	Results	Applications	Technology
Kamalov F. et al. (2023) [8]	The article presented contemporary IoMT security and privacy problems such as data breaches, unauthorized access, and cyber-attacks. It also investigated possible solutions such as encryption, authentication, and access control technologies, as well as the legislative frameworks that regulate data privacy and security.	Seizing control of the medical device, stealing sensitive patient health, personal and insurance data.	IoMT
Imad et al. (2022) [9]	In this paper, with sensors, wearables, and communication technologies, IoT might be utilized to combat the pandemic and develop smart healthcare systems.	Body-mounted sensors, fitness trackers.	HIoT
M. Rahman et al. (2022) [10]	According to the authors, the IoT has the potential to build social objects that may bring people together and stimulate social connections. The next stage is to embrace technology's social features.	Using remote monitoring for people with chronic diseases and long-term conditions, tracking patient medication orders, and tracking the location of patients admitted to hospitals.	IoT
Javaid M. et al. (2021) [11]	The COVID-19 pandemic has emphasized the need for novel techniques to halt disease propagation. IoT may be used to collect real-time data, monitor medical conditions, and deliver personalized treatment. It can also help with early viral identification, tracking, and tracing.	Remote patient monitoring, Glucose monitoring, Heartrate monitoring, Hand hygiene monitoring.	HIoT
Veena. et al. (2023) [12]	The article represented the benefits and drawbacks of employing biosensors and IoT in healthcare, including data privacy and security, standardization, and regulatory compliance.	Electrodermal activity sensors, PPG sensor.	IoT

(Continued)

TABLE 3.1 (CONTINUED)
Synopsis of Existing Studies

Authors	Results	Applications	Technology
Li W. et al. (2021) [14]	The paper presented IoT has the ability to build social objects and stimulate social connections, and the next step is to embrace the technology's social features.	Depression and mood monitoring, Parkinson's disease monitoring.	Machine-learning based big data analytics
Batista et al. (2021) [15]	The paper gave an in-depth look at security solutions for context-aware smart healthcare systems, such as authentication and access control methods, secure data transfer protocols, and intrusion detection systems.	electrocardiogram, thermometer, fluid level sensor, sphygmomanometer.	Sensor-based healthcare systems
Pateraki M. et al. (2021) [16]	The author discussed Biosensors and IoT are being employed in healthcare, with potential benefits including improved patient outcomes and cost savings.	defibrillators, nebulizers, pumps, or monitoring equipment with IoT sensor.	Biosensors and IoT technologies
Islam et al. (2021) [17]	IoT-based smart healthcare solutions such as sensors, wearable devices, and a cloud-based platform for data storage and analysis are important for monitoring COVID-19 patients.	Smartwatches, VR headsets and wearable electrocardiogram.	Wearable technology
Benerji et al. (2020) [18]	The relevance of IoT in healthcare includes remote monitoring and diagnosis of COVID-19 patients. It analyzes the accuracy, reliability, and security of wearable technology, sensors, and communication tools.	Smart patches, smart rings, cortisol (electronic epidermal tattoos).	Computational Intelligence and Virtual Environments for Measurement Systems

patients can be informed when their blood sugar levels are out of range, doing away with the need for manual record keeping.

3.3.3 Heart Rate Tracking

A patient in a hospital may find it challenging to monitor their heart rate and blood sugar levels. Conventional continuous cardiac monitoring devices in hospitals require patients to be permanently wired up, which limits their mobility, and routine heart rate checks do not shield patients from sudden changes in heart rate. Small IoT devices can now be used to continuously monitor heart rate, allowing patients to move around as they please. The vast majority of contemporary technologies are capable of 90% accuracy [12].

3.3.4 The Monitoring of Parkinson's Disease

In order to give Parkinson's patients, the best possible care, medical professionals must evaluate how their symptoms change throughout the course of the day [13]. IoT devices promise to greatly ease this process by continuously gathering data about Parkinson's symptoms. These devices also allow patients to live their lives in their own homes rather than requiring lengthy hospital stays for surveillance.

3.3.5 Associated Inhalers

Rapid attacks characterize conditions like COPD and asthma. Patients who use an IoT-connected inhaler can learn how frequently they are assaulted as well as obtain information about their environment to help medical professionals understand why an attack happened. Additionally, connected inhalers alert users when they've forgotten their inhalers at home, putting them at risk of having an attack without them or when they're using the device improperly [14].

3.3.6 Consumable Sensors

The process of collecting data from within the human body is frequently characterized by its lack of organization and disruptive nature. There is no such thing as a camera or probe that a person would enjoy having in their digestive system. Ingested sensors or consumable sensors can get information from digestive systems in less invasive methods [15]. These tests, for example, can be used to determine p^H levels and internal bleeding. These gadgets, which are small enough to swallow without difficulty, can reveal information about stomach p^H levels. The substance must also be able to wash through or disintegrate naturally in the human body. These requirements are being met by ingestible sensors that are being developed by numerous businesses [16].

3.3.7 Connected Contact Lenses

An additional method for the passive, non-intrusive collection of healthcare data is the use of smart contact lenses. In fact, firms like Google have already started to file patents for connected contact lenses, and we may soon be able to utilize our eyes as cameras. Whether employed to enhance health or for other reasons, intelligent lenses hold the possibility of making human eyes a potent tool for digital interactions [16].

3.3.8 Automated Surgery

Small robots connected to the internet allow a surgeon to perform complex operations that are difficult for human hands to handle. Small IoT devices will make it possible to perform robotic surgery with a smaller surgical incision, which will lessen patient trauma and speed up healing. These instruments must be compact and dependable in order to execute surgery with the least amount of disruption. They must also be able to decipher complex bodily situations in order to make wise decisions about how to continue during surgery. IoT robots can tackle these difficulties effectively because they are already employed in surgery [17].

3.3.9 Hearables

The newest product on the market for those with hearing loss is wearables, which are hearing aids. These days, hearing aids can be Bluetooth-paired with smartphones so that we can use headphones to listen to music. On real-world sounds, filters, equalizers, and layered effects can be used. Doppler Labs is one of the best examples [17].

3.3.10 Moodables

A moodable is a tool that improves our mood all day long. Though science fiction may seem unreal, it is actually quite close to reality. Thinc and Halo Neurosciences are working on it, and it's progressing incredibly well. The head-mounted wearables known as moodables work by sending low-intensity currents to your brain to improve your mood [18].

3.3.11 Integrating Computer Vision

A drone powered by AI and computer vision mimics visual perception and bases choices on it. Drones like Skydio employ computer vision technology to recognize obstacles and steer clear of them. Individuals who are blind or visually impaired can navigate more safely and effectively with the help of this technology [18].

3.3.12 Medical Charting

A doctor can spend less time manually charting patients thanks to a technology called Audmix. By using voice instructions, these gadgets collect data from the patients. The user can readily obtain patient data. The weekly time savings for doctors is about 15 hours [19].

3.3.13 Smart CGM and Insulin Pen

A specific smartphone app for real-time blood glucose monitoring is used to share data. Diabetics can use these devices to monitor their blood sugar and also to send information to their doctors [19].

3.3.14 Testing and Tracking with IoT

The IoT-enabled COVID-19 testing and tracing can stop the disease's spread, which is crucial in the fight against it. IoT adoption is accelerating because people are more likely to use it to test and track things now [20].

3.3.15 Wearable Technology

WHOOP Inc. Developed a method to identify COVID-19 using the WHOOP watch band to measure respiration according to Resting Heart Rate (RHR). WHOOP tape data is sent to the WHOOP system via the mobile application [20]. By day three of symptoms, their methods had found that 80% of people who were 20% two days earlier were positive for COVID-19. Philips has also developed a biosensor for early detection of negative COVID-19 patients and an array for early detection of COVID-19 patients [21].

Table 3.3 provides an overview of potential applications of IoT in smart healthcare [18–21].

3.4 FEDERATED LEARNING FOR THE IOMT

By utilizing IoMT devices, recent advancements in electronic technology and communication infrastructure have transformed the conventional healthcare system into a smart healthcare system. The information transmitted by IoMT devices is extremely private and is highly susceptible to opponents. In this regard, federated learning (FL), a distributive AI paradigm, has created new possibilities for maintaining participant privacy in IoMT without gaining access to their private information. Recent advances in deep learning have witnessed many success stories in smart healthcare applications that use data from insights to improve the quality of care provided by facilities.

Deep learning models that exhibit high performance are predominantly reliant on large volumes of data. Federated learning addresses the aforementioned challenges by utilizing a widely applicable deep learning model and a centralized aggregator server. Furthermore, the patient data is retained by the local party, so ensuring the security and confidentiality of the data. This study examines the progress of federated learning in healthcare applications during the past four years, focusing on several aspects such as data partition, data dissemination, data privacy attacks and protection, and benchmark datasets. The IoMT has enhanced healthcare administration, monitoring, and procedure while also enhancing life quality and overall human well-being. Healthcare systems are now personalized, user-centric, precise, and omnipresent.

FL is a distributed AI approach that facilitates the training of models by aggregating local model updates from several IoMT networks, without requiring direct access to the local data. Hence, by the utilization of the FL approach, it is possible to mitigate the potential hazards associated with the disclosure of user preferences and confidential medical information. Privateness in IoMT It's crucial to protect networks from a privacy standpoint, especially for electronic healthcare systems. Securing the network no longer suffices for it to function effectively in today's society [22].

3.4.1 Generalized FL-Enabled Healthcare System Framework

The FL-based healthcare system consists of a number of phases. Choosing the task, whether medical image processing or another human-related application, and

TABLE 3.3

Illustrating the Potential Applications of IoT for Smart Healthcare Solutions

Application	Description
Remote patient monitoring	Wearable devices that track vital signs, such as heart rate, blood pressure, and temperature, for remote monitoring and early detection of health issues.
Telemedicine and virtual care	Video conferencing platforms and connected medical devices for remote consultations, virtual examinations, and diagnostics.
Smart hospital infrastructure	The implementation of IoT technology in various systems, such as asset tracking, inventory management, and facility monitoring, has been shown to significantly improve operational efficiency and ensure patient safety.
Medication adherence monitoring	Smart pill dispensers with built-in sensors and reminders help patients adhere to their medication schedules, reducing errors and improving outcomes.
Chronic disease management	Connected devices that monitor and transmit data related to chronic conditions enable healthcare providers to monitor patients and provide personalized care remotely.
Ambient-assisted living	Smart home solutions with IoT sensors and devices that monitor activities of daily living, assisting elderly or disabled individuals to live independently.
Health and wellness tracking	Fitness trackers, smart scales, and mobile apps that monitor physical activity, sleep patterns, and nutrition encourage healthier lifestyles.
Infection control and monitoring	IoT-enabled systems for tracking hand hygiene compliance, monitoring air quality, and managing infection control protocols in healthcare facilities.
Predictive maintenance	IoT sensors in medical devices and equipment monitor performance and collect data to predict maintenance needs, reducing downtime and improving efficiency.
Data security and privacy	IoT security solutions ensure the protection and privacy of patient data transmitted between devices and stored in cloud platforms.
Real-time location tracking	IoT-based solutions that provide real-time tracking of medical equipment, patients, and healthcare staff for efficient resource utilization and improved patient flow.

identifying the algorithm based on the prediction or classification task are only a few of the network factors connected to healthcare systems that the central server first chooses. Additionally, the learning rates and many ML-related adjustable parameters are chosen. Additionally, the central server chooses which clients will take part in the FL process. The characteristics of medical data provide FL algorithms with a number of difficulties, including data partitions play crucial by combining a variety of customers' data, the FL approach tries to address the issue of small sample size when training a secure collaborative machine-learning model.

In medical applications, data security and privacy are crucial concerns [22]. Since there could be thousands or millions of participants, it is difficult to assume that every client in FL is trustworthy. Therefore, privacy-preserving procedures are required to safeguard medical information from unreliable patients or outside hackers. Data distribution (statistical challenge) plays a vital role in FL [23]. While developing a machine-learning model in a centralized manner, the training data are maintained and balanced centrally throughout. The size and quality of medical data sets have frequently hampered the creation of a reliable FL algorithm solution. While some datasets concentrate on network communication performance, others concentrate on the classification and segmentation of medical images. For medical datasets specifically, the benchmark datasets have not yet been assembled. Therefore, a reliable benchmark is required to assess the effectiveness of the FL that leverages a variety of medical data sources. Based on the aggregation schemes, FL is split into two groups: (a) centralized FL and (b) decentralized FL.

3.4.2 DATA PARTITION CHARACTERISTICS OF FL

When creating a model with a fixed sample size, the horizontal federated learning (HFL) data split is advised. The nodes in this data partition configuration could be various healthcare organizations or providers of health data applications. By combining patient sample data from many institutions without compromising patient privacy, the HFL intends to create a worldwide model. HFL data collection solves the main standardization problem in the reporting system as it consolidates data samples from all hospitals. For medical records, FL usually uses the HFL file format. In their survey, more than half of FL's medical practices used horizontally distributed medical data [23]. Vertical federated learning (VFL) data split. In this data partition design, two nodes shared the same user's profile but had distinct feature information. The nodes could be various healthcare organizations or suppliers of health data applications. By combining patient attributes from many institutions without directly transferring patient data, VFL seeks to create a global model. Each node has the same sample data but differing patients' traits (X) and labels (Y). In the same area, there are two separate healthcare organizations: a hospital and a health insurance provider. Because they are locals, the patients who use these two healthcare facilities may be largely similar. In contrast to the data configurations in HFL and VFL, the data partition in federated transfer learning (FTL) accounts for the situation when several nodes did not share the same user's profile or feature information. Numerous healthcare facilities or companies that offer health data applications might be the nodes, and they could be located anywhere in the world [23].

3.4.3 DATA PRIVACY ON FEDERATED LEARNING FOR MIoT

Two different data privacy attacks could be used against federated learning. The first assault, such as the model inversion attack, aims to duplicate the input data, while the second attack, such as the membership inference attack, aims to identify the training data. The data Privacy Protection with Differential Privacy (DP) Method is the integration of privacy protection and deep learning models. To protect the deep learning model, for instance, many researchers employ DP techniques [23].

3.4.4 CLASSIFICATION WORK FOR MEDICAL APPLICATIONS

According to a recent study, researchers used FL technology to develop machine-learning models for cancer diagnosis. FL is a potential method for integrating medical picture data from medical institutions for COVID-19 detection applications, allowing them to build models while protecting patient privacy. The IoHT and wearable technology are the subjects of growing study, and one technique to safeguard user privacy while constructing a model for human activity and emotion recognition is through the use of FL technology [24].

3.4.5 ADVANTAGES OF FL IN SMART MEDICAL APPLICATIONS

Within the framework of the FL-based intelligent healthcare system, the central server exclusively necessitates local updates, namely in the form of model gradients, to facilitate the training of AI. In contrast, the local health data is solely preserved within the confines of local medical establishments and their corresponding infrastructure. This proposed measure aims to improve user privacy by decreasing the probability of unlawful exposure of sensitive user information to external third parties [24]. The establishment of robust and protected intelligent healthcare systems necessitates the capacity to uphold the confidentiality of health user data in FL frameworks, owing to the progressively stringent regulations safeguarding the privacy of health information. In comparison to conventional centralized learning, FL has the capability to offer a satisfactory balance between accuracy and utility, while simultaneously improving privacy. The implementation of FL can effectively reduce communication costs, including latency and transmit power, associated with the transfer of high data volumes to the server.

3.4.6 LIMITATION AND PERSPECTIVE VIEW

The first drawback is that extant FL experiments only take into account one of the non-IID features, like label skew or data imbalance. However, there are no exhaustive experiments that look at a variety of non-IID attributes in the medical dataset. Additional methods will be found in the future view to deal with the problems posed by hybrid non-IID features. The hyperparameter framework search for FL is the second restriction. Hyperparameter tweaking is an important yet time-consuming step in the machine-learning pipeline. When models are trained across a distributed network of diverse data silos using federated learning, optimizing hyperparameters becomes noticeably more challenging. Consequently, a system or program that automatically chooses the best hyperparameters [25].

3.5 BENEFITS OF IOT IN HEALTHCARE

The healthcare industry is experiencing significant growth in the adoption of IoT solutions, driven by the multitude of benefits it offers. IoT enables enhanced patient monitoring, capturing vital signs and health metrics for remote patient monitoring and timely issue detection. Automation, improved efficiency, and reduced reliance on human intervention contribute to cost reduction in healthcare operations. Moreover, IoT enhances patient outcomes by improving care delivery and minimizing complications. For instance, IoT devices can support medication adherence, provide personalized feedback, and track patient progress. With its potential to revolutionize healthcare, IoT is expected to continue expanding based on the demonstrated market growth [26].

The IoT presents extensive opportunities for smart healthcare solutions, spanning various areas of healthcare delivery. Remote patient monitoring leverages IoT devices to collect real-time data on vital signs and activity levels, facilitating proactive monitoring and early detection of potential issues. Patients with chronic conditions can utilize IoT devices to track specific health parameters and share data with healthcare providers to inform treatment decisions. Fall detection systems utilizing IoT devices offer critical support for elderly patients, helping prevent accidents and identifying underlying health conditions [27]. IoT-based asset-tracking solutions improve hospital operations by efficiently monitoring the location of medical equipment and supplies, reducing losses and optimizing resource utilization. Surgical planning benefits from IoT devices capturing patient-specific data, enabling the creation of detailed 3D models for preoperative preparation and practice [28].

The potential applications of IoT in healthcare are diverse and expanding continuously. One significant area of improvement is in treatment, where IoT solutions enhance transparency and provide doctors with valuable insights for informed decision-making [29]. Cost reduction is achieved through real-time patient monitoring, minimizing unnecessary visits and readmissions. Additionally, IoT enables early disease diagnosis by continuously monitoring patients and analyzing real-time data, empowering clinicians to identify diseases before symptoms manifest [30]. Proactive medical treatment becomes feasible with constant health monitoring, ensuring timely interventions and personalized care. Furthermore, the IoT streamlines drug and equipment management, addressing complexities in the healthcare sector. By generating valuable data, IoT not only enables intelligent decision-making but also reduces errors, waste, and overall system costs [31].

Table 3.4 provides a comprehensive summary of the potential advantages and obstacles linked to the IoT within the healthcare industry.

3.6 FUTURE ASPECTS STAGES OF IOT IN HEALTHCARE

The integration of the IoT in hospitals offers significant benefits, including enhanced patient care, improved treatment outcomes, cost reduction, and an enhanced patient experience. Healthcare providers also stand to gain from improved processes, workflows, performance, and patient satisfaction. However, the extensive collection of

TABLE 3.4

The Potential Benefits and Challenges of IoT in Healthcare

Potential Benefits	Examples	Challenges
Improved patient monitoring	Wearable devices, remote patient monitoring	Security and privacy, interoperability, cost
Increased patient engagement	Patient-facing apps, telehealth	Data overload, user adoption
Reduced costs	Real-time data analytics, predictive analytics	Lack of standards, fragmented data
Improved outcomes	Personalized medicine, precision medicine	Regulatory hurdles, ethical concerns

private data by IoT-enabled devices raises concerns about data security. However, the IoT presents novel aspects of patient care with its ability to facilitate real-time health monitoring and provide access to medical information [32].

Figure 3.4 represents the deployment of sensors, actuators, monitors, detectors, video systems, and other networked equipment is necessary. The collected data, often in analog form, undergoes conversion to digital format for further processing. Subsequently, the data is pre-processed, standardized, and transmitted to cloud storage or data centers. Essential analyses and management of the finalized data are performed, followed by advanced analytics to derive valuable business insights.

The transformative potential of IoT in healthcare is significant, making it more effective, efficient, and economically viable, as depicted in Figure 3.5 [33]. The market for IoT in healthcare is expanding rapidly, and this upward trend is expected to continue in the foreseeable future. The Healthcare IoT market is driven by its numerous advantages. IoT devices play a crucial role in gathering vital signs, activity levels, and other health parameters, leading to improved patient monitoring and prompt issue detection through remote monitoring. Automation, increased efficiency, and reduced reliance on human intervention contribute to cost savings in healthcare. For example, IoT-enabled devices can autonomously manage supplies,

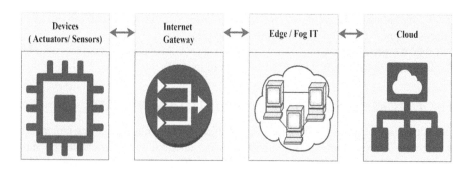

FIGURE 3.4   Future aspects stages of HIoT

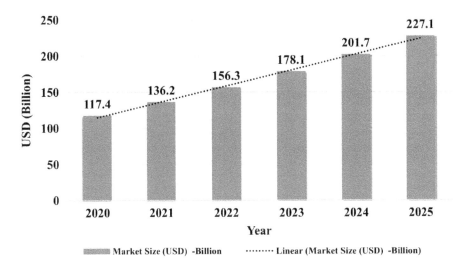

FIGURE 3.5 The potential of the IoT for smart healthcare solutions

maintain inventories, and facilitate medication delivery. Additionally, the IoT has the potential to enhance patient outcomes by providing better care and reducing complications. IoT devices enable tracking of patients' progress, provide feedback on activity levels, and offer medication reminders. Furthermore, the IoT offers a wide range of possibilities for creating smart healthcare solutions. Remote patient monitoring through IoT devices enables real-time collection of health parameters, benefiting patients with chronic conditions like diabetes or heart disease [34]. IoT devices also play a crucial role in fall detection among the elderly, helping prevent accidents and detecting potential health issues. Hospitals can leverage IoT to track medical supplies and equipment, reducing losses and optimizing costs. Real-time tracking using IoT gadgets attached to hospital beds and trolleys improves operational efficiency. Moreover, IoT devices contribute to surgical planning by gathering anatomical and physiological data, facilitating the creation of 3D models [35]. Surgeons can utilize this information to design surgeries and practice specific procedures before operating on real patients.

3.7 CONCLUSION

The IoT is rapidly changing the healthcare industry, which has enormous potential advantages. The sector has undergone a change thanks to real-time patient data collecting, remote monitoring, and individualized care. Healthcare professionals can remotely diagnose, monitor, and treat patients by using smart sensors, wearables, and linked gadgets. Remote diagnosis, monitoring, and treatment were made possible through the IoT in response to the COVID-19 epidemic. However, the full promise of IoT in healthcare has yet to be realized, necessitating significant investment. Improvements in patient outcomes, increased effectiveness, and cost savings are all advantages. Making informed decisions is made possible by real-time data, and automation increases operational effectiveness. Data privacy and cybersecurity issues require cooperation to be solved in order to reduce risks and increase patient confidence in IoT solutions. The IoT is transforming healthcare by enabling real-time patient data collection, remote monitoring, and personalized care through smart sensors and wearables. Although the full potential of IoT in healthcare requires further investment, it promises improved patient outcomes, increased efficiency, and cost savings while addressing data privacy and cybersecurity challenges to build patient trust in IoT solutions.

REFERENCES

1. Balasundaram, A., Routray, S., Prabu, A. V., Krishnan, P., Malla, P. P., & Maiti, M. (2023). Internet of things (IoT) based smart healthcare system for efficient diagnostics of health parameters of patients in emergency care. *IEEE Internet of Things Journal*, 10(21), 18563–18570. doi: 10.1109/JIOT.2023.3246065.
2. Samany, N. N., Liu, H., Aghataher, R., & Bayat, M. (2022). Ten GIS-based solutions for managing and controlling COVID-19 pandemic outbreak. *SN Computer Science*, 3(4), 269.
3. Nag, A., Mobin, G., Kar, A., Bera, T., & Chandra, P. (2022, December). A review on cloud-based smart applications. In *International Conference on Intelligent Systems Design and Applications* (pp. 387–403). Springer Nature Switzerland.
4. Elaziz, M. A., Dahou, A., Mabrouk, A., Ibrahim, R. A., & Aseeri, A. O. (2023). Medical image classifications for 6G IoT-enabled smart health systems. *Diagnostics*, 13(5), 834.
5. Nag, A., Das, A., Sil, R., Kar, A., Mandal, D., & Das, B. (2022, December). Application of artificial intelligence in mental health. In *International Conference on Intelligent Systems Design and Applications* (pp. 128–141). Springer Nature Switzerland.
6. Shabbir, A., Shabbir, M., Javed, A. R., Rizwan, M., Iwendi, C., & Chakraborty, C. (2023). Exploratory data analysis, classification, comparative analysis, case severity detection, and internet of things in COVID-19 telemonitoring for smart hospitals. *Journal of Experimental and Theoretical Artificial Intelligence*, 35(4), 507–534.
7. Patel, S. K. (2023). Attack detection and mitigation scheme through novel authentication model enabled optimized neural network in smart healthcare. *Computer Methods in Biomechanics and Biomedical Engineering*, 26(1), 38–64.
8. Kamalov, F., Pourghebleh, B., Gheisari, M., Liu, Y., & Moussa, S. (2023). Internet of medical things privacy and security: Challenges, solutions, and future trends from a new perspective. *Sustainability*, 15(4), 3317.
9. Imad, M., Hussain, A., Hassan, M. A., Butt, Z., & Sahar, N. U. (2022). IoT based machine learning and deep learning platform for Covid-19 prevention and control: A systematic review. In *Ai and IoT for Sustainable Development in Emerging Countries: Challenges and Opportunities* (pp. 523–536).
10. Rahman, M. M., Saha, S., Majumder, M. Z. H., Akter, F., Haque, M. A. S., & Anzan-Uz-Zaman, M. (2022, December). Design and development of an IoT-based smart system to monitor and control environment of a laboratory. In *2022 4th International Conference on Sustainable Technologies for Industry 4.0 (STI)* (pp. 1–8). IEEE.
11. Javaid, M., & Khan, I. H. (2021). Internet of Things (IoT) enabled healthcare helps to take the challenges of COVID-19 pandemic. *Journal of Oral Biology and Craniofacial Research*, 11(2), 209–214.

12. Veena, A., & Gowrishankar, S. (2023). Applications, opportunities, and current challenges in the healthcare industry. In *IoT in Healthcare Systems* (pp. 121–147). CRC Press.

13. Nag, A., Nath, B. K., Sil, R., & Chandra, P. (2023). Blood in need: An application for blood management. *International Journal of Computer Information Systems and Industrial Management Applications*, 15(1), 124–140.

14. Li, W., Chai, Y., Khan, F., Jan, S. R. U., Verma, S., Menon, V. G., ... Li, X. (2021). A comprehensive survey on machine learning-based big data analytics for IoT-enabled smart healthcare system. *Mobile Networks and Applications*, 26(1), 234–252.

15. Batista, E., Moncusi, M. A., López-Aguilar, P., Martínez-Ballesté, A., & Solanas, A. (2021). Sensors for context-aware smart healthcare: A security perspective. *Sensors*, 21(20), 6886.

16. Pateraki, M., Fysarakis, K., Sakkalis, V., Spanoudakis, G., Varlamis, I., Maniadakis, M., ... Koutsouris, D. (2020). Biosensors and Internet of Things in smart healthcare applications: Challenges and opportunities. In *Wearable and Implantable Medical Devices* (pp. 25–53). https://doi.org/10.1016/b978-0-12-815369-7.00002-1

17. Islam, M. M., Mahmud, S., Muhammad, L. J., Islam, M. R., Nooruddin, S., & Ayon, S. I. (2020). Wearable technology to assist the patients infected with novel coronavirus (COVID-19). *SN Computer Science*, 1(6), 1–9.

18. Banerjee, A., Chakraborty, C., & Rathi, M. (2020). Medical imaging, artificial intelligence, internet of things, wearable devices in terahertz healthcare technologies. In *Terahertz Biomedical and Healthcare Technologies* (pp. 145–165). Elsevier.

19. Mistry, C., Thakker, U., Gupta, R., Obaidat, M. S., Tanwar, S., Kumar, N., & Rodrigues, J. J. (2021, June). MedBlock: An AI-enabled and blockchain-driven medical healthcare system for COVID-19. In *ICC 2021-IEEE International Conference on Communications* (pp. 1–6). IEEE.

20. Al-Humairi, S. N. S., & Hajamydeen, A. I. (2022). IoT-based healthcare monitoring practices during Covid-19: Prospects and approaches. In *Healthcare Systems and Health Informatics* (pp. 163–185). CRC Press.

21. Dinesh, K., Vijayalakshmi, K., Nirosha, C., & Krishna, I. S. R. (2018). IoT based smart health care monitoring system. *International Journal of Institutional & Industrial Research*, 3(1), 22–24.

22. Kamalov, F., Pourghebleh, B., Gheisari, M., Liu, Y., & Moussa, S. (2023). Internet of medical things privacy and security: Challenges, solutions, and future trends from a new perspective. *Sustainability*, 15(4), 3317.

23. Lakshmi, G. J., Ghonge, M., & Obaid, A. J. (2021). Cloud based IoT smart healthcare system for remote patient monitoring. *EAI Endorsed Transactions on Pervasive Health and Technology*, 7(28), e4–e4.

24. Alam, T., & Gupta, R. (2022). Federated learning and its role in the privacy preservation of IoT devices. *Future Internet*, 14(9), 246.

25. Chauhan, S., Arora, N., & Arora, R. (2023). IoT and machine learning-based smart healthcare system for monitoring patients. In *Artificial Intelligence of Health-Enabled Spaces* (pp. 1–19). CRC Press.

26. Rieke, N., Hancox, J., Li, W., Milletari, F., Roth, H. R., Albarqouni, S., ... Cardoso, M. J. (2020). The future of digital health with federated learning. *NPJ Digital Medicine*, 3(1), 119.

27. Sheller, M. J., Edwards, B., Reina, G. A., Martin, J., Pati, S., Kotrotsou, A., ... Bakas, S. (2020). Federated learning in medicine: Facilitating multi-institutional collaborations without sharing patient data. *Scientific Reports*, 10(1), 12598.

28. Li, J., Meng, Y., Ma, L., Du, S., Zhu, H., Pei, Q., & Shen, X. (2021). A federated learning based privacy-preserving smart healthcare system. *IEEE Transactions on Industrial Informatics*, 18(3), 2021–2031.

29. Alotaibi, S., & Alshehri, A. (2022). Teledentistry approaches for dental assessments and consultation during the COVID-19 pandemic. *Smart Homecare Technology and TeleHealth*, 9, 11–25.

30. Anisha, P. R., Reddy, C. K., Nguyen, N. G., Bhushan, M., Kumar, A., & Mohd Hanafiah, M. (2022). *Intelligent Systems and Machine Learning for Industry: Advancements, Challenges, and Practices (1st ed.).* CRC Press. https://doi.org/10.1201/9781003286745.

31. Gomes, M. A. S., Kovaleski, J. L., Pagani, R. N., da Silva, V. L., & Pasquini, T. C. D. S. (2023). Transforming healthcare with big data analytics: Technologies, techniques and prospects. *Journal of Medical Engineering and Technology*, 47(1), 1–11.

32. Razdan, S., & Sharma, S. (2022). Internet of medical things (IoMT): Overview, emerging technologies, and case studies. *IETE Technical Review*, 39(4), 775–788.

33. Munnangi, A. K., UdhayaKumar, S., Ravi, V., Sekaran, R., & Kannan, S. (2023). Survival study on deep learning techniques for IoT enabled smart healthcare system. *Health and Technology*, 13(2), 215–228.

34. Chopade, S. S., Gupta, H. P., & Dutta, T. (2023). Survey on sensors and smart devices for IoT enabled intelligent healthcare system. *Wireless Personal Communications*, 131, 1957–1995. https://doi.org/10.1007/s11277-023-10528-8

35. Kumar, P., Kumar, R., Gupta, G. P., Tripathi, R., Jolfaei, A., & Islam, A. N. (2023). A blockchain-orchestrated deep learning approach for secure data transmission in IoT-enabled healthcare systems. *Journal of Parallel and Distributed Computing*, 172, 69–83.

4 Unveiling the Paradigm Shift—Industry 5.0 and the Rise of Intelligent Systems

P. R. Anisha, Vijaya Sindhoori Kaza, Rithika Badam, and Srinath Doss

4.1 INTRODUCTION

This introductory chapter lays the foundation for a profound exploration of the transformative journey from Industry 4.0 to Industry 5.0, heralding a new era of industrial evolution characterized by the seamless integration of intelligent systems [1]. As the echoes of Industry 4.0 begin to fade, Industry 5.0 emerges as a distinctive paradigm shift that transcends mere automation, inviting us into a realm where human ingenuity and technological prowess intertwine in unprecedented ways [2]. This chapter serves as an essential gateway to understanding the dynamics that shape the contemporary industrial landscape and the promising prospects it holds for the future.

4.1.1 EMERGENCE AND EVOLUTION OF INDUSTRIAL REVOLUTIONS

The journey of industrial revolutions commenced with the arrival of the first one in the late 18th century. This inaugural revolution was characterized by mechanization, the invention of the steam engine, and the transformation of agrarian economies into formidable industrial powerhouses. These developments laid the groundwork for urbanization, mass production, and significant social changes [3]. The second industrial revolution, powered by electricity and distinguished by mass production and assembly lines, propelled societies further into a new era of manufacturing prowess [3]. The third industrial revolution, often referred to as the digital revolution, witnessed the emergence of computers, automation, and information technology. This era ushered in the automation of production processes and the introduction of cyber-physical systems [3].

Industry 4.0, the latest of these revolutions, harnessed the potential of the Internet of Things (IoT), artificial intelligence (AI), and data analytics to interconnect machines, processes, and systems, thereby revolutionizing manufacturing processes

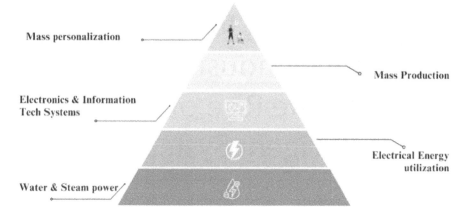

Mass personalization

Mass Production

Electronics & Information
Tech Systems

Electrical Energy
utilization

Water & Steam power

FIGURE 4.1 Evolution of industrial revolutions

and supply chains [1, 4–6]. As we now stand on the threshold of Industry 5.0, it is evident that this evolution represents not merely an incremental upgrade but a profound leap as depicted in Figure 4.1. Industry 5.0 is poised to redefine the relationship between humans and machines, transitioning from a focus solely on efficiency and automation to one that prioritizes collaboration, adaptability, and the synergy between humans and machines [2, 7–10].

The subsequent sections of this chapter delve deeper into the nuances of Industry 5.0, elucidating its defining characteristics, its impact on the human–machine relationship, the ethical considerations it necessitates, the challenges it poses, and the opportunities it presents.

4.1.2 Industry 4.0 as a Foundation for Technological Transformation

The evolution of industrial revolutions reached its pinnacle with Industry 4.0, marking a significant turning point in the ongoing technological revolution [1]. This phase emerged in response to the escalating demand for enhanced connectivity, automation, and data-driven decision-making in the realm of manufacturing and production as depicted in Figure 4.2 [1]. At its core, Industry 4.0 introduced the concept of the "digital thread," seamlessly integrating data across the entire product lifecycle, from design and manufacturing to distribution and consumption [1]. This digital thread enabled real-time monitoring and analysis, optimizing processes, reducing downtime, and enhancing efficiency [1]. Smart manufacturing systems, equipped with sensors, actuators, and data analytics, ushered in predictive maintenance and adaptive production, minimizing waste and resource consumption [1]. Furthermore, the IoT played a pivotal role by connecting physical devices and machines through the internet, fostering cyber-physical systems that improved productivity and reduced human intervention [1]. Industry 4.0's data-centric approach empowered businesses to make informed decisions and adapt to market demands [1].

While Industry 4.0 revolutionized automation and digitalization, it also emphasized the importance of human collaboration alongside machines [1]. This blurred the

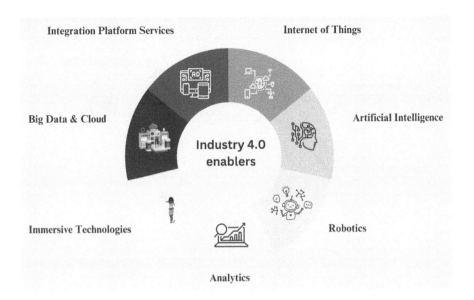

Integration Platform Services

Internet of Things

Big Data & Cloud

Artificial Intelligence

Industry 4.0 enablers

Immersive Technologies

Robotics

Analytics

FIGURE 4.2 Industry 4.0 enablers

traditional factory hierarchy as humans worked alongside smart machines, robots, and AI systems, necessitating a shift in workforce skills toward lifelong learning and adaptability [1]. However, Industry 4.0 had its limitations, primarily focusing on efficiency and sometimes neglecting concerns about job displacement and the potential overemphasis on technology over human creativity [1]. These shortcomings paved the way for Industry 5.0, which builds upon the foundation of Industry 4.0 while addressing these issues by emphasizing human–machine collaboration, ethical considerations, and broader societal impact [1, 2, 7]. In summary, Industry 4.0 serves as a vital precursor to Industry 5.0, providing the technological groundwork and insights required for the emergence of a new era where the boundaries between humans and machines continue to blur, shaping a collaborative and transformative industrial landscape [1, 2, 7].

4.1.3 TRANSITION FROM INDUSTRY 4.0 TO INDUSTRY 5.0

The transition from Industry 4.0 to Industry 5.0 represents a profound transformation in the course of industrial evolution. While Industry 4.0 laid the technological groundwork, Industry 5.0 reimagines industrial processes by elevating the role of humans and intelligent systems in a collaborative partnership as depicted in Figure 4.3. In this section, we explore the indications of Industry 4.0's maturity and the consequential impacts it generated, setting the stage for the emergence of Industry 5.0 [1, 6].

As Industry 4.0 matured, several unmistakable signs became apparent, signaling readiness for the transition to the next phase. These signs were accompanied by transformative impacts that underscored the imperative for a paradigm shift toward Industry 5.0. Notably, the widespread interconnectivity of machines, devices, and

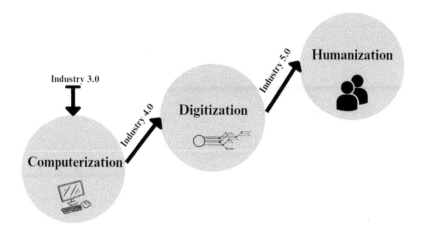

FIGURE 4.3   Industry 3.0 to Industry 5.0

systems within manufacturing environments emerged as a pivotal sign of Industry 4.0 maturity. The advent of the IoT fostered a complex network of data exchange, enabling real-time monitoring, analysis, and process optimization. This connectivity facilitated an unprecedented proliferation of data, forming the foundation for data-driven decision-making and continuous improvement [1, 6].

Automation, too, reached unprecedented heights during the Industry 4.0 era. Robotic systems became integral to various manufacturing processes, enhancing efficiency, precision, and speed [1]. Autonomous vehicles, guided by AI and sensors, seamlessly navigated factory floors and warehouses, streamlining logistics and minimizing errors [8]. This automation revolutionized factory floors into dynamic and efficient environments [1]. Furthermore, Industry 4.0 embraced advanced analytics and machine learning, translating data into actionable insights [11]. Predictive maintenance became a reality as AI algorithms analyzed sensor data to anticipate equipment failures, resulting in reduced downtime, cost savings, and heightened operational efficiency [11].

The Industry 4.0 era also brought about a shift toward customization and customer-centricity [12]. Smart manufacturing allowed for agile reconfiguration of production lines to accommodate diverse product variations [12]. Data-driven insights empower businesses to tailor products and services to individual customer preferences, thereby enhancing customer satisfaction and loyalty [12]. However, Industry 4.0 wasn't without its challenges, including concerns about job displacement due to automation [11] and ethical dilemmas surrounding data privacy and bias in decision-making [5]. These societal impacts highlighted the need for a more holistic approach to ensure the positive integration of technology [11]. The confluence of these signs and impacts laid the groundwork for the emergence of Industry 5.0—an era characterized by harmonious collaboration between humans and intelligent systems [2], transcending the confines of traditional automation. In the following sections, we delve deeper into the unique characteristics, collaborative dynamics [9], ethical considerations [13], challenges [14], and opportunities [15] that Industry 5.0 presents, encapsulating a future where human creativity and technological advancement intertwine to shape industries in unprecedented and transformative ways.

4.1.4 ANTICIPATING THE EMERGENCE OF INDUSTRY 5.0

As Industry 4.0 reached its zenith, it brought forth a series of technological advancements that reshaped industries and economies across the globe [1]. However, it also unveiled a set of challenges that prompted the anticipation and eventual birth of Industry 5.0 [2]. This new era wasn't just a natural progression; it represented a strategic response to the evolving needs, societal concerns, and technological possibilities that were brought to light during the Industry 4.0 journey.

4.1.4.1 Socioeconomic Transformation and Technological Potential

Industry 4.0 marked a technological revolution, highlighting the need for responsible harnessing of technology to mitigate job displacement and ethical concerns stemming from data-driven decision-making [11]. In response, Industry 5.0 embraces a balanced and inclusive approach to transform these challenges into opportunities [2]. Its key strength lies in blending human creativity with machine intelligence, moving beyond mere efficiency toward collaborative innovation [8]. Intelligent systems evolve into co-creative partners, enabling humans to harness technology in imaginative ways [16]. This collaborative synergy unlocks fresh possibilities for problem-solving, personalized product development, and industry-wide adaptability [2].

4.1.4.2 The Evolving Human–Machine Relationship

Industry 5.0 represents a pivotal shift in the human–machine relationship, building upon the foundations laid by Industry 4.0 [1]. While the previous era emphasized process optimization and predictive maintenance [1], Industry 5.0 takes this connection to the next level by placing humans and machines on equal footing, leveraging their unique strengths [8]. This evolving dynamic promises a more enriching work environment where routine tasks are handled by machines, freeing humans to engage in higher-order thinking, unleash their creativity, and tackle complex decision-making [8]. In this symbiotic relationship, continuous learning and upskilling become essential, as individuals adapt to a rapidly changing technological landscape [5]. This transformation calls for collaboration among educators, policymakers, and businesses to shape curricula and training programs that equip the workforce with the multidisciplinary skills necessary to thrive in a human-centered, technology-enhanced industrial ecosystem [1].

4.1.4.3 Ethical Considerations and Responsible Innovation

In the context of Industry 5.0, the profound integration of intelligent systems sparks crucial ethical considerations and emphasizes the imperative of responsible innovation [5]. This era acknowledges the weighty ethical responsibility that accompanies the immense technological power harnessed [5]. As machines actively engage in collaborative endeavors with humans across various industrial domains, pressing

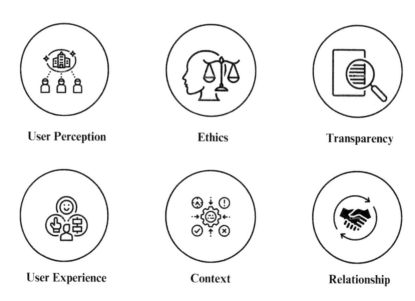

| User Perception | Ethics | Transparency |
| User Experience | Context | Relationship |

FIGURE 4.4 Ethical considerations and responsible innovation

concerns surface regarding data privacy, security, and the pervasive specter of algorithmic bias as depicted in Figure 4.4 [5]. To tackle these intricate ethical dilemmas, a multifaceted strategy is indispensable [5]. It demands the establishment of
comprehensive ethical frameworks that meticulously steer the development and
deployment of intelligent systems [5]. Simultaneously, the emphasis on transparent
and explainable AI becomes paramount, facilitating human comprehension of the
rationale underlying machine-driven decisions [5]. Ultimately, the responsible use
of technology transforms into a collective endeavor, uniting diverse stakeholders in
their commitment to fostering innovation that harmonizes with human values and
contributes to the betterment of society as a whole [5].

4.1.4.4 Redefining Industry Ecosystems and Value Chains

The transition from Industry 4.0 to Industry 5.0 goes beyond individual companies,
encompassing entire ecosystems. This shift underscores the necessity for novel
models of collaboration across businesses, educational institutions, governmental
bodies, and communities, emphasizing cross-disciplinary cooperation as industries
merge with research entities and policymakers to collectively steer the course of
innovation [9]. Simultaneously, value chains are undergoing a profound metamor-
phosis, departing from the traditional linear approach to become dynamic, interconnected networks where products and services are customized in real-time to
align with customer preferences [1]. Intelligent systems empower organizations to
scrutinize data spanning the entire value chain, offering invaluable insights that
guide decision-making, boost operational efficiency, and elevate the overall customer experience [10].

4.14.5 Holistic Societal Impact and Sustainability

Industry 5.0, with its emphasis on collaboration, transcends the boundaries of businesses and industries to promote a holistic societal impact rooted in environmental sustainability and well-being [17]. By leveraging the interconnectedness of intelligent systems, it holds the promise of optimizing resource usage, curbing waste, and mitigating environmental harm [12]. Furthermore, Industry 5.0 champions diversity and inclusivity, striving to make the benefits of technological progress accessible to all segments of society [8]. This vision closely aligns with the United Nations' Sustainable Development Goals, aspiring to shape a future where innovation serves the collective advancement of humanity [18].

In conclusion, Industry 5.0 represents more than just a technological leap; it signifies a profound conceptual shift that centers on human involvement in innovation. It addresses the challenges posed by Industry 4.0 by advocating a holistic and collaborative approach [2]. In doing so, Industry 5.0 sets the stage for a future where intelligent systems and human creativity coexist harmoniously, driving industries toward greater efficiency, innovation, and societal well-being [19]. The subsequent sections of this chapter delve deeper into this collaborative paradigm, exploring its defining characteristics, ethical considerations, challenges, and transformative potential.

The purpose of this chapter is to provide a comprehensive understanding of the transition from Industry 4.0 to Industry 5.0, highlighting the emergence of intelligent systems and the collaborative relationship between humans and machines [20]. It accomplishes this by examining the historical context, the evolution of industrial revolutions, and the limitations of Industry 4.0 [3]. These insights prepare the groundwork for a detailed exploration of Industry 5.0's unique features, ethical challenges, and opportunities [15]. This chapter's scope encompasses key objectives, including contextualizing Industry 5.0 within the industrial revolution continuum, delineating the evolution from Industry 4.0 to Industry 5.0, elucidating the characteristics of Industry 5.0 [1], addressing ethical considerations [5], outlining challenges and opportunities [14], and emphasizing interdisciplinary collaboration and holistic impact [21]. By fulfilling these objectives, this chapter aims to provide readers with a comprehensive understanding of the evolving industrial landscape and the promising future that Industry 5.0 represents. Subsequent sections further elaborate on the collaborative nature of Industry 5.0, its ethical dimensions [5], the challenges it poses [14], and the transformative possibilities it offers [9], inviting readers to envision the dynamic synergy between human ingenuity and technological advancement shaping the future of industries [10].

4.2 INDUSTRY 5.0: A PARADIGM SHIFT

The evolution from Industry 4.0 to Industry 5.0 marks a profound transition, redefining the way industries operate and humans collaborate with intelligent systems [1]. This section dissects the essence of Industry 5.0 through a series of subtopics that delve into its core attributes and implications. At the heart of Industry 5.0 lies a transformation that extends beyond conventional automation, heralding a new era

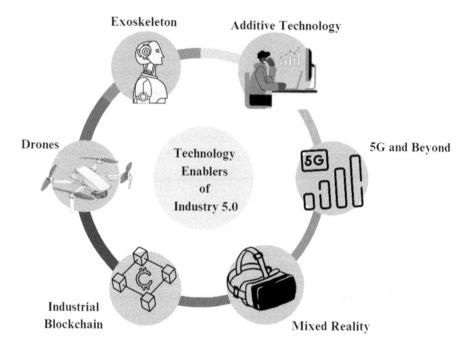

FIGURE 4.5   Technology enablers of Industry 5.0

where the lines between humans and machines are blurred in unprecedented ways as depicted in Figure 4.5 [2, 8]. This subsection delves into the nuanced aspects of Industry 5.0's definition, shedding light on its multifaceted nature and its role in shaping the contemporary industrial landscape [7, 19].

4.2.1   BEYOND AUTOMATION: REDEFINING INDUSTRIAL LANDSCAPES

While Industry 4.0 was characterized by automation and data-driven decision-making, Industry 5.0 takes a monumental leap forward by transcending the confines of automation. No longer limited to passive tools, intelligent systems in Industry 5.0 become active participants, collaborating with humans to co-create innovative solutions. This subsection explores how Industry 5.0 reimagines industrial landscapes by introducing dynamic partnerships between humans and machines, elevating the concept of collaboration to new heights [1, 2, 8, 9].

As the discussion unfolds, it becomes evident that Industry 5.0 represents a pivotal departure from the established norms of manufacturing and production, encompassing a holistic vision that places equal emphasis on human ingenuity and technological capabilities as depicted in Figure 4.6. The subsequent subsections continue to delve deeper into the defining characteristics and transformative potential of Industry 5.0, culminating in a comprehensive understanding of the paradigm shift that shapes the future of industries [1, 2, 8, 9].

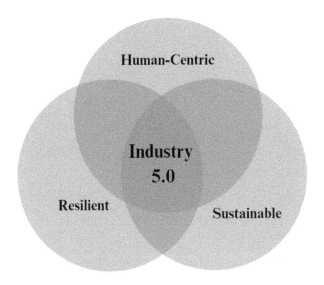

FIGURE 4.6 Components of Industry 5.0

4.2.2 INTEGRATION OF CYBER-PHYSICAL SYSTEMS AND HUMAN COLLABORATION

At the core of Industry 5.0's redefinition of industrial landscapes lies the seamless integration of cyber-physical systems and the collaborative partnership between humans and machines as depicted in Figure 4.7 [2]. This subsection delves into the intricate interplay between these two dimensions, highlighting how their synergy forms the foundation of Industry 5.0's transformative potential.

As cyber-physical systems become more sophisticated, the boundaries between the digital and physical worlds continue to blur [1]. Industry 5.0 leverages this integration to create a dynamic environment where intelligent machines and physical entities collaborate in real time [9]. This subsection explores the convergence of digital twins, which mirror physical processes in the virtual realm [1], and their real-world counterparts [9]. This symbiotic relationship empowers businesses to enhance decision-making, optimize operations, and mitigate risks by leveraging real-time insights from both realms [1, 9].

The true power of Industry 5.0 emerges when human collaboration is seamlessly woven into this interconnected fabric of cyber-physical systems [2]. As machines become active partners rather than mere tools, humans are positioned to interact with them in meaningful ways [2]. This subsection examines the role of human–machine collaboration in co-innovation, problem-solving, and adaptability [2]. It explores how cyber-physical systems facilitate the fluid exchange of information, enabling humans to contribute their creativity, intuition, and contextual understanding to decision-making processes [2].

The integration of cyber-physical systems and human collaboration extends beyond isolated processes and transcends organizational silos [2]. It reshapes

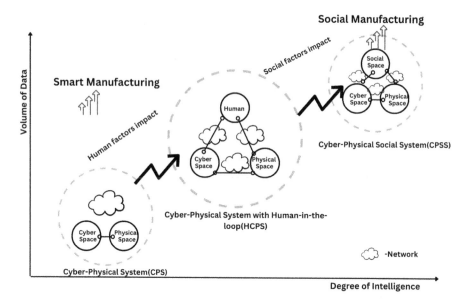

FIGURE 4.7 Integration of cyber-physical systems and human collaboration

traditional hierarchies, fostering a collaborative ecosystem where information flows freely across departments, industries, and even geographies [2]. By embracing this fusion, Industry 5.0 unleashes a new wave of productivity, agility, and innovation [2], catalyzing the potential for profound change across industries [2].

In sum, this subsection underscores the significance of the integration of cyber-physical systems and human collaboration in Industry 5.0 [2]. It emphasizes how this synergy transcends mere automation and ushers in an era where human–machine partnerships reshape the very fabric of industries [2], offering transformative possibilities that extend far beyond the boundaries of the factory floor [2].

4.3 EVOLUTION OF INTELLIGENT SYSTEMS

The evolution from Industry 4.0 to Industry 5.0 is not solely about technological advancements but also about the transformation of the role and capabilities of intelligent systems. This section traces this evolution, beginning with the passive automation prevalent in Industry 4.0 and subsequently delving into the active partnership that characterizes Industry 5.0 [1, 9].

4.3.1 Passive Automation in Industry 4.0

Industry 4.0 brought about a paradigm shift with the introduction of passive automation. This subsection delves into the foundational concepts of passive automation, exploring how it revolutionized industries by leveraging automated processes and data-driven decision-making [1].

4.3.1.1   Automated Processes and Data-Driven Decision-Making

In the realm of Industry 4.0, a pivotal element was the fusion of automated processes and data-driven decision-making, marking a shift toward passive automation [1]. This transformation revolutionized manufacturing by streamlining repetitive tasks, enhancing precision, and bolstering operational efficiency through increased automation, thus reducing human intervention and minimizing errors [1]. A key enabler of this paradigm shift was the strategic utilization of data obtained from various sources like sensors, devices, and production lines [1], which was then harnessed to yield actionable insights [11]. This involved the application of data analytics and machine learning algorithms for purposes such as predictive maintenance, demand forecasting, and real-time optimization [5, 11]. The consequence of these automated processes and data-driven insights was a profound alteration in industry operations, transitioning decision-making from a reactive stance to a proactive one [1], allowing businesses to anticipate market trends and customer preferences [8], ultimately leading to the creation of personalized products and services [1]. However, this passive automation approach had its limitations, as it occasionally overshadowed the value of human creativity and raised concerns about job displacement and ethical dilemmas stemming from data-driven decisions [5]. In sum, this subsection underscores the pivotal role of passive automation in Industry 4.0, setting the stage for the subsequent evolution to Industry 5.0, which will be explored in the following sections, emphasizing an active partnership where intelligent systems cease to be passive tools and instead become active collaborators in shaping the future of industries [2, 7].

4.3.1.2   Limitations and Challenges Encountered

Passive automation in Industry 4.0, while bringing substantial advancements, revealed a host of limitations and issues that propelled the transition toward Industry 5.0. This section explores these critical constraints. First, the exponential growth of data due to sensor and device proliferation posed challenges in terms of data management, quality assurance, and integration, casting doubt on the reliability of insights derived [1, 2, 12]. Second, the rigidity of predefined workflows hindered adaptability to dynamic changes, as automated processes struggled to respond swiftly to unforeseen disruptions [1]. Third, questions arose about the human–automation relationship, with concerns regarding job displacement and the potential sidelining of human expertise [11, 14]. Fourth, ethical dilemmas surrounding privacy, security, and bias emerged from heavy data reliance [13, 22, 23]. Lastly, an overreliance on technology posed vulnerabilities in the face of technical failures or cyberattacks [4]. In conclusion, these challenges spurred the evolution toward Industry 5.0, emphasizing active collaboration between humans and intelligent systems to create dynamic ecosystems of innovation and synergy [2, 8, 9]. Subsequent sections delve into how Industry 5.0 overcomes these limitations and transforms industries.

4.3.2   ACTIVE PARTNERSHIP IN INDUSTRY 5.0

The transition from passive automation to Industry 5.0 marks a shift from machines being passive tools to becoming active partners in collaboration with humans. This section explores the concept of active partnership in Industry 5.0 and begins with an examination of co-creation and co-innovation as fundamental components of this collaborative approach.

4.3.2.1 Co-Creation and Co-Innovation Between Humans and Machines

Industry 5.0 heralds a new era where humans and machines unite in co-creation and co-innovation, transcending conventional roles and redefining the landscape of creativity and problem-solving [2, 7]. This paradigm shift is characterized by the dynamic collaboration between humans and intelligent systems, working together to generate groundbreaking ideas, solutions, and products [2]. While machines offer data-driven insights, humans contribute invaluable intuition, empathy, and domain expertise [2]. This synergistic partnership yields innovative breakthroughs that neither humans nor machines could achieve in isolation [2].

Furthermore, co-innovation extends this collaboration to the realm of refining and iterating on concepts [2]. It highlights how intelligent systems enable rapid prototyping and controlled experimentation, reducing time-to-market and enhancing an industry's responsiveness to evolving market demands [1, 7]. This collaborative approach not only results in products and services that deeply resonate with customers, fostering loyalty and brand affinity [12, 15] but also fosters a culture of continuous learning and improvement within organizations [3].

Nevertheless, this transformative potential also comes with challenges, such as interoperability issues and communication gaps [11, 15], necessitating the cultivation of collaborative ecosystems that prioritize open communication, knowledge sharing, and mutual respect to fully harness the active partnership's potential [9]. In summary, Industry 5.0's active partnership between humans and machines paves the way for unprecedented collaboration, where the fusion of human creativity and machine intelligence propels innovation, problem-solving, and the evolution of industries [2, 7, 12, 15].

4.3.2.2 Contextual Awareness and Real-Time Adaptation

Industry 5.0 is characterized by its active partnership between humans and machines, and two key components that define this partnership are contextual awareness and real-time adaptation [1, 2]. Contextual awareness empowers intelligent systems to understand their environment, using sensors and data sources to gather information and process it with AI algorithms [2, 8]. This allows machines to recognize objects, analyze situations, and make informed decisions based on the data they receive [2, 11]. Real-time adaptation builds upon contextual awareness by enabling machines to dynamically adjust their operations based on their understanding of the context [1, 2]. Whether it is adapting to variations in raw materials in a manufacturing process or navigating complex environments, real-time adaptation ensures that machines optimize their actions to achieve desired outcomes [2, 8].

One striking example of the synergy between contextual awareness and real-time adaptation is the use of collaborative robots on factory floors [9, 15]. These robots can comprehend human gestures, movements, and intentions, adapting their behavior to facilitate seamless cooperation with human workers [9, 15]. This adaptive behavior creates a harmonious working environment where machines respond intuitively to human actions [9, 15]. However, implementing these capabilities is not without its challenges [5, 11], as this subsection also discusses. Processing diverse data sources [11, 23], ensuring data accuracy [11, 23], and addressing biases in AI algorithms [5, 11] are complex tasks. Ethical considerations [5, 22], particularly regarding the balance between autonomy and human control [5, 22], also require careful attention in the development of these intelligent systems.

In conclusion, the integration of contextual awareness and real-time adaptation is pivotal in Industry 5.0's active partnership between humans and machines [1, 2]. These attributes enhance collaboration and responsiveness, allowing machines to engage intelligently with their environment [2, 15]. As machines continue to become more contextually aware and adaptive [8, 9], they contribute to the vision of Industry 5.0 as a collaborative ecosystem where humans and machines work seamlessly together to achieve shared goals [1, 2, 15]. However, the journey toward achieving these capabilities is marked by technical complexities and ethical considerations [5, 11, 22] that must be addressed to ensure a successful and responsible implementation of Industry 5.0 technologies.

4.3.3 FROM TOOLS TO COLLABORATORS

Industry 5.0 signifies a transformative shift from viewing intelligent systems as mere tools to recognizing them as integral collaborators in the industrial landscape. This section explores this transition, beginning with a focus on the shift from a tool-centric to a collaborator-centric paradigm.

4.3.3.1 Shift from Tool-Centric to Collaborator-Centric Paradigm

In the context of Industry 4.0, intelligent systems were primarily regarded as tools aimed at automating various tasks and processes within industrial settings [1, 6]. However, Industry 5.0 brings about a significant shift in perspective, redefining the role of intelligent systems [2]. In this new paradigm, these systems are no longer passive tools but active collaborators, contributing holistically to both the creative and operational aspects of industries [2].

This transformation challenges the conventional tool-centric approach and introduces a collaborator-centric philosophy that emphasizes a more interactive and dynamic relationship between humans and machines [2]. The collaborator-centric paradigm in Industry 5.0 envisions a future where humans and machines work together in synergy, capitalizing on their respective strengths to create value that surpasses what either could achieve in isolation [1, 2]. While machines offer computational power, data processing capabilities, and precision, humans bring creativity, intuition, and emotional intelligence to the collaboration [1, 12]. This shift has far-reaching implications for the workforce, as job roles evolve from traditional task execution to roles that involve co-creation, problem-solving, and strategic decision-making [2, 12]. This necessitates a transformation in workforce skills, placing a greater emphasis on adaptability, critical thinking, and the ability to interact harmoniously with intelligent systems [2, 12].

However, the transition to a collaborator-centric paradigm also presents challenges [2, 15, 21]. Effective communication and mutual understanding between humans and machines, addressing concerns about job displacement, and fostering a culture of collaboration are essential considerations that need to be addressed to fully realize the potential of this paradigm [2, 15, 21]. In summary, the shift to Industry 5.0 highlights a transformative change from a tool-centric to a collaborator-centric approach, where intelligent systems actively engage as partners in co-creation, innovation, and synergy with human counterparts [2]. Embracing this shift holds the promise of unlocking unprecedented levels of creativity, efficiency, and value generation within industries [1, 2, 12].

4.3.3.2   Human-Centered Design of Intelligent Systems

In the dynamic landscape of Industry 5.0, the central role played by human-centered design in shaping intelligent systems cannot be overstated [2]. This subsection delves into the principles and practices that underpin the development of these systems, emphasizing their paramount significance in fostering seamless interaction and cooperation with human counterparts [7, 19]. At its core, human-centered design in this context begins with a profound understanding of user needs, goals, and the contextual environment in which intelligent systems are deployed [1, 8]. Extensive research, user surveys, and observations are employed to unearth insights that serve as the guiding compass for the design process [11, 15]. By empathizing with users, designers are empowered to create systems that not only meet expectations but also harmonize with users' behaviors and preferences [22].

User-friendly interfaces are pivotal to facilitating effective collaboration between humans and intelligent systems [4]. This subsection underscores the critical importance of interfaces that are intuitive and user-friendly, reducing cognitive load and enhancing transparency in interactions [3, 5]. Factors such as ease of use, clarity in information presentation, and adaptability to various user preferences are vital considerations in this regard [20, 24]. Moreover, as intelligent systems assume active roles in collaboration, the imperative for transparency in their decision-making processes becomes evident [16]. Designing interfaces that communicate the reasoning behind suggestions or actions, the data utilized, and the decision-making mechanisms employed is paramount. Explainable AI takes center stage, not only fostering trust but also enabling more productive and informed collaboration [23].

Human-centered design further recognizes the iterative nature of collaboration and the necessity for feedback loops and learning mechanisms [18, 25]. Systems should be designed to incorporate user input and rectify errors, enhancing the overall collaborative experience [12]. Additionally, intelligent systems should possess the capacity to learn from interactions and adapt to user preferences over time, evolving in tandem with the ever-changing collaborative landscape [9, 21]. Ethical considerations are woven into the fabric of this design process, addressing issues of potential bias, privacy, and data security [17]. This subsection also underscores the need to promote inclusivity in system interactions, ensuring that the collaborative environment is one where all users feel valued and respected [14].

The collaborator-centric paradigm of Industry 5.0 encourages co-design and co-creation between humans and intelligent systems [6]. This approach recognizes the pivotal role of users and stakeholders in shaping system functionalities, interfaces, and decision-making mechanisms [10, 13]. By actively involving them in the design process, a sense of ownership and relevance is cultivated, enhancing the adoption and effectiveness of intelligent systems [11, 17]. Furthermore, recognizing that collaboration with intelligent systems may necessitate users acquiring new skills, this subsection emphasizes the importance of providing accessible training resources and ongoing support [12]. Through the provision of responsive customer support and the establishment of user communities where knowledge can be freely shared, a smoother transition into this collaborative landscape is facilitated [4].

In summation, the human-centered design of intelligent systems stands as the bedrock of successful collaboration within the context of Industry 5.0 [19]. By placing paramount importance on user needs, intuitive interfaces, transparency, feedback mechanisms, ethical considerations, and co-creation, designers pave the way for harmonious interactions between humans and machines. This approach not only ensures the effective utilization of intelligent systems but also nurtures a culture of collaboration and continuous improvement in the industrial ecosystem.

4.4 THE COLLABORATIVE NATURE OF INDUSTRY 5.0

4.4.1 SYNERGY BETWEEN HUMANS AND MACHINES

4.4.1.1 Mutual Enhancement of Creativity and Precision

In the landscape of Industry 5.0, the central driving force is the collaborative synergy between humans and machines [1, 2, 8]. This dynamic interplay is where the creative capacities of humans intersect with the precision and computational capabilities of machines [1, 2]. Industry 5.0 recognizes that machines, while adept at data processing and analysis, lack the inherently imaginative and intuitive nature of humans [1, 2]. Human creativity is a cornerstone of innovation [2], and Industry 5.0 acknowledges the pivotal role of human creativity in ideation, problem-solving, and envisioning novel solutions that form the basis of progress [1, 2].

Intelligent systems in Industry 5.0 excel in precision and data-driven operations, processing vast amounts of information swiftly and accurately [2, 8]. Machines contribute significantly by refining processes, predicting trends, and making informed decisions based on intricate data patterns [2, 8]. Collaborative problem-solving emerges as a powerful approach [2], combining human creativity with machine precision to address complex challenges [2, 11]. This collaboration capitalizes on the strengths of both collaborators [2], culminating in well-rounded outcomes and fostering an iterative learning loop where insights gained inform future endeavors [11].

Furthermore, the collaborative synergy extends to enhanced decision-making processes [2, 11], where humans bring contextual factors, ethical implications, and emotional nuances into consideration [2, 5, 11]. When working in tandem with machines, humans contribute a holistic perspective [2, 11], while machines offer data-driven insights [2, 11], resulting in well-informed decisions that consider both qualitative and quantitative aspects [2, 11]. Cross-domain collaboration is also fostered in Industry 5.0 [12, 12], enabling humans and machines to leverage insights from diverse fields to develop innovative solutions [2, 12]. However, this collaborative relationship requires careful stewardship to ensure alignment with ethical guidelines [2, 5] and avoid unintended negative consequences, as ethical and social implications come to the forefront [2, 5].

In conclusion, the harmonious partnership between humans and machines in Industry 5.0 promises groundbreaking innovations, well-informed decisions, and cross-disciplinary solutions [2, 11, 12], but it must be guided by ethical responsibility for transformative positive outcomes [2, 5].

4.4.1.2 Bridging Skill Gaps and Enhancing Productivity

In the landscape of Industry 5.0, collaboration takes center stage, extending well beyond mere creative synergies. This paradigm shift embraces the profound merging of human ingenuity and technological prowess, with a focus on bridging skill gaps and elevating productivity [1, 2, 9]. In the first dimension, Industry 5.0 recognizes the importance of skill diversification. Here, humans leverage their cognitive and creative abilities, while machines deftly handle repetitive and data-intensive tasks [1, 2, 9]. This collaborative advantage redefines the workforce, empowering individuals to engage in higher-order tasks, ultimately enhancing overall productivity [1, 2, 9].

The second dimension delves into upskilling and reskilling, essential aspects of this partnership [2, 8, 9]. Collaborating with intelligent systems necessitates the development of new skills [2, 8, 9]. In response, tailored training programs and educational initiatives enable the workforce to adapt seamlessly to the evolving landscape [2, 8, 9]. These initiatives ensure that workers acquire expertise complementary to machine capabilities, fostering a dynamic and adaptable workforce [2, 8, 9].

In the final dimension, Industry 5.0 orchestrates efficiency through automation and data-driven insights [1, 2, 9]. It envisions a world where routine tasks are automated, liberating human resources for tasks demanding nuanced judgment and creativity [1, 2, 9]. Intelligent systems, adept at processing and interpreting vast datasets, provide humans with valuable insights, guiding informed decision-making and enhancing strategic planning [1, 2, 9]. Moreover, this collaborative ecosystem stimulates innovation, driving the development of novel products and solutions to meet the ever-evolving needs of consumers [1, 2, 9]. However, the societal implications of these advancements, such as shifts in employment structures and the ethical responsibility of organizations, must be thoughtfully considered, as Industry 5.0 reshapes our industrial landscape [11, 14, 15, 22].

In conclusion, the synergy between humans and machines in Industry 5.0 offers a multitude of benefits [1, 2, 9]. Skill gaps are addressed, productivity is boosted, and innovation thrives [1, 2, 9]. Yet, as this collaboration evolves, it is crucial to navigate its societal implications with care, ensuring a harmonious balance between efficiency and the well-being of the workforce [11, 14, 15, 22].

4.4.2   ROBOTS AND AI AS HARMONIOUS PARTNERS

4.4.2.1   Fluid Roles and Task Sharing

In the transformative landscape of Industry 5.0, the concept of collaboration, transcends the traditional boundaries of human–robot interaction. Here, robots and AI are not mere tools but poised to become harmonious partners across diverse industrial domains [1, 2, 8, 9].

This new era emphasizes the adaptability and versatility of this collaborative partnership, reshaping roles and responsibilities within the workforce [1, 2, 8, 9]. One fundamental shift in Industry 5.0 is the dynamic role allocation. Instead of fixed and predefined tasks, roles become fluid and adaptable in real-time [2, 8, 9]. Humans, robots, and AI work together in a dynamic ecosystem, with roles assigned based on immediate demands and the unique strengths of each collaborator [2, 8, 9]. This dynamic allocation optimizes efficiency and fosters a responsive industrial environment.

The collaborative landscape of Industry 5.0 also capitalizes on the cognitive and physical capabilities of robots and AI [1, 2, 8, 9]. Robots excel in physically demanding tasks, while AI shines in cognitive functions [1, 2, 8, 9]. By leveraging these complementary strengths, this collaborative system ensures that repetitive tasks are handled by robots, while AI assists in decision-making, data analysis, and complex problem-solving [1, 2, 8, 9]. This division of labor allows humans to focus on tasks that demand creativity, emotional intelligence, and intricate decision-making. These elements combined contribute to a collaborative ecosystem where efficiency and safety coexist, ultimately driving Industry 5.0 toward enhanced productivity and adaptability in the ever-evolving technological landscape [2, 8, 9]. Embracing this harmonious partnership ensures that industries can navigate the future with confidence, making the most of human–robot–AI collaboration [2, 8, 9].

4.4.2.2   Enabling Complex Problem-Solving

The collaborative synergy among robots, AI, and humans within Industry 5.0 extends its reach to enable the intricate domain of complex problem-solving, surpassing the capabilities of any single collaborator [1, 2, 8, 9]. This subsection delves into the intricacies of how this collaborative partnership leverages its diverse strengths to tackle complex challenges and drive innovative solutions.

Complex problem-solving often demands a multidimensional perspective that draws from various sources of insight [3, 5, 25]. The collaboration between robots, AI, and humans plays a crucial role in aggregating these insights [2, 8, 9]. While AI meticulously analyzes extensive datasets [4, 5], robots provide real-world data [1, 8, 9], and humans contribute their contextual understanding [2, 15]. Together, these collaborators form a comprehensive foundation that informs robust and well-rounded decision-making processes.

The inherent strength of AI lies in its data-driven decision-making capabilities [3, 5]. These dynamic complements the intuitive and experiential nature of human decision-making [2, 15]. By harnessing the power of AI's data analysis and pattern recognition alongside human intuition [5], the collaborative partnership is poised to forge novel problem-solving strategies and outcomes that are both informed and innovative.

Iterative problem-solving lies at the heart of addressing complex challenges, and the collaborative trio of humans, robots, and AI excels in this area [1, 2, 8, 9]. Robots and AI systems enable rapid prototyping and experimentation [1, 8, 9], accelerating the problem-solving process. In this iterative cycle, humans continually refine their solutions based on real-time feedback from insights generated by AI [5] and tasks executed by robots [1, 9], leading to efficient and effective problem resolution.

The breakdown of complex challenges into manageable components is an integral aspect of Industry 5.0's collaborative approach [2, 8, 9]. With the capability of AI to simulate various scenarios [5] and robots executing specific tasks [1, 9], humans can focus on overseeing and orchestrating the entirety of the problem-solving process. This collaborative effort results in a holistic understanding and approach to intricate challenges.

The complementarity between cognitive and physical assistance is a defining feature of Industry 5.0's collaborative problem-solving strategy [1, 2, 8, 9]. While robots excel in executing physical tasks with precision [1, 9], AI contributes to hypothesis generation, data analysis, and optimization [4, 5]. By aligning these capabilities, the collaboration ensures a comprehensive approach that addresses both cognitive and physical dimensions of complex challenges.

Creative solution generation thrives within the collaborative paradigm of Industry 5.0 [2, 8, 9]. Robots and AI systems contribute to this aspect by offering novel ideas based on data-driven analyses and pattern recognition [4, 5]. Humans then take on the role of refining and adapting these ideas [2], culminating in innovative solutions that leverage the collective strengths of all collaborators.

Resource allocation optimization becomes a seamless endeavor within the collaborative landscape of Industry 5.0's problem-solving [2, 8, 9]. AI's predictive capabilities assist in optimizing resource allocation [4, 5], while robots execute tasks with precision [1, 9]. Humans, in their overseeing capacity, make strategic decisions to ensure that the allocation aligns effectively with overarching objectives.

The collaborative partnership of Industry 5.0 extends to risk assessment and mitigation [2, 8, 9]. AI's simulation capabilities enable the identification of potential risks [5], robots gather real-time data [1, 9], and humans apply their judgment to effectively mitigate these risks [2]. This multifaceted approach ensures that challenges are approached with a keen awareness of potential pitfalls.

Innovation, often sparked by diverse perspectives, is embraced within Industry 5.0's collaborative problem-solving [2, 8, 9]. By combining human creativity [2], AI's analytical prowess [4, 5], and robots' precision [1, 9], the collaboration yields innovative solutions that might be difficult to attain through isolated efforts. The culture of continuous learning is inherent within this collaborative problem-solving approach [2, 8, 9]. Knowledge gained from solving one complex problem is readily applicable to future challenges [11, 21], fostering a cycle of ongoing improvement and refinement. Overall, the collaborative partnership among robots, AI, and humans within Industry 5.0 presents a powerful force that addresses complex problems comprehensively, drives innovation, and pushes the boundaries of what can be achieved through collective collaboration.

4.4.3 AMPLIFYING PRODUCTIVITY AND INNOVATION

4.4.3.1 Acceleration of Idea Generation and Prototyping

In the realm of Industry 5.0, the collaborative harmony between humans, robots, and AI serves as a catalyst for amplifying both productivity and innovation [1, 2, 3, 8, 9]. This section delves into how this partnership accelerates the generation of ideas and the prototyping process, thereby propelling industries toward novel heights of creativity and efficiency.

The collaborative synergy within Industry 5.0 sets the stage for the accelerated generation of ideas and concepts [1, 2, 3, 8, 9]. By harnessing the collective insights and diverse perspectives of humans, robots, and AI, this collaborative partnership becomes a fertile ground for the cultivation of innovative concepts [10, 11, 20, 25]. The analytical capabilities of AI, the experiential wisdom of humans, and the precision of robots amalgamate to spark creative ideation that transcends individual capabilities.

The prototyping phase, a critical juncture in innovation, also witnesses a remarkable acceleration through the collaborative efforts of humans, robots, and AI [1–3, 8, 9]. This subsection explores how the integration of diverse strengths expedites the transformation of concepts into tangible prototypes [5, 7, 15, 22]. Robots take on the role of swift and precise physical execution, while AI contributes real-time data analysis, aiding in the refinement of prototypes. Human oversight ensures that the prototypes align with overarching objectives and desired outcomes.

The multidimensional nature of collaboration between humans, robots, and AI paves the way for innovation that evolves beyond traditional boundaries [1–3, 8, 9]. This section discusses how diverse skills are amalgamated to break down barriers, leading to innovative solutions that might have otherwise remained undiscovered [12, 14, 21]. The combined strength of creative thinking, data-driven analysis, and technical execution fuels a holistic approach to innovation, driving industries toward pioneering breakthroughs.

The iterative nature of the collaborative partnership further enhances the innovation process [1–3, 8, 9]. Iteration and experimentation are integral components of creative refinement [5, 16]. Here, AI's ability to rapidly simulate and analyze various scenarios, robots' precision in executing changes, and human creativity in conceiving modifications together form a powerful cycle of iterative improvement. This subsection highlights how this continuous cycle accelerates innovation, leading to faster and more effective solutions.

As innovation accelerates, so does the overall productivity of industries within the framework of Industry 5.0 [1–3, 8, 9]. The collaborative partnership of humans, robots, and AI optimizes resource allocation, minimizes downtime through efficient task division, and leverages data-driven insights to make informed decisions swiftly [4, 17–19, 23]. This subsection delves into how this heightened productivity not only benefits individual organizations but also contributes to the economic growth of industries as a whole.

Moreover, this collaborative acceleration of productivity and innovation resonates with Industry 5.0's adaptability and responsiveness to evolving demands [1–3, 8, 9]. As industries face rapidly changing market landscapes, the ability to generate ideas swiftly and refine prototypes efficiently becomes a competitive advantage [12, 14, 17, 21]. This section examines how the harmonious partnership of humans, robots, and AI positions industries to remain agile in the face of disruptions and challenges, amplifying their resilience and sustained success.

In conclusion, the collaborative partnership among humans, robots, and AI in Industry 5.0 ignites a powerful synergy that accelerates idea generation, prototyping, and subsequently, innovation [1–3, 8, 9]. By harnessing the combined strengths of these collaborators, industries are primed to reach new levels of creativity, efficiency, and competitiveness. This amplification of both productivity and innovation not only transforms individual businesses but also shapes the trajectory of industries on a broader scale, ushering in a new era of industrial advancement.

4.4.3.2   Acceleration of Idea Generation and Prototyping

The collaborative landscape of Industry 5.0, driven by the harmonious partnership between humans, robots, and AI, has revolutionized idea generation and prototyping. This collaboration accelerates the creative process by leveraging diverse perspectives and expertise. AI's analytical power, robots' real-world data contribution, and human insights create a synergistic flow of ideas that transcend individual limitations [2, 7, 19].

In the prototyping phase, Industry 5.0's collaborative framework ensures rapid transformation of abstract concepts into tangible prototypes. Robots execute precise physical tasks, AI conducts real-time data analysis, and human oversight ensures alignment with objectives. This integration expedites the prototyping process, enhancing efficiency and effectiveness [1, 8].

Furthermore, the multifaceted collaboration dismantles traditional silos, facilitating innovation that spans industries and domains [15]. The accelerated iterative process within Industry 5.0's collaboration boosts creative refinement. The dynamic cycle of experimentation and improvement benefits from AI's scenario simulation, robots' precision in execution, and human creativity [11]. This iterative acceleration results in faster and more effective solutions, enhancing productivity and competitiveness. Overall, the collaborative synergy among humans, robots, and AI in Industry 5.0 propels industries toward heightened creativity, efficiency, and adaptability, shaping the trajectory of rapid advancement and progress [4, 5, 22].

4.5   SOCIOECONOMIC IMPLICATIONS OF INDUSTRY 5.0

The shift to Industry 5.0, characterized by collaborative partnerships between humans, robots, and AI, carries significant socioeconomic implications that warrant careful examination [2, 7]. This section dives into the multifaceted landscape of these implications, with a particular focus on the challenges and transformations the workforce faces, notably in terms of upskilling and adapting to the evolving industrial paradigm [19].

The advent of Industry 5.0 is reshaping conventional notions of work and the dynamics of the workforce [1]. This subsection delves into the transformative impact of the collaboration between humans, robots, and AI on the workforce [8]. As intelligent systems take on roles beyond automation, the workforce experiences a fundamental shift from mere task execution to encompassing co-creation, strategic decision-making, and problem-solving [15].

This transformation of the workforce necessitates a comprehensive effort in upskilling and reskilling [11]. With robots and AI becoming harmonious collaborators, humans are required to acquire new skill sets that complement and enhance the capabilities of these intelligent systems [22]. This subsection examines the challenges associated with upskilling, emphasizing the need for tailored training programs that empower workers to engage effectively with the evolving technological landscape [4].

Moreover, the upskilling challenge extends beyond technical competencies alone. The collaborative nature of Industry 5.0 places a premium on soft skills such as adaptability, critical thinking, emotional intelligence, and effective communication [5]. This section underscores the importance of nurturing a well-rounded workforce capable not only of harmonious interaction with robots and AI but also of contributing creatively and empathetically to collaborative efforts [3].

The socioeconomic implications extend to the potential disruption of job roles [20]. The integration of intelligent systems may lead to the displacement of certain routine and repetitive tasks, raising concerns about job security [24]. The subsection explores how industries must address these concerns through proactive measures, including reskilling initiatives, transition assistance, and the creation of new roles that leverage uniquely human attributes, such as creativity and complex decision-making [16].

The collaborative partnership also necessitates a shift in organizational culture [23]. The subsection examines the importance of fostering a culture that embraces change, innovation, and lifelong learning [25]. By cultivating a culture that values continuous improvement and embraces the possibilities that Industry 5.0 offers, organizations can navigate workforce transformations more effectively, creating an environment where upskilling becomes a continuous and integral part of the work experience [18].

Furthermore, the upskilling challenge is not confined to the existing workforce [12]. Preparing the next generation for the collaborative landscape of Industry 5.0 requires a reimagining of educational systems [21]. This section discusses the importance of integrating technology education, fostering interdisciplinary thinking, and emphasizing adaptability from early education stages to higher education curricula [9].

In conclusion, the socioeconomic implications of Industry 5.0, characterized by collaborative partnerships among humans, robots, and AI, underscore the imperative of workforce transformation and upskilling [14, 17]. As roles evolve and the nature of work changes, industries must navigate the challenges of upskilling with a strategic approach that encompasses both technical and soft skills [6]. By doing so, industries can create a resilient and agile workforce that not only thrives in the collaborative landscape but also drives innovation, productivity, and economic growth in the era of Industry 5.0 [13].

4.6 CHALLENGES AND OPPORTUNITIES

As the journey to Industry 5.0 unfolds, a landscape of challenges and opportunities emerges. This section delves into the complexities that industries face in navigating this transformative path, focusing on the challenges of paradigm shift and the strategies to overcome resistance to technological change.

4.6.1 OVERCOMING RESISTANCE TO TECHNOLOGICAL CHANGE

As industries transition to Industry 5.0, resistance to technological change can pose a significant challenge [2]. This section explores the various factors that contribute to resistance, such as fear of job displacement [2], unfamiliarity with new technologies [11], and concerns about privacy and security [19]. Addressing these concerns is paramount to fostering a culture that welcomes technological evolution [11].

To overcome resistance, industries must prioritize effective communication [2]. This subsection emphasizes the importance of transparent and empathetic communication that outlines the rationale behind the transition [2], clarifies misconceptions [15], and addresses concerns head-on [19]. By engaging with employees and stakeholders in a meaningful dialogue [15], industries can create a shared understanding of the benefits [1] and potential challenges of Industry 5.0 [19].

Additionally, showcasing tangible benefits is essential [1]. Demonstrating how Industry 5.0 can enhance efficiency [1], create new opportunities [12], and elevate the overall work experience [1] is vital in alleviating concerns and gaining buy-in. This section examines how industries can leverage pilot projects [9], case studies [7], and success stories [1] to showcase real-world advantages and build confidence in the transformative potential of Industry 5.0.

Change management strategies play a pivotal role in overcoming resistance [8]. This subsection explores the significance of comprehensive change management plans that encompass training [1], upskilling [4], and gradual implementation [9]. By providing the necessary tools and support [4], industries can empower employees to adapt to the evolving technological landscape with confidence and enthusiasm.

Cultivating a culture of innovation is instrumental in addressing resistance to technological change [12]. The collaborative nature of Industry 5.0 creates an environment where experimentation and creative problem-solving are valued [9]. This section discusses how industries can foster a culture that encourages employees to contribute their insights [9], embrace continuous learning [3], and actively participate in shaping the trajectory of Industry 5.0 [1].

Furthermore, involving employees in the decision-making process enhances their ownership of the transition [12]. This subsection examines the benefits of soliciting input [15], involving workers in the design of new processes [9], and allowing them to contribute to the strategic direction of Industry 5.0 [8]. By making employees co-creators of the transformation [12], industries can reduce resistance and ensure a smoother transition.

In conclusion, the paradigm shift to Industry 5.0 presents challenges, and overcoming resistance to technological change is a central endeavor [2]. By fostering transparent communication [15], showcasing benefits [1], implementing change management strategies [8], nurturing a culture of innovation [12], and involving employees in decision-making [12], industries can mitigate resistance and create a collaborative ecosystem that embraces the potential of Industry 5.0 [9]. This approach not only paves the way for a successful transition but also positions industries to seize the transformative opportunities that lie ahead [7].

4.6.2 MANAGING TRANSITION AND ADAPTATION STRATEGIES

In the era of Industry 5.0, where collaboration between humans, robots, and AI defines the industrial landscape, managing the transition and implementing effective adaptation strategies becomes a cornerstone of success [1, 2, 8, 9].

Navigating the transition to Industry 5.0 demands a systematic approach. This section emphasizes the importance of developing a clear roadmap that outlines the stages of transition, from the initial assessment of current capabilities to the full integration of collaborative systems [2, 9, 14, 21]. By creating a well-defined plan, industries can align efforts and set clear expectations for the journey ahead [14, 21].

Central to managing the transition is investing in workforce development. This subsection discusses the significance of robust upskilling and reskilling initiatives that equip employees with the skills required for the Industry 5.0 landscape [1, 2, 7, 12, 21, 23]. Industries should tailor training programs to individual roles, ensuring that workers can effectively collaborate with intelligent systems and leverage their unique strengths [1, 2, 7, 12, 21, 23].

Adaptation strategies should prioritize inclusivity. The subsection explores how industries must involve employees at all levels in the transition process [1, 2, 7, 15, 12, 14, 21]. By soliciting input, addressing concerns, and valuing diverse perspectives, industries can create a sense of ownership and empowerment that accelerates the integration of Industry 5.0 [1, 2, 7, 15, 12, 14, 21].

A phased approach to implementation is crucial. This section examines the value of gradual adoption, starting with pilot projects that allow for experimentation and learning [2, 9]. Industries can use these pilot initiatives to identify challenges, refine processes, and gather.

4.6.3 TECHNOLOGICAL ADVANCEMENTS FOR INDUSTRY 5.0—BREAKTHROUGHS IN AI, ROBOTICS, MATERIALS, AND ENERGY SYSTEMS

In the landscape of Industry 5.0, marked by the collaborative synergy between humans, robots, and AI, technological advancements play a pivotal role [1, 2, 8]. The evolution to Industry 5.0 is underpinned by groundbreaking advancements in various technological domains. This subsection highlights the transformative breakthroughs in AI [4, 11], robotics [9, 10], materials science [13], and energy systems [4] that propel Industry 5.0's collaborative landscape.

Advancements in AI enable intelligent systems to perceive, reason, and learn [5, 11]. This section explores how machine learning [5], neural networks [5], and natural language processing [8] empower robots and AI to understand complex contexts, engage in meaningful interactions, and provide invaluable insights. AI's ability to comprehend human inputs and collaborate effectively marks a pivotal shift in Industry 5.0.

Robotics experiences unprecedented advancements in dexterity, mobility, and collaboration capabilities [9, 10]. The subsection discusses how collaborative robots (cobots) equipped with tactile sensors, adaptable grippers, and safe interactions enhance their ability to work alongside humans [9]. These advancements usher in a new era of co-creation, where robots contribute not only strength but also precision and versatility.

Materials science innovations lead to the development of smart and responsive materials [13]. This section examines how materials with self-healing properties, shape-memory characteristics, and adaptive functionalities enhance the capabilities of intelligent systems. These materials enable robots to adapt to changing environments and contribute to collaborative efforts with enhanced agility.

Energy system advancements contribute to sustainable and efficient collaboration [4, 12]. The subsection delves into how emerging energy storage solutions, renewable energy integration, and energy-efficient technologies support the continuous operation of intelligent systems [4]. By reducing downtime and optimizing resource usage, these advancements drive productivity and environmental responsibility in Industry 5.0.

4.7 ENVISIONING THE FUTURE

As Industry 5.0 ushers in a new era of collaborative partnership between humans, robots, and AI, the vision of the future becomes both exciting and transformative. This section delves into the far-reaching impact of Industry 5.0, focusing on its influence on industries, economies, reshaping business models, and its contributions to economic growth and global competitiveness.

4.7.1 IMPACT ON INDUSTRIES AND ECONOMIES

The advent of Industry 5.0 resonates across industries and economies, catalyzing a wave of transformation that ripples through various sectors [2]. Industry 5.0 disrupts traditional industrial paradigms, fostering collaborative ecosystems that redefine how industries operate. This section explores how the seamless integration of humans, robots, and AI transcends linear value chains and ushers in dynamic networks where co-creation, agility, and innovation become paramount [1, 2].

Industries undergo a shift from isolated entities to interconnected ecosystems. The subsection discusses how Industry 5.0 enables real-time data sharing, predictive insights, and agile responses, promoting collaboration across suppliers, manufacturers, and customers. This transformation blurs industry boundaries, accelerates innovation cycles, and ushers in a new era of interdependent industries [9, 19].

Market dynamics evolve with the collaborative landscape of Industry 5.0. This section examines how personalized products, on-demand manufacturing, and agile supply chains reshape market demands. Intelligent systems' ability to swiftly adapt to changing preferences and deliver tailored solutions fosters customer-centricity and elevates consumer experiences [12, 17].

The collaborative future of Industry 5.0 offers immense contributions to economic growth and global competitiveness. This section explores how the collaborative landscape drives innovation, productivity, and strategic advantage [9, 12].

4.7.2 Shaping the Human–Machine Ecosystem

As Industry 5.0 transforms the collaborative landscape between humans, robots, and AI, the evolution of the human–machine ecosystem becomes a central focus. This section delves into the ways in which Industry 5.0 reshapes workflows, and decision hierarchies, and cultivates a culture of lifelong learning and adaptability.

4.7.2.1 Redefining Workflows and Decision Hierarchies

Industry 5.0 heralds a new era where workflows and decision-making structures are reimagined to harness the strengths of both humans and intelligent systems [1, 2]. This section explores how Industry 5.0 reshapes traditional workflows and empowers decision-making hierarchies.

Workflows become collaborative processes. The subsection discusses how Industry 5.0's co-creation model replaces linear workflows with interactive processes where humans and machines seamlessly contribute [1, 2]. Intelligent systems offer data-driven insights, while humans provide intuition, creativity, and contextual understanding, resulting in optimized outcomes.

Decision hierarchies transform into dynamic networks [1, 2]. This section examines how Industry 5.0 disperses decision-making across various levels, empowering individuals with relevant expertise to contribute insights. Decisions become informed by data analytics, real-time insights, and expert input, resulting in more agile and adaptive organizational responses.

The role of supervisors evolves into orchestrators of collaboration [1]. The subsection explores how supervisors transition from mere task managers to facilitators of human–machine interactions. Supervisors ensure effective collaboration, allocate tasks based on strengths, and foster an environment where both humans and machines thrive [1, 9].

4.7.2.2 Cultivating a Culture of Lifelong Learning and Adaptability

Industry 5.0's collaborative ecosystem demands a workforce that is adaptable, curious, and committed to continuous learning [2, 7]. This section delves into how Industry 5.0 cultivates a culture of lifelong learning and adaptability.

Lifelong learning becomes essential for workforce resilience [2]. The subsection discusses how Industry 5.0 encourages employees to embrace continuous learning, upskilling, and reskilling [7]. Lifelong learners are equipped to navigate evolving roles and tasks, contributing to a dynamic and agile workforce [2, 7].

Adaptability becomes a hallmark of Industry 5.0 professionals [2]. This section examines how the ability to pivot, embrace change, and adopt new technologies becomes a sought-after skill [2]. Employees who exhibit adaptability thrive in Industry 5.0's collaborative landscape, as they seamlessly integrate with evolving technologies and processes [2].

Collaborative learning bridges human–machine knowledge gaps [1, 19]. The subsection highlights how humans and machines can learn from each other, leveraging AI's data analysis and humans' contextual understanding [1, 19]. Collaborative learning environments promote mutual knowledge sharing, contributing to an ecosystem of continuous improvement [1, 19].

In conclusion, Industry 5.0 shapes the human–machine ecosystem by redefining workflows, and decision hierarchies, and cultivating a culture of lifelong learning and adaptability [2]. By harnessing the collective strengths of humans and machines, industries create a dynamic and innovative collaborative landscape where individuals thrive, roles evolve, and adaptability becomes a cornerstone of success [2]. Through these transformative shifts, Industry 5.0 paves the way for a future where humans and machines coexist harmoniously, contributing to a collaborative and agile world [2].

4.8 CONCLUSION

The transition from Industry 4.0 to Industry 5.0 marks a profound shift that is reshaping industries, economies, and societies in ways that were previously unimaginable. This transformative journey underscores the dynamic relationship between human creativity and technological progress, paving the way for a future where humans, robots, and AI not only coexist but also flourish through collaboration. Industry 5.0 is more than just a technological upgrade; it signifies a paradigm shift toward fostering collaboration, driving innovation, and promoting responsible advancement.

At the core of Industry 5.0 lies a shift from a tool-centric approach to a collaborator-centric one. Intelligent systems evolve from passive tools to active collaborators, augmenting human capabilities in terms of creativity, precision, and decision-making. This transformation presents both challenges and opportunities, emphasizing the importance of effective communication, change management, and a culture of innovation. Interdisciplinary collaboration emerges as a critical factor for Industry 5.0's success, drawing expertise from fields such as engineering, psychology, ethics, and more to construct a comprehensive and holistic collaborative ecosystem.

REFERENCES

1. Xu, X., Lu, Y., Vogel-Heuser, B., & Wang, L. (2021). Industry 4.0 and industry 5.0—Inception, conception and perception. *Journal of Manufacturing Systems*, *61*, 530–535.
2. Leng, J., Sha, W., Wang, B., Zheng, P., Zhuang, C., Liu, Q., ... Wang, L. (2022). Industry 5.0: Prospect and retrospect. *Journal of Manufacturing Systems*, *65*, 279–295.

3. Popkova, E. G., Ragulina, Y. V., & Bogoviz, A. V. (Eds.). (2019). *Industry 4.0: Industrial Revolution of the 21st Century* (Vol. 169, p. 249).Springer.

4. Ahmad, T., Zhu, H., Zhang, D., Tariq, R., Bassam, A., Ullah, F., … Alshamrani, S. S. (2022). Energetics systems and artificial intelligence: Applications of industry 4.0. *Energy Reports, 8*, 334–361.

5. Ahmed, I., Jeon, G., & Piccialli, F. (2022). From artificial intelligence to explainable artificial intelligence in industry 4.0: A survey on what, how, and where. *IEEE Transactions on Industrial Informatics, 18*(8), 5031–5042.

6. Xu, X., Lu, Y., Vogel-Heuser, B., & Wang, L. (2021). Industry 4.0 and industry 5.0—Inception, conception and perception. *Journal of Manufacturing Systems, 61*, 530–535.

7. Tiwari, S., Bahuguna, P. C., & Walker, J. (2022). Industry 5.0: A macroperspective approach. In *Handbook of Research on Innovative Management Using AI in Industry 5.0* (pp. 59–73). IGI Global.

8. Wang, F. Y., Yang, J., Wang, X., Li, J., & Han, Q. L. (2023). Chat with chatgpt on industry 5.0: Learning and decision-making for intelligent industries. *IEEE/CAA Journal of Automatica Sinica, 10*(4), 831–834.

9. Gladysz, B., Tran, T. A., Romero, D., van Erp, T., Abonyi, J., & Ruppert, T. (2023). Current development on the Operator 4.0 and transition towards the operator 5.0: A systematic literature review in light of industry 5.0. *Journal of Manufacturing Systems, 70*, 160–185.

10. Xian, W., Yu, K., Han, F., Fang, L., He, D., & Han, Q. L. (2023). Advanced manufacturing in industry. 5.0: A survey of key enabling technologies and future trends. *IEEE Transactions on Industrial Informatics*, 1–15. doi: https://doi.org/10.1109/TII.2023.3274224.

11. Jan, Z., Ahamed, F., Mayer, W., Patel, N., Grossmann, G., Stumptner, M., & Kuusk, A. (2022). Artificial intelligence for industry 4.0: Systematic review of applications, challenges, and opportunities. *Expert Systems with Applications, 216*, 119456.

12. Tang, Y. M., Chau, K. Y., Fatima, A., & Waqas, M. (2022). Industry 4.0 technology and circular economy practices: Business management strategies for environmental sustainability. *Environmental Science and Pollution Research International, 29*(33), 49752–49769.

13. Longo, F., Padovano, A., & Umbrello, S. (2020). Value-oriented and ethical technology engineering in industry 5.0: A human-centric perspective for the design of the factory of the future. *Applied Sciences, 10*(12), 4182.

14. Gagnidze, I. (2023). Industry 4.0 and industry 5.0: Can clusters deal with the challenges? (A systemic approach). *Kybernetes, 52*(7), 2270–2287.

15. Jafari, N., Azarian, M., & Yu, H. (2022). Moving from industry 4.0 to industry 5.0: What are the implications for smart logistics? *Logistics, 6*(2), 26.

16. Anisha, P. R., Reddy, C. K. K., Nguyen, N. G., Bhushan, M., Kumar, A., &Hanafiah, M. M. (Eds.). (2022). *Intelligent Systems and Machine Learning for Industry: Advancements, Challenges, and Practices.* CRC Press.

17. Carayannis, E. G., & Morawska-Jancelewicz, J. (2022). The futures of Europe: Society 5.0 and industry 5.0 as driving forces of future universities. *Journal of the Knowledge Economy, 13*(4), 3445–3471.

18. Kumar, M., Thakur, S., Bangarwa, K., Kumar, R., & Pooniya, S. (2022). Economic and financial challenges after COVID-19. *NeuroQuantology, 20*(5), 1246–1250.

19. Akundi, A., Euresti, D., Luna, S., Ankobiah, W., Lopes, A., & Edinbarough, I. (2022). State of industry 5.0—Analysis and identification of current research trends. *Applied System Innovation, 5*(1), 27.

20. Anisha, P. R., Nguyen, N. G., & Sreelatha, G. (2021, November). A text mining using web scraping for meaningful insights. In *Journal of Physics: Conference Series* (Vol. 2089, No. 1, p. 012048). IOP Publishing.

21. Mourtzis, D., Angelopoulos, J., & Panopoulos, N. (2022). A literature review of the challenges and opportunities of the transition from industry 4.0 to society 5.0. *Energies, 15*(17), 6276.

22. Hassoun, A., Aït-Kaddour, A., Abu-Mahfouz, A. M., Rathod, N. B., Bader, F., Barba, F. J., ... Regenstein, J. (2022). The fourth industrial revolution in the food industry—Part I: Industry 4.0 technologies. *Critical Reviews in Food Science and Nutrition, 63*(23), 6547–6563.

23. Anisha, P. R., Reddy, C. K. K., & Nhu, N. G. (2022). Big data: Trends, challenges, opportunities, tools, success factors, and the way toward pandemic analytics. In *Handbook of Research for Big Data* (pp. 297–318). Taylor and Francis.

24. Tungana, B., Hanafiah, M. M., & Doss, S. (2023). *A Study of Machine Learning Methods Based Affective Disorder Detection Using Multi-Class Classification.* Europe PMC. https://doi.org/10.21203/rs.3.rs-2888288/v1

25. Reddy, C. K. K., Anisha, P. R., & Mohana, R. M. (2021, November). Assessing wear out of tyre using Opencv & convolutional neural networks. In *Journal of Physics: Conference Series* (Vol. 2089, No. 1, p. 012001). IOP Publishing.

5 Securing the Predicted Disease Data using Transfer Learning in Cloud-Based Healthcare 5.0

V. S. Anusuya Devi, Arunadevi Thirumalraj,
Balasubramanian Prabhukavin, Gan Hong Seng

5.1 INTRODUCTION

The concept of healthcare version 5.0 has risen to prominence in recent years as a result of developments in information technology. By streamlining processes and increasing individualization, Healthcare 5.0 represents a radical departure from the status quo in the medical industry [1]. Technology innovations like the Internet of Things (IoT), artificial intelligence (AI), Big Data Analytics (Big Data), and computing are used to achieve this goal. The 5.0 iteration of healthcare is more than just a technology revolution [2]. The traditional disease-centered style of medicine is giving way to a more patient-centric approach. Medical informatization has moved from a focus on individual clinics to encompass entire regions [3]. Furthermore, medical management has shifted from a broad approach to one that is more tailored to the individual. This shift may be seen, for instance, in the rise of the concept of preventive medicine. It involves putting equal emphasis on both curative and preventive medicine [4, 5].

The healthcare business has recently undergone a change from a hospital-centric to a patient-centric perspective, giving patients more say in their own medical decisions [6]. Artificial intelligence, the IoT, Big Data, and aided fog and edge networks all play a role in realizing and sustaining this transformation. Smart sensors are used in digital health to create prediction models and commercial analytics in real time [7]. Healthcare 4.0 refers to an analytical approach to healthcare that is both patient-centric and sensor-driven [8]. The healthcare sector has shifted its practices in line with the Healthcare 4.0 vision, but another major paradigm shift is on the horizon [9]. Smart control, would all be part of this change, which is being called Healthcare

5.0 [10]. As a result, analytics-driven innovations in the healthcare industry would be widespread, highly tailored, dynamic, and reason-based [11].

The goal of Healthcare 5.0 is to deliver digital wellness, and enhanced healthcare metrics [12] through the integration of millions of sensors that would transfer data over infrastructure. The integration of smart mobile wearables with mobile communication and medical technology enables convenient and remote delivery [13]. This scenario is enabled by 5G, the Internet of Things, and artificial intelligence. Attached to patients, cutting-edge Internet of Things sensors gather vital signs, track improvement, and report diagnoses to doctors and hospitals with minimal human intervention. A 10 Gbps speed, 10 ms latency, secure infrastructures in the future, expanded cellular coverage, improved network presentation, and extended battery life by roughly 90% are just some of the promises of 5G in the Internet of Things [14]. Image and text recognition, imaging, accurate illness prediction and diagnosis, and remote health care are just some of the complicated operations that can be performed on created big data sets using artificial intelligence algorithms like (CNN) or deep neural networks (DNN).

Concerns have been raised about the potential social and personal effects of the widespread use of various forms of AI technology. Therefore, it is important to make ethical, transparent, and accountable use of AI. Furthermore, Healthcare 5.0 faces a variety of problems and obstacles, such as "security threats, regulatory difficulties," etc. [15]. Replay, man-in-the-middle (MiTM), impersonation, (DoS), and other information security-related threats are all feasible in Healthcare 5.0. As a result of these intrusions, potentially sensitive patient information may be compromised, altered, or lost. As a result, Healthcare 5.0 requires a solid security infrastructure to protect patient information. The study effort introduced the Hybrid Capsule Network for illness prediction and offered an encryption method for protecting data before it is processed in the cloud, filling a gap between the two fields. Lung cancer illness is analyzed from a variety of perspectives in order to validate the model.

The chapter is structured as follows: The relevant studies are presented in Section 5.2, and the suggested model is briefly labeled in Section 5.3. In Section 5.4, the results of the experiment and their commentary are presented. Future research is discussed to wrap up the chapter.

5.2   RELATED WORKS

A deep learning-based brain tumor classification model was proposed by Haq et al. [16]. To categorize meningioma, glioma, and pituitary brain cancers, an enhanced convolutional neural network was employed in the development of the suggested technique. Brain MRI scans are used to put a multi-level convolutional neural network model to the test. Data augmentation and transfer learning were used to enhance the MCNN model's classification performance. In addition, the suggested MCNN model uses hold-out and performance assessment criteria. The experimental findings demonstrate that the suggested model achieved 99.89% classification accuracy, which is greater than the state-of-the-art methods. We conclude that the suggested method is superior for the detection of brain cancer in IoT-healthcare systems and so recommend it.

In order to increase accountability and transparency, Ali et al. [17] have created an audit log of all data exchanges. That has allowed for a comparison to be made with conventional models, one that takes into consideration things like the cost of transmission, the number of transactions, and the level of security given. Our trials have shown that our technique effectively preserves data privacy while allowing for efficient data processing and analysis. In conclusion, for healthcare applications that make use of the IoT, the combination of homomorphic encryption with blockchain knowledge offers a key that is both robust and protective of users' privacy. This method ensures the privacy of patients while providing a secure environment for the management and communication of sensitive medical statistics.

For our proposed edge-assisted IoT-healthcare scheme, Trivedi et al. [18] designed a homomorphic cryptosystem-based secure data model to enable safe data collection and aggregate offloading on edge nodes. End-to-end privacy and data integrity are achieved using Paillier ID-based signatures. Key-escrow resilience is also enabled by a semi-trusted authority in HC-SDPM. Under the computational Diffie-Hellman assumptions, the HC-SDPM security analysis guarantees the unforgeability of signatures in the random oracle model. In terms of computational cost, communication overhead, and storage complexity, HC-SDPM proves superior to similarly modeled methods.

Using the Rider Horse Herd Optimization Algorithm (RHHO), Yempally et al. [19] developed a safe method of generating keys for use in the data-sharing method. Here, eight stages are used for safe verification and data decryption. The model is by combining the Rider Optimization Algorithm (ROA) with the suggested RHHO. With a computation cost of 0.235, an accuracy of 0.935%, and a memory need of 2.425 MB, the suggested RHHO model outperformed prior models.

A method for ensuring the reliability of data has been developed by Chandol and Kameswara Rao [20]. This architecture consists of four parts: the Data Owner, the Internet of Things server, the Key Generator Center, and the Auditor. The IoT server in this setup can attest to the veracity of the data being outsourced. The data integrity model consists of the initialization, storage, and validation steps. Here, we produce integrity keys in the most optimal way feasible using the suggested optimization. Here, we suggest a variation of BCCO that takes inspiration from both the Taylor series and the Border Collie cat, or Taylor-based BCCO. The suggested method is implemented using the programming language Python. When tested on a dataset of data related to cardiovascular illness, the suggested technique demonstrated improved performance, with a normalized alteration of 0.710, a privacy of 2.880, and a calculation time of only 0.179 seconds.

In order to choose between two different types of gateways in the healthcare network, Ali et al. [21] suggest a mathematical model. Transmission power and infrastructure expenses are optimized to be as low as possible. The computation difficulty problem was solved by swarm intelligence-based optimization techniques. These evolutionary algorithms combine a set of local search techniques into either a "fireworks" or "artificial bee colony" approach. The genetic algorithm is used to evaluate how well they function. Results from simulations show that the proposed healthcare infrastructure may reduce power consumption by up to 33%, which will have a major impact on the efficiency and cost-effectiveness of healthcare data transmission.

5.3 PROPOSED SYSTEM

This research presents an intelligent scheme for predicting lung illness in the health-care business version 5.0 using transfer learning and the Internet of Medical Things. Figure 5.1 depicts the suggested model. In order to forecast patients utilizing a smart healthcare scheme, the following steps make up the projected IoMT-enabled Brainy Scheme with a TL model:

Figure 5.1 is a flowchart depicting the proposed model's breakdown into its con-stituent parts. These parts are as follows validation layer. The IoMT is used to import all of the raw data produced by these installations into a central repository. The patient data acquired through a wireless link might become noisy during transmis-sion, requiring further processing before analysis. All patient data is handled by each hospital's preprocessing layer, which is responsible for filling in missing values and normalizing the data before it is processed further. The training layer is composed of the performance layer. Diseases are classified based on processed patient data

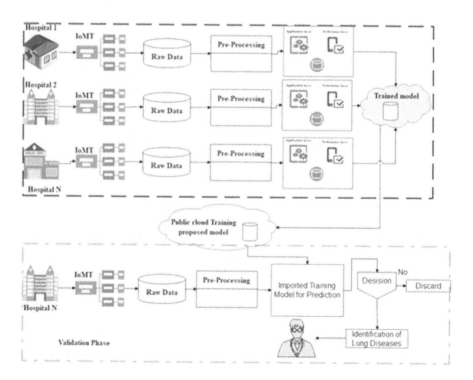

FIGURE 5.1 Projected transfer learning perfect

using a TL model at the application layer. After the layer, the performance layer receives the TL model's outputs for verification of correctness. The TL model should be retrained on the provided dataset if its performance falls short of the criteria. This procedure is repeated until all prerequisites have been satisfied.

5.3.1   PREDICTION OF DISEASE USING DL

After deriving three completely connected layers in the original CapsNet (see Figure 5.2) [22], these layers are joined as a decoder network at the very top of the network.

Minimizing the squared difference between the reconstructed and input images is an effective learning strategy for input picture reconstruction. The sum of the margin loss plus the reconstruction loss equals the total loss (12). The reconstruction loss is scaled down with a very tiny coefficient (= 0.0005) to guarantee that the margin loss is the dominant loss throughout the training stage.

$$Loss = margin\ loss + (\alpha.reconstruction\ loss) \qquad (5.1)$$

5.3.1.1   Proposed Hybrid Capsule Neural Network

In this section, we lay out how our proposed architecture came to be. Deeper layer structures in computer vision can improve feature extraction and perhaps even model performance, although in most cases the opposite is true. Disease classification is not a natural fit for the original CapsNet model because it was developed for more traditional computer vision pictures. Therefore, the suggested HCapsNet's primary workflow is broken down into the following three stages (see Figure 5.3) to generate a model that is acceptable for classification. What follows is an explanation of these three parts.

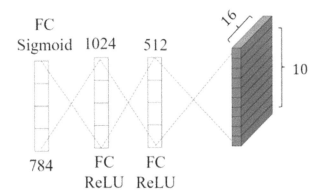

FIGURE 5.2   The decoder comprises three fully associated layers with the sum of neurons 784, 1024, 512

FIGURE 5.3 Proposed HCapsNet block diagram

1. Redundancy is reduced by using principal components analysis (PCA) on a labeled dataset, which is the first step in dimensionality reduction. The data is compressed, which lessens the range of frequencies. The related image is then segmented into labeled patches centered on the central pixel, without the need for feature engineering. Extraction of the spectral-spatial feature map is accomplished using 2-D and 3-D CNNs. *Capsule Connections:* For a single capsule in the CapsNet architecture, the output is first reshaped into nD vectors u_i ($i = 1, ..., I$), where n is the vector length. ClassCapsule $u\_ij(j = 1, ..., J)$.

2. The length of one ClassCapsule's vector is denoted here by m. After that, the squash operation is performed, and finally the weighted sum S_j is computed. Then, the ClassCapsule will be communicated with the PrimaryCapsule that is most closely associated with it via the DR procedure. One capsule per class can be used to create a classifier in the final layer. It indicates accurate encoding of the spatial connections between features and their respective attributes.

3. The instantiation parameters are encoded from input data using a higher-level capsule called ClassCapsule, which is driven by a reconstruction loss in the decoder. The decoder acts like a regularizer by including the margin loss in the training process to avoid overfitting, but the scaling factor (0.0005)

In this scenario, 25 principle components (PCs) are chosen from the lung cancer dataset to illustrate the structure of the many layers, each of which has a unique input and output form. Output is produced using both a 3-D-CNN and 2-D-CNN. The DR method for classification then reformats the output into capsules (PrimaryCaps) and forwards them to the best-fitting ClassCapsule in the subsequent layer. The decoder is included in the model at its final stage.

5.3.2 SECURING THE DATA USING LIGHTWEIGHT ENCRYPTION TECHNIQUE

The suggested image encryption approach and supporting documentation form the framework of this chapter. Figure 5.4 shows the encoding and extrication modules employed. The visual.net structure has been implemented as a part of an image cryptosystem [23, 24].

The encryption–decryption mechanism used in medical picture security must not hinder system performance and must adhere to the principle of least privilege. Two distinct categories may be made for the suggested encryption methods, and their respective procedures are shown in Figure 5.5. The current method is utilized, and improvements are made as.

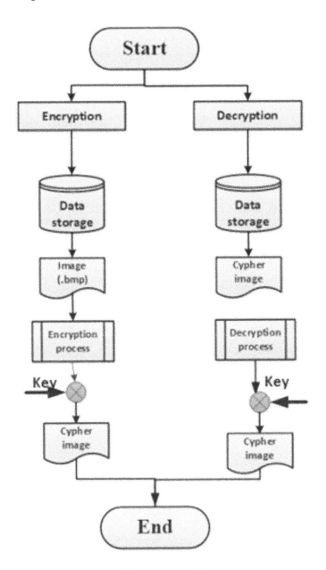

FIGURE 5.4 The working process of the projected scheme

- First, an image will be designated.
- Pixel blocks are then shaped from the designated image by separating.
- Approximating the pixel–block D horizontal.

To do this, we need to make a vertical estimate of 10 pixels based on the height of the D-block picture. Counting pixel blocks (pixel blocks vertical pixel blocks) leads to the next approximation. The subsequent step is to verify the pixel count by: Number of pixels should be adjusted to equal the number of pixels plus one if pixel blocks = 2 W D 0.

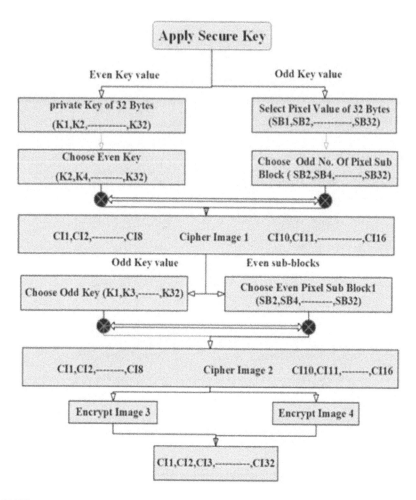

FIGURE 5.5 Projected system architecture phase I (a)

1. *Split the pixel blocks into sub-blocks (SB1, SB2 ...)*
2. *Then select variables I = 0 and R = 0*
   (R => random variable).
   While (I<SB1.R = random number between (0, Sub – Block1 – 1))
3. *Set the new location of block R <= pixel–block*
   I = I + 1
   End While.
4. *Likewise for SB.2.I = 0 and R = 0*
   While (I < SB.R = random number between (0, SB2–1) R <= pixel–block).
   I = I + 1
   End While.
5. *Finally, we get the new location of the pixels block in SB1 and SB2 [25].*

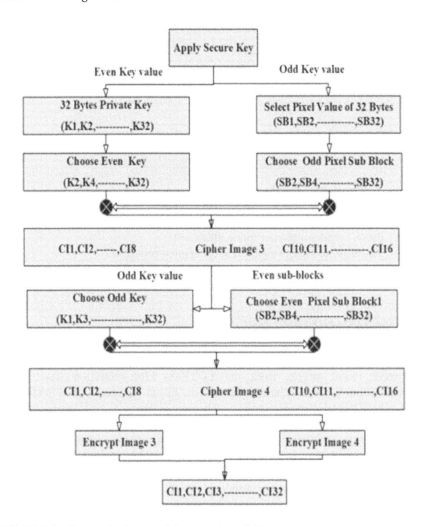

FIGURE 5.6   Proposed scheme architecture phase II (b)

The proposed encryption technique is built in three distinct phases. The output from the transition mechanism served as an input in the first stage, the output from that stage served as an input in the second stage, and so on. All the data is shuffled using a 256-bit key value and a logical operation. A diagram of the suggested scheme architecture is presented in Figure 5.5. The following is a summary of the recommended methods procedure:

1. *At first, we configure the parameters.*
2. *Then Applying Key for the brain images.*
3. *Start Key nomination and Image nomination process.*
4. *The compute and apply:*

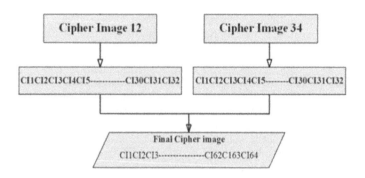

FIGURE 5.7 Proposed system architecture phase III (c)

- Block-based image encryption alteration
- The projected lightweight Twin encryption procedure
- Checkered for the calculated best data.

5.4   RESULTS AND DISCUSSION

5.4.1   Dataset

The cancer tissue images from the LC25000 [26] collection were used. Adenocarcinoma, carcinoma, and benign are the five (5) categories used to classify images of lung tissue; adenocarcinoma and benign are the two (2) categories used to classify images of colon tissue.

When the picture dataset is received, the images must be pre-processed to remove noise. The picture dataset is then split in two for use with machine learning models during training and validation, after preprocessing. In the second stage, the TL model is trained using a dataset of dispersed pictures. This continues until the necessary learning conditions are satisfied. We then transferred the trained TL perfect to the cloud server for testing and validation in the third stage. To further validate the efficacy of the proposed model, we used a widely used dataset for lung cancer categorization as a case study in this research. This data collection serves as the foundation for the analysis and simulation.

The LC25000 data collection was mostly made up of 1,250 lung and colon tissue pathology slides. By switching the pictures' orientations in a number of ways, we were able to increase the quality of the lung cancer dataset from 15,000 to 25,000, with five sets of 5,000 photos each. The images were reduced in size to 768 pixels by 768 pixels before the enhancement was blurred. Figure 5.8 depicts an example of the collection's photographic material. As can be seen in Figure 5.3, the collection's picture classes are each identified by a unique name and ID. Benign colon tissue (a), malignant colon adenocarcinoma (b), benign lung tissue (c), adenocarcinoma (d), and malignant carcinoma of the lung (e) from the LC25000 dataset.

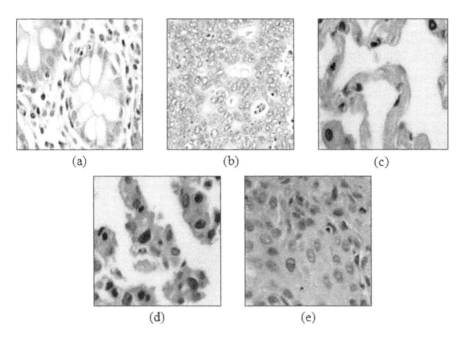

FIGURE 5.8   Histological imageries of each class from the dataset

5.4.2   ENVIRONMENTAL SETUP

This study employs the usage of MATLAB 2020a. The levels of the pre-trained perfect are revised to meet the needs of this study. To accommodate the size requirements of the model, images were scaled to 227 227 3. Partitioning the lung cancer dataset only 30% of the photographs were used for checking accuracy while 70% were used for instruction. The simulation's deployment setting is detailed in Table 5.1. The preferences and other training elements are shown in Table 5.2. In this study, we examined and verified these training options and parameters under a variety of conditions, and they produced the best results.

TABLE 5.1
Implementation Environment

Tool/Device name	Description
Desktop System	Windows 10 (Version 21H1)
Processor	Intel(R) Core(TM) 4770 CPU@3.40GHz
RAM	18.0GB
MATLAB	2021a

TABLE 5.2
Training Selections and Limits

Training preferences	Consideration
Shuffle	Every-epoch
Validation Frequency	1
Repetitions per epoch	273
Entire iterations	1092
Early learning rate	0.0001
Momentum	0.9
Solver	SGDM
Execution Situation	Auto
Minibatch Size	64
Scope of image	227*227*3
Sum of epochs	04

TABLE 5.3
Encryption Time Comparison

Key Sizes	64	128	256	512	1024
AES	9	100	150	410	720
Blowfish	7	10	100	220	650
LWEM	1	2	5	80	350

5.4.3 PERFORMANCE ANALYSIS FOR PROPOSED ENCRYPTION MODEL

Table 5.3 represents the encryption time comparison. In the analysis, we used different keys and different methods. In AES, the model reached the 64 key size at an encryption time of 9, the 128 key size at an encryption time of 100, the 256 key size at an encryption time of 150, the 512 key size at an encryption time of 410, and the 1024 key size at the encryption time as 720, respectively. Then in the Blowfish 7 model the 64 key size was reached at an encryption time of 10, the 128 key size at an encryption time of 100, the 256 key size at an encryption time of 220, and the 512 key size at an encryption time of 650, respectively. Then the LWEM model reached the 64 key size at an encryption time of 1, the 128 key size at an encryption time of 2, the 256 key size at an encryption time of 5, the 512 key size at an encryption time of 80, and the 1024 key size at an encryption time of 350, respectively.

5.4.3.1 Decryption Time

The sum of time needed to convert ciphertext to plaintext is known as the decryption time.

TABLE 5.4
Decryption Time Comparison

Key Sizes	64	128	256	512	1024
AES	70	145	280	520	830
Blowfish	60	120	270	400	710
LWEM	0	8	10	90	400

The *Jn* values that are displayed above in Table 5.4 represent the comparison of the decryption times. During the course of the investigation, we made use of a variety of keys and approaches. The AES model achieved the 64-bit key size at the encryption time of 70, the 128-bit key size at the encryption time of 145, the 256-bit key size at the encryption time of 280, the 512-bit key size at the encryption time of 520, and the 1024-bit key size at the encryption time of 830, respectively. The Blowfish model eventually arrived at the 64-key size at the encryption time of 60, the 128-key size at the encryption time of 120, the 256-key size at the encryption time of 270, the 512-key size at the encryption time of 400, and the 1024-key size at the encryption time of 710, respectively. The LWEM model eventually arrived at the point where the 64-bit key size at encryption time was equal to zero, the 128-bit key size at encryption time was equal to 8, the 256-bit key size at encryption time was equal to 10, the 512-bit key size at encryption time was equal to 90, and the 1024-bit key size at encryption time was equal to 400.

5.4.4 PERFORMANCE ANALYSIS OF PROJECTED CLASSIFIER

The results of this comparison can be seen in the table that can be found above titled "Analysis of Proposed Classifier with Existing Techniques." In this analysis, we evaluated the performance of various models using a variety of metrics, which vary from model to model. In the investigation of the VGGNet model, the accuracy was found to be 89.02, while the precision was found to be 90.87. Additionally, the

TABLE 5.5
Analysis of Proposed Classifier with Existing Techniques

Pre-trained models	ACC	Pre	Recall	F1
VGGNet	89.02	90.87	89.02	89.26
AlexNet	91.50	92.94	91.39	91.71
DenseNet	92.12	93.62	92.12	92.34
CapsuleNet	92.94	93.08	92.68	92.80
Hybrid Capsule Network	94.19	94.54	94.19	94.28

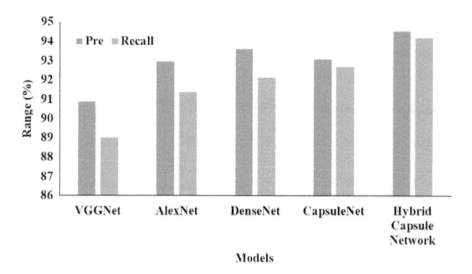

FIGURE 5.9 Analysis of various models

recall value was found to be 89.02, and the F1 score was found to be 89.26. Following the AlexNet 91.50 and 92.94 scores, the recall value was calculated as 91.39, and the F1-score was determined to be 91.71, respectively. The DenseNet model achieved an accuracy of 92.12, as well as a precision of 93.62, as well as a recall value of 92.12, and finally an F1-score of 92.34, respectively. The CapsuleNet model attained an accuracy of 92.94, a precision of 93.08, a recall charge of 92.68, and an F1-score of 92.80, respectively, the next step was to calculate the recall value. When the

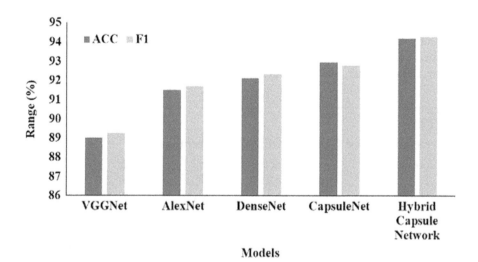

FIGURE 5.10 Comparative study of different models

accuracy of the Hybrid Capsule Network model reached 94.19, the precision of the model reached 94.54, the recall value was 94.19, and the F1-score reached 94.28, respectively.

5.5 CONCLUSION

It is challenging to predict human diseases, especially cancer, to give improved and more timely treatment. Cancer is a devastating illness that can spread to many parts of the body and ultimately prove fatal. To rapidly and effectively anticipate cancer sickness without compromising patient privacy, a fifth-generation intelligent scheme for the healthcare sector is being created using IoMT. In order to lessen response time while upholding high accuracy, a deep ML perfect and a secure IoMT-based TL approach are employed. The suggested technique accurately lung cancer based on the subtypes of lung cancer. To test the feasibility of the projected IoMT-enabled intelligent scheme for the healthcare industry 5.0, a simulation is run in MATLAB 2020a using a secure IoMT-based TL model. In comparison to prior state-of-the-art procedures for predicting sector 5.0, the suggested IoMT-enabled intelligent system with the proposed methodology obtained 94% accuracy. In addition, LWEM is used to encrypt the data beforehand it is sent to the cloud. Although lung cancer was the only condition studied in the study's diagnostics, this method will be used for other diseases in the future.

REFERENCES

1. Wazid, M., Das, A. K., Mohd, N., & Park, Y. (2022). Healthcare 5.0 security framework: Applications, issues and future research directions. *IEEE Access*, 10, 129429–129442. doi: 10.1109/ACCESS.2022.3228505.
2. Mbunge, E., Muchemwa, B., & Batani, J. (2021). Sensors and healthcare 5.0: Transformative shift in virtual care through emerging digital health technologies. *Global Health Journal*, 5(4), 169–177.
3. Saraswat, D., Bhattacharya, P., Verma, A., Prasad, V. K., Tanwar, S., Sharma, G., … Sharma, R. (2022). Explainable AI for healthcare 5.0: Opportunities and challenges. *IEEE Access*, 10, 84486–84517. doi: 10.1109/ACCESS.2022.3197671.
4. Lee, S. A., Byth, K., Gifford, J. A., Balasubramanian, M., Fozzard, C. A., Skapetis, T., & Flood, V. M. (2020). Assessment of health research capacity in Western Sydney Local Health District (WSLHD): A study on medical, nursing and allied health professionals. *Journal of Multidisciplinary Healthcare*, 13, 153–163. doi: 10.2147/JMDH. S222987.
5. Taimoor, N., & Rehman, S. (2021). Reliable and resilient AI and IoT-based personalised healthcare services: A survey. *IEEE Access*, 10, 535–563.
6. Van Wyk, T., Mahomed-Asmail, F., & Swanepoel, D. W. (2019). Supporting hearing health in vulnerable populations through community care workers using mhealth technologies. *International Journal of Audiology*, 58(11), 790–797.
7. Mohanta, B., Das, P., & Patnaik, S. (2019, May). Healthcare 5.0: A paradigm shift in digital healthcare system using artificial intelligence, IoT and 5G communication. In *2019 International Conference on Applied Machine Learning (ICAML)* (pp. 191–196). IEEE.

8. Nester, M. S., Hawkins, S. L., & Brand, B. L. (2022). Barriers to accessing and continuing mental health treatment among individuals with dissociative symptoms. *European Journal of Psychotraumatology*, 13(1), 2031594.

9. Gupta, R., Bhattacharya, P., Tanwar, S., Kumar, N., & Zeadally, S. (2021). GaRuDa: A blockchain-based delivery scheme using drones for healthcare 5.0 applications. *IEEE Internet of Things Magazine*, 4(4), 60–66.

10. Bonnevie, E., Gallegos-Jeffrey, A., Goldbarg, J., Byrd, B., & Smyser, J. (2021). Quantifying the rise of vaccine opposition on Twitter during the COVID-19 pandemic. *Journal of Communication in Healthcare*, 14(1), 12–19.

11. Rehman, A., Abbas, S., Khan, M. A., Ghazal, T. M., Adnan, K. M., & Mosavi, A. (2022). A secure healthcare 5.0 system based on blockchain technology entangled with federated learning technique. *Computers in Biology and Medicine*, 150, 106019.

12. Natarajan, R., Lokesh, G. H., Flammini, F., Premkumar, A., Venkatesan, V. K., & Gupta, S. K. (2023). A novel framework on security and energy enhancement based on Internet of medical things for Healthcare 5.0. *Infrastructures*, 8(2), 22.

13. Garg, P. K., Tripathi, N. K., Kappas, M., & Gaur, L. (Eds.). (2022). *Geospatial Data Science in Healthcare for Society 5.0*. Springer.

14. Chi, H. R., de Fátima Domingues, M., Zhu, H., Li, C., Kojima, K., & Radwan, A. (2023). Healthcare 5.0: In the perspective of consumer internet-of-things-based fog/cloud computing. *IEEE Transactions on Consumer Electronics*.

15. Bhattacharya, P., Obaidat, M. S., Savaliya, D., Sanghavi, S., Tanwar, S., & Sadaun, B. (2022, July). Metaverse assisted telesurgery in healthcare 5.0: An interplay of blockchain and explainable AI. In *2022 International Conference on Computer, Information and Telecommunication Systems (CITS)* (pp. 1–5). IEEE.

16. Haq, A. U., Li, J. P., Kumar, R., Ali, Z., Khan, I., Uddin, M. I., & Agbley, B. L. Y. (2023). MCNN: A multi-level CNN model for the classification of brain tumors in IoT-healthcare system. *Journal of Ambient Intelligence and Humanized Computing*, 14(5), 4695–4706.

17. Ali, A., Al-Rimy, B. A. S., Alsubaei, F. S., Almazroi, A. A., & Almazroi, A. A. (2023). HealthLock: Blockchain-based privacy preservation using homomorphic encryption in Internet of things healthcare applications. *Sensors*, 23(15), 6762.

18. Trivedi, H. S., & Patel, S. J. (2023). Homomorphic cryptosystem-based secure data processing model for edge-assisted IoT healthcare systems. *Internet of Things*, 22, 100693.

19. Yempally, S., Singh, S. K., & Sarveshwaran, V. (2023). A secure and efficient authentication and multimedia data sharing approach in IoT-healthcare. *The Imaging Science Journal*, 71(3), 1–22. doi: 10.1080/13682199.2023.2180140.

20. Chandol, M. K., & Kameswara Rao, M. (2023). Blockchain-based cryptographic approach for privacy enabled data integrity model for IoT healthcare. *Journal of Experimental and Theoretical Artificial Intelligence*, 1–22.

21. Ali, H. M., Bomgni, A. B., Bukhari, S. A. C., Hameed, T., & Liu, J. (2023). Power-aware fog supported IoT network for healthcare infrastructure using swarm intelligence-based algorithms. *Mobile Networks and Applications*, 1–15.

22. Khodadadzadeh, M., Ding, X., Chaurasia, P., & Coyle, D. (2021). A hybrid capsule network for hyperspectral image classification. *IEEE Journal of Selected Topics in Applied Earth Observations and Remote Sensing*, 14, 11824–11839.

23. Elhoseny, M., Ramirez-Gonzalez, G., Abu-Elnasr, O. M., Shawkat, S. A., Arunkumar, N., & Farouk, A. (2018). Secure medical data transmission model for IoT-based healthcare systems. *IEEE Access*, 6, 20596–20608.

24. Hasan, M. K., Ismail, A. F., Islam, S., Hashim, W., Ahmed, M. M., & Memon, I. (2019, February). A novel HGBBDSA-CTI approach for subcarrier allocation in heterogeneous network. *Telecommunication Systems*, 70(2), 245–262.

25. Elhoseny, M., Shankar, K., Lakshmanaprabu, S. K., Maseleno, A., & Arunkumar, N. (2020, August). Retracted article: Hybrid optimization with cryptography encryption for medical image security in Internet of Things. *Neural Computing and Applications*, 32(15), 10979–10993.

26. Borkowski, A. A., Bui, M. M., Thomas, L. B., Wilson, C. P., Deland, L. A., & Mastorides, S. M. (2019). Lung and colon cancer histopathological image dataset (LC25000) [Online]. Available: https://github.com/beamandrew/medical-data.

6 Sustainable Agriculture
A Critical Analysis of Internet of Things—Based Solutions

Anindya Nag, Ayontika Das,
Nisarga Chand, Nilanjana Roy

6.1 INTRODUCTION

IoT has shown a fresh path for cutting-edge study in the agricultural sector. But the agricultural industry faces many enduring problems, such as high costs, a labor shortage, endemic diseases of plants, unfavorable climatic changes, etc. Currently, the migration of people from rural to urban areas is hampering agriculture [1]. Agricultural organizations can adopt IoT in farming to optimize production and improve their sustainability with precision agriculture. Precision agriculture uses information technology advancements like sensors, robotics, drones, and autonomous vehicles in farming processes. Remote sensing systems can provide information to help detect and monitor agricultural plants. Global Positioning System (GPS) receivers are used in farming machines to determine the position of farm fields and adjust their operation appropriately.

A Geographic Information System (GIS) is a system which consists of a database to store, retrieve, analyze, and display the geographical data of the field for analysis. The yield monitor is a device coupled with other sensors to calculate and record yield. Field scouting is the method of examining pest levels in fields. Autonomous machines replace hand tools, reducing the farmers' tasks and risks of hand-harvesting. Variable rate technology enhances fertilizer application for farmers. High-Throughput Plant Phenotyping (HTPP) technology combines genetics, sensors, and robotics. Agricultural drones improve strategy and planning based on real-time information gathering and processing. Analyzing the soil, planting seeds, spraying crops, keeping an eye on growth, irrigating, etc., all these aerial and ground-based drones can be used for agricultural needs [2].

For the farmer, the IoT-based solution is the answer to their issues. In smart agriculture, the IoT help with automatic greenhouse management. Parameters from WSN-based systems were used for innovative irrigation water management. This included temperature, soil moisture, leaf wetness sensors, etc. Using camera technology, farmers can keep their crops safe from animals. The density of insect populations

DOI: 10.1201/9781032642789-6

is calculated using image processing. Crop & Plant Growth and Monitoring are done using IoT-based innovative technology. Farmers can access all information on their smartphones using Information and Communication Technology (ICT) tools. Plant crop disease is predicted using machine learning (ML) techniques, and farmers are provided with appropriate solutions [3].

IoT facilitates data collection from various sensors deployed in the field. Insect population, pest detection, plant growth, etc., may all be tracked using sensors that monitor environmental conditions in the soil. IoT and smartphone technology have enabled farmers to check their crops from afar [4]. Wireless sensor network nodes gather information about the environment and produce it in the field and send the data through the ZigBee network to the server node. The farm's processes are then automatically monitored and controlled using microcontrollers. Cameras are installed on farms to visualize crop conditions. Automated irrigation systems, pest management, plant growth monitoring, insect population control, etc., are all made possible with the help of the IoT, transforming conventional farming into mechanized agriculture.

Various authors in the past have researched IoT-based sustainable agriculture [5]. A robot can carry out weeding, spraying, moisture detection, scaring birds and animals, and more. Real-time data is used to support intelligent decision-making and smart control for irrigation. Brilliant warehouse management includes monitoring temperature and humidity levels and detecting theft. Using sensors and an Arduino board, this system can track environmental factors that could affect crop success, such as the weather and the whereabouts of animals that could cause harm [6]. Similar works have been brought to our attention. Information technology, decision-making control systems, GPS guidance, sensors, robots, autonomous vehicles, drones, GPS-based soil sampling, variable rate technology, automated hardware, software, telematics, and so on are all covered, as well as the work based on these innovations. On the other hand, everything will be controllable from a single location on any computer or mobile device with an internet connection [7]. Sensors, Wi-Fi or ZigBee modules, cameras, and actuators will be integrated with microcontrollers and Raspberry Pi to perform the required actions.

The integration of IoT smart technology has facilitated the advancement of sophisticated horticultural methodologies. In contemporary times, the need of addressing prevailing issues has underscored the indispensability of innovation. Consequently, numerous industries are embracing cutting-edge improvements to streamline and automate their operational processes. The incorporation of IoT technologies within the agricultural sector is anticipated to augment the efficacy of fertilizer utilization, consequently empowering farmers to mitigate wastage and amplify productivity. The projected outcome of this breakthrough is expected to bring about a significant transformation in advanced agricultural practices. Technology offers farmers increased control over various aspects of their agricultural operations, including animal management, crop production, resource allocation, and cost minimization. The following list provides a comprehensive overview of the benefits connected with the application of technology in the agricultural sector.

- The automatic adjustment of farming machinery to regulate elements such as temperature and moisture levels is facilitated by the integration of data, including crop yields, climate conditions, and equipment specifications.
- In the context of broad agricultural settings, the utilization of a drone integrated with IoT technology enables the collection of up-to-date crop data and real-time imagery of the farms.
- Through the implementation of on-site study of agricultural land and its associated resources, valuable insights can be obtained regarding the current condition of fields and cultivated plants.

The challenges encountered during the creation of the IoT platform are as follows:

- An all-encompassing solution capable of effortlessly integrating with several categories of IoT devices.
- The biggest obstacle encountered by the IoT within the agriculture industry pertains to the matter of availability. Inadequate network connectivity is reported in several geographical areas.
- The second most prominent challenge encountered by Advanced Farming relying on the IoT is the inadequate knowledge possessed by potential buyers.
- An adaptable system capable of seamless integration with a wide range of IoT devices, designed to meet the requirements of expansive agricultural operations.

This chapter highlights IoT-based sustainable agriculture by utilizing automation and IoT technologies to make agriculture smarter. A literature review and analysis are conducted in this chapter to identify the shared objectives and characteristics of IoT-based sustainable smart farming. Based on the current state of the agricultural system, this chapter has evaluated the literature on integrating IoT sensor technology and wireless networks.

Section 6.2 describes an overview of agriculture based on IoT. Section 6.3 states the sustainable farming revolution. Section 6.4 discusses the various research topics in IoT-based sustainable agriculture systems. Section 6.5 describes farmers' problems and their IoT-based solutions. Section 6.6 gives an idea about use-case challenges and their IoT-based solutions related to the sustainability goal. Section 6.7 provides a statistics scenario about sustainable smart agriculture. Section 6.8 concludes the paper and discusses the future scope of the work.

6.2 IOT IN AGRICULTURE

The development of an agricultural country depends heavily on the farm system. Most projects use wireless sensor networks to collect data from multiple sensors located at different nodes and transmit it using a wireless protocol. Nutrient fertilization is crucial for maintaining soil fertility and improving crop quality and output. It's not just the producer who pays a high price for traditional fertilizers; they can

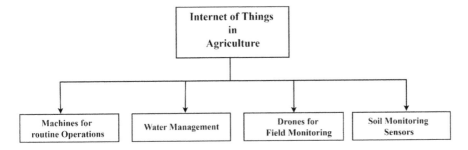

FIGURE 6.1   The Agri-IoT overview

also harm humans and the environment [8]. IoT has recently significantly influenced the agriculture sector with various sensors utilized for different innovative agricultural aims. Year after year, the number of IoT applications has grown dramatically.

Figure 6.1 illustrates the application of IoT technology in smart agriculture, explicitly focusing on monitoring and controlling IoT devices. This integration involves deploying sensors, actuators, and other intelligent devices throughout the agricultural ecosystem to gather data and automate various processes. By leveraging IoT devices in smart agriculture, farmers can access real-time data, make informed decisions, optimize resource allocation, reduce expenses, boost yields, and ultimately enhance the sustainability and effectiveness of their agricultural practices.

The Agri-IoT, short for the agricultural IoT, offers an innovative and transformative approach to modernizing agriculture. It involves integrating IoT technology into agrarian practices, enabling farmers and stakeholders to monitor, manage, and optimize various aspects of farming and agricultural processes. Agri-IoT leverages smart sensors, actuators, and other IoT devices to collect real-time data from the farming environment, including soil conditions, weather patterns, crop health, water levels, and livestock well-being. The collected data is then transmitted and processed through interconnected systems and cloud-based platforms, where advanced analytics and artificial intelligence algorithms are employed to extract valuable insights. These insights empower farmers to make data-driven decisions, enabling precision agriculture and tailored interventions based on specific field conditions.

Applications of the IoT in the agricultural industry rely heavily on the participation of several different sensors. It can connect various sensors, drivers, and other types of smart devices to portable computers over the internet. IoT services now feature data sharing with sophisticated control and decision-making tools. This is made possible by cloud-based remote data capturing. The field of smart agriculture stands to gain a great deal from the availability of such skills, making it possible to boost output and efficiency. The conventional approach to improving modern horticulture is investigating the IoT area of interest in agriculture [9]. The past decade has witnessed enormous advancements in the IoT, greatly benefiting every sector of the economy.

Figure 6.2 is Agri-IoT, an intricate platform intricately engineered to simplify the administration of geo-spatial agriculture data. The figure highlights Agri-IoT, a

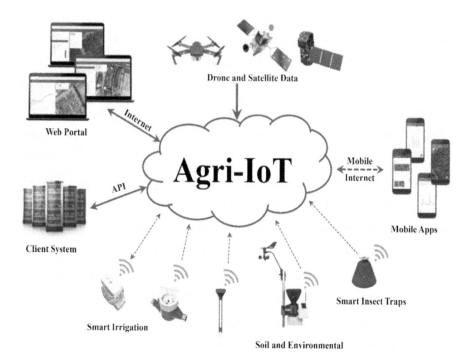

FIGURE 6.2   Geo-spatial agriculture data management platform Agri-IoT

sophisticated platform thoughtfully created to streamline the management of geo-spatial agriculture data. This inventive resolution provides a smooth method for overseeing and structuring intricate agricultural information. Its specialized functionalities are customized to amplify the effectiveness of data management within contemporary farming methodologies.

Smart farming relies on the IoT because it allows for the seamless integration of scalable software, hardware, cost-effective procedures, autonomy, and intelligent decisions. Measurement components of the smart architecture are depicted in Figure 6.1. Irrigation, plant development, leaf-level disease diagnosis, and production management are just some of the tasks that can be planned for in the smart agriculture industry. Smart agriculture, which relies on the IoT, provides affordable alternatives for farmers [10]. As a means of increasing agricultural output, researchers devised several interconnected modern technologies. This way, numerous cutting-edge innovations can be integrated with time-tested farming practices to yield the desired results. Multiple sensors and descriptions of natural environments are just the beginning of how IoT can intelligently construct agriculture.

6.3 SUSTAINABLE AGRICULTURE REVOLUTION

Sustainable Agriculture Revolution in the IoT refers to integrating IoT technologies and practices in the agricultural sector to promote sustainable and efficient farming

methods. IoT connects various devices, sensors, and machinery through the internet, enabling data collection, analysis, and automated real-time decision-making.
IoT can revolutionize farming practices and contribute to a more sustainable and
environmentally friendly approach when applied to agriculture [11]. By integrating
IoT technologies into agriculture, farmers can achieve higher yields, reduce waste,
minimize the use of resources, and make more sustainable choices. Combining data
analytics, automation, and informed decision-making can transform the agricultural
sector into a more sustainable and environmentally responsible industry. However,
it's essential to address potential challenges related to data privacy, cybersecurity,
and the digital divide in rural areas to ensure the equitable adoption of the IoT in
agriculture.

Figure 6.3, the Sustainable Agriculture Revolution in the IoT, represents the convergence of cutting-edge IoT technology with sustainable agricultural practices, further enhancing farming efficiency, productivity, and environmental stewardship. The
integration of IoT technology in sustainable agriculture contributes to the overall
goal of achieving a more resilient and environmentally responsible food system [12].
By leveraging real-time data, automation, and precision, IoT-enabled sustainable
agriculture enables farmers to optimize their operations while minimizing negative environmental impacts. It represents a significant step toward building a more

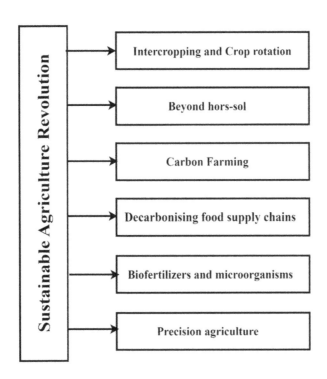

FIGURE 6.3   Sustainable Agriculture Revolution

sustainable future for agriculture and ensuring food security for a growing global population.

Overall, the Sustainable Agriculture Revolution in IoT combines cutting-edge technology with sustainable agriculture principles to create a more efficient, environmentally responsible, and socially equitable agricultural system. As the world faces mounting challenges in food security and environmental sustainability, the integration of IoT in agriculture holds tremendous potential to address these issues and pave the way for a more sustainable future. Table 6.1 represents the benefits and new threats of the Sustainable Agriculture Revolution.

Overall, the Sustainable Agriculture Revolution in the IoT combines cutting-edge technology with sustainable agriculture principles to create a more efficient, environmentally responsible, and socially equitable agricultural system. As the world faces mounting challenges in food security and environmental sustainability, the integration of the IoT in agriculture holds tremendous potential to address these issues and pave the way for a more sustainable future.

6.4 LITERATURE REVIEWS

After extensively reviewing the most recent seven years of academic papers, we have extracted valuable insights from various IoT-based sustainable agriculture systems studies in Table 6.2 The research has shed light on incorporating IoT solutions to optimize resource usage, minimize waste, and improve overall efficiency in farming operations. Addressing challenges such as data privacy and security, energy-efficient IoT device design, and e-waste management emerged as critical focus areas in building sustainable agricultural systems. Furthermore, the literature highlights the importance of standardization, scalable infrastructure, and regulatory support to foster the adoption of IoT-based solutions in agriculture.

6.5 FARMERS' PROBLEMS AND THEIR IOT-BASED SOLUTIONS

Table 6.3 presents an in-depth analysis of the challenges faced by farmers and proposes potential IoT-based solutions to address these issues. Through this examination, the authors aim to gain valuable insights into farmers' real-world problems and explore how technology can play a transformative role in mitigating these challenges.

Table 6.3 demonstrates the potential of IoT-based solutions to revolutionize agriculture by addressing various challenges farmers face. By adopting these technologies, farmers can enhance resource management, optimize agrochemical usage, improve livestock health, and make well-informed decisions, fostering sustainable and prosperous agricultural practices.

6.6 USE-CASE CHALLENGES AND THEIR IOT-BASED
SOLUTIONS RELATED TO THE SUSTAINABILITY GOAL

IoT-based solutions have the potential to significantly contribute to sustainability goals by optimizing resource usage, reducing waste, and enhancing overall efficiency.

TABLE 6.1

Benefits and New Threatening of Sustainable Agriculture Revolution

Sustainable Revolution	Description	Benefit	New Threatening
Beyond hors-sol	Vertical farming, hydroponics, soil-free growth, and controlled indoor environments are alternatives to traditional farming settings [6–7].	• Reduced land-intensive farming. • Farming in urban/suburban areas or arid lands is an option. • Supply chain reduction.	• High initial investment cost and operational risk (infrastructure). • Pollination requires a lot of effort if no insects (bees, bumblebees) are involved.
Carbon farming	Various agricultural methods aim at actively increasing carbon adoption (sequestration) in soil and plant material [8].	• Carbon in the atmosphere has decreased net. • Improved soil health improves biodiversity.	• Potential harm to ecosystem services if incentive structures encourage land clearing and monoculture. • Regenerative (carbon-sequestering) agriculture may not be scalable enough in some arid regions.
Decarbonizing food supply chains	Taking on emissions in the broader agri-food system, such as emissions from transportation and packaging and waste management [8].	• GHG emissions are reduced as supply chains become shorter and more regional. • Increased food waste control.	Potential compromises to be made during the period of change.
Precision agriculture	Benefits of using information technology advances (e.g., sensors, robotics, drones, autonomous vehicles) in farming processes like pest control or watering [9].	• Productivity has increased. • Reduced labor intensity. • Fertilizer use has been reduced.	• Cyber-attacks can disrupt operations and have an impact on production. • Increased risk of service disruption is associated with reliance on external resources such as the internet, software, and data suppliers.

(Continued)

TABLE 6.1 (CONTINUED)
Benefits and New Threatening of Sustainable Agriculture Revolution

Sustainable Revolution	Description	Benefit	New Threatening
Microorganisms and other biological fertilizers	Fertilizers based on bacteria or algae can be used instead of carbon-intense chemical fertilizers; microbes and bacteria (such as rhizobacteria) can be used instead of chemical pesticides and herbicides [10].	• Reduced reliance on synthetic fertilizers. • Environmental degradation has been reduced. • Crop resistance to abiotic stress has increased.	• Possibility of using the incorrect type of bacteria, resulting in crop damage. • Scalability to high productivity is unknown. • Inadequate adaptation to local conditions
Intercropping and crop rotation	Plants of different species grow together or in succession [11–12].	• Fewer synthetic fertilizers are needed, and natural resources may be used more efficiently. • Improving soil health, biological methods of pest management, and biodiversity. • Environmental degradation/pollution has been reduced.	• Short shelf life necessitates a lean supply chain and proper storage. • Lower initial yields when compared to monoculture. However, some believe yields will increase once crops and soil have adjusted and matured.

TABLE 6.2
Literature Review

Authors	Objectives
V. Suma. (2021) [13]	This research provided a comprehensive overview of integrating predictive analysis, IoT devices with cloud administration, and security units into multi-culture agriculture. It highlighted the challenges and complexities of merging modern technology with traditional farming practices. This agricultural system was poised for revolutionary changes by leveraging statistical and quantitative approaches. IoT drones, sensors, and advanced monitoring techniques facilitate efficient crop management, irrigation, and disease detection on green fields.
Sjaak Wolfert et al. (2022) [14]	The research conducted case studies in five different agricultural industries to demonstrate the practicality and validity of the method. Despite the influence of external factors that were challenging to control, the results suggested that IoT implementation positively impacted sustainability. The technique introduced tools for practitioners to evaluate and monitor the sustainability effects of emerging technologies like IoT, making it valuable for large-scale initiatives aligning with strategic sustainability objectives.
Nikesh Gondchawar. (2016) [15]	This project presented several unique features, including a smart GPS-based remote-controlled robot capable of performing various tasks such as weeding, spraying, moisture detection, bird and animal scaring, and surveillance. It utilized real-time field data to enable intelligent decision-making and efficient irrigation control. Additionally, the project implemented intelligent warehouse management, incorporating temperature and humidity monitoring and theft detection within the warehouse. Integrating microcontrollers, Raspberry Pi, sensors, Wi-Fi or ZigBee modules, cameras, and actuators allowed remote management through internet-connected smart devices and computers.
Anusha Vangala et al. (2020) [16]	This article presented a comprehensive literature analysis focusing on the latest developments in blockchain-based information security techniques for smart agriculture. It identified critical criteria for smart agriculture and proposed a generalized blockchain-based security architecture. The article included a detailed cost study of analyzed projects and conducted a thorough comparative investigation, highlighting the limitations of earlier research efforts. Additionally, through a literature review, the article identified the targeted security goals and suggested potential opportunities for future research in artificial intelligence.
Junhu Ruan et al. (2019) [17]	Based on the findings, several recommendations were proposed to guide the development of agricultural IoT infrastructure. These included focusing on robust data security and sharing mechanisms to protect sensitive information. Implementing sustainable energy solutions was advised to ensure the long-term viability of IoT systems in agriculture. Economic analyzed and operation management practices should be integrated to optimize efficiency and resource allocation. Additionally, leveraging IoT-based finance solutions and e-business models could enhance precision farming practices. These recommendations aimed to support academics and professionals in achieving precision farming goals with the help of IoT technologies.

(Continued)

TABLE 6.2 (CONTINUED)
Literature Review

Authors	Objectives
S. R. Prathibha et al. (2017) [18]	The project involved implementing a comprehensive system for agricultural monitoring and management. It utilized GPS-based remote monitoring and various sensors, such as moisture, temperature, leaf wetness, and security sensors, to gather data from the farm and its surroundings. The data was transmitted through wireless sensor networks, and farm sensor nodes were strategically distributed across the farm. The system allowed remote control and regulation of these parameters through any remote device or online service by connecting sensors, Wi-Fi, and webcams to microcontrollers. Developing this concept as a product significantly benefits farmers by enhancing their well-being and improving farm management practices.
Mohamed Amine Ferrag et al. (2020) [19]	This study categorized and compared existing security and privacy technologies for IoT applications and explored their adaptations for IoT-based green agriculture. The authors also investigated IoT consensus algorithms and blockchain-based privacy-oriented solutions and their potential applications in IoT-based green agriculture. Based on their findings, the authors suggested future research directions in security and privacy for IoT-based green agriculture. They identified open research issues and challenges that need to be addressed.
Partha Pratim Ray (2017) [20]	This article discussed contemporary software issues. Several research and application paths were suggested. Low cost, autonomous, energy-efficient, interoperable, standardized, heterogeneous, and AI/DSS solutions were in demand. Many IoT components must be met for intelligent, widespread agriculture.
Jayvant Devare et al. (2019) [21]	The study revealed that IoT technology brings numerous benefits to various aspects of agriculture, including smart irrigation, pest management, insect control, and plant development, ultimately leading to improved productivity and reduced farmer mortality. The farm utilized nodes with diverse sensors and wireless sensor network technology to collect real-time environmental data, bug population, pest status, and yield information. This data was analyzed and prepared for examination, with smartphones using the GSM network to transmit the data. Actuators played a role in controlling and implementing corrective actions. Farmers benefit from IoT's automation of laborious tasks and efficient crop monitoring, resulting in enhanced crop production, monitoring, and insect management. IoT also enabled farmers to remotely monitor their farms, helping them address uncontrollable factors like rainfall and drought and optimizing water and pesticide usage. Integrating cloud computing, machine learning, and image processing further facilitates smart farming practices.
K. A. Patil et al. (2016) [22]	This paper focused on integrating sensor technology and wireless networks into IoT technology within an agricultural system. It introduced the Remote Monitoring System (RMS) as a proposed approach that utilized the internet and wireless communication to collect real-time data on farming conditions. The main objective of the RMS was to provide farmers with easy access to agricultural services, including SMS alerts and crop advice, based on the real-time data collected from the sensors.

(Continued)

TABLE 6.2 (CONTINUED)
Literature Review

Authors	Objectives
Prathibha S R1 et al. (2017) [23]	The included temperature and humidity monitoring in agricultural environments using sensors based on a single CC3200 chip. The camera used the CC3200 to capture images and send them via MMS to farmers' mobile phones via Wi-Fi.
M. Newlin Rajkumar et al. (2017) [24]	The main goal of this project was to enhance crop growth and optimize water availability by implementing various agricultural technologies. A microcontroller controlled the pump motor, turning it on and off based on soil moisture levels. Additionally, a GSM phone line measures and monitors temperature, humidity, and soil moisture, providing valuable data for efficient irrigation and crop management.
Ramya Venkatesan et al. (2017) [25]	This project used a Raspberry Pi camera to feed live video from the server and automatically monitor the agricultural land. Farms measure soil moisture, temperature, and humidity. Temperature, humidity, and soil moisture sensors would manage autonomous irrigation. IoT devices monitor field data, process it, and inform field owners of countermeasures.
Haikal Hafiz Kadar et al. (2019) [26]	The IoT solution presented in this project is based on the AGRI2L smart water management system prototype. This system's architecture and physical scenario were designed for IoT data management platforms, enabling efficient management and sharing of water resources. The smart water level and leakage monitoring system utilizes real-time data, empowering analyzed to make prompt, cost-effective decisions. Integrating data and IoT technologies enabled innovative agriculture practices through the AGRI2L system.
Pradyumna K. Tripathy et al. (2021) [27]	IoT technology offers significant advantages for smart greenhouse farming by enabling early problem detection through various sensors that monitor crucial parameters such as humidity, nutrient levels, pH, temperature, UV light intensity, CO_2 levels, mist, and pesticide usage. A Decision Support System (DSS) efficiently organized all the data and efforts. This study addressed greenhouse rose-to-farm challenges and proposed a sustainable and innovative IoT-based approach. The work introduced a redefined concept of sustainability through its adaptable model for smart greenhouse farming.
Junhu Ruan et al. (2019) [28]	This article addressed the challenges in implementing agricultural IoT applications by categorizing them into controlled environment planting, open-field planting, animal breeding, aquaculture, and aquaponics. It emphasized the importance of expanding agricultural IoT systems and considering energy efficiency in farm IoT systems—the integration of green IoT systems throughout the agri-product life cycle interests farmers. In green IoT systems in agriculture, the life cycle framework encompasses aspects such as IoT finance, supply chain management, data financing, network node recharge, maintenance, and data management. Novel approaches to address FOM (Finance, Operations, and Management) issues are essential for advancing agricultural production and agribusinesses.

(Continued)

TABLE 6.2 (CONTINUED)
Literature Review

Authors	Objectives
Et-Taibi Bouali et al. (2021) [29]	This study introduced an affordable integrated sustainable agriculture (SA) solution, catering to the needs of small farmers who might need access to commercial solutions. The solution was built on three key pillars: • Real-time data from a cloud-based IoT system enabled optimized groundwater use and conservation practices. • Renewable energy integration reduced fossil fuel consumption for water-table pumping, promoting energy-efficient agriculture. • Smart irrigation techniques enhanced crop quality and quantity while safeguarding soil and water-table ecosystems. The open-source approach allowed other academics to adopt and adapt the solution, promoting a specialized cloud-based platform for water-table usage, particularly beneficial in the desert and Sub-Saharan African regions.
E. T. Bouali et al. (2020) [30]	The qualitative sustainability analysis of FarmFox in this paper demonstrated its dependability. FarmFox's practical application was anticipated to result in an economically smart solution for sustainable agriculture.
Laura García et al. (2019) [31]	This study focused on irrigation system monitoring factors related to soil, weather, and water quality. The authors reviewed various wireless technologies and nodes commonly used in agricultural IoT irrigation systems. They also examined popular metrics for evaluating irrigation, soil, and weather water quality. Additionally, the study explored the latest IoT irrigation and agriculture management applications. The authors proposed a four-layer crop irrigation architecture to address sensor-based irrigation system installation challenges and suggested best practices.
G. Sushanth et al. (2018) [32]	This study introduced an Arduino board sensor system to monitor temperature, humidity, wetness, and crop-damaging animals in agricultural fields. The system was designed to send SMS and Wi-Fi/3G/4G notifications to the farmer's smartphone if any irregularities are detected. An Android app analyzed the data and scheduled irrigation through the system's duplex cellular-Internet interface. The system's low cost and energy independence make it particularly suitable for remote water-scarce regions, providing valuable assistance to farmers.
Salinee Santiteerakul et al. (2020) [33]	This study focused on applying innovative technology in sustainable agriculture, mainly plant factories. The study evaluated the impact of employing intelligent technology in these facilities through a case study methodology. The findings reveal that innovative technology improved sustainability by enhancing production productivity, crop yield, product quality, resource utilization efficiency, food safety, and overall staff quality of life in plant factories.
Kanwalpreet Kour et al. (2022) [34]	This article analyzed various agronomical variables affecting the growth of saffron. The study identified corm size, temperature, water availability, and minerals as the main factors influencing saffron growth. Interestingly, there needs to be more research on using IoT technology for sustainable saffron cultivation in smart cities. The article proposed an IoT-based system that controlled and monitored critical saffron growth factors during cultivation, aiming to enhance the sustainability and efficiency of saffron farming in urban environments.

(Continued)

TABLE 6.2 (CONTINUED)
Literature Review

Authors	Objectives
Nawab Khan et al. (2021) [35]	This overview article explored advanced farming practices, encompassing techniques related to farming, packaging, shipping, and sowing. It suggested using uncrewed aerial vehicles (UAVs) for agricultural monitoring and optimizing production processes. The article delved into modern IoT-based applications in agriculture. Furthermore, the authors uncover intriguing IoT applications for ecological farming, showcasing the potential benefits of incorporating IoT technology in sustainable agricultural practices.
I. Danlard et al. (2020) [36]	This paper focused on recent developments in precision agriculture and presented engineering solutions to enhance sustainable agriculture while maintaining environmental quality. The study explored innovative approaches to improve agricultural practices by integrating advanced technologies and precision techniques to promote more efficient and eco-friendly farming methods.

Table 6.4 outlines the specific challenges related to sustainability goals and presents corresponding IoT-based resolutions that offer innovative solutions to address these pressing issues. Through this detailed examination, we aim to highlight the transformative potential of IoT technology in achieving sustainable development across various sectors.

6.7 RESEARCH STATISTICS

After conducting an extensive survey covering 1986 to 2023, we have witnessed an astonishing transformation in sustainable smart agriculture. Over the years, technological advancements and a growing emphasis on sustainability have driven remarkable developments in this domain. From traditional farming practices to integrating cutting-edge IoT solutions, sustainable smart agriculture's evolution has been extraordinary.

Looking toward to the future, our analysis leads us to anticipate a notable increase in publications in 2022 compared to the previous year, 2021 [40]. The momentum gained in recent years indicates a positive trend toward more comprehensive exploration and dissemination of knowledge in this vital field. Figure 6.4 depicts the PubMed reports from the search query "sustainable smart agriculture" from 1986 to 2023 (June).

6.8 CONCLUSION AND FUTURE WORK

Between 1986 and 2023, the field of sustainable smart agriculture experienced a remarkable transformation. This survey revealed an astonishing shift in the industry and anticipated a surge in publications in 2022 compared to the previous year, indicating growing interest and advancements. This research thoroughly examined the state of precision agriculture today and proposed engineering-based solutions to

TABLE 6.3
Survey—Farmers' issues and Their IoT-Based Solutions

Parameters of the survey	Farmers' issues	Problem-Solving based on IoT
Smart Agriculture [30]	• Problems with Greenhouse Management.	• Automatic greenhouse management.
Smart Irrigation [30]	• Water distribution based on plant type. • Insufficient water supply and inappropriate water use.	• WSN-based water management using temperature, soil moisture, and leaf wetness sensors. • Drip-irrigation.
Insect Population Controlling [30]	• Protecting field-stored grains and crops from animals. • Insect Population Control.	• The implementation of video surveillance systems had the potential to effectively deter animals from encroaching upon agricultural fields and vegetation. • The insect population density could be determined and relayed to farmers through image processing.
Crop/Plant Growth and Monitoring [31]	• Proportional fertilizer distribution. • Methods and strategies for crop growth that consider climate and soil type differences.	• WSN systems made it simple to monitor large-scale farming. • Soil testing is used to distribute fertilizer proportionately to the available neutrinos. As a result of the availability of this data on their mobile devices, farmers can boost their crop yields by using ICT technologies. • Robots controlled by remote control are used to disperse fertilizers and insecticides evenly. • Choice of pesticides for a variety of plants and crops. • Plant and environment-specific ratios of pesticides. • The real-time tracking of a massive agricultural operation. It would accurately keep tabs on the state of the environment.
Applied Technology [32–33]	• Inappropriate use of technology.	As a result of the availability of this data on their mobile devices, farmers could boost their crop yields by using ICT technologies.
Pest Control [34]	• Disease detection in plants and crops. • Pest control and seed germination. • Pest and insect population control without the use of pesticides.	• Plant crop disease would predict using ML techniques, and farmers were provided with appropriate solutions. • Alternative methods for controlling pest populations using ultrasonic sound and saving farmers' lives.

TABLE 6.4

Use-Case Challenges—IoT-Based Solutions and Sustainability Goal

Sector	Name	Use-case issue	IoT solution	Sustainability goal
Vegetables (Indoor) [35]	Commercial greenhouse cultivation with a closed-loop supply chain.	Developing a comprehensive sensor–actuator-based system could enhance the integration of the value chain and facilitate the generation of high-quality innovations in the context of greenhouse-grown tomato production.	Web-based decision support systems incorporate greenhouse sensors, field, laboratory, and model data. End-users could leverage supply chain production and management information to make decisions and provide value-added crop growth, climate, and irrigation set points to meet quality, sustainability, and traceability requirements.	Crop monitoring and sensing would boost productivity and reduce environmental impact.
Vegetables (outdoor) [36]	Valuable information for weedings.	Using cutting-edge vision technology to collect data on weeding in organic vegetable production increases the value chain.	The cloud is updated with crop information collected by a wedding machine's sensor and camera system. Measurements of crop size, crop health, and weed pressure were all calculated with the help of image processing. Decisions are made on the farm and further up the value chain using this information and other data.	Farmar's could boost output and cut costs by reducing the time spent weeding (by hand). Using fewer herbicides during weeding had a beneficial effect on the environment.
Dairy [37]	Happy Cow.	The implementation of cloud-based ML and 3D monitoring of cow activity had the potential to enhance productivity at dairy farms.	When a cow is equipped with a sensor, it is possible to monitor its whereabouts in 3D. Everything is uploaded to the cloud, where AI may analyze it and draw conclusions. The information was sent to the farmer using a mobile app that suggests ways to manage cows better.	Reduce the use of antibiotics and other medicines while improving cow health. To maximize output, the interval between births should be shortened.

(Continued)

TABLE 6.4 (CONTINUED)

Use-Case Challenges—IoT-Based Solutions and Sustainability Goal

Sector	Name	Use-case issue	IoT solution	Sustainability goal
Meat [38]	Pig farm management.	Pig production management was improved with data from on-farm sensors that would be compatible with slaughterhouse data.	Individual pigs were tracked using sensors that recorded data on diet, water consumption, growth rate, and environmental factors. The dashboard incorporated analytics, early alerts, and predictions alongside supply chain data.	Lessen your influence on the planet and boost output by enhancing animal sensing, monitoring, and utilizing fewer resources.
Arable [39]	Zoning for in-field management purposes.	The creation of customized field management zones could be achieved through the integration of sensing and actuating equipment with external data sources.	An electromagnetic soil scanner produced a soil map, which an algorithm processes into a variable rate application (VRA) map (spraying, fertilizing, and haulm destruction). LoRa networks allow machines to communicate.	Site-specific sensing and monitoring allow variable rate application to conserve pesticides and fertilizers by targeting the spatial and temporal disparities between management zones.

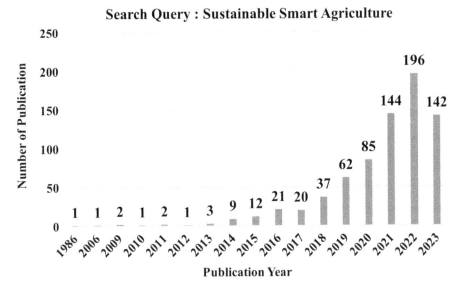

FIGURE 6.4 PubMed results for the search query "sustainable smart agriculture"

enhance ecologically sustainable farming practices. Additionally, the chapter delved into wireless communication technology, specifically its connection to the IoT and its potential applications in the agricultural sector. This chapter highlighted the critical distinctions between Smart Agriculture and Conventional Farming and emphasized the urgent need for technological updates and adaptations to achieve sustainability in the current agricultural practices. By harnessing technology, farmers can gain the ability to design and implement management strategies that optimize input usage, leading to increased output and profitability.

Looking toward the future, we envision developing a chatbot application that will enable direct communication between farmers and agricultural specialists. This platform will provide farmers with real-time SMS alerts regarding crucial information such as weather forecasts and crop insights on their mobile devices. To further assist farmers, plan to deploy Raspberry Pi cameras and server-side monitoring software to monitor the farm remotely. These cameras will capture images, transmit them over the internet, and convert them into SMS messages that can be conveniently delivered to farmers' cell phones. A server-side web page will also be regularly updated to provide the latest agricultural market information for informed decision-making. Our vision is to empower farmers with cutting-edge technology, facilitating sustainable practices and enhancing overall agricultural productivity.

REFERENCES

1. Zhang, X., Xu, M., Su, J., & Zhao, P. (2023). Structural models for fog computing based internet of things architectures with insurance and risk management applications. *European Journal of Operational Research*, 305(3), 1273–1291.

2. Fotia, L., Delicato, F., & Fortino, G. (2023). Trust in edge-based internet of things architectures: State of the art and research challenges. *ACM Computing Surveys*, 55(9), 1–34.

3. Ray, P. P. (2018). A survey on Internet of Things architectures. *Journal of King Saud University – Computer and Information Sciences*, 30(3), 291–319.

4. Furstenau, L. B., Rodrigues, Y. P. R., Sott, M. K., Leivas, P., Dohan, M. S., López-Robles, J. R., ... Choo, K. K. R. (2023). Internet of things: Conceptual network structure, main challenges and future directions. *Digital Communications and Networks*, 9(3), 677–687.

5. Alavi, A. H., Jiao, P., Buttlar, W. G., & Lajnef, N. (2018). Internet of Things-enabled smart cities: State-of-the-art and future trends. *Measurement*, 129, 589–606.

6. Reddy, L. (2021). Smart technology in farming. *Journal of Advanced Research in Instrumentation and Control Engineering*, 8(1 & 2), 22–26.

7. Sylvester, G. (Ed.). (2018). E-Agriculture in Action: Drones for Agriculture. Food and Agriculture Organization of the United Nations and International Telecommunication Union.

8. Szmeja, P., Fornés-Leal, A., Lacalle, I., Palau, C. E., Ganzha, M., Pawłowski, W., ... Schabbink, J. (2023). ASSIST-IoT: A modular implementation of a reference architecture for the next generation Internet of Things. *Electronics*, 12(4), 854.

9. Peters, A. (2018). This strawberry-picking robot gently picks the ripest berries with its robo-hand. Fast Company. Available online: www.fastcompany.com/40473583/this-strawberry-pickingrobot-gently-picks-the-ripest-berries-with-its-robo-hand(accessed on 2 March 2021).

10. Khan, N., Ray, R. L., Sargani, G. R., Ihtisham, M., Khayyam, M., & Ismail, S. (2021). Current progress and future prospects of agriculture technology: Gateway to sustainable agriculture. *Sustainability*, 13(9), 4883.

11. Turck, M. (2018). Growing pains: The 2018 internet of things landscape. *Mattturck. Comput*, 33. January 09 (accessed on 20 June 2018).

12. Jasper, C. (2018). Take control of your connected devices and manage your M2M worldwide. *CIS Syst*, 1–35. Available online: https://www.business.att.com/content/dam/businesscenter/pdf (accessed on 13 December 2018).

13. Suma, D. V. (2021). Internet of things (IoT) based smart agriculture in india: An overview. *Journal of IoT in Social, Mobile, Analytics, and Cloud*, 3(1), 1–15.

14. Wolfert, S., & Isakhanyan, G. (2022). Sustainable agriculture by the Internet of Things–A practitioner's approach to monitor sustainability progress. *Computers and Electronics in Agriculture*, 200, 107226.

15. Gondchawar, N., & Kawitkar, R. S. (2016). IoT based smart agriculture. *International Journal of Advanced Research in Computer and Communication Engineering*, 5(6), 838–842.

16. Vangala, A., Das, A. K., Kumar, N., & Alazab, M. (2020). Smart secure sensing for IoT-based agriculture: Blockchain perspective. *IEEE Sensors Journal*, 21(16), 17591–17607.

17. Ruan, J., Jiang, H., Zhu, C., Hu, X., Shi, Y., Liu, T., ... Chan, F. T. S. (2019). Agriculture IoT: Emerging trends, cooperation networks, and outlook. *IEEE Wireless Communications*, 26(6), 56–63.

18. Prathibha, S. R., Hongal, A., & Jyothi, M. P. (2017, March). IoT based monitoring system in smart agriculture. In *2017 international conference on recent advances in electronics and communication technology (ICRAECT)* (pp. 81–84). IEEE.

19. Ferrag, M. A., Shu, L., Yang, X., Derhab, A., & Maglaras, L. (2020). Security and privacy for green IoT-based agriculture: Review, blockchain solutions, and challenges. *IEEE Access*, 8, 32031–32053.

20. Ray, P. P. (2017). Internet of things for smart agriculture: Technologies, practices and future direction. *Journal of Ambient Intelligence and Smart Environments*, 9(4), 395–420.
21. Devare, J., & Hajare, N. (2019, July). A survey on IoT based agricultural crop growth monitoring and quality control. In *2019 International Conference on Communication and Electronics Systems (ICCES)* (pp. 1624–1630). IEEE.
22. Patil, K. A., & Kale, N. R. (2016, December). A model for smart agriculture using IoT. In *2016 international conference on global trends in signal processing, information computing and communication (ICGTSPICC)* (pp. 543–545). IEEE.
23. Prathibha, S. R., Hongal, A., & Jyothi, M. P. (2017, March). IoT based monitoring system in smart agriculture. In *2017 international conference on recent advances in electronics and communication technology (ICRAECT)* (pp. 81–84). IEEE.
24. Rajkumar, M. N., Abinaya, S., & Kumar, V. V. (2017, March). Intelligent irrigation system—An IoT based approach. In *2017 International Conference on Innovations in Green Energy and Healthcare Technologies (IGEHT)* (pp. 1–5). IEEE.
25. Kumar, R., Sinwar, D., Pandey, A., Tadele, T., Singh, V., & Raghuwanshi, G. (2022). IoT enabled technologies in smart farming and challenges for adoption. *Internet of Things and Analytics for Agriculture*, 3, 141–164.
26. Kadar, H. H., & Sameon, S. S. (2019, November). Sustainable water resource management using IoT solution for agriculture. In *2019 9th IEEE International Conference on Control System, Computing and Engineering (ICCSCE)* (pp. 121–125). IEEE.
27. Tripathy, P. K., Tripathy, A. K., Agarwal, A., & Mohanty, S. P. (2021). MyGreen: An IoT-enabled smart greenhouse for sustainable agriculture. *IEEE Consumer Electronics Magazine*, 10(4), 57–62.
28. Ruan, J., Wang, Y., Chan, F. T. S., Hu, X., Zhao, M., Zhu, F., ... Lin, F. (2019). A life cycle framework of green IoT-based agriculture and its finance, operation, and management issues. *IEEE Communications Magazine*, 57(3), 90–96.
29. Sengupta, A., Debnath, B., Das, A., & De, D. (2021). FarmFox: A quad-sensor-based IoT box for precision agriculture. *IEEE Consumer Electronics Magazine*, 10(4), 63–68.
30. Bouali, E. T., Abid, M. R., Boufounas, E. M., Hamed, T. A., & Benhaddou, D. (2021). Renewable energy integration into cloud & IoT-based smart agriculture. *IEEE Access*, 10, 1175–1191.
31. García, L., Parra, L., Jimenez, J. M., Lloret, J., & Lorenz, P. (2020). IoT-based smart irrigation systems: An overview on the recent trends on sensors and IoT systems for irrigation in precision agriculture. *Sensors*, 20(4), 1042.
32. Sushanth, G., & Sujatha, S. (2018, March). IoT based smart agriculture system. In *2018 International Conference on Wireless Communications, Signal Processing and Networking (WiSPNET)* (pp. 1–4). IEEE.
33. Santiteerakul, S., Sopadang, A., Yaibuathet Tippayawong, K., & Tamvimol, K. (2020). The role of smart technology in sustainable agriculture: A case study of wangree plant factory. *Sustainability*, 12(11), 4640.
34. Kour, K., Gupta, D., Gupta, K., Juneja, S., Kaur, M., Alharbi, A. H., & Lee, H. N. (2022). Controlling agronomic variables of saffron crop using IoT for sustainable agriculture. *Sustainability*, 14(9), 5607.
35. Khan, N., Ray, R. L., Sargani, G. R., Ihtisham, M., Khayyam, M., & Ismail, S. (2021). Current progress and future prospects of agriculture technology: Gateway to sustainable agriculture. *Sustainability*, 13(9), 4883.
36. Danlard, I. (2020). IoT based sustainable agriculture-advances, challenges and opportunities. *SSRN Electronic Journal*. https://doi.org/10.2139/ssrn.3734063

37. Ranganathan, J., Waite, R., Searchinger, T., & Hanson, C. (2018). *How to Sustainably Feed 10 Billion People by 2050, in 21 Charts*. World Resources Institute, Washington DC.

38. Khan, N., Ray, R. L., Sargani, G. R., Ihtisham, M., Khayyam, M., & Ismail, S. (2021). Current progress and future prospects of agriculture technology: Gateway to sustainable agriculture. *Sustainability*, 13(9), 4883.

39. Miranda, B. S., Yamakami, A., & Rampazzo, P. C. (2019). A new approach for crop rotation problem in Farming 4.0. In *Technological Innovation for Industry and Service Systems: 10th IFIP WG 5.5/SOCOLNET Advanced Doctoral Conference on Computing, Electrical and Industrial Systems, DoCEIS 2019, Costa de Caparica, Portugal, May 8–10, 2019. Proceedings 10* (pp. 99–111). Springer International Publishing.

40. Kour, K., Gupta, D., Gupta, K., Dhiman, G., Juneja, S., Viriyasitavat, W., ... Islam, M. A. (2022). Smart-hydroponic-based framework for saffron cultivation: A precision smart agriculture perspective. *Sustainability*, 14(3), 1120.

7 Autonomous Agriculture Robot for Smart Farming

Mohammad Rafi B. Shaik, U. Vinay,
S. Althaf, G. Aravind

7.1 INTRODUCTION

Agricultural robots are advanced machines revolutionizing modern agriculture. These Agricultural robots are designed to optimize farming practices, improve efficiency, and address real-time problems in crop cultivation. Equipped with robotics, artificial intelligence, and sensing technologies, they perform tasks such as planting, harvesting, weeding, pest control, and crop monitoring [1, 2]. Autonomous agriculture robots have been gaining traction in the recent decade. Harvesting is the stage where most robots are being employed. The agricultural landscape is witnessing the rise of robots for diverse tasks, dealing with activities like weed elimination, seed planting, crop reaping, ecological surveillance, and soil assessment. They can potentially improve farm productivity and perform precision-targeted activities.

Several vegetative crops in India are grown in parallel rows [3]. For navigating autonomously in the fields, the typical solution for most of the developed agriculture robots is to use the high-precision dual-frequency RTK-GNSS receiver to steer the robot along a preprogrammed path [4]. The high cost of these systems is a roadblock for production-ready agriculture robots. In this chapter, we showcase navigation in row-crop fields only based on camera observations and exploit the intrinsic row structure to guide the robot and cover the field [5, 6, 7]. After successfully entering the crop row, the next important task is to detect the plants and weeds, as we have many state-of-the-art object detection algorithms which can easily detect and classify the objects in the training dataset. Plants and weeds are not in the original dataset of Faster-RCNN. We train with a custom dataset from our fields. Faster-RCNN gives the best accuracy and is the most used model for object detection tasks [8, 9].

Alireza Ahmadi et al. [10] presented a robust approach for autonomously navigating row-crop fields. Mechanical design, watering, and precision weed cutting are presented in a RIPPA Robot [11], developed by the University of Sydney. A RIPPA is capable of autonomously identifying and shooting at targets when stationary and can do targeted spraying of water and herbicide or fertilizer. Another robot BoniRob [12], developed by Bosch Deep Field Robotics, can perform plant breeding and weed removal. BoniRob identifies a weed based on color, shape, and size and smashes the weed with a ramming rod. However, the weeding mechanism is very efficient in

DOI: 10.1201/9781032642789-7

carrot fields only. BoniRob and RIPPA use RTK-GPS for navigation, which becomes cost-ineffective for production.

Soluciones Robóticas Agrícolas develop Agrobot E-Series. Agrobot can identify the ripeness of the fruits, and it has 24 robotic arms to pick strawberries. The Small Robotic Farm Vehicle (SRFV) [13] developed by the Queensland University of Technology mainly focuses on mechanical design and energy utilization efficiency. Also, the open-source precision agriculture CNC farming system consists of a Cartesian coordinate robot. The main drawback of such systems is that they cannot be scaled to large farms. Recently, Motohisa Fukuda et al. [14] presented CROP (Central Roundish Object Painter), which recognizes and paints the object at the center of an RGB image.

The above-listed problems and challenges allow us to develop a low-cost robot, Agriculture Application Robot (referred to now as AAR). So we propose a Semi-Autonomous Robot AAR, which roams in the field, stops at every plant and waters it, sprays pesticides, reads weather information and soil moisture, and logs it in the database for future research. The AAR is equipped with an automatic weed-cutting mechanism. This would reduce a lot of human labor, which is a significant problem for Indian farmers. An AAR combines robotics, artificial intelligence (AI), Internet of Things (IoT), and algorithms. A ground robot with four wheels roams the crop row in a field above the plants. The development of AARs is a mixture of several works inspired by different areas. The major contributions of the work include: (i) developing a customized farm bot with pesticide sprinkler and weed-cutting mechanism, (ii) training and development of computer vision algorithms that can detect crop rows, fruit or vegetable segmentation, and weeds in real-time, and (iii) development of a web interface to track and record field attributes like moisture, temperature, humidity. The rest of the chapter is organized as follows. Section 7.2 deals with the design aspects of the bot. Section 7.3 introduces the communication mechanism of the bot. The computer vision algorithms for plant characteristic analysis are discussed in Section 7.4. Finally, Section 7.5 concludes the chapter with experimental observations and future directions.

7.2 DESIGN ASPECTS OF AAR

Advancements in agriculture through intelligent systems and machine learning have been greatly explored in recent times [15]. The three-dimensional model of the Agriculture Application Robot, as shown in Figure 7.1, is a rover-like robot with four wheels and a roof rack. It is designed in such a way that it can go above the plants without affecting the rows. Each of the four legs has a wheel attached to a motor, each with an equal rpm of 300 to avoid unwanted path deflections. These wheels are suitable for moving in all kinds of terrain. The processor controls these motors for navigation in different directions. The basic movements like forward, backward, left, and right are given by programming instructions written in Python and executed by the processor. It has a camera set up to send the video content to the processor. The water sprinkling mechanism is attached to the downside of the roof rack. The sprinkling mechanism comprises an electronic water pump which the processor controls.

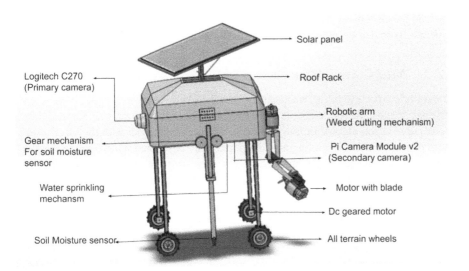

Solar panel

Logitech C270
(Primary camera)

Roof Rack

Robotic arm
(Weed cutting mechanism)

Gear mechanism
For soil moisture
sensor

Pi Camera Module v2
(Secondary camera)

Water sprinkling
mechansm

Motor with blade

Dc geared motor

Soil Moisture sensor

All terrain wheels

FIGURE 7.1 Three-dimensional design of the AAR with labeled parts

The roof rack has a solar panel that delivers electrical energy to the battery from which the controller draws a power supply. AAR has a soil moisture sensor mechanism to periodically collect moisture content in the soil at various field regions.

7.2.1 GENERAL MECHANISM

The Logitech C270, with a 3MP resolution, is used as the front camera for row detection and tracking. Another camera, Raspberry Pi Camera Module v2, is a 5MP camera facing toward the ground and is used as the image source for the plant–weed detector. Raspberry Pi 4 with 4GB RAM is the processor that runs the plant–weed detection model. The AAR holds two sensors: a DHT22 temperature and humidity sensor [16] and a soil moisture sensor [17]. A soil moisture sensor is fitted on the robot's left side, and DHT22 is attached to the roof rack. They collect diverse parameters throughout the day and transmit them to both a local database and cloud storage, similar to the IoT concept. These readings will enable us to estimate and forecast the weather. Essentially, the water requirement for a plant is primarily guided by these three measurements. With more research, we could predict the exact amount of water required for a plant and water them precisely by using time-series analysis techniques. However, this analysis is specific to various crops and requires further probing.

7.2.2 WATER SPRINKLING MECHANISM

The water sprinkling mechanism is fitted below the roof rack of the robot. It consists of a water pump and a small 1-L water storage tank. If a plant is detected, the robot holds that the plant is exactly below the water sprinkler, and 25 mL of water is released for each plant. So, a full tank can water up to 40 plants. The capacity of the tank can be scaled based on the number of plants and the area of the field.

7.2.3 WEED-CUTTING MECHANISM

The robotic structure of the weed-cutting mechanism resembles a hand, incorporating three servo motors that enable three degrees of freedom. Upon weed detection by a computer vision algorithm, the robotic hand precisely aligns with the weed using the coordinates of the bounding box. A couple of metallic blades are fitted to the axis of the motor, cutting the detected weed. The servo motors adjust to varying angles based on the calibration between their positions and the coordinates of the weed.

7.3 INTERFACING COMMUNICATION

This section describes inter-system communication between sensors, processors, and actuators. The robot's motion is purely based on the forward camera, and a motion planning algorithm controls the velocity and direction. A survey on motion planning algorithms can be found here [18]. The water sprinkling mechanism operates only when there is a plant right below the water sprinkler. The weed-removing mechanism will get work after successfully classifying the weed and taking action to remove the weed.

7.3.1 MOTION MECHANISM

The primary camera captures the video feed in the forward direction. This video feed contains rows of plants in the field. The row detection algorithm described in Section 7.4.2 is used to detect rows, so lanes are marked accordingly. The robot uses these lanes to move forward. This communication is essential to ensure the AAR is on the right path. The primary camera detects the lane in which the robot is moving whenever it is deflected from the path, the processor recognizes it and sends the triggers to reorient itself to ensure no damage to the crop, and it keeps the robot on the right course.

7.3.2 WATER SPRINKLING MECHANISM

Precision farming uses minimal external life support, i.e., water, nutrients, and fertilizers. The water sprinkling mechanism in AAR ensures that the crop utilizes the right amount of water. There has to be a minimal delay between sensing the plant and triggering the water pump. The custom-trained plant detection algorithm detects the plant and instructs AAR to halt. This process requires a small amount of time, to ensure that water is being pumped at the exact location, we orient the camera to detect the plant ahead of its occurrence. This spares us some time for sending the instructions.

7.3.3 Weed-Cutting Mechanism

The secondary camera is used for detecting both plants and weeds. The communication process is the same for both plants and weeds; it is done as mentioned above in Section 7.3.2. But there will be a minute change in delay because the weed cutter is behind the robot and needs more time to reach the targeted weed. So, we allow the robot to move a little distance to let the weed near the cutter. When the weed is in the position processor instructs the cutter to turn it on and suppress it, and the weed cutter will return to its resting position immediately after the action.

7.4 COMPUTER VISION AND ASSOCIATED ALGORITHMS

This section deals with all the soft computing algorithms that we used in the functioning of multiple modules of AAR. We employed suitable deep-learning models that were successful in various aspects of object detection and classification. The component-wise software algorithms and their description are given below.

7.4.1 Processing Pipeline

Figure 7.2 illustrates the data flow from the sensor to the processor and the processor to the actuators and user interface. The processor sends control instructions to the actuators. A web interface is made available where we can get live camera feeds, sensor data visualizations, and control actions given by the processor. Sensor data from moisture and DHT22 is directly logged in the IoT cloud. An active internet connection is made available to the processor all the time.

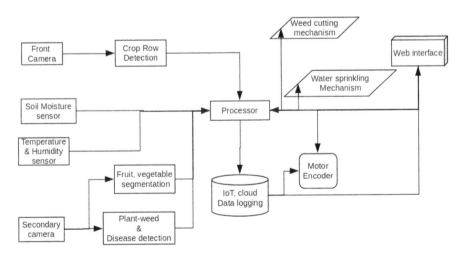

FIGURE 7.2 Flowchart of agricultural application robot

7.4.2 NAVIGATION

In row-crop fields, crops are organized in the patterns of numerous parallel curves or lines [19]. We use such an arrangement to enable a mobile robot to maneuver and perform desired tasks in the field autonomously. We used a vision-based navigation system that depends only on local visual features and exploits the crops' row-wise arrangement in fields to navigate in row-crop fields autonomously without needing an explicit map. We restricted ourselves to developing AAR for low-height horticulture crops for convenience and ease of making. The front-facing camera is fitted with a tilt angle so it can only see the crop row in front of the robot. To separate plants from the soil, we use a straightforward approach Excess Green Index (ExG), often used in agriculture applications. It is given by $I_{EXG} = 2I_G - I_R - I_B$ where I_G, I_R, and I_B correspond to the red, green, and blue components of the image. Visual-servoing method enables the robot to track the continuous path marked on the field. We have used OpenCV [20] for all image processing tasks. Figure 7.3 to Figure 7.6 shows the initial, intermediate, and final results for crop-row detection.

7.4.3 PLANT–WEED CLASSIFICATION

Plant–weed classification is performed by deep-learning algorithms that employ convolutional neural networks. Convolutional Neural Networks (CNNs) successfully extract meaningful representations from the images that convey essential image input characteristics [21]. We are one of the teams participating in the AI Hackathon 2019, organized by CDAC and NVIDIA. Our problem statement is to find the density of plants from aerial images. We use the Faster R-CNN Object Detection model [22]. The results are stunning, with 99% detection of all plants. This helped us to train the

FIGURE 7.3   Original crop-row image

FIGURE 7.4   Green filter applied image

plant–weed detection model. Faster R-CNN comprises a two-step procedure, result-ing in an enhanced performance over SSD in accuracy. However, the SSD model infers faster than the Faster R-CNN. In our task, accuracy is more important than execution time. We collected plant image data from a small field, which we planted for training purposes. Nearly 500 images have been captured and labeled manually using the LabelImg [23] tool. This exact process has been followed for weeds. We

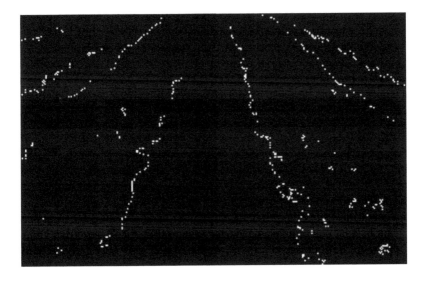

FIGURE 7.5   Edge-detected image

FIGURE 7.6   Final rows detected and marked with white lines

used TensorFlow Object Detection API to train the model. It was backed with the Faster R-CNN Object Detection model. Faster R-CNN is a DNN architecture that presents box proposals that deal with scales and shifts of the object. A Faster R-CNN comprises two parts: a region proposal network (RPN) and a region classifier.

7.4.4 Fruit–Vegetable Detection

Besides the plant–weed classification, we used a pre-trained deep-learning model [14] to detect vegetables and fruits. This model segments vegetables and fruits in the frame [24]. The method involves image segmentation by the more profound version of the original U-Net, which is essentially a deep neural network's architecture [25].

FIGURE 7.7   Image with clearly visible guava fruit

FIGURE 7.8 Guava fruit segmented with pink color masking

The segmentation of fruits or vegetables will help in predicting the production of the crop by counting the total number of vegetables. This technique allows us to monitor the growth of the vegetables on the farm. Based on the number of individual vegetables and fruits detected, and the standard weight of each vegetable to estimate the yield. Figure 7.8 and Figure 7.9 shows the detected guava fruit with a color mask.

7.4.5 PLANT DENSITY ESTIMATION

Plant density is defined as the number of plants in a specified area. The aerial images are acquired by surveying the field through a readily available drone [26]. The aerial images of the crops are used for this estimation. The images acquired through this process are high resolution, with height = 4000 pixels, and width = 3000 pixels. The input size to our detection algorithm is width = 300px and height = 300px. Since the aerial image is high in resolution, the image is split into several blocks, and the detection algorithm is applied to each block by keeping a count of plants in each one of them.

FIGURE 7.9 Fruit and background are segmented

FIGURE 7.10   Areal detection of the crop

Once the detection is done, all the blocks are combined together to form the original high-resolution image. A heat map can be generated to visualize the density with the count of plants as a metric. This density is used to know the germination rate of the seeds in different fields. It helps us improve the germination rate if we avoid sowing seeds in the parts with less density [27]. A crop field and the corresponding heatmap indication density of plants are shown in Figures 7.10 and 7.11.

7.5   EXPERIMENTAL OBSERVATIONS

In a 400 square meter field, we planted groundnut and vegetables like Okra and bottle guard for initial experimentation of data logging and plant detection. Initially, a drip irrigation system is used to water the plants in this field. Recognizing the presence of the plant marks the initial achievement, as every subsequent task execution by the robot hinges on its ability to detect the plant. The Faster R-CNN model provides both the bounding boxes and class labels, as illustrated in Figure 7.11, where we performed detection as well as classification on the groundnut crop. Experiments on plant detection resulted in 99% accuracy for plant vs weed classification for groundnut crops. Thus obtained bounding box coordinates detect a plant and labels are used to instruct the robot to do the tasks of water/pesticide sprinkling or weed removal. When a plant is detected, the robot checks the class label; it finds the label

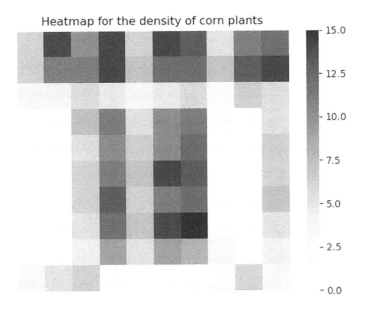

FIGURE 7.11   Corresponding heatmap of the field

as *plant* and triggers the pump to turn on and sprinkle the water/pesticide. Guided by the sensor values like temperature, humidity and soil moisture, we can set the timer to stop the sprinkler module based on the amount of water required by the plant. Similarly, when a weed is detected, with the help of the bounding box coordinates, the weed-cutting mechanism points toward the weed and cuts it through the blades.

Figure 7.12 shows the implemented prototype of an AAR with all the mechanisms. The robot's weed-cutting mechanism, sprinkler mechanism, and moisture-sensing mechanism are controlled with the help of Arduino programs integrated with Python scripts. The AAR is tested in this field, and the robot movement is not ideally accurate in following the path due to soil and terrain variations. However, the design is sufficient following the groundnut crop rows. Hence there is a need to explore alternate designs like metal tracked wheels, etc. As programmed, the robot stops at every plant and waters it correctly. When the robot recognizes the weed, it targets the weed accurately but partially eliminates it. Further improvements have to be made to get more accuracy in the algorithms and hardware calibrations.

7.5.1 Conclusion

In conclusion, the development of agriculture application robots marks a significant milestone in the field of agricultural robotics and intelligent systems, particularly in India. However, there is a need to develop low-cost customized robots to match specific crops. In this work, we developed a cost-effective intelligent robot that can perform multiple functionalities to cut weeds and sprinkle pesticides or spray water. Through our design and integration of cutting-edge technologies like computer

FIGURE 7.12   A view from the corner of the field

FIGURE 7.13   Real-time detection of groundnut

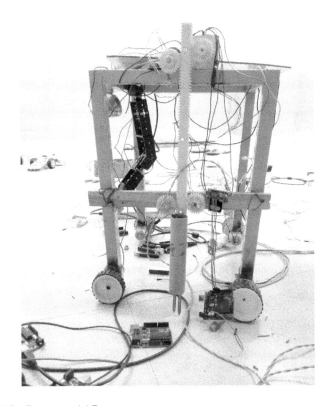

FIGURE 7.14   Prototype AAR

vision (AI), and IoT, we have achieved a competent and versatile autonomous robot. Its performance across various tasks like detecting crop lanes, fruits/vegetables, plant disease, and weeds showcases the potential impact of intelligent systems in the agriculture industry.

7.5.2   FUTURE WORK

As discussed in the introduction, there is much research to be done in this field. Our future plans include precision watering, disease detection, spraying fertilizers, and medicine. With the sensor data available, we could predict the amount of water required for a specific plant with time-series data analysis. We could use this time-series data to predict future weather conditions with the help of recurrent neural networks like LSTM or GRU. Disease detection is a much more difficult task as it requires much domain knowledge of botany and a large dataset. Moreover, adding RTK-GPS would allow us to generate maps of the entire field by stitching the images by the AAR at different locations. Therefore, we can get a bird's eye view of the field without using an aerial drone. We can even estimate the production of the crop with stereo cameras and three-dimensional rendering. We could develop a user interface to monitor and surveil the field. Code for some of the algorithms used is available here: https://github.com/ummadiviany/Agriculture-Application-Robot

REFERENCES

1. Rachapudi, Sai Maruthi, Nithin Tulasi, Sai Chandu Bonagiri, Anil Kumar Bollu, and Sandeep Bansal. "Farming robot: A smart solution to agriculture problems." In *Futuristic Sustainable Energy & Technology*, pp. 55–63. CRC Press, 2022.
2. Zhang, Dan, and Bin Wei, eds. *Robotics and Mechatronics for Agriculture*. CRC Press, 2017.
3. Sivanappan, R. K. "Prospects of micro-irrigation in India." *Irrigation and Drainage Systems* 8(1) (1994): 49–58.
4. Stempfhuber, W., and M. Buchholz. "A precise, low-cost RTK GNSS system for UAV applications." *The International Archives of the Photogrammetry, Remote Sensing and Spatial Information Sciences* 38 (2012): 289–293.
5. Romeo, J., G. Pajares, M. Montalvo, J. M. Guerrero, M. Guijarro, and A. Ribeiro. "Crop row detection in maize fields inspired on the human visual perception." *The Scientific World Journal* 2012 (2012): 1–10.
6. García-Santillán, Iván, José Miguel Guerrero, Martín Montalvo, and Gonzalo Pajares. "Curved and straight crop row detection by accumulation of green pixels from images in maize fields." *Precision Agriculture* 19(1) (2018): 18–41.
7. Tu, Chunling, Barend Jacobus Van Wyk, Karim Djouani, Yskandar Hamam, and Shengzhi Du. "An efficient crop row detection method for agriculture robots." In *2014 7th International Congress on Image and Signal Processing*, pp. 655–659. IEEE, 2014.
8. Girshick, Ross. "Fast r-cnn." In *Proceedings of the IEEE International Conference on Computer Vision*, pp. 1440–1448, 2015.
9. Redmon, Joseph, Santosh Divvala, Ross Girshick, and Ali Farhadi. "You only look once: Unified, real-time object detection." In *Proceedings of the IEEE Conference on Computer Vision and Pattern Recognition*, pp. 779–788, 2016.
10. Ahmadi, Alireza, Lorenzo Nardi, Nived Chebrolu, and Cyrill Stachniss. "Visual servoing-based navigation for monitoring row-crop fields." In *2020 IEEE International Conference on Robotics and Automation (ICRA)*, pp. 4920–4926. IEEE, 2020.
11. Lee, James Ju Heon, Kris Frey, Robert Fitch, and Salah Sukkarieh. "Fast path planning for precision weeding." In *Australasian Conference on Robotics and Automation*, ACRA, 2014.
12. Ruckelshausen, Arno, Peter Biber, Michael Dorna, Holger Gremmes, Ralph Klose, Andreas Linz, Florian Rahe et al. "BoniRob–an autonomous field robot platform for individual plant phenotyping." *Precision Agriculture* 9(841) (2009): 1.
13. Bawden, Owen, David Ball, Jason Kulk, Tristan Perez, and Raymond Russell. "A lightweight, modular robotic vehicle for the sustainable intensification of agriculture." In *Proceedings of the 16th Australasian Conference on Robotics and Automation 2014*, pp. 1–9. Australian Robotics and Automation Association (ARAA), 2014.
14. Fukuda, Motohisa, Takashi Okuno, and Shinya Yuki "Central object segmentation by deep learning for fruits and other roundish objects." arXiv Preprint ArXiv:2008.01251, 2020.
15. Anisha, P. R., C. Kishor Kumar Reddy, N. G. Nguyen, M. Bhushan, A. Kumar, and M. M. Hanafiah. *Intelligent Systems and Machine Learning for IndustryAdvancements, Challenges, and Practices*. CRC Press, 2022.
16. Mihai, B. "How to use the DHT22 sensor for measuring temperature and humidity with the Arduino board." *Acta Uiversitatis Cibiniensis–Technical Series* 68 (2016): 22–25.

17. Kizito, F., C. S. Campbell, G. S. Campbell, D. R. Cobos, B. L. Teare, B. Carter, and J. W. Hopmans. "Frequency, electrical conductivity and temperature analysis of a low-cost capacitance soil moisture sensor." *Journal of Hydrology* 352 (2008): 367–378.

18. Goerzen, Chad, Zhaodan Kong, and Bernard Mettler. "A survey of motion planning algorithms from the perspective of autonomous UAV guidance." *Journal of Intelligent and Robotic Systems* 57(1–4) (2010): 65–100.

19. Ji, Ronghua, and Lijun Qi. "Crop-row detection algorithm based on random Hough transformation." *Mathematical and Computer Modelling* 54(3–4) (2011): 1016–1020.

20. Bradski, Gary. "The openCV library." *Dr. Dobb's Journal of: Software Tools for the Professional Programmer* 25(11) (2000): 120–123.

21. Girshick, Ross, Jeff Donahue, Trevor Darrell, and Jitendra Malik. "Rich feature hierarchies for accurate object detection and semantic segmentation." In *Proceedings of the IEEE Conference on Computer Vision and Pattern Recognition*, pp. 580–587, 2014.

22. Faster, R. C. N. N. "Towards real-time object detection with region proposal networks." *Advances in Neural Information Processing Systems* 9199 10(5555) (2015): 2969239–2969250.

23. Tzutalin LabelImg. https://github.com/tzutalin/labelImg, 2015.

24. Zhang, Li, Guan Gui, Abdul Mateen Khattak, Minjuan Wang, Wanlin Gao, and Jingdun Jia. "Multi-task cascaded convolutional networks based intelligent fruit detection for designing automated robot." *IEEE Access* 7 (2019): 56028–56038.

25. Ronneberger, Olaf, Philipp Fischer, and Thomas Brox. "U-net: Convolutional networks for biomedical image segmentation." In *Medical Image Computing and Computer-Assisted Intervention–MICCAI 2015: 18th International Conference, Munich, Germany, October 5–9, 2015, Proceedings, Part III 18*, pp. 234–241. Springer International Publishing, 2015.

26. Velumani, Kaaviya, Raul Lopez-Lozano, Simon Madec, Wei Guo, Joss Gillet, Alexis Comar, and Frederic Baret. "Estimates of maize plant density from UAV RGB images using Faster-RCNN detection model: Impact of the spatial resolution." *Plant Phenomics* 2021 (2021).

27. Bradford, Kent J. "A water relations analysis of seed germination rates." *Plant Physiology* 94(2) (1990): 840–849.

8 Agricultural Development in Industry 5.0
Food Manufacturing and Development

S. Sivagami, D. Hemalatha, Carmel Mary Belinda, and A. Saleem Raja

8.1 INTRODUCTION

Modern technologies and established industries coming together has always been a catalyst for revolutionary transformation. The most recent phase of industrial evolution, known as Industry 5.0, promises to impact industries outside of manufacturing, including agriculture [1]. The dynamic relationship between Industry 5.0 and agriculture is explored in-depth in this chapter, along with its definition, guiding principles, the difficulties faced by contemporary agriculture, and the critical role played by technological advancement in advancing agricultural growth into a new era [2].

8.1.1 Definition and Key Principles of Industry 5.0

Industry 5.0 emphasizes harmonious cooperation between people and machines as a result of the confluence of human inventiveness and technological prowess [3]. Industry 5.0 goes beyond simple automation, while Industry 4.0 concentrates on the digitization and interconnection of machinery. It imagines a coexisting ecology where humans and robots cooperate, each bringing special skills to bear to maximize productivity, innovation, and adaptation. The following Figure 8.1 represents the emerging technologies beyond Industry 5.0.

In the dynamic landscape of technological evolution, Industry 5.0 emerged in the 2020s as a synergy of innovation and industry [4]. Progressing into the 2030s, nanotechnology took center stage, enabling precise nutrient delivery and pest management. By the 2040s, synthetic biology harnessed DNA mastery for robust crops and heightened yields. The 2050s unveiled quantum computing's enigmatic potential, refining crop modeling and climate foresight. As time marched on to the 2060s,

DOI: 10.1201/9781032642789-8

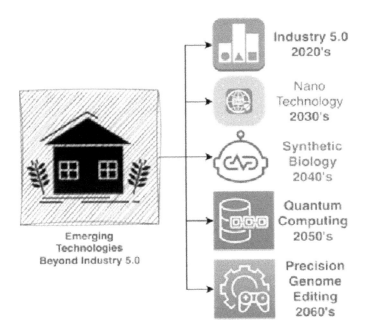

FIGURE 8.1   Emerging technologies beyond Industry 5.0

precision genome editing wielded genetic scissors, crafting bespoke crops with enhanced traits. Together, these milestones compose a visionary journey propelling agriculture into a realm of limitless possibilities.

Fundamentally, Industry 5.0 aims to break free from the limitations of completely automated processes and bring back the human touch to manufacturing and other sectors. In order to do this, production lines that are inflexible and linear must give way to flexible, networked systems that encourage human–robot interaction. Important ideas include:

1. *Human-Centric Focus:* Industry 5.0 puts people first, recognizing their originality, analytical skills, and emotional intelligence. Humans supply the knowledge and experience required for complicated decision-making, while machines handle repetitive chores and data-intensive processes.
2. *Collaboration in Robotics:* Robots are no longer isolated machines used only for predetermined duties. Instead, they work in harmony with people, sharing resources and tasks. This teamwork-based strategy improves adaptability, productivity, and safety.
3. *Customization and Personalization:* Industry 5.0 supports the idea of mass customization, in which production procedures are adaptable enough to address the unique needs of each customer. This level of personalization is made possible by combining cutting-edge technology with human understanding.

4. *Decentralized Decision-Making:* Decentralized, agile methods are used in place of conventional top-down decision-making frameworks. This encourages quick reactions to shifting conditions and empowers frontline employees.

8.1.2 Overview of Challenges in Modern Agriculture

A number of issues that threaten modern agriculture's sustainability and capacity to supply the world's food demand have brought it to a crossroads [5]. To secure food security, environmental protection, and economic viability, these issues demand novel solutions. Among the principal difficulties are:

1. *Population Increase:* By 2050, it is anticipated that there will be 9 billion people on the planet, placing tremendous pressure on agricultural systems to increase food production. Increases in crop yield must be significant in order to meet this demand, and resources must be used effectively.
2. *Climate Change:* Disruptions to established agricultural practices due to erratic weather patterns, shifting growing seasons, and extreme weather events result in lower yields and more vulnerable crops.
3. *Resource Scarcity:* Sustainable agriculture has considerable obstacles due to the diminishing amount of arable land, water limitations, and restricted access to necessary resources.
4. *Labor Shortages:* Aging agricultural workers and rural-to-urban migration cause labor shortages, endangering food production and supply systems.
5. *Environmental Effects:* Conventional agricultural methods exacerbate environmental deterioration and the loss of biodiversity by causing deforestation, soil degradation, and excessive chemical use.

8.1.3 Importance of Technological Integration
in Agricultural Development

Agriculture and Industry 5.0 coming together will have a significant impact on how these issues are resolved and how farming will be done in the future.

A diversified approach to agricultural development is made possible by the incorporation of new technologies. Figure 8.2 represents the integration of AI and machine learning in agriculture.

1. *Precision Farming:* Precision farming techniques are made possible by Industry 5.0 technologies like sensors, drones, and satellite imagery. Irrigation, fertilization, and pest management decisions are informed by real-time data gathering and analysis, minimizing resource waste and adverse environmental effects.
2. *Smart Farming:* Robotics and automated equipment automate labor-intensive chores to ensure effective and timely operations. Robotic planting,

INTEGRATION OF AI AND MACHINE LEARNING IN AGRICULTURE

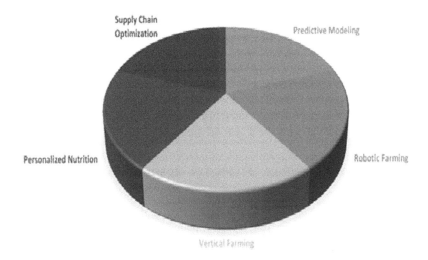

FIGURE 8.2 Integration of AI and machine learning in agriculture

harvesting, and monitoring increase output while addressing the labor shortage.

3. *Data-Driven Decision-Making:* Farmers are given useful information thanks to Industry 5.0's focus on data analytics. Crop management, disease detection, and yield prediction are optimized through predictive modeling and AI-driven algorithms.

4. *Sustainable Practices:* By minimizing chemical use, optimizing resource allocation, and lowering waste, technological integration promotes sustainable farming practices.

5. *Supply Chain Enhancement:* Real-time connection enabled by Industry 5.0 improves supply chain visibility and permits seamless coordination from farm to customer. Produce stays fresher and there is less food waste as a result.

Blending of agriculture and Industry 5.0 heralds a fundamental change in how to view food production, distribution, and sustainability [6]. The dynamic interaction of human skill and cutting-edge technology offers hope for overcoming the difficulties facing modern agriculture. Industry 5.0's guiding principles and technological integration provide a ray of hope for guaranteeing food security, environmental responsibility, and the vitality of agricultural communities so as to traverse its complex landscape. This transformative journey aims to create a more robust and peaceful relationship between people, technology, and the natural environment, not just through reinventing farming.

8.2   INDUSTRY 5.0 APPLICATIONS IN AGRICULTURE

The convergence of Industry 5.0 and agriculture has become a revolutionary force in a time of unprecedented connectivity and rapid technology innovation. Industry 5.0, the development of manufacturing and industry, penetrates agricultural areas and landscapes in addition to factory floors.

This innovative blending of modern technology and time-tested farming methods ushers in a new era of creativity, effectiveness, and sustainability and Figure 8.3 gives the technologies involved in advanced agriculture. Industry 5.0 is transforming industries outside of manufacturing, and it has numerous and significant applications in agriculture that are changing the way food is produced, distributed, and managed.

8.2.1   COLLABORATIVE FARMING AND HUMAN–ROBOT INTERACTION

The idea of harmonic collaboration between humans and robots is essential to the Industry 5.0 philosophy [7]. This idea is never clearer than in collaborative farming, a ground-breaking strategy that transforms how farmers and technology interact. The relationship between human competence and technological accuracy is shown through collaborative farming. In this paradigm, robots serve as intelligent partners who work with farmers to increase productivity, efficiency, and the quality of the agricultural experience as a whole. They are not merely automated tools. Collaborative farming is centered on human–robot interaction. Farmers can easily speak with robots to direct them through chores, give them directions, and adjust to changing conditions thanks to easy interfaces that ease this contact. By bridging the gap between human intuition and robotic capabilities, these interfaces guarantee that the best elements of both worlds come together to produce the best outcomes.

Collaboration in agriculture has effects that go beyond individual farms. With this strategy, labor shortages and rural-to-urban migration issues could be addressed,

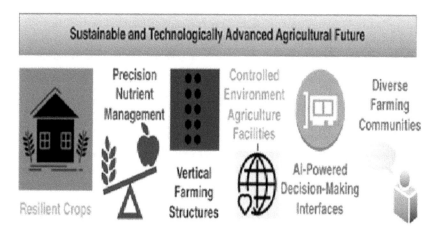

FIGURE 8.3   Vision for a sustainable and technologically advanced agricultural future

potentially reshaping the labor market in agriculture. Additionally, when farmers connect with one another and with technology, collaborative farming encourages information sharing by creating a communal pool of ideas and best practices. The future of agriculture is characterized by increased production, optimized resource utilization, and a redefined role for the modern farmer as Industry 5.0 permits this peaceful coexistence between people and machines.

8.2.2 Smart Farming and Precision Agriculture

The development of "smart farming" and "precision agriculture" is another illustration of Industry 5.0's effects on the agricultural sector [8]. These ideas are supported by the seamless fusion of automation, data analytics, and sensors, resulting in a network of interconnected systems that collectively optimize farming operations. Farmers now use real-time data to make informed decisions and increase resource efficiency in smart farming, which is a shift from traditional, linear approaches to agriculture.

Precision agriculture, a method that specifically tailors interventions to the demands of each crop and field, is at the core of modern farming. Data on temperature, moisture content, nutrient content, and other important characteristics is gathered through sensors buried in the soil and crops. This information is transmitted to central platforms, where it is processed by sophisticated algorithms to produce insights that farmers may use.

Precision farming makes it possible to make precise interventions like timed pest control, customized fertilization, and targeted watering. Farmers can now use resources only where they are required, minimizing waste and lessening the impact of farming operations on the environment, as opposed to equally treating entire fields. This method improves agricultural productivity and quality while also conserving essential resources.

In addition, smart farming incorporates a number of cutting-edge technologies, including as satellite imagery and drones. Drones that have cameras and sensors can watch fields from above while gathering data and taking high-resolution pictures. This overhead viewpoint provides a thorough view of crop health, growth trends, and prospective problems, enabling farmers to decide quickly and with knowledge.

Precision agriculture and smart farming are two examples of how data-driven decision-making can be effective in Industry 5.0. Farmers switch from reactive to proactive practices as the agricultural landscape becomes more integrated, anticipating problems and making quick adjustments to shifting conditions. By combining technology and agriculture in this way, food production enters a more sustainable and effective era while also improving productivity.

8.2.3 Supply Chain Optimization and Real-Time Data Management

Agriculture is a vital link in the intricate web that links farms to consumers; it is not a solitary activity. This supply chain is transformed by Industry 5.0 by including real-time data management and optimization techniques. The smooth transition of food from farm to table is made possible by supply chain optimization, which also reduces waste and inefficiencies while improving the entire customer experience. The agricultural supply chain can be tracked at every stage thanks to the integration of real-time data management. Perishable commodities are kept fresh and safe for consumption by sensors and IoT devices that monitor variables including temperature, humidity, and transport conditions [9]. Farmers, wholesalers, and retailers can make wise decisions and act quickly in the event of any deviations from the ideal conditions thanks to this degree of visibility.

Additionally, the real-time connection of Industry 5.0 enables flexible changes to supply chain logistics. Real-time data enables stakeholders to reroute shipments, modify inventory levels, and optimize delivery routes when demand changes and outside factors have an impact on transportation and distribution. This flexibility makes sure that goods get to customers quickly and that food waste is kept to a minimum.

Consumer tastes and needs are also taken into account during supply chain optimization. Retailers and distributors can foresee consumer wants and modify their offerings by continuously analyzing buying behaviors and market developments. With this demand-driven strategy, surplus inventory is decreased, shortages are avoided, and customer satisfaction is increased.

Industry 5.0 applications in agriculture are fundamentally altering how food is produced and distributed [10]. The role of farmers is being redefined and productivity is being increased by collaborative farming and human–robot interaction. Precision farming and smart farming improve sustainability by maximizing resource use. Food goes effectively from farm to table thanks to supply chain optimization and real-time data management, reducing waste and satisfying customer demands. Agriculture is being transformed by Industry 5.0 as it moves forward, ushering in a new era of innovation, efficiency, and sustainability that will change how to produce, distribute, and consume food globally.

8.3 MACHINE LEARNING IN FOOD MANUFACTURING

A new era of creativity and efficiency has emerged as a result of the integration of technology and food production [11]. Machine learning, a kind of artificial intelligence that enables systems to learn from data and enhance their performance over time, is at the core of this shift. This chapter examines the underlying ideas behind machine learning, as well as its various subsets and significant contribution to the modernization of the food manufacturing industry. This article explores the practical applications that are changing the face of food processing through incisive case studies.

8.3.1 Introduction to Machine Learning and Its Subsets

Industry 5.0's machine-learning technology gives machines the power to learn and decide for themselves based on data [12]. This includes a wide range of methods, from conventional algorithms to advanced deep-learning models. Unsupervised learning, which finds hidden patterns in unlabeled data, supervised learning, which teaches models using labeled data, and reinforcement learning, which teaches systems by interacting with their surroundings, are all subsets of machine learning.

8.3.2 ROLE OF MACHINE LEARNING IN OPTIMIZING FOOD PRODUCTION PROCESSES

The intricate and varied nature of food production necessitates accuracy, effectiveness, and quality assurance. Machine learning enters the picture as a game-changer, providing a number of advantages:

1. *Predictive Analysis:* Manufacturers may optimize production schedules, avoid overstocking, and cut waste by using machine-learning algorithms to estimate demand [13].
2. *Quality Assurance:* Machine learning can be used to analyze real-time sensor data to look for anomalies and ensure consistent quality along the whole production line.
3. *Process Optimization:* Algorithms adjust variables like pressure and temperature to increase productivity and product quality, which results in cost and energy savings.
4. *Supply Chain Management*: Machine learning supports the timely sourcing of raw materials, forecasting supply chain interruptions, and dynamic inventory management.
5. *Personalized Nutrition:* Product formulas are adjusted using machine learning to take into account consumer preferences, dietary needs, and health trends.

8.3.4 CASE STUDIES OF MACHINE-LEARNING APPLICATIONS IN FOOD MANUFACTURING

Predictive Maintenance: Machine learning is used by the dairy industry to forecast equipment breakdowns, reducing downtime and improving maintenance plans.

How Flavors Are Formulated: Product creation is revolutionized by an inventive beverage maker who utilizes machine learning to design new flavors based on consumer preferences.

Quality Control: A company that makes snack foods incorporates machine learning to spot flaws in items in real time, ensuring that only flawless goods get to customers.

Optimization of the Supply Chain: A multinational food corporation uses machine learning to predict changes in demand, improving inventory control and lowering stockouts.

Nutritional Labeling: To produce accurate labels that promote compliance and transparency, machine learning algorithms analyze ingredients and nutritional data.

Industry 5.0 has the ability to revolutionize efficiency, quality, and innovation through its symbiotic relationship with the food manufacturing industry. Food producers may improve processes, develop new products, and provide consumers with more value by leveraging the power of data-driven decision-making. The uses of machine learning in food manufacturing will be covered in more detail in the following sections of this chapter, with a focus on how they affect quality control and preventive maintenance.

8.4 QUALITY ASSURANCE AND PREDICTIVE MAINTENANCE

In the food manufacturing industry, quality control and maintenance are crucial to assuring consumer protection and superior products [14]. With its ability to analyze massive volumes of data and spot patterns, machine learning has emerged as a crucial tool for ensuring quality and anticipating equipment maintenance requirements.

8.4.1 USING MACHINE LEARNING FOR REAL-TIME QUALITY ASSESSMENT

Real-time quality assessment is crucial in a sector where reliability and security are top priorities. Machine-learning algorithms examine each step of the production process using data gathered from sensors and cameras [15]. These algorithms quickly identify departures from accepted norms, allowing for prompt corrective action. Machine learning aids in a quick and accurate quality assurance procedure by helping to recognize aberrant colors, shapes, or sizes. This protects customer health and brand reputation by ensuring that defective or contaminated items are quickly discovered and taken off the production line.

8.4.2 PREDICTIVE MAINTENANCE OF AGRICULTURAL MACHINERY AND PROCESSING EQUIPMENT

Unexpected equipment breakdown downtime can result in production delays, higher expenses, and reduced efficiency. A proactive approach to this problem is predictive maintenance, which is enabled by machine learning. Machine-learning algorithms can predict when machinery or equipment will break down by examining previous data, sensor readings, and environmental factors. Because of their foresight, manufacturers may plan maintenance tasks in advance of a failure, reducing downtime and extending the life of crucial assets. As a result, production lines run efficiently, cutting down on unscheduled downtime and maximizing resource use.

8.4.3 ENSURING FOOD SAFETY THROUGH AUTOMATED QUALITY CONTROL

Food safety cannot be compromised, and automated quality control using machine learning has completely changed the game in this area [16]. Incorporated into production lines, machine-learning systems continuously check items for flaws or impurities. These systems are able to differentiate between safe compounds and those that may be dangerous, warning operators and stopping production if any deviations are found. Manufacturers may proactively address safety concerns and stop contaminated items from reaching the market by relying on machine learning to spot even minute irregularities. In a larger sense, the union of artificial intelligence with food production fosters consumer confidence by reassuring them that products are subject to stringent quality control procedures. In turn, this encourages brand loyalty and helps create a safer, more reliable food supply.

8.4.4 USE CASE: PREDICTIVE MAINTENANCE IN FOOD PROCESSING

Maintaining the efficient operation of machinery is essential in the hectic world of food processing to satisfy production demands and guarantee product quality. However, equipment malfunctions can result in expensive downtime, delaying production schedules and compromising the quality of the final product. This is where machine-learning-powered predictive maintenance enters the picture to completely transform the sector.

Challenge

Unpredictable equipment failures are a challenge for a large-scale food processing facility. Frequent equipment breakdowns cause production delays, higher maintenance costs, and inefficient resource use.

Solution

The food processing facility uses machine-learning techniques to build a predictive maintenance solution.

Functions

1. *Data Collection:* Throughout the whole production line, sensors are placed strategically on important machines. Numerous characteristics, including temperature, vibration, pressure, and energy usage, are continuously monitored by these sensors. Data from the past is gathered and kept.
2. *Data Analysis and Model Development:* To find patterns and connections between sensor readings and previous equipment failures, machine-learning algorithms examine historical data. The system gains the ability to identify the signs and symptoms of possible failures.
3. *Predictive Models:* Predictive models are created based on the knowledge discovered through data analysis. These models are able to forecast the probability of equipment failure within a specific time range. When the danger of failure surpasses a set level, they also produce alerts and warnings.
4. *Real-time Observation:* The real-time predictive maintenance system continuously compares the most recent sensor readings to the pre-set patterns. The system sends notifications to maintenance staff as soon as any deviation is found.
5. *Proactive Maintenance:* Maintenance staff are alerted ahead of time to anticipated problems, enabling them to plan preventive maintenance procedures ahead of a breakdown. This could entail changing out worn-out parts, lubricating moving components, or making changes to stop a breakdown.

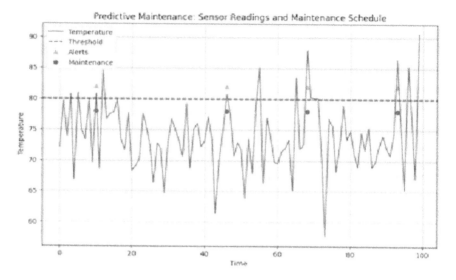

FIGURE 8.4 Maintenance prediction in food processing

An illustration of preventive maintenance in the food processing industry using graphs to display sensor data, alarms, and maintenance activities over time is shown in Figure 8.4.

Key Ideas

- Plotted over time are simulated temperature sensor values.
- The alarm threshold for preventive maintenance is represented by a red dashed line.
- Alerts that were sent when sensor readings exceeded the threshold are shown as orange triangles.
- According to alerts and a predetermined period, green circles represent scheduled maintenance occurrences.

Benefits

Decreased Downtime: Predictive maintenance reduces unplanned downtime by addressing equipment problems before they become serious failures. This leads to continuous production and reliable product output.

Optimized Resource Allocation: Maintenance tasks are efficiently scheduled and carried out, minimizing the need for urgent repairs and lowering maintenance expenses in general.

Longer Equipment Lifespan: Regular preventive maintenance increases a machine's lifespan and delays the need for costly upgrades and replacements.

Enhanced Product Quality: Reliable machinery operation guarantees that products maintain the desired quality and requirements.

Improved Safety: Predictive maintenance makes the workplace safer for workers by avoiding unforeseen problems.

The food processing facility successfully handles the issue of unforeseen machinery failures by incorporating machine-learning-based predictive maintenance into its operations. As a result, the production process is more productive, economical, and dependable and maintains product quality while causing the fewest number of disruptions. This use case serves as an example of how machine learning has the ability to alter the food manufacturing process and contribute to the goal of Industry 5.0, which calls for smarter, more effective industries.

8.5   QUALITY CONTROL AND PREDICTIVE MAINTENANCE IN FOOD MANUFACTURING

The pursuit of excellence in quality, efficiency, and safety has become crucial in the dynamic world of food processing. Machine learning's skills in quality control and predictive maintenance emerge as revolutionary forces that change how the industry views manufacturing methods and product integrity [17]. In order to show how machine learning is revolutionizing the food manufacturing industry, this chapter looks deeply into the fields of real-time quality assessment, predictive maintenance of machines, and automated quality control.

8.5.1   Using Machine Learning for Real-Time Quality Assessment

A key component of the food manufacturing process is the capacity to guarantee consistent product quality. Real-time quality assessment is made possible by machine-learning algorithms, which minimize fluctuations and flaws that can jeopardize customer pleasure. These algorithms look at data from sensors, cameras, and other sources to find abnormalities and departures from predetermined quality standards [18]. Machine-learning algorithms, for instance, track the texture, color, and form of candies as they pass along a production line in a confectionery factory. Every time there is a departure from the required parameters, there are immediate notifications that allow for quick corrections. Similar to this, in the preparation of meat, machine learning may examine photos to find flaws or impurities, guaranteeing that only high-quality, safe goods are sold to consumers.

8.5.2   Predictive Maintenance of Agricultural Machinery and Processing Equipment

The foundation of food production is comprised of agricultural and processing machinery. To avoid disruptions and sustain productivity, it is imperative to ensure their optimal performance. A crucial use of machine learning is predictive maintenance, which enables proactive detection of maintenance needs prior to equipment problems.

Machine-learning models forecast when machinery parts are likely to break using sensor data, previous maintenance logs, and environmental conditions. This enables producers to organize maintenance work during predetermined downtime, minimizing production stops and cutting maintenance expenses in general. Predictive maintenance in the context of agriculture makes sure that tractors, harvesters, and irrigation systems run without a hitch throughout crucial planting and harvesting seasons.

8.5.3 ENSURING FOOD SAFETY THROUGH AUTOMATED QUALITY CONTROL

In the food manufacturing sector, food safety is a given. Machine-learning-driven automated quality control offers a thorough and effective way to uphold strict safety standards. In order to identify potential contamination, foreign objects, or departures from hygiene standards, machine-learning algorithms analyze enormous volumes of data from production lines. Machine-learning algorithms, for instance, analyze the microbiological composition of milk samples in real time in a dairy processing facility. Actions are taken right away to stop contaminated batches from reaching consumers whenever bacteria are detected that could jeopardize consumer safety. Similar to how it may discover damaged seals or packaging flaws that could cause food to spoil, machine learning can also analyze sensor data from packaging lines.

8.5.4 UTILIZING MACHINE LEARNING FOR QUALITY CONTROL AND PREDICTIVE MAINTENANCE

Predictive maintenance and quality control are the foundations of excellence and resiliency in the food manufacturing industry. These pillars are strengthened through the use of machine learning, giving manufacturers access to real-time insights, proactive maintenance plans, and reliable safety measures. Machine learning and food production work together in a synergistic way that not only improves productivity and product quality but also protects customer health. The use of machine learning in quality control and predictive maintenance provides a view into the future of food manufacturing—a future characterized by accuracy, safety, and innovation—as it continues to negotiate the challenging landscape of Industry 5.0.

8.5.5 USE CASE: IMPROVED PREDICTIVE MAINTENANCE AND QUALITY CONTROL IN DAIRY PROCESSING

Challenge

Milk, yogurt, and cheese are just a few of the many dairy products that are produced in a dairy processing facility. To meet regulatory requirements and preserve consumer confidence, it is crucial to guarantee constant product quality and prevent contamination. The facility also has maintenance issues with essential processing machinery, which might result in production halts and compromised product integrity.

Solution

The dairy processing facility uses machine learning to power an extensive quality control and predictive maintenance system.

Quality Assurance Using Machine Learning

Analysis of Microbial Composition: At several processing stages, the facility gathers samples of milk. Real-time microbial composition analysis by machine-learning algorithms compares the composition to predetermined safety standards. When bacteria start to develop or become contaminated, alarms are sent out right once to stop production and look into the problem.

Packaging Inspection: To identify compromised seals, packaging flaws, or foreign items, machine-learning models analyze sensor data from packing lines. Automation removes defective packing from the manufacturing process when quality criteria are violated.

Evaluation of Texture and Consistency: Machine-learning algorithms are used with machine vision systems to analyze the textures and consistency of products. For example, yogurt consistency is checked to make sure it complies with specifications before packaging.

Machine Learning for Predictive Maintenance

Equipment Sensor Data: On crucial processing machinery, sensors are mounted to collect information on characteristics like temperature, pressure, vibration, and others. Machine-learning models are trained using historical sensor data and maintenance logs.

Failure Prediction: Based on sensor data and past trends, machine-learning models forecast when equipment parts are likely to fail. These models take into account things like past maintenance, usage, and environmental variables.

Scheduling for Maintenance: Real-time alerts and forecasts of impending equipment breakdowns are sent to the plant. In order to prevent production interruptions, maintenance schedules are modified to proactively resolve problems during scheduled downtime.

Figure 8.5 shows two subplots that use simulated data to show how quality control and predictive maintenance are implemented in a dairy processing facility.

Subplot 1: Microbial Composition and Quality Alerts

- A temporal plot of the microbial composition of milk samples is shown in above Figure 8.5.
- High microbial composition-related quality alarms are indicated by red triangles.

Subplot 2: Equipment Temperature and Anticipated Maintenance

- Temperature readings from the equipment are plotted over time.
- Based on simulated data, the orange dashed line shows anticipated maintenance events.

Benefits

Enhanced Product Safety: Real-time quality assessment guarantees that only secure and uncontaminated goods get to consumers, protecting public health and adhering to rules.

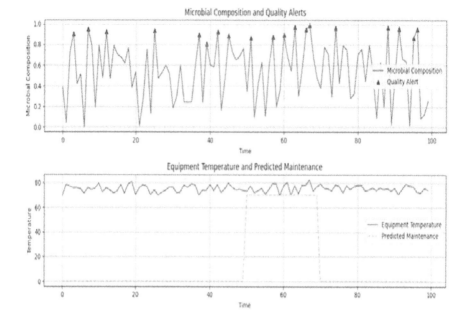

FIGURE 8.5   Quality control and predictive maintenance in dairy processing

Consistent Quality: Machine-learning-based quality control eliminates variances in product quality, upholding a brand's reputation and retaining customer confidence.

Reduced Downtime: With predictive maintenance, unplanned equipment failures are kept to a minimum, minimizing downtime and maintaining continuous production.

Cost Savings: Schedules for proactive maintenance optimize resource use and lower overall maintenance costs.

Efficient Resource Utilization: Predictive maintenance and quality control enable the effective use of labor, energy, and raw materials.

The dairy processing facility achieves a higher level of product quality, safety, and operational efficiency through the integration of machine learning in quality control and predictive maintenance. A more robust and creative environment for food manufacturing can be achieved by using data-driven decision-making and preventive maintenance techniques, as shown by the convergence of Industry 5.0 concepts with cutting-edge technologies. This use case is a great illustration of how machine learning can revolutionize the food business by improving quality and sustainability.

8.6   ENHANCING CROP YIELD AND NUTRITIONAL CONTENT

The need for agriculture to increase crop output and nutrient content is unprecedented due to the world's expanding population, difficulties from climate change, and resource constraints. The integration of technology and agriculture offers creative solutions to these problems as stands at the nexus of Industry 5.0 [19]. This chapter highlights the crucial role of technology in the revolution in food production by examining the revolutionary potential of predictive modeling for crop yield estimation, machine learning for crop breeding optimization, and nutrition optimization through personalized agriculture.

8.6.1 PREDICTIVE MODELING FOR CROP YIELD ESTIMATION

The way think about agricultural yield estimation is changing as a result of predictive modeling, which is supported by machine-learning algorithms. Traditional approaches frequently made use of historical data and crude computations. Contrarily, machine learning makes use of a wide range of factors, such as weather patterns, soil characteristics, and crop health data, to produce precise and immediate predictions [20]. Farmers get high-resolution information on their fields by combining sensors, drones, and satellite photography. Then, machine-learning models examine this data to reveal information on the health, rate of growth, and prospective yields of the crop. Farmers can decide on irrigation, fertilization, and pest management with the use of this information. Crop yields are increased, waste is minimized, and resource allocation is optimized as a result.

8.6.2 MACHINE LEARNING FOR OPTIMIZING CROP BREEDING AND GENETIC IMPROVEMENT

Machine learning is driving a revolution in crop breeding, a long-standing practice. Crop breeding, once a time-consuming and error-prone process, is now sped up and improved thanks to the power of data-driven algorithms. In order to discover desirable features and forecast the results of various breeding combinations, machine-learning models analyze genetic data. This method hastens the development of crops that have characteristics like higher nutritional value, disease resistance, and drought tolerance. Additionally, it lessens the need for time- and money-consuming field tests. Even the discovery of previously unknown unique genetic combinations made possible by machine learning has resulted in the development of more hardy and fruitful agricultural varieties.

8.6.3 NUTRIENT OPTIMIZATION AND PERSONALIZED AGRICULTURE USING MACHINE LEARNING

Machine learning is emerging as a powerful tool for optimizing nutrient delivery to crops as the idea of personalized nutrition gets hold. Machine-learning models can make exact fertilizer formulation recommendations that are suited to the particular requirements of each field by examining data on the features of crops, weather patterns, and soil types. This focused strategy guarantees ideal nutrient intake, minimizes waste, and has a minimal negative impact on the environment. Additionally, machine learning supports the idea of personalized agriculture, in which each plant is given a unique regimen of care. Real-time monitoring of each plant's health and growth trajectory is made possible by sensors and data analytics. Then, using machine-learning algorithms, irrigation, fertilization, and other inputs are modified to meet the particular needs of each plant, improving crop health, yield, and nutrient content.

Agriculture is about to become a more effective, resilient, and sustainable industry thanks to the integration of predictive modeling, machine learning, and personalized agriculture. Farmers may increase crop yields, create genetically better kinds, and provide nutrient-rich produce to fulfill the demands of a growing world population by utilizing the potential of technology. The use of machine learning to improve agricultural productivity and nutrient content is a prime example of how innovation and sustenance may coexist harmoniously as they progress in Industry 5.0.

8.6.4 Use Case: Personalized Agriculture to Increase Crop Yield and Nutritional Content

Challenge
The difficulty for a large-scale agricultural farm is to increase crop productivity while preserving the nutritional value of its produce. Achieving consistent and high-quality yields across several fields is a challenging endeavor because different fields have diverse soil types, weather patterns, and crop varieties. The farm wants to use technology to improve dietary quality and crop productivity on an individual basis.

Solution
The farm uses machine learning to construct an extensive personalized agriculture system.

Predictive Modeling for Estimating Crop Yields
Collection of Data: The farm uses a network of sensors, drones, and satellite imaging to gather information on crop health, soil moisture, temperature, and humidity. This information is paired with past yield information and weather predictions.

Models for Machine Learning: The gathered data is analyzed by machine-learning algorithms to create forecasting models for crop production estimation. These models account for a variety of variables affecting yield, including soil characteristics, changes in the weather, and insect concerns.

Real-Time Insights: Farmers are given immediate information on the anticipated crop yields for each farm. This makes it possible to make well-informed decisions on pest management methods, fertilization schedules, and watering schedules.

Optimizing Nutrients and Using Personalized Agriculture
Analysis of the Soil Composition: The composition and amounts of nutrients are examined in soil samples collected from various fields. The correlations between soil properties and crop nutrient requirements are discovered using machine-learning algorithms.

Specific Nutritional Advice: Machine-learning models suggest customized nutrient compositions for each field based on crop types, weather data, and soil composition. These formulas have been carefully chosen to maximize crop health and nutrient uptake.

Real-Time Monitoring: Real-time monitoring of plant health, growth rates, and nutrient levels is done with the use of sensors. These data are analyzed by machine learning algorithms to modify fertilizer and irrigation supply to each individual plant.

Optimization of crop yield and nutritional content is shown in Figure 8.6; two subplots that use simulated data to show how personalized agriculture may be used to maximize crop output and nutrient content.

Subplot 1: Soil Nutrient Levels and Projected Yield

- Plots of soil nutrients show changes throughout time.
- The graph shown in Figure 8.6 the predicted crop production, which was determined using the temperature, humidity, and nutrient levels.

Subplot 2: Weather Conditions and Expected Yield

- Readings for temperature and humidity are plotted over time.
- The simulated formula's predicted crop production is displayed along with the current weather.

Benefits

Maximized Yield: Because predictive modeling optimizes resource allocation, crop yields across fields are higher and more uniform.

Nutrient-Rich Produce: Personalized nutrient recommendations raise crops' nutritional value, giving customers access to foods that are more nourishing and healthier.

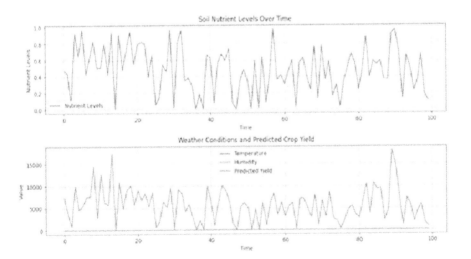

FIGURE 8.6   Optimization of crop yield and nutritional content

Resource Efficiency: Accurate irrigation and nutrient supply cut down on waste and encourage effective resource use.

Accelerated Breeding: Using machine learning, crop varieties with desired features can be developed faster, increasing total productivity.

Machine-learning-powered personalized agriculture helps the agricultural farm strike a healthy balance between high crop productivity and improved nutrient content. The farm helps to produce healthy and sustainable food by utilizing technology to expedite crop breeding, allocate resources more effectively, and provide individualized care to each plant. This use case serves as an example of how Industry 5.0 has the ability to transform agriculture and tackle issues related to a growing world population and shifting environmental conditions.

8.7 FOOD PRODUCT DEVELOPMENT AND PERSONALIZATION

The area of food product creation is witnessing a tremendous transition in an era where customer preferences and tastes are as varied as the world's population. Food producers are revolutionizing how they develop, forecast, and customize food products to suit different tastes thanks to the powers of machine intelligence [21]. This chapter explores the intriguing fields of flavor prediction, product customization, formulation utilizing machine-learning algorithms, and the significant effects these developments have on speeding up food innovation while shortening development times.

8.7.1 Customizing Food Products Based on Consumer Preferences

The days of producing food using a one-size-fits-all strategy are over. Industry 5.0 ushers in a new paradigm where personalization takes center stage. Machine-learning algorithms process a variety of customer data, including flavor preferences, cultural influences, and dietary restrictions and allergies. This extensive dataset supports the development of customized food products that connect with customers personally. Imagine a situation where a cereal blend is created by a food producer to suit the preferences of a particular consumer, ensuring that it has the right amount of sweetness, crunch, and nutrition. Manufacturers can design a wide range of items that appeal to various demographics thanks to machine-learning-driven personalization, which ultimately improves customer pleasure and loyalty.

8.7.2 Flavor Prediction and Formulation Using Machine Learning Algorithms

A key component of enjoying food is flavor, which is a complex fusion of taste and fragrance. The rules of flavor prediction and formulation are being rewritten by machine-learning algorithms, which are armed with a wealth of sensory data and ingredient knowledge. Machine learning can precisely anticipate how several ingredients will combine to produce a particular taste experience by examining the chemical make-up of materials, historical flavor profiles, and even the cultural context of some flavors. The formulation of food is revolutionized by this predictive capability. This eliminates the need for expensive and time-consuming physical trials by enabling producers to test out innovative ingredient combinations virtually. Machine-learning algorithms direct the formulation process, optimizing flavor profiles while minimizing the trial-and-error process often involved in product development, whether it's a savory snack or a delicate dessert.

8.7.3 ACCELERATING FOOD INNOVATION AND REDUCING DEVELOPMENT TIMELINES

Food innovation has historically been a time- and labor-intensive process. However, the rate of innovation is now growing exponentially as a result of the development of machine learning. Machine-learning algorithms help anticipate upcoming food trends by utilizing historical data, customer feedback, and ingredient information. This enables businesses to proactively build goods that resonate with changing consumer tastes. Additionally, by speeding the iterative process of recipe testing and optimization, machine learning reduces the development time. Manufacturers can quickly develop and improve food goods thanks to virtual simulations powered by algorithms, which eliminates the need for rigorous physical testing. This adaptability decreases expenses related to unsuccessful tests while simultaneously speeding up time to market.

A new era of unmatched personalization, flavor innovation, and faster creativity is brought about by the combination of machine learning and food product creation. Food producers are in a good position to satisfy the expectations of a wide and discriminating customer base by customizing food items to individual preferences, anticipating and optimizing flavors, and accelerating development timelines. The use of machine learning in the production of food products is an excellent example of how technology and culinary artistry might coexist in the future, when every mouthful is a unique culinary masterpiece as to navigate the complex landscape of Industry 5.0.

8.7.4 USE CASE: PERSONALIZED CEREAL BLEND CREATION USING MACHINE LEARNING

The food sector is embracing the power of machine learning to revolutionize the process of developing and customizing food items in a world where consumer preferences for food goods vary widely. Take the example of a cereal producer that specializes in breakfast foods and wants to develop a custom cereal mix for each customer.

Step 1: Data Collection and Analysis

The food producer compiles a plethora of information regarding consumer preferences. Dietary restrictions, flavor preferences, dietary needs, and cultural influences are all part of this information. This heterogeneous dataset is processed by machine learning algorithms to find patterns and correlations that can be used to create custom cereal combinations.

Step 2: Making Customized Profiles

Machine-learning algorithms develop unique profiles for each customer based on the insights obtained from the data analysis. The optimal qualities of the cereal blend are described in these profiles, including the amount of sweetness, crunchiness, types of grains, and additional additives (such as fruits, nuts, or seeds).

Step 3: Flavor Prediction and Formulation

Machine-learning algorithms evaluate the interactions between various ingredients, the chemical make-up of various compounds, and historical flavor profiles. These algorithms forecast how various component combinations would affect the overall flavor and scent of the cereal blend based on user-specific profiles.

Step 4: Virtual Prototyping and Testing

A new cereal blend would typically go through several iterations of physical prototype and taste testing. In contrast, the producer can use machine learning to generate virtual prototypes of various cereal combinations based on the projected flavor profiles. With no need for massive physical production, the producer may swiftly evaluate the flavor and texture of these virtual prototypes by testing them in a simulated setting.

Step 5: Iterative Refinement

Virtual taste testing provides data that machine-learning algorithms analyze to improve the formulation of the cereal mixtures. The algorithms continually incorporate feedback to improve their formulation and prediction accuracy.

Step 6: Production and Customization

The company can use the customized profiles to alter the production process after virtual prototyping and refinement have established the best cereal blend formulas. Each custom cereal blend is meticulously created to satisfy each customer's unique preferences.

A graphical representation of flavor profiles predicted using machine-learning methods for custom cereal combinations is shown in Figure 8.7. The y-axis displays the projected flavor intensity scores for each cereal blend, and the x-axis displays various cereal blend compositions. The graph's lines are color-coded according to several flavor attributes, such as sweetness, crunchiness, and nuttiness. The graph graphically illustrates how machine-learning algorithms may tweak component combinations to optimize flavor profiles, resulting in cereal blends that are specifically suited to each consumer's preferences.

Benefits: Customers receive cereal mixtures that are customized to their specific preferences, increasing customer happiness and brand loyalty.

Efficiency: By eliminating the need for substantial physical testing and experimentation, machine learning shortens the time required for product creation.

Waste Reduction: Virtual prototyping reduces waste by lowering the amount of resources needed for physical production and testing.

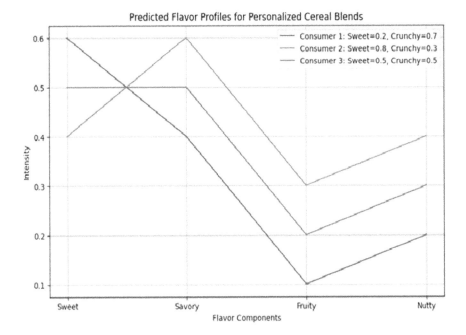

FIGURE 8.7   Predicted flavor profiles for personalized cereal blends

Innovation: The producer can experiment with new ingredient pairings and flavor profiles thanks to machine learning, leading to innovations in product offers.

The development of customized cereal blends is an example of how machine learning is changing the industry of food product development. Machine Learning enables producers to produce distinctive and cutting-edge food products that are tailored to individual preferences by utilizing customer data, forecasting flavor interactions, and enabling virtual prototyping. This use of machine learning not only improves customer experiences but also hastens food sector innovation.

8.8   SUSTAINABILITY AND RESOURCE MANAGEMENT

The need for sustainable food production methods has never been more pressing as the world's population expands and environmental concerns grow. With its technological competence and data-driven skills, Industry 5.0 has a special chance to handle these difficulties. In the context of food production, this chapter examines the transformative significance of machine learning in maximizing resource allocation, lowering waste and energy consumption, and promoting sustainable practices [22].

8.8.1   USING MACHINE LEARNING TO OPTIMIZE RESOURCE ALLOCATION

Sustainable food production is significantly hampered by resource constraint, which ranges from water and land to fertilizers and electricity. Real-time data and machine-learning techniques enable precise and dynamic resource allocation [23]. These algorithms offer insights that help farmers optimize irrigation, fertilization, and pest control practices by examining soil properties, weather patterns, and crop growth data.

Decisions in agriculture are now influenced by data and adjusted to the unique requirements of each field rather than being solely based on intuition. Farmers can increase yields, reduce waste, and maximize resource efficiency thanks to machine learning. As machine-learning algorithms assist in managing energy-intensive operations, such as irrigation and equipment operation, to lessen the carbon footprint of food production, this resource optimization also extends to energy consumption.

8.8.2 Waste Reduction and Energy Efficiency in Food Production

A sustainable food production ecosystem must include waste reduction and energy efficiency. Machine learning provides creative ways to reduce waste and improve energy usage. For instance, data on temperature, humidity, and energy use is collected by smart sensors placed all along the production line. This data is analyzed by machine-learning algorithms to find inefficiencies and irregularities, enabling manufacturers to make adjustments in real time.

By optimizing cutting techniques, ingredient utilization, and packaging in the food processing industry, machine learning helps to reduce product waste. Based on variables like ingredient quality and processing circumstances, algorithms forecast yield fluctuations, allowing producers to modify output as necessary. This data-driven strategy promotes a more sustainable and effective food manufacturing process by lowering production costs and food waste.

8.8.3 Sustainable Practices Through Data-Driven Decision-Making

Decisions must be made with knowledge if sustainable practices are to be adopted. Making ecologically responsible decisions is made possible by machine learning, which provides stakeholders with actionable insights drawn from massive databases. Supply chain managers, for instance, can use machine learning to compare the carbon footprints of several transportation routes and choose the greenest one.

Beyond operations, data-driven decision-making is used in product creation. Machine learning assists firms in developing goods that are in line with sustainability objectives by examining consumer preferences and market trends. Additionally, machine-learning algorithms can forecast the environmental impact of various packaging materials, enabling knowledgeable decisions that lower waste and support recycling.

In a time of growing environmental concerns, the combination of machine intelligence and sustainable food production offers optimism. Industry 5.0 ushers in a new era of ethical food production by streamlining resource allocation, cutting waste, and encouraging data-driven decision-making. The uses of machine learning in sustainability highlight the sector's commitment to protecting our planet's resources while feeding a growing global population as to navigate the uncharted waters of a fast-changing world.

8.8.4   Use Case: Optimizing Resource Allocation and Waste Reduction in Sustainable Farming

Background

Although agriculture is essential to feeding the world's expanding population, it also faces difficulties like resource scarcity and environmental issues. In order to secure food security while minimizing harm to the environment, sustainable agricultural techniques are important. By maximizing resource allocation and minimizing food production waste, machine learning, a major element of Industry 5.0, provides a potent answer to these problems.

Green Acres Farm is a forward-thinking agricultural enterprise that uses machine learning to improve resource management and cut waste. It has adopted sustainable farming technique

1. Optimized Fertilization and Irrigation

Real-time data from soil moisture sensors, weather predictions, and crop health monitors are analyzed using machine-learning algorithms. To establish the precise irrigation and fertilization needs for each field and crop, this data is processed. Green Acres Farm maximizes water and nutrient efficiency by customizing resource applications to specific demands. This reduces water use and minimizes fertilizer runoff.

2. Disease Management and Pest Management

Based on past data and present circumstances, machine-learning models are taught to forecast the risk of pest infestations and disease epidemics. Early warning notifications are produced, enabling farmers to take specific precautionary measures. With less need for excessive pesticide application, less chemical residue in the environment, and healthier produce, this proactive strategy reduces the need for overuse of pesticides.

3. Energy-Efficient Operations

Machine-learning algorithms are used by Green Acres Farm to track patterns in the energy used by its equipment, lighting, and climate control systems. The farm reduces its carbon footprint and energy expenses by identifying energy-intensive processes and scheduling operations during off-peak hours.

4. Exact Harvesting and Sorting

On harvesting machinery, sensors and cameras powered by machine learning are fitted to identify and classify food according to ripeness and quality. Only the best product is picked and provided to consumers as a result. Green Acres Farm minimizes food waste and raises consumer satisfaction by minimizing the proportion of subpar or underripe products.

5. Decisions Regarding Sustainable Packaging

To help with packaging decisions, machine-learning algorithms analyze consumer preferences, market trends, and data on environmental impacts. Green Acres Farm utilizes packaging components and styles that support sustainability objectives, minimizing the use of plastic and fostering recyclable materials.

Predicted Soil Moisture Levels for the Next Seven Days:

Day 31: Predicted Soil Moisture = 0.874
Day 32: Predicted Soil Moisture = 0.891
Day 33: Predicted Soil Moisture = 0.908
Day 34: Predicted Soil Moisture = 0.925
Day 35: Predicted Soil Moisture = 0.941
Day 36: Predicted Soil Moisture = 0.958
Day 37: Predicted Soil Moisture = 0.975

The graph uses current and anticipated soil moisture levels to show how irrigation scheduling for Crop X is done as shown in Figure 8.8. From the beginning through the end of the crop's growth cycle, the days on the x-axis denote time. The y-axis shows the range of soil moisture, from very low to very high. On the graph, the blue line represents the actual soil moisture levels that were measured over the course of the crop's growth. It illustrates how variations in soil moisture are caused by factors such as weather, irrigation methods, and natural water absorption. The soil moisture levels anticipated by a machine-learning algorithm are represented by the

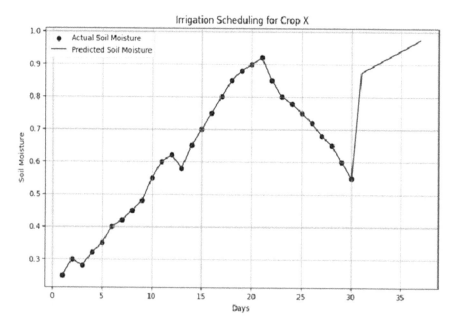

FIGURE 8.8   Irrigation scheduling for Crop X—actual and predicted soil moisture levels

orange line. These estimates are based on a number of variables, including historical soil moisture data, weather predictions, and irrigation inputs. As new data become available, the system continuously improves its predictions. Farmers and irrigation managers can choose when and how much to water by comparing the actual and forecast soil moisture levels. Adjustments to the irrigation schedule may be necessary if there are deviations between the two lines, which can signify periods of over- or under-irrigation. In order to ensure that Crop X receives the appropriate amount of water at the appropriate time, this graph graphically illustrates the importance of machine learning in irrigation practice optimization. Predicting soil moisture levels promotes crop health, water resource conservation, and efficient, sustainable food production.

BENEFITS

Green Acres Farm achieves the following advantages by employing machine learning:

Resource Efficiency: Accurate resource distribution reduces the need for fertilizer and water, maximizing crop growth while reducing waste.

Lower Environmental Impact: Lessened energy use and pesticide use result in a healthier ecosystem and lower carbon emissions.

Minimized Food Waste: Careful selection and harvesting techniques guarantee that only the highest-quality produce is taken, minimizing waste after harvest.

Cost Savings: The farm experiences cost savings as a result of energy optimization and reduced resource utilization.

Consumer Trust is Increased by Environmentally Friendly Practices and Clear Packaging Options

The accomplishments of Green Acres Farm serve as a testament to the transformative power of machine learning in advancing resource efficiency and sustainability in food production. The farm not only contributes to a more ecologically friendly approach to agriculture by optimizing irrigation, cutting waste, and making data-driven decisions, but also offers an example for others to follow in establishing a more sustainable food future.

8.9   CHALLENGES AND ETHICAL CONSIDERATIONS IN THE AGE OF INDUSTRY 5.0

Unprecedented opportunities and challenges arise as lead Industry 5.0, a revolutionary wave that fuses technology and industry. The adoption of cutting-edge technologies, data analytics, and machine learning across a range of industries, including agriculture, promises to have significant advantages [24]. But this quick technical development also raises difficult ethical questions that need close examination. This chapter explores the problems with data security and privacy, the need for unbiased and open-source machine-learning algorithms, and the pressing need to close the digital divide and provide equal access to technology in the field of agriculture.

8.9.1 Data Privacy and Security in Agricultural Data Management

An era of data-driven decision-making where productivity and sustainability are improved by insights gained from sensors, drones, and other devices is ushering in the digitization of agriculture. However, the security and privacy of all this data are a problem. Agricultural data, which might include information on crop production statistics and weather forecasts, is extremely valuable to both farmers and agribusinesses and other data-driven firms.

Both individual farmers and the larger agricultural ecosystem are significantly threatened by data breaches and unauthorized access. The wrong people could gain access to confidential information regarding planting techniques, pest control methods, and market trends, which could lead to financial losses and weakened competitive advantages. Therefore, to protect agricultural data, strong data encryption, secure cloud storage, and rigorous access controls are necessary.

8.9.2 Ensuring Unbiased and Transparent Machine-Learning Algorithms

Numerous technical developments in agriculture, such as predictive modeling and crop management, are based on machine-learning algorithms. The objectivity and transparency of these algorithms, however, are what determines their dependability. While opaque algorithms pose questions about accountability and decision-making procedures, biased algorithms can worsen already existing imbalances.

Biased algorithms may favor particular crops or geographical areas in agriculture while ignoring the demands of disadvantaged groups. To combat this, algorithms must be trained on diverse, representative data that accurately depicts the rich tapestry of agriculture. Furthermore, open machine-learning models and thorough documentation of the decision-making procedures give stakeholders the ability to comprehend and question the results.

8.9.3 Addressing the Digital Divide and Access to Technology in Agriculture

The digital gap is a significant barrier despite Industry 5.0's promises of a future filled with technological progress. Unfair access to digital infrastructure and technology has the potential to widen already existing gaps between metropolitan centers and rural areas, as well as between major and small agribusinesses. This gap impedes equitable development while also stifling Industry 5.0's potential benefits for all parties involved in agriculture. It will take coordinated efforts to offer marginalized populations affordable and accessible digital solutions in order to close this gap. Initiatives that provide technical assistance, affordable gadgets, and training can equip farmers with the resources they need to take advantage of Industry 5.0. To make sure that technological improvements are inclusive and suited to address the varied needs of various agricultural contexts, policymakers, stakeholders, and inventors must work together. Industry 5.0 is characterized by both exciting technological advances and complex ethical quandaries. The concerns of data privacy,

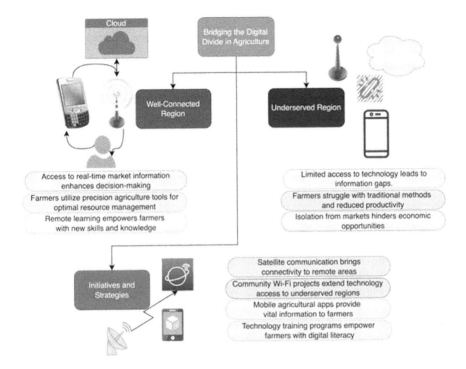

FIGURE 8.9 Addressing the digital divide in agriculture

algorithmic bias, and digital equity deserve our undivided focus as technology enters every aspect of agriculture, from data-driven decision-making to predictive modeling. AI can make sure that Industry 5.0 advances agriculture while simultaneously fostering a more fair, open, and sustainable future for all parties involved by proactively addressing these ethical concerns.

The above Figure 8.9, illustrates the digital divide by showing a comparison between well-connected regions with advanced technology adoption and underserved regions with limited access to technology.

8.9.4   USE CASE: ETHICAL CONSIDERATIONS IN PRECISION AGRICULTURE

A ground-breaking experiment in precision agriculture is being conducted in the verdant fields of Green Valley Farm under the direction of Industry 5.0. To improve every part of crop production, cutting-edge technologies including sensors, drones, and machine-learning algorithms have been combined. The ethical issues that must support this technological transition, however, stand out among the technological marvels.

Data Security and Privacy: The farm's data hub gathers a wide range of data, including soil moisture content, temperature, crop health, and anticipated yields. To make wise decisions, farmers and agribusinesses rely on this data. Green Valley

Farm has put strict controls in place to ensure data security and privacy. Sensitive agricultural data is kept private and protected from unauthorized access thanks to encryption, multi-factor authentication, and regular security audits.

Algorithms that are Transparent and Unbiased: The use of machine-learning algorithms is essential for determining planting plans and foreseeing disease outbreaks. The farm is dedicated to preventing prejudice and advancing openness in algorithmic decision-making. Algorithms are trained using a variety of datasets that account for different soil types, crop varieties, and environmental factors. Every algorithm's decision-making procedure is also recorded and made available to farmers, encouraging accountability and enabling ongoing improvement.

Digital Divide and Equitable Access: The digital gap between large-scale agricultural operations and smallholder farmers must be closed, according to Green Valley Farm. The farm has engaged with neighborhood communities to promote fair access, giving technology seminars and supplying sensors and gadgets at a reasonable price. Green Valley Farm is fostering an inclusive culture and a shared prosperity by equipping farmers with the knowledge and resources they need to capitalize on Industry 5.0's promise.

The above Figure 8.10, illustrates the correlation between historical crop yield data and soil moisture as well as temperature. It also showcases a predicted crop yield marked by a red "x" for a specific input of soil moisture and temperature. The core values of Industry 5.0 at Green Valley Farm are inseparable from ethical issues; they go beyond technological advancement. The farm is dedicated to managing the

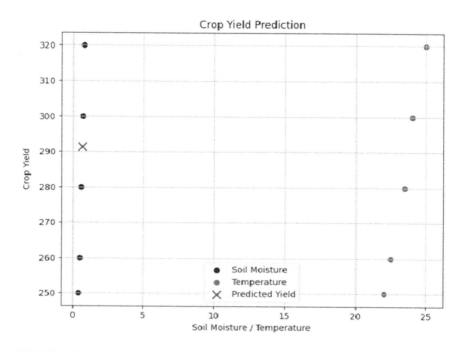

FIGURE 8.10   Crop yield prediction based on soil moisture and temperature

ethical aspects of Industry 5.0 even as it forges a sustainable future where technology improves productivity and land management. By doing this, Green Valley Farm cultivates not only crops but also a future in which innovation and morality coexist in harmony.

8.10   FUTURE TRENDS AND OUTLOOK: A VISION OF AGRICULTURE BEYOND INDUSTRY 5.0

The agricultural environment is about to undergo a significant change as Industry 5.0 reshapes industries and redefines the limits of what is possible. Beyond the boundaries of Industry 5.0, a tapestry of new technologies, the ongoing advancement of machine learning and artificial intelligence (AI), and a vision for a sustainable and technologically advanced agricultural future come together to create a picture of unmatched innovation and development [25]. In order to establish a new era of agricultural greatness, this chapter investigates the enticing future trends and provides a visionary outlook that transcends the present.

8.10.1   EMERGING TECHNOLOGIES BEYOND INDUSTRY 5.0

While Industry 5.0 is at the forefront of industrial growth, future technologies have the potential to transform agriculture in far more profound ways. By manipulating materials at the molecular level, nanotechnology, for instance, can improve insect control, nutrient delivery, and even the development of intelligent fertilizers. Crops having features not present in nature, such as resistance to particular illnesses or harsh environmental conditions, could be engineered via synthetic biology.

Crop modeling, weather forecasting, and the optimization of intricate biological processes can all be transformed by quantum computing thanks to its incredible computational capability. Furthermore, improvements in biotechnology allow for precise genome editing, resulting in crop varieties that are adapted to flourish in changing climates and generate produce that is high in nutrients. Together with Industry 5.0, these technologies advance agriculture into a previously sci-fi-only area of innovation.

8.10.2   CONTINUED INTEGRATION OF AI AND MACHINE LEARNING IN AGRICULTURE

The integration of AI and machine learning in agriculture is still in its early stages. In fact, it is about to become more complex and varied, affecting every aspect of food production. More advanced predictive models will provide granular insights into market patterns, disease outbreaks, and planting times. Machine-learning algorithms will decipher the complex interactions between soil microorganisms, plants, and climate, resulting in improved soil health and nutrient cycling.

Robotics powered by AI will take center stage, with sophisticated tasks like the careful harvesting of delicate fruits and the precise application of pesticides being carried out by intelligent machines on their own. Field monitoring will be transformed by the combination of AI and drone technology, enabling quick response to new problems. AI-powered solutions will also make it possible for consumers to have highly customized experiences, including real-time nutritional insights and personalized dietary suggestions.

8.10.3   Vision for a Sustainable and Technologically Advanced Agricultural Future

Emerging technology, Industry 5.0 concepts, and AI integration come together to create a vision of agriculture that goes beyond basic survival. It imagines a time when sustainability is not only a high ideal but rather a fundamental quality. Crops that are resource-efficient, climate-adaptive, and pest-resistant are abundant in fields. Precision nutrient management improves soil health while reducing pollutants and maintaining ecosystem balance.

As automated technologies manage every stage of the food supply chain, from planting to delivery, waste is essentially eliminated in this scenario. Urban areas are thriving with energy-efficient vertical farms and controlled environment agriculture, minimizing the environmental impact of food production. Biodiversity is praised as AI-driven genetic engineering makes it easier to cultivate rediscovered crops and restore native species, improving nutrition and resiliency.

The benefits of this agricultural future do not only benefit the wealthy few. Strong digital infrastructure and cooperative projects close the digital gap, giving smallholder farmers access to information, technology, and markets. Platforms driven by AI democratize agricultural decision-making, enabling farmers from a variety of backgrounds to prosper in a sector that is fast-changing.

Examining Agriculture's Future Beyond Industry 5.0

The agricultural sector is about to undergo a colossal upheaval that will push the limits of creativity to new heights as Industry 5.0 sweeps across industries. Beyond Industry 5.0, a compelling story of new technologies, the constant advancement of AI, and a vision of a technologically advanced, sustainable agricultural future converge, creating a vivid tapestry of unprecedented progress. This chapter explores the fascinating contours of emerging trends and offers a transcendent aspirational perspective.

Beyond Industry 5.0, Embracing Revolutionary Technologies

While Industry 5.0 is in the spotlight right now, the future holds a wave of innovations that have the potential to fundamentally alter agriculture. With its capacity to alter matter at the atomic level, nanotechnology has the potential to improve nutrition delivery, insect control, and the development of intelligent fertilizers. Synthetic biology provides a way to design crops with innovative characteristics like resistance to particular diseases or harsh climatic conditions.

With its unmatched processing power, quantum computing has the potential to revolutionize complex biological processes, crop modeling, and weather predictions. Precision genome editing is now possible because of technological advancements, ushering in crop kinds specifically bred to flourish in shifting climates and provide food that is incredibly nutrient-dense. These developments propel agriculture into a domain that was previously reserved for science fiction when combined with Industry 5.0.

The Deepening Fusion of Agriculture and AI

Every aspect of food production will be impacted by the ongoing integration of AI and machine learning into agriculture in ever more complex and varied ways. The most effective planting windows and market trends will be revealed by sophisticated forecasting models. The complicated dance between soil microbes, plants, and climate will be revealed by machine-learning algorithms, promoting soil health and nutrient cycling.

Robots driven by AI will take the stage, skillfully handling chores like the exact application of pesticides and the delicate harvesting of fruits. Field monitoring will change as drones powered by AI enable quick responses to new issues. Real-time nutritional advice and customized dietary recommendations will be made available to consumers thanks to AI-driven solutions.

Figure 8.11 displays how well a machine-learning model performed in forecasting the growth of crops over a given time frame. The y-axis shows the crop growth percentage, and the x-axis shows the time in weeks. The orange line on the graph indicates the anticipated crop growth produced by the machine-learning model, while the blue line on the graph represents the actual crop growth seen in the field. Both the actual and anticipated growth rates gradually rise in the first several weeks,

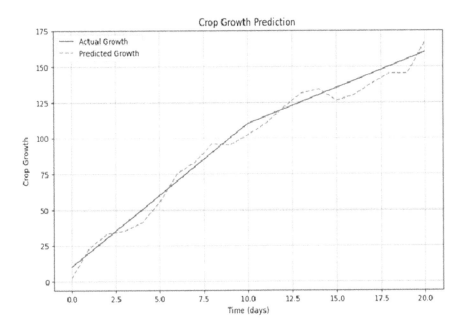

FIGURE 8.11   Crop growth prediction—actual vs. predicted

demonstrating how closely the model's predictions match actual observations. A small difference between the two lines can be seen as time goes on. The model's propensity to predict a faster growth rate than the actual field conditions is indicated by the predicted growth's slightly steeper slope.

The actual and expected growth rates significantly increase around the half-way point of the timeline, which could signify a time of good weather or efficient resource use. But as the crop cycle progresses, a significant difference between the actual and anticipated growth rates appears. The real growth begins to plateau while the anticipated growth stays very high, suggesting that the model may not be able to fully capture the later stages of crop development. The graph demonstrates the machine-learning model's initial ability to reasonably anticipate crop growth, but it also emphasizes the difficulties in continuing to make accurate predictions as the crop lifecycle develops. This visual comparison sheds important light on the model's advantages and weaknesses, highlighting the significance of ongoing improvement to boost its predictive power and support better agricultural decision-making.

8.11 CONCLUSION

The investigation of numerous aspects of agriculture under the aegis of Industry 5.0 illuminates a period of unmatched change and innovation. The landscape of agriculture is set for dramatic changes as cutting-edge technology, data analytics, and machine learning continue to merge. In the era of Industry 5.0, ethical concerns must be carefully navigated, from algorithmic prejudice and data privacy to equal access to technology. A futuristic perspective also exposes the incorporation of cutting-edge technologies outside of Industry 5.0, where quantum computing, synthetic biology and nanotechnology expand the potential for sustainable practices and crop development. Every aspect of food production is being revolutionized by the continued integration of AI and machine learning, from fine-grained market data to autonomous field monitoring, providing customers with customized experiences. It imagines a world where waste is reduced, resource-efficient crops thrive, and various ecosystems coexist peacefully with cutting-edge technologies. The benefits of this future, it's important to note, are extended through accessible technology and inclusive decision-making. In essence, Industry 5.0's integration of technology and agriculture results in a harmonic union of innovation and sustenance. All have the chance to guide in a new era of responsible and resilient food production by embracing these developments, and addressing global concerns while nourishing a growing population. The applications of Industry 5.0 in agriculture hold out hope for a future when development, ethics, and sustainability will come together to create a better world for all.

REFERENCES

1. Paschek, D., Luminosu, C.T. and Ocakci, E., 2022. Industry 5.0 challenges and perspectives for manufacturing Systems in the Society 5.0. In *Sustainability and Innovation in Manufacturing Enterprises: Indicators, Models and Assessment for Industry 5.0* (pp. 17–63).

2. Carayannis, E.G., Draper, J. and Bhaneja, B., 2021. Towards fusion energy in the Industry 5.0 and Society 5.0 context: Call for a global commission for urgent action on fusion energy. *Journal of the Knowledge Economy*, *12*(4), pp. 1891–1904.

3. Xu, X., Lu, Y., Vogel-Heuser, B. and Wang, L., 2021. Industry 4.0 and Industry 5.0— Inception, conception and perception. *Journal of Manufacturing Systems*, *61*, pp. 530–535.

4. Maddikunta, P.K.R., Pham, Q.V., Prabadevi, B., Deepa, N., Dev, K., Gadekallu, T.R., Ruby, R. and Liyanage, M., 2022. Industry 5.0: A survey on enabling technologies and potential applications. *Journal of Industrial Information Integration*, 26, p. 100257.

5. Devlet, A., 2021. Modern agriculture and challenges. *Frontiers in Life Sciences and Related Technologies*, *2*(1), pp. 21–29.

6. Kasinathan, P., Pugazhendhi, R., Elavarasan, R.M., Ramachandaramurthy, V.K., Ramanathan, V., Subramanian, S., Kumar, S., Nandhagopal, K., Raghavan, R.R.V., Rangasamy, S. and Devendiran, R., 2022. Realization of sustainable development goals with disruptive technologies by integrating Industry 5.0, Society 5.0, smart cities and villages. *Sustainability*, *14*(22), p. 15258.

7. Newman, B.A., Aronson, R.M., Srinivasa, S.S., Kitani, K. and Admoni, H., 2022. HARMONIC: A multimodal dataset of assistive human–robot collaboration. *The International Journal of Robotics Research*, *41*(1), pp. 3–11.

8. Yazdinejad, A., Zolfaghari, B., Azmoodeh, A., Dehghantanha, A., Karimipour, H., Fraser, E., Green, A.G., Russell, C. and Duncan, E., 2021. A review on security of smart farming and precision agriculture: Security aspects, attacks, threats and counter-measures. *Applied Sciences*, *11*(16), p. 7518.

9. Leveling, J., Edelbrock, M. and Otto, B., 2014, December. Big data analytics for supply chain management. In *2014 IEEE International Conference on Industrial Engineering and Engineering Management* (pp. 918–922). IEEE.

10. Ramirez-Asis, E., Vilchez-Carcamo, J., Thakar, C.M., Phasinam, K., Kassanuk, T. and Naved, M., 2022. A review on role of artificial intelligence in food processing and manufacturing industry. *Materials Today: Proceedings*, *51*, pp. 2462–2465.

11. Zhou, Y., Xia, Q., Zhang, Z., Quan, M. and Li, H., 2022. Artificial intelligence and machine learning for the green development of agriculture in the emerging manufacturing industry in the IoT platform. *Acta Agriculturae Scandinavica, Section B—Soil & Plant Science*, *72*(1), pp. 284–299.

12. Badillo, S., Banfai, B., Birzele, F., Davydov, I.I., Hutchinson, L., Kam-Thong, T., Siebourg-Polster, J., Steiert, B. and Zhang, J.D., 2020. An introduction to machine learning. *Clinical Pharmacology and Therapeutics*, *107*(4), pp. 871–885.

13. Alex David, S., Varsha, V., Ravali, Y. and Naga Amrutha Saranya, N., 2022. Comparative analysis of diabetes prediction using machine learning. In *Soft Computing for Security Applications: Proceedings of ICSCS 2022* (pp. 155–163). Singapore: Springer Nature Singapore.

14. Parpala, R.C. and Iacob, R., 2017. Application of IoT concept on predictive mainte-nance of industrial equipment. In *MATEC Web of Conferences* (Vol. 121, p. 02008). EDP Sciences.

15. Bhardwaj, A., Dagar, V., Khan, M.O., Aggarwal, A., Alvarado, R., Kumar, M., Irfan, M. and Proshad, R., 2022. Smart IoT and machine learning-based framework for water quality assessment and device component monitoring. *Environmental Science and Pollution Research International*, *29*(30), pp. 46018–46036.

16. Kyaw, K.S., Adegoke, S.C., Ajani, C.K., Nwabor, O.F. and Onyeaka, H., 2022. Toward in-process technology-aided automation for enhanced microbial food safety and qual-ity assurance in milk and beverages processing. *Critical Reviews in Food Science and Nutrition*, *62*(1), pp. 1–21.

17. He, Y., Gu, C., Chen, Z. and Han, X., 2017. Integrated predictive maintenance strategy for manufacturing systems by combining quality control and mission reliability analysis. *International Journal of Production Research*, *55*(19), pp. 5841–5862.

18. Kumar, K. A., and Kumar, S. R., 2016. Vision-based Vehicle Detection Survey. *International Journal of Recent Contributions from Engineering, Science and IT (iJES)*, *4*(1), pp. 31–35.

19. Tester, M. and Langridge, P., 2010. Breeding technologies to increase crop production in a changing world. *Science*, *327*(5967), pp. 818–822.

20. Kulkarni, S., Mandal, S.N., Sharma, G.S. and Mundada, M.R., 2018, September. Predictive analysis to improve crop yield using a neural network model. In *2018 international conference on advances in computing, communications and informatics (ICACCI)* (pp. 74–79). IEEE.

21. Usha, V., Saranya, J.C. and Ravikumar, S., 2017. Effective manless vehicle charging system with RFID. *International Journal of Civil Engineering and Technology*, *8*(9), pp. 733–740.

22. Ravikumar, S., David, S.A., Jothi, C.S., Usha, V. and Saravanan, K.A., 2017, August. Adolescent sheltered tracking to evade quandary via observant using android app. In *2017 IEEE International Conference on Smart Technologies and Management for Computing, Communication, Controls, Energy and Materials (ICSTM)* (pp. 151–154). IEEE.

23. Ravikumar, S. and Kannan, E., 2018. A swift unrest horde system for curtail SDO hit in cloud computing. *International Journal of Engineering and Technology (UAE)*, *7*(2), pp. 156–160.

24. Longo, F., Padovano, A. and Umbrello, S., 2020. Value-oriented and ethical technology engineering in industry 5.0: A human-centric perspective for the design of the factory of the future. *Applied Sciences*, *10*(12), p. 4182.

25. ElFar, O.A., Chang, C.K., Leong, H.Y., Peter, A.P., Chew, K.W. and Show, P.L., 2021. Prospects of Industry 5.0 in algae: Customization of production and new advance technology for clean bioenergy generation. *Energy Conversion and Management: X, 10*, p. 100048.

9 Novel Approaches for Applied Intelligent Systems in GIS

Elakkiya Elango, Mohamed Imran Kareem Basha,
B. Sundaravadivazhagan, and
Balasubramanian Shanmuganathan

9.1 INTRODUCTION

Artificial intelligence-geographic information system (AI-GIS) technology is now a significant field of study. However, the majority of studies only focus on one or two application scenarios and typically never include investigation and evaluation into the AI-GIS framework, therefore a quick summary regarding the AI-GIS software technological architecture is inadequate. To achieve this, Song Guanfu, President of SuperMap, emphasized the outcomes, and an instance for each component of the platform's development using the geo-intelligence pyramid offers the foundation of AI-GIS software technologies. He emphasized the expected development path of AI-GIS and clarified the design for AI-GIS application using SuperMap GIS as an example.

9.1.1 Geographic Information Systems

An AI-GIS is a combination that includes artificial intelligence and various GIS features, especially spatial data processing and analysis algorithms (GeoAI) that integrate AI, in addition to a general term embracing a variety of technologies that allow AI and GIS to cooperate. AI-GIS has been steadily becoming the primary focus of geoscience study and implementation in recent years as shown in Figure 9.1.

9.1.2 Geo-Intelligence Pyramid

Geo-intelligence is a broad term that encompasses geographic visualization, evaluation, decision-making processes, layout, as well as management that utilizes GIS, sensors, and satellite navigation technologies. The primary attribute which differentiates GIS from other kinds of data systems is geo-intelligence [1]. It contains four steps that enhance the geo-visualization, geo-decision, geographic-design, and

DOI: 10.1201/9781032642789-9

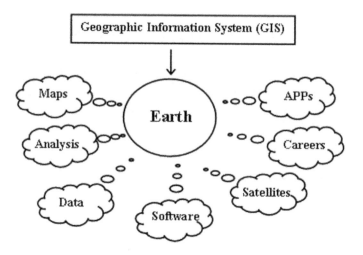

FIGURE 9.1 Geographic information system (GIS)

geo-control, each representing all parts of the geo-intelligence pyramid as illustrated in Figure 9.2. The intricacy of the pyramid increases from bottom to top, while maturity decreases. Geo-intelligence will usher in an era of technological advancement and produce more value through the advent of AI.

9.2 GEOAI UTILIZING LAND ANALYSIS

By using sophisticated methods of learning and integrating varied geospatial and environmental data, GeoAI has contributed significant improvements to urban land use research. [2] It employs a neural network (TR-CNN) to identify urban land use

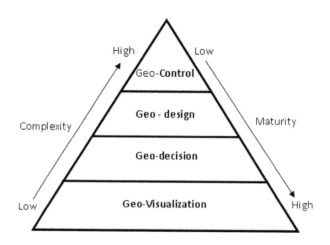

FIGURE 9.2 Geo-intelligence pyramid

patterns by fusing remote sensing data with high spatial and temporal accuracy time-series electrical data that incorporate socioeconomic aspects [3]. It uses a combined classification technique that utilizes vector-based buildings as well as POIs, as well as an improved graph convolution neural network (GCNN) and a Word2Vec approach, to classify urban functional areas, achieving more accurate classification compared to a single-source data-driven application and being multisource data collection techniques. Gevaert and Belgiu (2022) utilize a supervised classification model, Fully Convolutional Network (FCN), to analyze the resemblance of testing and training photographs for land use categorization and building identification in three African cities [4].

Pan et al. (2022) examine urban expansions by combining a convolution neural network (U-Net) as well as a recurrent neural network (LSTM), resulting in high-accuracy zoning categorization because of U-Net's multi-scale nearby information and LSTM's longitudinal data regarding past urban expansion. GeoAI is utilized in land use research across usual settings, like coastal lands and wetlands, alongside urban land use classifications. For example, De Carvalho et al. (2022) use multi-spectral panoptic segmentation using WorldView-3 photographs to identify items in beach environments, allowing for specific mapping and enumeration of tourist infrastructure and background aspects of beach locations [5].

Chen et al. (2022) use tasseled cap transformation and morphological investigation of multi-temporal remote sensing photographs to gather coastal knowledge and analyze the temporal and spatial development of the archipelago shoreline [6]. The strategy efficiently handles suspended sediments and complicated coasts, and it gives insights into the archipelago's coastal preservation efforts. Jamali et al. (2022) use a deep learning framework that utilizes 3D Generative Adversarial Networks (3D GAN) and Vision Transformers to perform wetlands identification with few training variables, which holds significant promise for massive amounts of remote sensing wetland classification [7].

9.3   GEO-INTELLIGENCE AND AI USING GIS

There has been an enormous connection between AI with GIS throughout the decade before this one. Although GIS is a strong technology with enormous amounts of artificial intelligence enables improved approaches for GIS projects by using data and a wide range of AI applications. The term "AI-GIS" describes the fusion of AI technology with various GIS processes, such as spatial data analysis algorithms (GeoAI), which combine AI technology and a number of AI and GIS-enabled technologies.

In recent years, geoscience research and applications have increasingly focused on AI-GIS. A cost-effective solution to the current intelligence difficulty facing GIS systems was to use AI-GIS to enhance and sustain the next stage of growth for GIS technology platforms [8]. AI-GIS initially began to achieve visual collection of geographical data from pictures and videos of satellite images. In addition, AI technologies like voice recognition and synthetic speech may be launched, leading to increased empowerment.

9.3.1 WHEN AND WHY SHOULD WE USE GIS?

GIS serve as excellent training datasets over AI systems because they include an enormous amount of information based on geographical location. In view of recent advancements in computing technology and image recognition, this artificial intelligence is acceptable [9]. Additionally, there have been multiple successful attempts to utilize GIS and AI to reduce pollution and fend off disease. Satellite communication images offer data at a wide range of levels of specificity, which is vastly underused. Yet, there are additionally some issues with identifying roadways, structures, and various other things. Another example of simplified applications includes the utilization of GIS and Internet of Things (IoT) information to offer practical responses to urban industrial challenges. These platforms may also collect information from public entities, including health surveys and environmental measures.

9.3.2 ANTHROPOGENIC LIMITATIONS

Data science, machine learning, and geography expertise are required for both users and administrators of GIS systems. The fundamentals of the industry in which they operate must be understood by experts, and they must be able to work collaboratively with experts from other fields [10]. The majority of the moment, these end-users don't have a strong grasp of GIS systems; therefore they cannot give effective assistance and seldom supply significant finances.

9.3.3 GIS IN 2D AND 3D

In 2010, cloud-based GIS services gained popularity because they allowed users to store and distribute geographic data on remote servers, increasing GIS's usability and scalability. It saw a widespread usage of Google Earth that showed viewpoints and 2D and 3D information. It didn't take long for GIS to show that 3D GIS were also useful and practical. Even though the expected GIS could handle and analyze 3D vector data, the procedure was lengthy and difficult and could handle merely simple 3D data. By 2010, it was possible to use GIS to create straightforward 3D scenarios, such as offshore wind farms, in which depths and sea levels could be precisely represented together with additional data.

Vertical coordinate systems and ISO time and date standards were introduced for the initial time of 2D and 3D. As a result, the utilization of GIS in conjunction with additional geospatial technologies like remote sensing, LiDAR, and drone photography increased. Technologies like Pix4D, Drone2Map, and other mapping applications remained accessible for transforming the survey data to shareable formats via GIS until a few years later, in 2010. The precision farming and agricultural sectors have expanded as a result of being capable of visualizing and managing the agricultural estate using a GIS-based structure, as well as crop, yield, and meteorological expertise, as well as the development of IoT sensors that might provide real-time feedback across regions such as pest control.

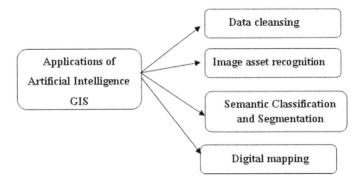

FIGURE 9.3   Applications of AI-GIS

9.4   APPLICATIONS OF AI-GIS

Artificial intelligence in GIS has a wide range of application scenarios as shown in Figure 9.3.

GIS are sophisticated computer systems that aid with the capturing; gathering, storing, verifying, processing, analysis, and management of data related to geography (for example, vector data, raster imagery, grid data, and others). These programs present a wide range of data, like roads, structures, plants, and others. GIS is utilized by hundreds of thousands of organizations worldwide to build precise charts, communicate information, spot challenges, monitor changes, handle and react to emergent incidents, and recognize patterns. Additional applications that use this complex software involve epidemic control, climate forecasting, assessing the potential for energy from renewable sources, and handling logistics, among other commonplace applications such as mobility (Uber, Lyft, Bolt, FlightRadar) and food delivery (Glovo Delivery, Uber Food, Bolt Food), in addition to the Armed Forces.

- *Data cleansing*
  When missing or incorrect data must be removed from assets that are hidden under the surface, data cleansing and augmentation require time. Engineers typically retain GIS service data—a generally active gathering of different kinds of (historical) data—instead of saving it. This is where machine learning may give the utility of business with distinct benefits.
- *Image asset recognition*
  Image-recognition technology that was recently taught to identify particular assets and validate how assets are interrelated is used to analyze the image collections. The program additionally evaluates typeface attributes and measures meters like gas pressure from images [5]. When photographs contain a geotag, image-recognition software functions well; however, it can also work when images have links to particular items within a GIS. Beyond that, we must establish the relevant asset type solely on the image, and finally validate and fix the data within the GIS database.

- *Semantic Classification and Segmentation*
  Image segmentation and classification are additional significant GIS components. These enable geographical observation, namely infrastructure design, network extraction, land cover, and other tasks [11]. Artificial intelligence used for automated vision may help in examining pixels, segmenting them into segments based on related spectral properties, grouping segments into objects, and classifying objects.
- *Digital mapping*
  Numerous graphics exist within the utilities GIS field, often representing various network circumstances. Instead of automatically supplying the appropriate information into a GIS framework, sketch data of different uses and standards is typically manually stored in the utility asset registration process. Data professionals may utilize machine learning techniques to identify and fix poor data circumstances [12]. An algorithm, for example, may determine which lacking valve type needs to be installed while examining the diameter of the connected pipes. Considering numerous obstacles in advance, it might be tough to properly train AI to become perfectly suited for these roles.

9.4.1 AI-GIS Technology System

The first functional layer of the AI-GIS is made up of the three components that were previously specifically specified (see Figure 9.4).

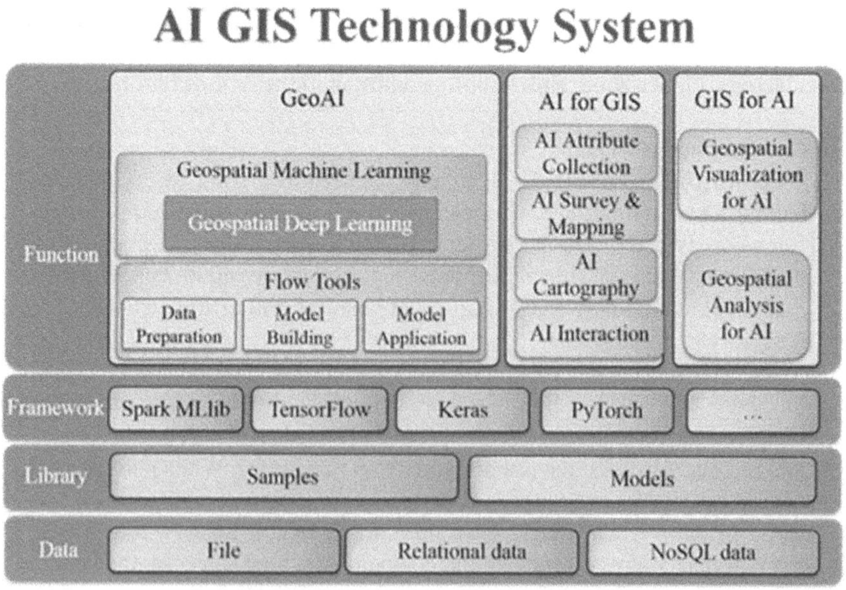

FIGURE 9.4   AI-GIS technology systems

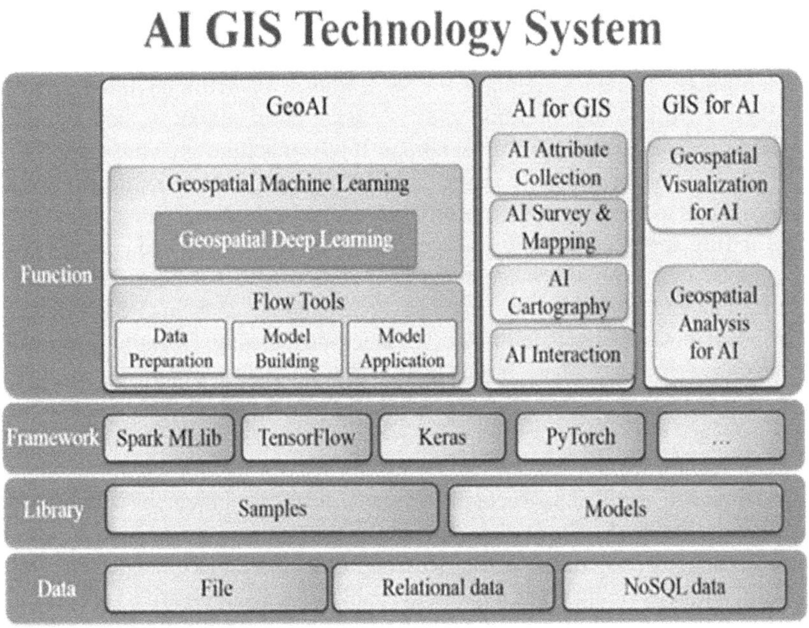

AI GIS Technology System

Function	GeoAI			AI for GIS	GIS for AI
	Geospatial Machine Learning			AI Attribute Collection	Geospatial Visualization for AI
	Geospatial Deep Learning			AI Survey & Mapping	
	Flow Tools			AI Cartography	Geospatial Analysis for AI
	Data Preparation	Model Building	Model Application	AI Interaction	

Framework	Spark MLlib	TensorFlow	Keras	PyTorch	...

Library	Samples	Models

Data	File	Relational data	NoSQL data

FIGURE 9.5 AI-GIS technology system

Four-layer architecture could be built from the bottom upwards to establish a rather full AI-GIS technology framework with the goal of efficiently handling the three aspects of AI-GIS. The data layer occupies the bottom, and then comes the domain-specific library. The structure of the layers has the capacity to appropriately combine and include a variety of artificial intelligence platforms.

AI technology should be thoroughly linked with various GIS software programs, including Components GIS, Portable GIS, Server GIS, and others, in order to jointly develop the AI-GIS product architecture depicted in Figure 9.5.

9.4.2 AI Technologies in GIS

In the past ten years, as digitization has rapidly permeated every business, GIS have been significantly and favorably impacted by a variety of modern innovations, including artificial intelligence [13]. In recent times, enhanced GIS including embedded artificial intelligence has grown critical in geoscience research.

Among the technologies used are:

- **Handwritten text recognition (HTR)**—Handwriting recognition (HWR), at times referred to as HTR, is the ability of computers to handle and analyze legible handwriting input that comes from sources that include paper documents, photographs, touch screen, and other devices.
- **Optical character recognition (OCR)**—The process of converting a text picture into a machine-readable text format is known as OCR. When we

scan a form or receipt, for example, our computer stores the scan as an image file.

- **Computer vision**—Computer vision, a subset of artificial intelligence, allows robots to interpret and analyze visual data, emulating how people see and comprehend their surroundings. It uses machine learning models to recognize and categorize items in digital photos and videos before allowing computers to respond to the information individual's view.
- **Machine and deep learning**—Deep learning solves issues and makes forecasts by using computer-generated neural networks that have been influenced by and mimic the human brain. The spatial analysis in GIS continues to grow mostly dependent on ArcGIS machine learning. Utilizing geo-processing technology, these methods and tools have been effectively applied to address problems in three key areas. We could employ vector machine techniques to generate land-cover classification layers using classification.
- **Face recognition**—Face recognition using AI is a method based on computer vision utilized to recognize an individual or object in a video or image. It employs a variety of technologies such as deep learning, computer vision algorithms, and image processing. Face detection, recognition, and verification techniques are utilized to enable systems to identify, recognize, and verify faces in digital photos or videos. The technology is growing in popularity in a wide range of applications, including Smartphone gaining access, door unlocking, passport verification, surveillance systems, medical devices, and so on. Machines may even recognize emotions based on their facial expressions.
- **Speech recognition**—Whenever we utilize smartphones and tablets, we generally need to enter a huge amount of text information. Keyboard inputs and handwritten inputs are both of the most common typing options. However, the limited input speed associated with both of these methods has a significant influence on GISers' job efficiency. According to the investigation's results, the keyboard input speed is below 40 characters per minute. There are also additional issues, such as the difficulty in learning Chinese phonetics for unusual characters, accents, and dialects. Speech recognition is an innovative input method offered by SuperMap iMobile. It represents the industry's top multi-scene speech recognition technique. It is capable of transferring "sounds" to "characters." As a result, the input efficiency is considerably improved.
- **Virtual reality**—A specific field of study involves developing VR apps that provide accurate visualizations of information about traffic, with an emphasis on their value for managing traffic. The combination of actual time data and virtual reality enables traffic controllers to further readily examine various modes of transportation as well as obtain the capacity to anticipate trends according to past or expected patterns. Applying it in web-based technology also provides for better data exchange, since managers and individuals utilizing transportation can easily get relevant data. APCRDA has integrated 3D developing model information, resident data,

and real-time and historical traffic reports into its platform, enabling an effective comprehension of metropolitan areas in which all that from present traffic structures to up-to-date residential data can be utilized within a human–computer interaction.

Complex data-intensive applications have grown into a major challenge for VRGIS, especially since these applications include spatial query operations to make it easier to find needed multi-dimension data, permitting users to more effectively take benefit of analytical features inside GIS whereas retaining VR visualization. Addressing this difficulty has entailed the use of multitasking simultaneous scheduling techniques which can analyze complex information more rapidly rather than merely looking at large amounts of data. Such technologies enable speedier data processing, allowing visuals and query data to emerge faster than in conventional PC contexts. In reality, data has grown complicated in architecture and in volume, and VR systems are uniquely suited to visualizing such complicated data in its right aspects.

- **Artificial creativity**—AI, as defined by Ed Newton-Rex in his post Innovative AI—a reading list, is the simulation of machine intelligence. Similarly, Innovative AI represents the emulation of innovation in robots.

9.4.3 AI's Role in GIS and Mapping

With the emergence of AI, the area of GIS as well as connecting has gone through a significant transformation in recent years. AI has proved to be a game-changer in GIS and mapping because it can analyze enormous quantities of geospatial data, detect emerging trends and patterns, classify imagery from satellites, and streamline tasks including related emergence as well as information processing. The present study investigates the role of AI in GIS and mapping, focusing on its possible advantages and implications [14]. AI may analyze massive volumes of geographical data to detect trends and patterns.

With an exponential increase of geographic data, it is becoming more and more challenging to efficiently handle and analyze this data [15]. However, AI-powered algorithms are able to help in addressing this difficulty by simplifying the data processing process. For example, AI may be used to analyze satellite photos to recognize alterations to land cover, detect regions of deforestation or urbanization, and track the environmental effects of natural catastrophes. Furthermore, AI may be utilized to analyze data from social networks, retagged pictures, and various other geographic data sources to uncover patterns and trends in human behavior, such as migration patterns or urbanization trends. Machine learning algorithms may be trained to recognize things such as houses and roads in satellite data.

Finding objects in satellite images has previously entailed manual interpretation, which can be time-consuming and prone to mistakes [16]. However, AI-powered machine learning algorithms may be trained to accurately identify items in satellite photos. These machine learning algorithms, for example, may be taught to recognize buildings, roads, and other types of infrastructure, which can be helpful for urban planning, disaster recovery, and various other purposes. Furthermore, the application of AI in satellite imagery processing can assist in minimizing the cost and time necessary for manual interpretation. AI-powered GIS technologies may assist in automating operations like map development and data processing, enhancing mapping productivity and accuracy.

Mapping is an essential component of GIS and entails the generation of maps as well as the analysis of geographical data. However, creating maps and processing data may be time-consuming and tiresome, especially when working with large volumes of data. AI-powered GIS solutions can assist in automating these operations, lowering the amount of time and effort necessary for map construction and data processing. AI, for example, may be used to build maps automatically depending on user-defined factors such as surface area or land usage. Furthermore, AI may be used to process and analyze geographical data, including terrain models, in order to extract useful information. AI can additionally be employed for the analysis and processing of geographical data, including terrain models, in order to find appropriate data, including as elevation or slope.

9.4.4 Knowledge-Based Expert System-GIS Development

Expert Systems Based on Knowledge GIS is characterized as a combined GIS and Expert System which is specifically built to respond to the three questions [17]. The GIS component is made up of two major components that help solve the "What" and "Where" inquiries: the GIS databases and the analysis of spatial data. The expert system element is made up of two essential modules that help address the "Why" question: the database of knowledge and the inference engine. An expert system's knowledge base is constructed using the results of knowledge acquisition in the manner of production rules. The production strategy is made up of heuristic sets. The employing of IF ... THEN phrases to convey information or rules by which a system can be handled is a common feature of heuristics.

A basic understanding processing tool forming an expert system's aspect is a mechanism for inference. Its major goal is to integrate facts and regulations in order to produce, deduce, or make inferences regarding novel information. If knowledge base guidelines are particular to a given subject or expertise, inference engine rules are more generic controls and searching techniques for generating conclusions determined by evaluation, sorting, and pruning mechanisms. The integration module, which connects the GIS spatial analysis and inference engine via the GIS database and knowledge base, is the most significant component of a knowledge-based GIS [18]. For expert system processing in this study, ERDAS Macro Language (EML) was employed.

9.4.5 Challenges Facing Continued Development
and Implementation of GIS

Even while it is inspiring to consider what we may do in the future, it is not possible without some manual exertion. In order to ensure that significant sectors are managed and given authority, organizations and regulations will need to be put in place. The need for exact and high-quality data is one of GIS's problems. The accuracy and correctness of the data must be ensured via GIS. Even while small quantities may be possible, expanding this worldwide will require careful consideration.

The need to merge data from numerous sources, forms, and platforms is a further challenge for GIS. GPS, survey information, satellite photos, and other data sources are all used by GIS. Integrating this data can be time-consuming and challenging [19]. It will be crucial to standardize information formats via steering groups and international laws in order to make sure that GIS data is able to be communicated and utilized effectively across systems. The growing usage of GIS has raised major questions about data safety and confidentiality. GIS data protection is essential since it usually includes sensitive information, including location data.

The creation and use of GIS require a high level of technical knowledge. Making sure there are enough skilled professionals available to develop and maintain GIS systems is extremely tough. Additionally, it may be expensive to create and maintain GIS systems and financing and other resources for these systems might be difficult to come by. Data formats have to be standardized in order to guarantee that GIS data can be reliably shared and utilized throughout various platforms.

9.4.6 Comparative Analysis of GIS: Demand, Forecasts, and Research

We have seen an enormous increase in attention as well as the need for geospatial information systems over the last few years. The utilization of cloud technology and the growing accessibility of useful geographical information are major factors in how widely used it is [20]. The rising desire for personalized enterprise geographic information systems is an additional significant influencing element. Based on the aforementioned variables, researchers forecast that the sector would create $24,607.7 million in revenue by 2030. IS a technique providing an effective way to examine and comprehend social and environmental issues?

More researchers are utilizing remote sensing and other specialized techniques primarily as a result of the accessibility of numerous reliable information, quick and effective analyses of the collected data, and solutions that facilitate the sharing of discoveries. The continuous deployment of nanosatellites, used to collect data via known as radio occultation, an approach for detecting temperatures, etc., is a case study of the real-world application of contemporary GIS software. For instance, in 2010, the University of Southern California scientists developed and launched nanosatellites, such as CAERUS, that became a part of the NASA satellite MAYFLOWER in 2010.

9.4.7 Raising Investments in GIS Solutions

Over the past few years, governments have invested more in GIS applications. Additionally, the United Nations issued its geospatial plan for 2021–2022, in April 2021, with the purpose of facilitating the availability of location data for many sectors. The goal is to make geographic information management investments and

TABLE 9.1
GIS Market Scope

GIS Market

Report Coverage	Details		
Base Year:	2022	Forecast Period:	2023–2029
Historical Data:	2018 to 2022	Market Size in 2022:	US $ 10.24 Bn
Forecast Period 2023 to 2029 CAGR:	12.5%	Market Size in 2029:	US $ 23.37 Bn
Segments Covered:	By component	Hardware Software	
	By function	Mapping Surveying Telematics and Navigation Location-Based Services	
	By application	Aerospace and Defense Oil and Gas Exploration Water and Wastewater Government Agriculture Construction Utilities and Mining Transportation & Logistics Engineering & Business Services Oil and Gas Refining Telecommunications Healthcare	

consumption easier. Additionally, this approach attempts to strengthen collaboration across analytical entities and information providers, enabling integrated situational awareness to handle emergencies and improving the exchange of data between them. Although the market outlook through 2029 depends using the actual output, demand, and availability of 2022 as shown in Table 9.1, 2022 statistics are also approximated on the basis of the genuine numbers released by major companies as well as all significant participants worldwide.

9.5   CONCLUSION

The current artificial intelligence problem of GIS systems may be effectively solved by using AI-GIS to design and upgrade the next-generation GIS technology platforms. The first application of AI-GIS was the computer vision acquisition of geographic data from remote sensing photos and videos. Additionally, one might realize greater empowerment by using AI technologies like speech recognition and language processing. GeoAI is a fast-expanding area with several potential future paths. A handful of these approaches are listed below. To begin, most AI approaches are now used to perform pre-defined and very precise geographical analytic objectives.

Can there be a generic GeoAI assistant, akin to Amazon's Alexa or Google Assistant? What about Apple's Siri? A GeoAI helper of this type may be able to grasp a GIS practitioner's demands, automatically formalize and describe tasks, and select relevant tools from a broad GIS toolbox. Second, because most AI models currently are built on a training dataset, they inherently inherit any possible bias in the data. In geographic research, training data are frequently obtained from a specific geographic region, making it challenging for models that were trained using data from one geographic area to function effectively with data from other places.

As a result, one significant aim is to enhance model architectures (or the training process) such that the resulting GeoAI models may be transported across diverse geographic locations. Third, most previous GeoAI research just uses AI approaches to solve geographic challenges rather than developing or discovering novel approaches. Although this can be good for solving challenges, geographers must not only acquire methodologies from other fields but also export geographic knowledge into additional domains. To capture the distinctiveness, geographically informed or spatially explicit AI models might be constructed.

9.6 FUTURE IN GIS AI

All things considered, the future of GIS is pretty bright. As more organizations understand the immense commercial value geospatial data can provide, it is primed toward even broader scale use than that which has occurred in previous generations. As data analytics, mobility, augmented reality, and the Internet of Things continue to grow and take off throughout the globe, we can anticipate geographic information science and technology not only being revolutionized, but additionally to positively influencing how organizations use these advances. One of the guiding principles of USC's graduate GIS degrees and certifications is to educate students for the future, regardless of how related technologies advance.

REFERENCES

1. Kruiger, J. F., Kasalica, V., Meerlo, R., Lamprecht, A. L., Nyamsuren, E., Scheider, S. Loose programming of GIS workflows with geo-analytical concepts. *Transactions in GIS* 2021, 25(1), 424.
2. Liu, T., Yao, L., Qin, J., Lu, N., Jiang, H., Zhang, F., Zhou, C. Multi-scale attention integrated hierarchical networks for high-resolution building footprint extraction. *International Journal of Applied Earth Observation and Geoinformation* 2022, 109, 102768. https://doi.org/10.1016/j.jag.2022.102768.
3. Ahmad, I., Dar, M. A., Andualem, T. G., Teka, A. H., Tolosa, A. T. GIS-based multi-criteria evaluation for deciphering of groundwater potential. *Journal of the Indian Society of Remote Sensing* 2020, 48(2), 305.
4. Gevaert, C. M., Belgiu, M. Assessing the generalization capability of deep learning networks for aerial image classification using landscape metrics. *International Journal of Applied Earth Observation and Geoinformation* 2022, 114, 103054. https://doi.org/10.1016/j.jag.2022.103054.
5. Ferreira de Carvalho, O. L., Abílio de Carvalho Júnior, O., Olino de Albuquerque, A., Nickolas Castro, S., Leandro Borges, D., Luiz, A. S., Gomes, R. A. T., Guimarães, R. F. Multispectral panoptic segmentation: Exploring the beach setting with worldview-3 imagery. *International Journal of Applied Earth Observation and Geoinformation* 2022, 112, 102910. https://doi.org/10.1016/j.jag.2022.102910.

6. Chen, C., Liang, J., Xie, F., Hu, Z., Sun, W., Yang, G., Jie, Y., Chen, L., Wang, L., Wang, L., Chen, H., He, X., Zhang, Z. Temporal and spatial variation of coastline using remote sensing images for Zhoushan archipelago, China. *International Journal of Applied Earth Observation and Geoinformation* 2022, 107, 102711. https://doi.org/10.1016/j.jag .2022.102711.

7. Jamali, A., Mahdianpari, M., Mohammadimanesh, F., Homayouni, S. A deep learning framework based on generative adversarial networks and vision transformer for complex wetland classification using limited training samples. *International Journal of Applied Earth Observation and Geoinformation* 2022, 115, 103095. https://doi.org /10.1016/j.jag.2022.103095.

8. Iddianozie, C., McArdle, G. Towards robust representations of spatial networks using graph neural networks. *Applied Sciences* 2021, 11(15), 6918.

9. Bosisio, A., Berizzi, A., Merlo, M., Morotti, A., Iannarelli, G. A GIS-based approach for primary substations siting and timing based on Voronoi diagram and particle swarm optimization method. *Applied Sciences* 2022, 12(12), 6008.

10. Lunga, D. Artificial intelligence tools and platforms for GIS. The Geographic Information Science & Technology Body of Knowledge (4th Quarter 2019 Edition), John P. Wilson (ed.) 2019, https://doi.org/10.22224/gistbok/2019.4.16.

11. Muhadi, N. A., Abdullah, A. F., Bejo, S. K., Mahadi, M. R., Mijic, A. Deep learning semantic segmentation for water level estimation using surveillance camera. *Applied Sciences* 2021, 11(20), 9691.

12. Xu, C., Li, F., Xia, J. Fusing high-resolution multispectral image with trajectory for user next travel location prediction. *International Journal of Applied Earth Observation and Geoinformation* 2023, 116, 103135.

13. Alastal, A. I., Shaqfa, A. H. GeoAI technologies and their application areas in urban planning and development: Concepts, opportunities and challenges in smart city (Kuwait, study case). *Journal of Data Analysis and Information Processing* 2022, 10(2), 110–126.

14. Janowicz, K., Gao, S., McKenzie, G., Hu, Y., Bhaduri, B. GeoAI: Spatially explicit artificial intelligence techniques for geographic knowledge discovery and beyond. *International Journal of Geographical Information Science* 2020, 34(4), 625.

15. Baer, M. F., Purves, R. S. Window Expeditions: A playful approach to crowdsourcing natural language descriptions of everyday lived landscapes. *Applied Geography* 2022, 148, 102802.

16. Anisha, P. R., Kishor Kumar Reddy, C., Nguyen, N. G., Bhushan, M., Kumar, A., Hanafiah, M. M. *Intelligent Systems and Machine Learning for Industry Advancements, Challenges, and Practices*. CRC Press, 2022.

17. Sadly, M., Hendiarti, N., Sachoemar, S. I., Nurdin, N., Faisal, Y., & Awaluddin, A. Application of knowledge-based expert system model for fishing ground prediction in the tropical area. The Second APEC Workshop of SAKE. https://karya.brin.go.id/id/ eprint/12361/.

18. Zhang, Z., Song, Y., Luo, P., Wu, P. Geocomplexity explains spatial errors. *International Journal of Geographical Information Science* 2023, 37(7), 1449–1469.

19. Liu, Z., Guan, R., Hu, J., Chen, W., Li, X. Remote sensing scene data generation using element geometric transformation and GAN-based texture synthesis. *Applied Sciences* 2022, 12(8), 3972.

20. Zhao, G., Li, Z., Yang, M. Comparison of twelve machine learning regression methods for spatial decomposition of demographic data using multisource geospatial data: An experiment in Guangzhou City, China. *Applied Sciences* 2021, 11(20), 9424.

10 Federated Learning-Based Variational Auto-Encoder for Prediction of Breast Cancer in Cloud-Based Healthcare 5.0

Santosh Kumar, Tarunika Sharma, Balasubramanian Prabhu Kavin, and Gan Hong Seng

10.1 INTRODUCTION

Global healthcare systems are expected to undergo a significant transformation as a result of digital technologies in modern healthcare. Smart healthcare links individuals, services, and organizations through digital technology, navigates health data swiftly, and responds right away to the needs of the medical environment [1]. The numerous parties involved in the medical system—patients, doctors, hospitals, and insurance companies—all gain from smart healthcare's capacity to connect them. Artificial intelligence (AI), the Internet of Things (IoT), fog figuring computation cloud services, army blockchain observing machines, 5G technology, and the IoMT are examples of new and developing technologies that make this possible [2]. These technologies must assist with the shift to the healthcare 5.0 paradigm. Deprived of the requirement for computer-to-computer or human-to-human contact, it is now possible to communicate data via a network, which has aided in protecting data transmission, managing responsibilities, assessing opportunities, and connecting devices [3]. Healthcare 5.0 will be significantly impacted by the IoT. Medical IoT equipment is already widely used by healthcare institutions for online patient record sharing. There are several novel sensor-based IoT applications being employed in healthcare, each with unique properties [4]. The IoHT, IoNT, and IoMT, for example—all abbreviations for numerous internet-based health and cognitive healthcare framework—were made possible by the IoT [5].

Therefore, contemporary IoT variations provide networked healthcare, enabling the smooth integration of contemporary medical devices and the distant, comprehensive interchange of health information [6]. For instance, the concept of traditional

DOI: 10.1201/9781032642789-10

healthcare has changed into "smart healthcare" due to the availability of technology that enables a monitoring system in medical services [7]. In sequence to improve the standard of care they offer, healthcare practitioners will be able to somewhat hook up to, analyze, and assess the well-being info sensed by biomaterials and interactional wearable technologies via variations of the IoT [8]. As a result of evolving digital technology and gadgets, portable healthcare is emerging, enabling wireless communication and aiding patients with chronic illnesses outside of healthcare facilities. Therefore, biosensors have a lot of potential as instruments for managing and detecting diseases [9, 10].

In recent years, breast cancer has become the highest cause of death among women. 15% of all deaths in women are caused by breast cancer [11]. The World Health Organization (WHO) predicts that 2.7 million additional cases of breast cancer will occur globally by 2040 [12]. Many developing countries are fearful of this scenario as a result of the COVID-19 epidemic's burden on hospital employees [13]. Early cancer diagnosis can be challenging, thus techniques that could improve accurate breast cancer detection are continuously being researched. An accurate discovery of cancer can lead to a quicker treatment and an increase chance of survival. Mist computing services are necessary for the development of improved living conditions [14]. Furthermore cloud computing can help patients, the elderly, and relatives with disabilities in far-off towns and towns where there are few medical facilities and resources [15]. Breast cancer patients in these areas commonly receive incorrect diagnoses, and by the time they locate a physician in a larger city, it is typically too late. Using cloud computing, doctors may diagnose patients who are unable to see them in person due to financial constraints [16]. Mist computing can be used for communicating through telehealth and telemedicine, which involves transmitting and receiving biomedical images and audio-visual footage, from smaller less equipped sites to larger sites, where specialized physicians and sizable hospitals are located.

Essential services like a fast search tool for blood and organ donors as a backup are also made possible by cloud computing [17].

In this study, features are retrieved using a combination of AlexNet and GLCM and utilized to classify breast cancer using FL-VAE. The validation analysis uses a publicly accessible dataset. The rest of the chapter is structured as follows: Relevant works are described in Section 10.2, and a brief clarification of the suggested model is provided in Section 10.3. Section 10.4 provides an investigation of the projected model's compatibility with current methodologies. Finally, Section 10.5 provides the work's conclusion.

10.2   RELATED WORKS

Transfer deep learning with an assured IoMT-founded technique is taken into consideration by Abbas et al. [18]. In the smart healthcare sector, the Google network's deep machine-learning tool is utilized for precise illness prediction. Using this, we can predict cancer in the human body simply and reliably using an IoMT-based transfer approach. Additionally, the consequences of the recommended secure

IoMT-based transfer learning methodologies are used to confirm the best cancer detection forecast in the industry. In comparison to prior approaches used in the smart healthcare industry for cancer prediction, the recommended safe IoMT-based transfer learning strategy obtained 98.8%, which is highest.

In order to safeguard patient data and ensure speedy data transfer, Abbas et al. [19] suggested an intelligent system for the identification of lung illnesses incorporating federated learning entwined with an edge strategy. In the projected intelligent scheme, lung illness is predicted using federated deep extreme machine-learning data. A deep approach is applied to improve the suggested model's demonstration of lung disease prediction. The simulation and output are governed by the MATLAB 2020a implementation. By using the proposed federated learning model, the smart healthcare model is developed for predicting the most common cancer called lung cancer. The proposed fused extreme machine-learning algorithm produced a result of 97.2%, which is superior to the most recent techniques that have been published.

Natarajan et al. [20] developed a special energy-efficient routing protocol (ECC-EERP) based on elliptic curve cryptography in order to deliver an energy-efficient system for ECC-EERP, a key-based encryption technique that can be used to encrypt data. Pairs of keys are used to encrypt and decrypt web traffic, which reduces the amount of energy used by a WSN overall. Analysis evaluated the effectiveness of the recommended approach in comparison to a number of other current methods. Utilizing common attributes and effects, such as security encryption throughput energy effectiveness, network life cycle communication overload, processing time, and running cost, the proposed technique was assessed. The consequences show that the suggested technique provides improved safety and power efficiency.

Nigar et al. [21] offer a unique IoT-based fusion approach for the early identification and monitoring of six major chronic diseases, including COVID-19, heart disease, brain tumors, and Alzheimer's. This approach takes other factors into account. The outputs from various ML models are assessed using performance measures, including accuracy. With the use of benchmark and real-world datasets, the suggested technique is verified in a cloud-based environment. ANOVA tests were used in the statistical analysis of the datasets to demonstrate that there are notable differences in the accuracy consequences of various classifiers. This will facilitate the early identification of chronic conditions by healthcare experts.

Lilhore et al. [22] introduced an IoT cloud-based system that is chiefly based on fuzzy cluster-focused augmentation and an optimum support vector machine set in order to anticipate infection through routine inspection and enhance the quality of healthcare by providing recommendations. The recommended model effectively segments pictures using the fuzzy clustering approach, with a focus on transition region filtration. In order to identify the characteristics of the transition period region and extract features from it, SVMs are also utilized. The testing of parameter optimization, feature selection, and optimal SVM are the three elements of the experimental phase. The suggested enhanced SVM methodology beat various machine-learning methods, feature selection, precision, TPR, FPR, and F1-score, rendering to the trial phase results.

To address the challenge of recognizing early-stage cancer, Ogundokun et al. [23] introduced a medical IoT-based diagnostic system that successfully distinguishes between malignant and benign individuals in an IoT situation. Support was used as a baseline classifier for comparison. Then, to discriminate between malignant and benign tumors, ANN with hyperparameter tuning was employed. Because they directly alter the behavior of the effectiveness of machine-learning models, hyperparameters are algorithms. When employing MLP and SVM to recover the classification presentation of the breast cancer dataset, we use a feature selection approach called unit swarm optimization (PSO). A grid-based search was used to discover the ideal hyperparameter value for CNN and ANN models. The hypothesis was tested using the WDBC dataset. With CNN and ANN, the suggested perfect has a classification accuracy of 98.5% and 99.2%, respectively.

10.3 PROPOSED SYSTEM

10.3.1 CLOUD-BASED BREAST CANCER DIAGNOSIS PERFECT

The creation of a cloud-based breast cancer discovery system is suggested in this chapter, along with health information monitoring for the recognition of cancer. When examining data kept on cloud servers, the approach is adaptable and sufficient to detect and categorize a range of ailments. But the main focus of this investigation was the categorization of the illness as "cancerous" or "noncancerous." Figure 10.1 depicts the general layout of the model design that we suggest. The patient visits a nearby remote healthcare facility, where a healthcare service provider gathers the patient's data, including x-rays and extra well-being indicators, and then delivers the data to a medic through the internet. A cloud-based application is then used by the doctor to submit the patient's data for additional analysis. analysis and management.

Processing takes place twice in the cloud. Researchers in the past have demonstrated that attribute choice enhances the effectiveness of machine knowledge techniques.

10.3.2 FEATURE EXTRACTION

10.3.2.1 Gray-Level Co-Occurrence Matrix (GLCM) Topographies

For textural characteristics, GLCM is used [24]. It offers a thorough analysis of the image. It determines how two brightness levels in a picture are related to one another. The co-occurrence matrix is created first, and then the texture characteristics are calculated, to calculate the GLCM. The first step is to calculate the investigation of the GLCM between two adjacent values using the displacement $d = 1$ and the angles = ($0°$, $45°$, $90°$, $135°$). The co-occurrence matrix is then employed to extract a number of statistical variables, the specifics of which may be found in the work by Sadad et al. [25].

10.3.2.2 AlexNet Architecture

A variant of the CNN paradigm is the AlexNet architecture [26]. Five convolutional layers were utilized to create the proposed AlexNet model. Because WBCD pictures

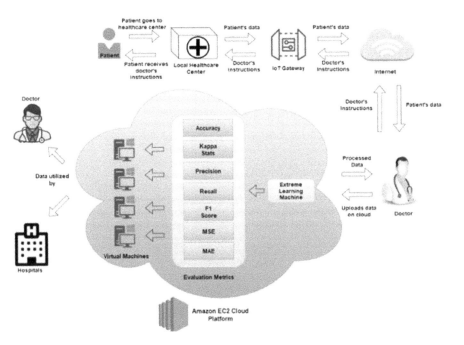

FIGURE 10.1 Components of the proposed architecture

are provided consistent with the AlexNet architecture, this approach is used after transforming the WBCD from two dimensions to three dimensions. As a result, before being entered into CNN's layers, pictures are converted into three dimensions. Additionally, the AlexNet model has an FC8 layer as well; however, it only contains 1024-dimensional features. So, for the purpose of extracting 4096 characteristics from each picture in the MIAS database supplied to the AlexNet architecture, we take into account the FC6 and FC7 layers. We are interested in the maximum accuracy and the amount of automatically calculated extracted characteristics. The proposed AlexNet architecture is shown in Figure 10.4.

10.3.2.3 Fusion of Features

The object's capacity to be interpreted or classified may only be limited to one feature extraction approach [27]. However, this feature fusion produces a unique lesion categorization descriptor. As a result, before performing the classification stage in the proposed technique, we concatenated GLCM and AlexNet features. As a result, we were able to create the fusion (Alexnet, GLCM) characteristics that are shown in Equation (10.1). In the end, 5016 three-dimensional characteristics were completed, as shown in Table 10.1.

$$Fusion_{(Alexnet, GLCM)} = Conc\left[Feature_{AlexNet}, Feature_{GLCM}\right] \qquad (10.1)$$

TABLE 10.1
Fusion Feature Explanation

Features	Explanation	Size
GLCM	Feature second-order technique	1×20
AlexNet	Produce deep topographies	1×4096

10.3.3 FEDERATED LEARNING MODEL

The system's two subsystems are the clients (certain hospitals/GH) and the central server (cloud). The middle waitron gives the clients the initial load values to commence the federated learning educating process. Following one or more phases of exercise by each client, the obtained data are broadcast to the server for update after being aggregated from all users. The middle server does this via FedAvg. The FedAvg technique essentially averages the data gathered from all clients. This is supported by

$$w_{k+1} = \sum_{c=1}^{C} \frac{n_c}{n} \nabla w_c \qquad (10.2)$$

where w_{k+1} is the reorganized weights provided by the dominant attendant in the $_{k+1}$th is the masses sent by client c to the middle server. The limit n shows the entire sum of opinions used in a global model, whereas the parameter n_c shows the client c.

This iterative process among clients and server lasts until the required level of training accuracy is attained. The middle waitron transmits the revised data back for training. This procedure demonstrates how FedAvg tries to fit a general perfect to the data of the clients, and how perfect based on the volume of data is utilized for training. As can be seen, this uses a three-layer IoT design. Smart indicators that detect energy use and transmit it to the central server make up the perception and network levels. A middle waitron that does calculations on the data received from the client is part of the application layer. The internet protocol suite TCP/IP and MQTT are used by the smart device to transfer data to the main server. Each smart gadget queries the central server for weight updates and uploads weight data to it. Throughout this work, each smart device is described by its specific client. Deep learning-based VAE performs the prediction process, which is described in the section below.

10.3.3.1 CVAE

Kingma et al. created the Variational Auto-Encoders (VAE) model, which enhances the latent variable of the auto-encoder [28]. A deep Bayesian network, which combines statistics and neural networks, serves as the foundation for the variational auto-encoder. The fundamental principle of VAE is that the hidden variable z is programmed to follow a certain conventional customary delivery, in contrast to auto-encoders (AE). Due to its constraint on latent variable independence, the VAE feature extraction approach could be more effective.

The CVAE used in this study is to replace the fully connected layer of the VAE with a convolutional layer and a pooling layer, where the encoder and decoder are convolutional neural networks (CNN). As a consequence, the computational and learning capabilities of the system are considerably enhanced while the geographical information of the input data is preserved.

The loss function formula and the CVAE model's architectural layout are shown in Figure 10.2. The unseen variable's mean and variance are indicated by Conv2D, and each section of the hidden variable follows the associated common sharing $N_{x,x2}$. Resampling is used, and the network includes $N_{0,I}$ Gaussian noise.

The latent variable quantity z is obtained by:

$$z = \mu + \sigma \Delta \varepsilon \tag{10.3}$$

where the element-wise multiplication symbol, stands for the Hadamard operator.

To maximize the confirmation lower constrained (*ELBO*), it might be stated as follows:

$$ELBO = E_{z \sim q(z|x)} \left[\log p(x|z) \right] - KL\left[q(z \mid x) \parallel p(z) \right] \tag{10.4}$$

Where $KL[]$ stands for the Kullback-Leibler difference, which calculates the change relating to two distributions, and $E_{zq(z|x)}$ [] is a calculated expectation calculator. Please consult the available literature [29] for further information about ELBO.

The network's loss function may be represented as the following Equation (10.5) after being simplified.

$$L^*(\theta) = KL[q(z \mid x) \mid p(z)] + \varsigma L(x, y; \theta) \tag{10.5}$$

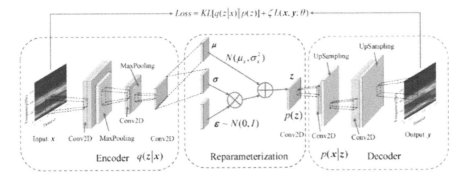

FIGURE 10.2   Construction of CVAE perfect

The hyperparameter combines the two components of the loss function. The projected delivery $q_{(z|x)}$ of the encoder, which may be described by KL divergence, is different. This difference is represented by the hidden layer loss, which is the first component. KL is computed as follows after being streamlined.:

$$KL[q(z \mid x) \mid\mid p(z)] = \int \left(q(z|x) \log \frac{q(z|x)}{(z)} \right) dz$$
$$= \int (q(z|x) \log q(z|x) - q(z \mid x) \log p(z)) dz \qquad (10.6)$$
$$= \frac{1}{2} \sum_{i=1}^{N} \left(\sigma_i^2 + \mu_i^2 - 1 - \log \sigma_i^2 \right)$$

The argument involving the input and output files is represented by the second component, the reconstruction loss. The RMSE, which is determined using Equation (10.7), is typically employed.

$$RMSE = \sqrt{\frac{1}{n} \sum_{i=1}^{n} (y_i - \hat{y}_i)^2} \qquad (10.7)$$

A destruction level is established as the criterion to determine whether the data includes abnormalities. The harm is regarded as being existent when the RMSE exceeds this limit. According to Ren et al.'s investigation, the self-confidence maximum is presented as the break maximum under the assumption that RMSE follows the common break $N_{r,r}$. The following is the formula:

$$L_{1-a} = \mu_r + Z_{1-a} \sigma_r \qquad (10.8)$$

where $_r$ and $_r$ stand for the mean and RMSE, respectively, and L_{1-a} is the upper confidence limit. The upper bound of the one-misleading sureness interval of $_{1-a}$ is the confidence level of Z_{1-a}. Z_{1-a} may be determined using statistical information as follows.:

$$Z_{1-a} = \frac{t_{1-a}(n-1)}{\sqrt{n}} \qquad (10.9)$$

The preferred value for an in this model is 0.05, which denotes that the sample data may be regarded as normal then that the RMSE is within the one-weighted 95% self-confidence intermission. If not, the data might be deemed odd and could point to damage to the tunnel.

10.4   RESULTS AND DISCUSSION

10.4.1   CLOUD ENVIRONMENT

The ELM simulations that were assessed on a separate system were deployed in the cloud. The major goals of moving the simulations to the bank of the cloud were to shorten the execution time and improve accuracy. Additionally, moving the models to the cloud makes them accessible from anywhere at any time. The LINUX operating system is the foundation for all of the virtual computers utilized in the cloud environment. Later, the outcomes from the standalone system and cloud environment were compared.

Additionally, the Amazon EC2 cloud infrastructure was used to put up this process. While other elements such as the amount of CPUs, and RAM changed, Ubuntu (Canonical Ltd., London, United Kingdom) functioned as the operating logic for the virtual system that ensued wrought on the rain cloud program. We utilized instances with the m4.xlarge and c5.xlarge Intel Xeon (Intel CPUs). To choose the highlighted subset, Weka 3.8 (University of Waikato, Innovative Zealand) was utilized [30].

10.4.2 STANDALONE ENVIRONMENT

The hardware setup for the standalone system that was utilized to conduct the experiment was as follows: 8 GB of RAM; an Intel i5-7200 u processor with a 1 TB hard drive. Using PyCharm integrated development environment ver. 2020.2 (JetBrains s.r.o., Prague, Czech Republic) [31] in this setting, multiple classification models were developed on the WBCD dataset and assessed using a variety of assessment criteria.

10.4.3 COLLECTION OF DATA

The investigation made use of the WBCD [32] dataset. The diagnostic property indicated whether the 569 items in the dataset were malignant or benign. The 32 properties are described in Table 10.2.

These qualities' serial numbers ranged from 24 to 29, then from 29 to 8, then from 8 to 28, then from 4 to 5, from 15 to 7, from 12 to 14, and finally from 27 to 14.

10.4.4 PERFORMANCE MEASURE

The WI Chest Cancer Finding (WBCD) [32] dataset was used in the investigation. The 569 objects in the dataset were classified as diagnostic characteristics. Table 10.2 provides descriptions of the 32 attributes.

Real positive occurrences that are appropriately categorized as positive are referred to as true positive (TP). The false positive (FP) is that the categorized true positive is actually a false negative (FN).

The symbols in Equations (10.10), (10.11), (10.12), and (10.13) stand for of ACC, F-m, PR, and RC.

$$Accuracy = \frac{TN + TP}{TP + TN + FN + FP} \times 100 \tag{10.10}$$

$$F - measure / F - Score = \frac{2TP}{\left(2TP + FP + FN\right)} \times 100 \tag{10.11}$$

TABLE 10.2
Dataset Explanation

Account	Attribute Name
Id Sum	Id
The analysis of tissues (M = malignant, B = Benign)	Diagnosis
Mean of distances from the perimeter	Radius_Mean
Standard nonconformity of grayscale standards	Texture_Mean
Mean scope of the core tumor	Perimeter_Mean
Mean part of the core tumor	Area_Mean
Mean of local variation in range lengths	Smoothness_Mean
Mean of $perimeter^2/area$—1	Compactness_Mean
Mean of the harshness of the concave slice of the contour	Concavity_Mean
Mean concave helpings of the outline	Concave points_mean
Mean for $coastline\ estimate$—1	Fractal_dimension_mean
Deviation of the circumference's distances to the center in standard deviation	Radius_se
Standard mistake for SD for grayscale standards	Texture_se
error for local differences in area lengths	Smoothness_se
Standard error for $perimeter^2/area$—1	Compactness_se
Standard mistake for harshness of concave helpings of the contour	Concavity_se
Standard error concave servings of the contour	Concave points_se
Standard error for $coastline\ estimate$—1	Fractal_dimension_se
"worst" or major mean worth for the nasty of perimeter	Radius_worst
"worst" standard deviation of grayscale morals	Texture_worst
"worst" or largest nasty worth for resident variation length	Smoothness_worst
"worst" or major mean worth for $perimeter^2/area$—1	Compactness_worst
"worst" or largest mean value for the harshness of concave helpings of the outline	Concavity_worst
"worst" or prime mean value for the sum of concave helpings of the contour	Concave points_worst
"worst" rate for $coastline\ estimate$—1	Fractal_dimension_worst

TABLE 10.3
Confusion Matrix

	Predicted Positive	Predicted Negative
Actual Positive	True Positive (TP)	False Positive (FP)
Actual Negative	False Negative (FP)	True Negative (TN)

$$Precision = \frac{TP}{\left(FP + TP\right)} \times 100 \qquad\qquad (10.12)$$

$$Recall = \frac{TP}{\left(FN + TP\right)} \times 100 \qquad\qquad (10.13)$$

Table 10.4 represents feature extraction analysis. In this analysis we used different metrics and models to evaluate the presentation. The LeNet model reached an accuracy range of 79.67, a precision rate of 78.14, a recall range of 84.92, and finally a f-measure calculation of 80.72, respectively. Then the ResNet model reached an accuracy range of 80.24, a precision rate of 84.17, a recall range of 86.66, and finally a f-measure calculation of 88.28, respectively. Then the VGGNet model reached an accuracy range of 86.86, a precision rate of 91.94, a recall range of 95.61, and finally an f-measure calculation of 95.78 consistently. Then the AlexNet model reached an accuracy range of 94.13, aprecision rate of 96.84, a recall range of 97.24, and finally a f-measure calculation of 98.97, respectively.

Table 10.5 in the preceding section indicates that the Validation Analysis of the Proposed Classifier was performed. During the investigation of the DBN model, the accuracy range reached 90.24, the precision rate reached 91.47, the recall range reached 92.89, then the f-measure calculation reached 93.41. After that, the AE model arrived at an accuracy of 94.47, a precision rate of 95.14, a recall range of 95.68, and an f-measure calculation of 95.27. Finally, the f-measure calculation was successful. The VAE model eventually arrived at an accuracy of 95.78, a precision rate of 96.79, a recall rate of 96.74, and finally a f-measure calculation of 96.49. The FL-CVAE then arrived at an accuracy range of 96.57, as well as a precision degree of 97.48, a recall range of 97.69, and finally an f-measure calculation of 98.35, respectively.

10.5   CONCLUSION

Using FL-CVAE as a classifier, this chapter provided a system for cloud-based breast cancer detection. Because the healthcare sector may use the system at any time,

---

TABLE 10.4
Feature Extraction Analysis

Feature Extraction with GLCM	Parameter Evaluation			
	Accuracy (%)	Precision (%)	Recall (%)	F-measure (%)
LeNet	79.67	78.14	84.92	80.72
ResNet	80.24	84.17	86.66	88.28
VGGNet	86.86	91.94	95.61	95.78
AlexNet	**94.13**	**96.84**	**97.24**	**98.97**

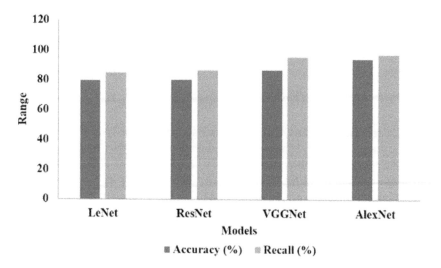

FIGURE 10.3   Graphical comparison of the proposed FE model

cloud computing got benefits from these sectors. It can offer continuous services everywhere and at any time. Additionally, the cloud environment offers resources that raise the suggested model's total classification accuracy. The key benefit of FL-CVAE is that the suggested approach is entirely unsupervised and does not need data collected in a variety of scenarios to train the network. In this context, this study proposed a cloud-based architecture for the diagnosis of breast cancer, which collected the data of the patient at remote healthcare centers and sent the data using cloud services to specialist doctors for analysis. We used a variety of classifiers to diagnose breast cancer using the WBCD dataset. Additionally, the suggested

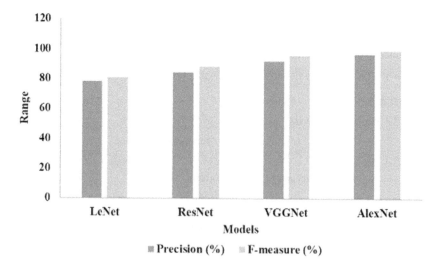

FIGURE 10.4   Analysis of various pre-trained models

TABLE 10.5
Validation Analysis of Proposed Classifier

Classifiers	Parameter Assessment			
	Accuracy (%)	Precision (%)	Recall (%)	F-measure (%)
DBN	90.24	91.47	92.89	93.41
AE	94.47	95.14	95.68	95.27
VAE	95.78	96.79	96.74	96.49
FL-CVAE	96.57	97.48	97.69	98.35

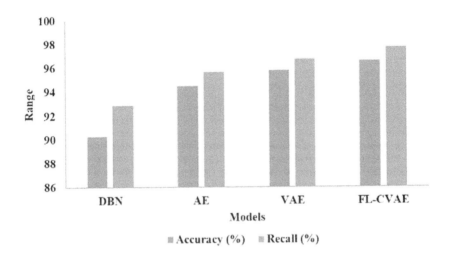

FIGURE 10.5   Classification analysis

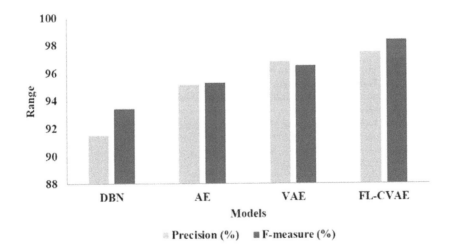

FIGURE 10.6   Graphical comparison of different models

approach was implemented on the EC2 cloud stage. As a result, cloud computing will offer a reliable platform in this situation since it offers more precision and faster execution times than a standalone platform. The FL-CVAE approach based on the cloud outperforms other strategies, according to the findings obtained on the WBCD dataset. The best performance results of FL-CVAE were taken from both the standalone and cloud environments, and a comparison has been made. The accuracy reached was 0.96, the recall was 0.97, the precision was 0.97, then the f-measure was 0.98, according to the experimental data. In the future, this framework may be expanded to perhaps improving categorization accuracy.

REFERENCES

1. Gopal, V. N., Al-Turjman, F., Kumar, R., Anand, L., & Rajesh, M. (2021). Feature selection and classification in breast cancer prediction using IoT and machine learning. *Measurement*, 178, 109442.
2. Memon, M. H., Li, J. P., Haq, A. U., Memon, M. H., & Zhou, W. (2019). Breast cancer detection in the IOT health environment using modified recursive feature selection. *Wireless Communications and Mobile Computing*, 2019, 1–19.
3. Liu, Q., Liu, Z., Yong, S., Jia, K., & Razmjooy, N. (2020). Computer-aided breast cancer diagnosis based on image segmentation and interval analysis. *Automatika*, 61(3), 496–506.
4. Salvi, S., & Kadam, A. (2021, March). Breast Cancer Detection Using Deep Learning and IoT Technologies. *Journal of Physics: Conference Series*, 1831(1), 012030.
5. Savitha, V., Karthikeyan, N., Karthik, S., & Sabitha, R. (2021). A distributed key authentication and OKM-ANFIS scheme based breast cancer prediction system in the IoT environment. *Journal of Ambient Intelligence and Humanized Computing*, 12(2), 1757–1769.
6. Talari, A. C., Rehman, S., & Rehman, I. U. (2019). Advancing cancer diagnostics with artificial intelligence and spectroscopy: Identifying chemical changes associated with breast cancer. *Expert Review of Molecular Diagnostics*, 19(10), 929–940.
7. Zahir, S., Amir, A., Zahri, N. A. H., & Ang, W. C. (2021, February). Applying the deep learning model on an IoT board for breast cancer detection based on histopathological images. *Journal of Physics: Conference Series*, 1755(1), 012026.
8. ELOUERGHI, A., BELLARBI, L., Amal, A. F. Y. F., & TALBI, T. (2020, March). A novel approach for early breast cancer detection based on embedded micro-bioheat ultrasensitive sensors: IoT technology. In *2020 International Conference on Electrical and Information Technologies (ICEIT)* (pp. 1–4). IEEE.
9. Kaur, P., Kumar, R., & Kumar, M. (2019). A healthcare monitoring system using random forest and internet of things (IoT). *Multimedia Tools and Applications*, 78(14), 19905–19916.
10. Muhsen, I. N., Rasheed, O. W., Habib, E. A., Alsaad, R. K., Maghrabi, M. K., Rahman, M. A., ... Hashmi, S. K. (2021). Current status and future perspectives on the Internet of Things in oncology. *Hematology/Oncology and Stem Cell Therapy*. https://doi.org /10.1016/j.hemonc.2021.09.003
11. Klyushin, D., Golubeva, K., Boroday, N., & Shervarly, D. (2021). Diagnosis of breast cancer by malignant changes in buccal epithelium using artificial intelligence, Internet of things, and cloud storage. In *The Fusion of Internet of Things, Artificial Intelligence, and Cloud Computing in Health Care* (pp. 67–85).

12. Suresh, A., Udendhran, R., Balamurgan, M., & Varatharajan, R. (2019). A novel internet of things framework integrated with real time monitoring for intelligent healthcare environment. *Journal of Medical Systems*, 43(6), 1–10.

13. Zuluaga-Gomez, J., Al Masry, Z., Benaggoune, K., Meraghni, S., & Zerhouni, N. (2021). A CNN-based methodology for breast cancer diagnosis using thermal images. *Computer Methods in Biomechanics and Biomedical Engineering: Imaging and Visualization*, 9(2), 131–145.

14. Din, I. U., Almogren, A., Guizani, M., & Zuair, M. (2019). A decade of Internet of Things: Analysis in the light of healthcare applications. *IEEE Access*, 7, 89967–89979.

15. Malathi, P., & Kalaivani, A. (2021). A survey on early detection of women's breast cancer using IoT. In *Ai Innovation in Medical Imaging Diagnostics* (pp. 208–219). IGI Global.

16. Kumar, Y., Gupta, S., & Gupta, A. (2021, November). Study of machine and deep learning classifications for IOT enabled healthcare devices. In *2021 International Conference on Technological Advancements and Innovations (ICTAI)* (pp. 212–217). IEEE.

17. Pradhan, K., & Chawla, P. (2020). Medical Internet of things using machine learning algorithms for lung cancer detection. *Journal of Management Analytics*, 7(4), 591–623.

18. Abbas, T., Fatima, A., Shahzad, T., Alissa, K., Ghazal, T. M., Al-Sakhnini, M. M., ... Ahmed, A. (2023). Secure IoMT for disease prediction empowered with transfer learning in healthcare 5.0, the concept and case study. *IEEE Access*.

19. Abbas, S., Issa, G. F., Fatima, A., Abbas, T., Ghazal, T. M., Ahmad, M., ... Khan, M. A. (2023). Fused weighted federated deep extreme machine learning based on intelligent lung cancer disease prediction model for Healthcare 5.0. *International Journal of Intelligent Systems*, 2023, 2023. https://doi.org/10.1155/2023/2599161

20. Natarajan, R., Lokesh, G. H., Flammini, F., Premkumar, A., Venkatesan, V. K., & Gupta, S. K. (2023). A novel framework on security and energy enhancement based on Internet of medical things for Healthcare 5.0. *Infrastructures*, 8(2), 22.

21. Nigar, N., Jaleel, A., Islam, S., Shahzad, M. K., & Affum, E. A. (2023). IoMT meets machine learning: From edge to cloud chronic diseases diagnosis system. *Journal of Healthcare Engineering*, 2023, 2023. https://doi.org/10.1155/2023/9995292

22. Lilhore, U. K., Simaiya, S., Pandey, H., Gautam, V., Garg, A., & Ghosh, P. (2022). Breast cancer detection in the IoT cloud-based healthcare environment using fuzzy cluster segmentation and SVM classifier. In *Ambient Communications and Computer Systems: Proceedings of RACCCS 2021* (pp. 165–179). Singapore: Springer Nature Singapore.

23. Ogundokun, R. O., Misra, S., Douglas, M., Damaševičius, R., & Maskeliūnas, R. (2022). Medical internet-of-things based breast cancer diagnosis using hyperparameter-optimized neural networks. *Future Internet*, 14(5), 153.

24. Rehman, A. (2021). "Light microscopic iris classification using ensemble multi-class support vector machine." *Microscopy Research and Technique*, 84(5), 982–991.

25. Sadad, T., Hussain, A., Munir, A. et al. (2020). "Identification of breast malignancy by marker-controlled watershed transformation and hybrid feature set for healthcare." *Applied Sciences*, 10(6), 1900.

26. Krizhevsky, A., Sutskever, I., & Hinton, G. E. (2012). "ImageNet classification with deep convolutional neural networks." *Advances in Neural Information Processing Systems*, 25. https://proceedings.neurips.cc/paper/2012/file/c399862d3b9d6b76c84 36e924a68c45b-Paper.pdf

27. Abunadi, A. A., Albraikan, J. S., Alzahrani et al. (2022). "An automated glowworm swarm optimization with an inception based deep convolutional neural network for COVID-19 diagnosis and classification." *Healthcare*, 10(4), 697.

28. Kingma, D. P., & Welling, M. Auto-encoding variational bayes. arXiv:1312.6114.
29. Xu, H., Chen, W., Zhao, N., Li, Z., Bu, J., Li, Z., Liu, Y., Zhao, Y., Pei, D., Feng, Y. (23–27 April 2018). Unsupervised anomaly detection via variational auto-encoder for seasonal kpis in web applications. In *Proceedings of the 2018 World Wide Web Conference*, Geneva (pp. 187–196).
30. Frank, E., Hall, M. A., & Witten, I. H. (2016). *The WEKA Workbench. Online Appendix for "Data Mining: Practical Machine Learning Tools and Techniques"*, 4th ed. Burlington: Morgan Kaufmann.
31. PyCharm: The python IDE for professional developers by JetBrains. https://www.jetbrains.com/pycharm/.
32. Lahoura, V., Singh, H., Aggarwal, A., Sharma, B., Mohammed, M. A., Damaševičius, R., ... Cengiz, K. (2021). Cloud computing-based framework for breast cancer diagnosis using extreme learning machine. *Diagnostics*, 11(2), 241.

11 Securing the MANET by Detecting the Intrusions Using CSO and XGBoost Model

*V. S. Anusuya, Swathi Baswaraju,
Arunadevi Thirumalraj, and A. Nedumaran*

11.1 INTRODUCTION

The prevalence of malicious software makes it extremely difficult to design intrusion detection systems (malware) [1]. A tool for tracking and looking into computer system occurrences is the intrusion detection system. An IDS contains sophisticated tools as well as modeling and anomalous behavior discovery approaches. They attempt to ascertain whether or not the network is experiencing any malicious activity [2]. The benefit of utilizing and installing the IDS is that it examines all network traffic going in and out and finds any security issues [3]. IDS can be divided into two categories based on the methods used for data gathering and for detection. Network-based IDS (NIDS) and host-based IDS (HIDS) are two different types of IDS that are based on the method of data collection [4]. The HIDS aims to monitor computer systems' internal operations. The goal of the NIDS is to monitor the network traffic logs in real time [5]. Depending on how they detect threats, IDS solutions can be categorized into three categories: hybrid, anomaly, and signature. In general, known assaults respond well to a signature-based strategy, while unknown attacks respond well to an anomaly-based approach. Because it can identify zero-day threats and requires fewer human inputs, anomaly-based IDS detection has an edge in the Internet of Things. The hybrid strategy incorporates both approaches based on anomalies and signatures [6].

Due to the fact that MANETs are typically self-configuring, infra-structureless networks, any attackers can directly target them [7]. The (IoT) can be thought of as an umbrella that incorporates key features of wireless sensor networks (WSN) and MANET and functions as an interface to the cloud or the internet [8]. The medium is easily observable, the network topology is dynamic, the networking protocols depend on the dispersed cooperation of the nodes, and the nodes have limited capabilities, making wireless MANETs particularly vulnerable to attackers [9].

DOI: 10.1201/9781032642789-11

ML-based models are effective in increasing scalability and reducing energy use [10]. Teams of IDS developers use a range of methods for detecting and preventing intrusions. A handful of these tactics concentrate on machine learning techniques. ML systems are able to predict and identify attacks before they become serious cyber risks [11]. In order to classify or value attacks, ML techniques first discover their statistical characteristics using tiny amounts of data [12]. Labeled datasets are needed for machine learning (ML) approaches in order to train a classification or prediction mode [13]. This research developed a method for detecting MANET intrusions using an ML classification algorithm that exploits the randomly fluctuating nature of network statistics.

The contributions of this paper are,

- The datasets are pre-processed using CSE-CIC-IDS2018 datasets.
- Cat Swarm Optimization is performed for feature selection.
- A scalable ML model XGBoost classifier is used for classification of MANET intrusions.
- After classification, grasshopper optimization (GOA) is used to perform optimal selection for the weight of XGBoost.

The remaining sections of the study are organized in the form of shadows: The relevant works are summarized in Section 11.2, the suggested model is briefly explained in Section 11.3, the results and validation analysis are shown in Section 11.4, and the summary and conclusion are provided in Section 11.5.

11.2   RELATED WORKS

In a paper by Ninu [14], a Deep Neuro-Fuzzy Network-based method for MANET vulnerability scanning based on the Exponential Henry Gas Solubility Optimization is presented. The freshly developed EHGSO algorithm is used in the early phases of safe routing to select the optimum routes. These four fitness metrics—power, duration, neighborhood quality, and connection quality—are used to assess the effectiveness of this tactic. The proposed EHGSO combines Exponential Weighted Moving Average (EWMA) and Henry Gas Solubility Optimization (HGSO). During the second step, which entails altering the sent data packets and extracting Knowledge Engineering in Databases (KDD) features, the intrusion detection phase begins at the base station. Following the extraction of the KDD features, data augmentation takes place. Before executing the intrusion detection, the Deep Neuro-Fuzzy Network is trained using the suggested EHGSO approach. The proposed method outperforms any existing technology. When factors like energy, throughput, packet loss, jitter, performance and development review (PDR), precision, and recall are taken into account, the suggested approach yields values of 0.342 J, 134,975 kbps, 4.123, 0.086, 95.877%, 0.950, and 0.924 in the absence of attacks.

The "Malicious Packet Dropping Attack" on the network layer is examined in research by Vijayalakshmi et al. [15]. We propose a novel strategy game theory to counter this assault. The proposed system monitors the behavior of the neighboring nodes and overcomes limitations like false positives inherent in standard IDS in order to offer safe communication between nodes that connect with each other in order to process traffic from source to destination. Even in the vicinity of hostile nodes, the suggested method raised packet delivery by 42%.

Additional elements of this study include the network setup, sample labeling, feature extraction, data creation, intrusion detection method, and performance reliability evaluation model. These are all covered in a paper by Prasad et al. [16]. The assessment model calculates the defined system of based processes using a fuzzy logic system after assessing the functionality and hardware reliability of intrusion detection methods. The results show that, as a result of an uneven sample ratio, while one statistical performance grows, another statistical performance lowers. The two top results have thus been examined by the suggested evaluation model. It rates intrusion detection systems and offers a comparison with a rough performance as scheme reliability. The experimental results show that the suggested detection methodology outperforms existing methods in retaining high scheme dependability.

A study by Abbood et al. [17] focused on security standards by determining efficiency, identifying malicious nodes, and mitigating network attacks using the three presented algorithms: the Cascading Back Propagation Neural Network (CBPNN), FNN, and CBPNN. It used MANET to recognize complex patterns (FFNN). These fundamental types of deep neural network (DNN) building designs, in addition to CNN, are frequently applied to enhance the performance of IDS and the usage of IDS in conjunction with ML. Additionally, ML approaches offer MANET network learning capabilities and promote adaptation to various settings above their statistical and logical counterparts. The proposed model performs better end-to-end (E2E) and average receiving packet (ARP) metrics when compared to another current model. The results were 74%, 82%, and 85% from CBP, FFNN, and CNN, respectively.

In order to improve IDS in MANET, a study by Meddeb [18] provides a stacked auto-encoder technique. The study recommends a stacked auto-encoder-based technique for MANET in order to lessen correlation and model pertinent properties with high-level representation (Stacked AE-IDS). This method creates the output using an auto-encoder, and then feeds it to a DNN classifier to duplicate the input with reduced correlation (DNN-IDS). The proposed Deep Learning-based IDS harnesses the majority of probable assaults that can hinder the routing capabilities of mobile networks and concentrates on denial-of-service (DoS) attacks within the suitable allowed that really are available for intrusion prevention. The suggested Stacked AE-IDS technique increases IDS's ability to recognize attacks in MANETs by reducing correlation. The suggested strategy is particularly pertinent for MANET security since it focuses on DoS attacks and how they affect routing services in mobile networks. The suggested Stacked AE-IDS method could be used to increase IDS efficiency and hence increase MANET security. This method can be used to identify various attacks, including DoS attacks, and their effects on the routing services offered by mobile networks.

For the purpose of precisely predicting the classified label, this research will use integrated optimization and classification approaches. This framework includes the operational modules of pre-processing, feature extraction, optimization, and classification by Prashanth [19]. The initial step in pre-processing is to add missing values to the input datasets and normalize the contents of duplicate cells. Then, the principal component analysis (PCA) method is utilized to choose the collection of characteristics that will improve the performance of the classification. In order to choose the most ideal characteristics based on the best fitness value, the Gray Wolf Optimization (GWO) technique is used, which lowers the total complexity of IDS. Last but not least, the classification results are used to determine if attacks or normal outcomes will occur using the DCNN technique. The generated results are then compared to present condition models, and a number of performance criteria were reviewed throughout the investigation to validate the results.

11.3   PROPOSED WORKS

11.3.1   PROPOSED ID SYSTEM

There are four basic steps in the suggested effective IDS. Pre-processing from the original IDS dataset constitutes the first step of the suggested methodology. Using Cat Swarm Optimization (CSO), the second stage involves feature selection. The third stage uses XGBoost to implement traditional ML classifiers for intrusion detection, while the fourth stage makes use of GOA for optimization. The proposed IDS system utilizes the modern real-time heterogeneous CSE-CIC-IDS 2018 dataset and combines the advantages of the capable XGBoost with ML. Each stage is thoroughly described in the following subsections.

11.3.2   DATA PRE-PROCESSING

The suggested IDS framework's initial phase is represented by this. The ten days of tagged flow make up the CSE-CIC-IDS2018. More than 80 attributes may be extracted from the raw IDS dataset using CICFlowMeter-V3 and saved in CSV format for subsequent use in network traffic analysis. Initially, just a small number of factors like IP address and time stamp have a marginal effect on whether network traffic is malicious or benign in CSE-CIC-IDS2018. This study has removed this column of the property because the IDS categorizes network traffic based on its behavioral characteristics. This also removes the timestamp feature because it has little effect on training the network. The dataset was then split into train, test, and validation groups. For a rapid evaluation of the model, the validation data is helpful. Utilizing test data, the model is ultimately evaluated after being trained with training data. It is acknowledged that the CSE-CIC-IDS2018 is a diversified real-world IDS dataset that is frequently insufficient because it lacks necessary specialized characteristics, or feature values, or is simply cumulative. Outliers or errors are concealed by noise, and name as well as code differences are concealed by inconsistent noise. This chapter has adopted over-sampling as a solution to the imbalance problem, which requires increasing the number of instances of the minority class by arbitrarily repeating them in order to show a stronger representative of the minority group throughout the sample. No data is removed, despite the risk of overfitting the data. However, it outperforms the under-sampling strategy. The trained and tested datasets utilized in this investigation are listed in Table 11.1.

TABLE 11.1
Distribution of Training and Test Data

Class	attack categorization	Testing	Flow Quantity	Training
DoS attacks	DoS-attacks-Hulk	4667	466,664	18,667
—	DDoS attacks LOIC-UDP	346	1730	1384
DDoS attacks	DDoS attacks- GoldenEye	4151	41,508	16,603
—	SQL-injections	17	87	70
—	FTP-Brute force	122	611	489
Brute force	SSH-Brute force	46	230	184
—	DoS-attacks-SlowHTTPTest	13,989	139,890	55,956
Benign	—	12,698	12,697,719	50,791
—	Brute-Force-XSS	1876	187,589	7504
—	DDoS attacks HOIC	6860	686,012	27,441
Infilteration	Infilteration	1620	161,934	6478
—	DDoS attacks LOIC-HTTP	5762	576,191	23,048
Bot	Bot	2862	286,191	11,448
—	DoS-attacks Slowlories	1099	10,990	4396
Web attack	Brute-Force-Web	3867	193,360	15,469
Total	—	57,782	15,450,706	231,127

11.3.3 FEATURE SELECTION

The application of feature selection, a crucial step in data categorization, comes next. Reduced computing complexity, improved learning algorithm efficiency, the elimination of redundant data, and an improvement in the generalization and comprehension of the data are some benefits of feature selection. Tree boosting using the CSO algorithm, as described in. The CSO's performance in a number of data mining and machine learning issues has received widespread recognition. As a result, it used the CSO algorithm, which applies the feature importance score to feature selection. A series of decision trees make up the CSO.

The set of decision trees used for the prediction is

$$y_i' = \sum_{m=1}^{m} f_k \qquad (11.1)$$

where m = various decision trees, f_k = decision tree predictions, x_i = the ith data point's feature vector. It is important to optimize a loss function in order to train the model. The following is the loss function for our binary feature selection:

$$L = -\frac{1}{N}\sum_{i}^{N}\left(\left(y_i \log p_i\right)+\left(1-y_i\right)\log\left(1-p_i\right)\right) \qquad (11.2)$$

Another crucial component of the CSO method is regularization, which is provided by

$$\Omega = Y^T + \frac{1}{2}\lambda\sum_{j=1}^{T} wj^2 \qquad (11.3)$$

where T = amount of leaves and wj^2 = a score on the jth leaf.

The model's goal is stated as follows:

$$obj = L + \Omega \qquad (11.4)$$

where L = The model's training loss impacts how accurately it can be predicted.

Ω = Overfitting is prevented and the model complexity is regulated by the regularization function.

In CSO, the objective function is improved using the mean and variance as the sequence of gradient descents.

Consequently, the step's goal function is written as

$$obj(t) = \sum_{i=1}^{n}\left[g_i f_t(x_i) + \frac{1}{2}h_i f_t^2(x_i)\right] + \Omega(f_t) \qquad (11.5)$$

11.3.3.1   Cat Swarm Optimization

The principles of CSO are based on how cats hunt and rest. For these skills, the searching mode (SM) and tracing mode (TM) models are employed, respectively. The cat is continually vigilant even though it spends most of SM sleeping. In SM, the cat moves slowly. Cats attack their prey with remarkable speed and vigor in TM, in contrast to SM, where they are less active.

11.3.3.1.1   Seeking Mode

Four parameters are employed in SM.

These are:

  i. SMP—seeking memory pool,
 ii. SRD—seeking range of the selected dimension for mutation,
iii. CDC—count of dimensions to change,
 iv. SPC—self-position consideration.

A mixing ratio (MR) is also utilized in SM and TM to lessen the cat population. The SM process is described below:

1. Choose a random portion of the population to be cat-seeking.
2. For each cat in SM, repeat steps 3–6.
3. Make SMP duplicates of the cat that is searching.

4. Execute the following operations based on the value of CDC.
   i.   Add or subtraction of SRD fraction from the value of the current position is done at random for each copy of the ith cat.
   ii. For each of the copies, swap out the previous values.
5. Calculate each copy's fitness.
6. Choose the copy with the best fitness out of all the copies, then transport it to the position of the seeker.

In SM, a number of problem space regions are examined that correspond to the locations of cats; but, the scan is only conducted in the vicinity of the cat that is actively looking. As a result, for the given solutions, it works as a local search.

11.3.3.1.2 Tracing Mode

During TM, cats adjust their position and speed to move toward the best possible position based on the current best position. The steps for tracing mode are as follows:

1. The speed of each dimension of the cat's positioning is updated by Equation (11.6).
2. The revised velocities are adjusted to the limit if they are outside of the acceptable range.
3. Using Equation (11.7), the positions of the cats are updated.
4. The positions are adjusted to the limit if they are not within the range.

$$v_k^d(t+1) = w \times v_k^d(t) + c \times r \times \left(x_{best}^d(t) - x_k^d(t) \right) \tag{11.6}$$

$$x_k^d(t+1) = x_k^d(t) + v_k^d(t+1) \tag{11.7}$$

where $x_k^d(t)$ and $x_k^d(t+1)$ are position of the dth dimension of kth cat at time t and $t+1$, respectively, $v_k^d(t)$ and $v_k^d(t+1)$ z1 are the dth dimension's speeds of kth cat at time t and $t+1$, respectively, $(x_{best}^d(t))$ is the position of the best cat's dth dimension found so far, w is the weight of inertia, c is a constant that has an impact on the rate of change for each dimension, while r is a random value between $[0, 1]$.

A cat's position may alter significantly during TM, but its objective is to identify the best possible solution using what is known at this time about the best possible position so far.

Due to the local searching behaviors that CSO displays in SM and TM, it is possible for it to become trapped in local optima. Second, because of SRD, the duplicates of cats in SM are now located in locations that are somewhat close to where they originally were. The new positions of cats in TM also are roughly comparable to the greatest positions reached thus far. Therefore, there is less variety within the population, particularly when the initial set is not distributed uniformly across the search area, leading to early convergence. The chosen attributes for categorizing MANET intrusions are then sent to XGBoost.

11.3.4 CLASSIFICATION USING XGBOOST ALGORITHM

1. for n repetitions
   (a) Build a tree all the way to the bottom.
      i. Decide on the ideal separation point.
      ii. Give the two new leaves a weight.
   (b) The nodes with negative gain are removed from the tree in bottom-up sequence.
2. End for

The XGBoost model's trees are built using the aforementioned procedures. Let the feature set, v_i be v_1, v_2, ..., v_m where $i = 1, 2, 3, ..., m$. Then, the score for feature relevance IS_i is calculated based on how often each feature is used to distribute the data for training among all of the trees. This results in the score for feature relevance set being expressed as

$$IS_i = \{x \mid x = w_i v_i\} \tag{11.8}$$

Where v_i denotes the feature set and w_i denotes each feature's relative weight. The best feature significance scores from the CSE-CIC-ID 2018 dataset are plotted with the XGBoost technique.

In the literature, the XGBoost has been applied as a single classification model by Chen Z et al. [20]. Extensive tests using various categorization thresholds are used to evaluate the accuracy of the XGBoost method.

11.3.4.1 Grasshopper Optimization

In this case, GOA is employed to carry out optimal selection for an XGBoost weight. The GOA is a novel chaotic swarm-based optimization method that takes cues from the behavior of grasshopper insects. A random swarm of the populace enters GOA in the beginning just like any other swarm optimization method, in order to search for and identify the problem's global optimal (maximum or lowest) solution. P_i which is stated as follows, predicts how the ith grasshopper will evolve in relation to the objective grasshopper

$$P_i = GF_i + SA_i + WA_i, \tag{11.9}$$

where GF_i is the gravitational force on the ith grasshopper, SA_i is an interaction with others, and WA_i is a wind convection.

Here, P_i is the ith grasshopper's position, which is determined as follows:

$$P_i = R_1 SA_i + R_2 GF_i + R_3 WA_i \qquad (11.10)$$

where R_1, R_2, and R_3 are constants at random in the range [0,1].

The grasshopper's social interactions (SA_i) depend on the two social forces that prevent collisions between the two grasshoppers a repulsion force and an attraction force over a short distance. The following social interaction is simulated:

$$SA_k = \sum_{\substack{l=1 \\ l \neq i}}^{N} SA(D_{kl}) D_{kl} \qquad (11.11)$$

$$D_{lk} = X_k - X_l \qquad (11.12)$$

$$\hat{D}_{lk} = \frac{X_k - X_l}{D_{lk}} \qquad (11.13)$$

where D_{lk} is the Euclidian's length of the kth with the lth position grasshopper, and $\hat{D}_{lk}$ describes presently, a unit vector connecting the kth and lth grasshoppers. The strength of the social forces is identified by SF, which is assessed using the formula below:

$$SF(R) = f_i e^{-R/L} - e^{-R} \qquad (11.14)$$

where L denotes the attraction's length scale, and f_i describes the strong attraction that exists.

The formula for the strength of attraction's intensity is as follows:

$$X_k^d = c \left(\sum_{\substack{l=1 \\ l \neq 1}}^{N} c \frac{U_B^d - L_B^d}{2} SF\left(\left|X_i^d - X_k^d\right|\right) \frac{X_l - X_k}{D_{lk}} + \hat{T}_d \right), \qquad (11.15)$$

where SF discusses the impact of grasshoppers on interpersonal interactions.

The GF element is assessed by,

$$GF_i = -GF\hat{e}_g \qquad (11.16)$$

where $\hat{e}_g$ describes a single vector pointing toward the planet's core and G_i represents the gravitational force's constant.

Finally, WA_i is the model of wind advection created by

$$WA_i = U\hat{e}_g \tag{11.17}$$

where U is a constant drift, and $\hat{e}_g$ describes a unity vector along with the wind.

It is possible to achieve the following formula by substituting the previously specified parameters:

where SF is a function and The entire population of grasshoppers is N.

A formula is created for measuring the connections among grasshopper swarms under the assumption that gravity and wind always point in the direction of the intended target:

$$X_I^d = c\left(\sum_{\substack{l=1 \\ l \neq 1}}^{N} c\, \frac{U_B^d - L_B^d}{2} SF\left(\left|X_k^d - X_I^d\right|\right) \frac{X_I - X_k}{D_{lk}} \right) + \hat{T}_d, \tag{11.18}$$

$$c = c_{max} - l\, \frac{c_{max} - c_{min}}{L}, \tag{11.19}$$

where U_B^d and L_B^d are the upper and lower limitations in a dth dimension, respectively, $\hat{T}_d$ is the actual magnitude of the target grasshopper's dth dimension, c describes the moderating factor in the appropriate repulsion and attraction zones, c_{max} and c_{min} are the maximum value of component c and the lowest value, respectively, and l and L are the number of iterations both currently and overall, respectively.

11.4 RESULT AND DISCUSSION

Several tests have been conducted to demonstrate the effectiveness of the suggested IDS on a contemporary heterogeneous dataset CSE-CIC-IDS2018. The sections below contain a detailed discussion of this work.

11.4.1 DATASET DESCRIPTION

The IDS data used to describe the simulated features of the proposed IDS system in this research were chosen because it is vital to take crucial factors into account when choosing relevant data to assess an IDS system. Although there are many publicly available standard IDS datasets, some of them contain undevitrified, traditional, irreproducible, and rigid incursion. For our proposed high-performance efficient IDS system, it has used the most recent heterogeneous IDS datasets, such as CSE-CIC-IDS2018, to eliminate the shortcomings of IDS datasets [21]. The CIC and the CSE worked together on a project to create this dataset.

TABLE 11.2
Confusion Matrix for the Proposed IDS

Actual classes	Predicated		
	Anomaly	FP	TN
	Normal	TP	FN

11.4.2 PERFORMANCE PARAMETERS

This work has examined models by testing them as they are trained. Then, the confusion matrix is used to calculate performance metrics. The confusion matrix element displays the expected and actual classification. Two classes the incorrect class and the proper class are used to categorize the classification results. The confusion matrix's element must be calculated under four crucial circumstances. As indicated in Table 11.2, this has the confusion matrix in the IDS environment.

- The phrase "true positive" (*TP*), denoted by the letter "*x*," denotes that the model's forecasts are both accurate and pessimistic.
- False negative (*FN*) is represented by the letter *Y*, which stands for the wrong prediction. A high degree of abnormality instances are categorized as regular, and the model predicts negative consequences incorrectly.
- False positive (*FP*) prediction: Although the actual number of attacks is normal, the model predicts a positive outcome incorrectly, as seen by the z-axis.
- The term "true negative" (*TN*), which is represented by the letter "*t*," denotes instances in which an assault has been appropriately identified to foretell unfavorable outcomes.

Precision compares the proportion of correctly classified objects to those that are incorrectly classified.

$$precision = \frac{TP}{TP + FP} \qquad (11.20)$$

Recall is calculated by dividing the total correctly classified items by the total number of missing entries.

$$Recall = \frac{TP}{TP + FN} \qquad (11.21)$$

The *F*1 score calculates the harmonic mean of recall and precision.

$$F1 - Score = \frac{Precision.Recall}{Precision + Recall} \qquad (11.22)$$

As *DR* and *FAR* are the two crucial and frequently used factors for evaluating IDS, it is possible to determine the performance of the suggested IDS using the confusion matrix mentioned above. *DR* stands for the proportion of anomalous classes that the IDS model has identified. *FAR* stands for the number of incorrectly assigned normal classes.

$$DR = TP / (TP + FN) = x / (x + y) \tag{11.23}$$

$$FAR = FP / (TN + FP) = z / (t + z) \tag{11.24}$$

The effectiveness of the suggested IDS for intrusion detection without CSO feature selection is shown in Table 11.3. In the analysis of precision, the proposed model achieved nearly 93%, LR achieved 37%, DT achieved 58%, SVM achieved 75%, RF achieved 89%. The reason is that all the manual features are given as an input to the XGBoost classifier. When the model is tested for Recall, F1-Score, FAR, and DR achieved 95%, 96%, 97% and 96%, respectively.

Table 11.4 shows the outcomes after the features have been optimally chosen by CSO and after the relevant characteristics have been fed into the classifiers. LR has 89%, DT has 86%, SVM has 64%, RF has 56%, and the proposed model has 99% of

TABLE 11.3
Analysis of Various ML Classifiers Without CSO

Classifier	precision	Recall	F1-score	FAR	DR
LR	0.373	0.641	0.415	0.91	0.64
SVM	0.752	0.852	0.806	6.92	0.75
DT	0.583	0.731	0.654	4.95	0.72
RF	0.891	0.924	0.867	9.55	0.79
Proposed model	0.933	0.952	0.969	12.57	0.96

TABLE 11.4
Analysis of Various ML Classifiers with CSO

Classifier	precision	Recall	F1-Score	FAR	DR
LR	0.456	0.694	0.656	0.93	0.74
SVM	0.845	0.896	0.852	7.64	0.89
DT	0.662	0.791	0.765	5.64	0.78
RF	0.901	0.941	0.903	10.45	0.88
Proposed model	0.995	0.999	0.998	15.23	0.98

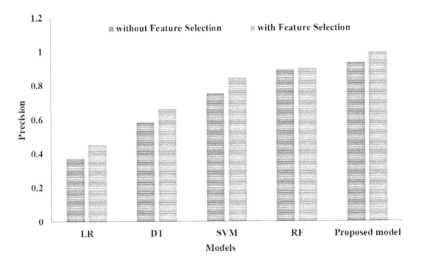

FIGURE 11.1 Precision comparisons

precision. When the models are tested with Recall, LR has 86%, DT has 88%, SVM has 89%, RF has 92%, and the proposed model has 99% of Recall. While the models are tested with F1-Score LR has 85%, DT has 89%, SVM has 91%, RF has 96%, and the proposed model has 99% of F1-Score. When the models are tested with FAR, LR has 88%, DT has 89%, SVM has 93%, RF has 95%, and the proposed model has 98% of FAR. When compared with all other models, the proposed model achieved better performance in accuracy analysis with 98%. Figures 11.1 to 11.5 offer a graphical description of the projected model.

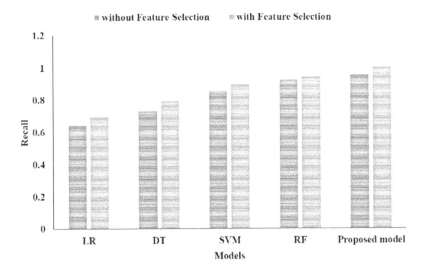

FIGURE 11.2 Recall analysis

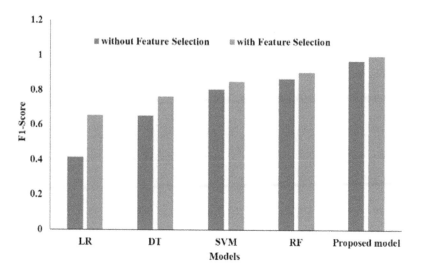

FIGURE 11.3   F1-Score

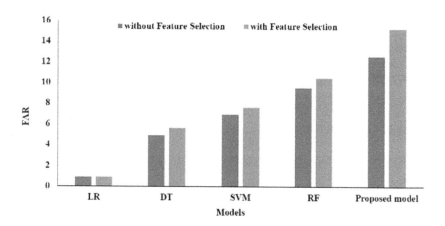

FIGURE 11.4   FAR analysis

11.5   CONCLUSION

IDS in MANETs are of paramount importance in securing these dynamic and decentralized networks. They provide active monitoring, threat detection, and mitigation capabilities, protecting the integrity, confidentiality, and availability of data. IDS enable the efficient utilization of resources, facilitate secure IoT integration, and contribute to the overall resilience and reliability of MANETs. For feature selection this paper has made use of the Cat Swarm Optimization algorithm's feature importance score. This feature selection technique is the first of its kind to be utilized for intrusion detection, and it uses the CSE-CIC-ID 2018 dataset. The main application of the XGBoost model is classification. GOA is used to perform an optimal selection

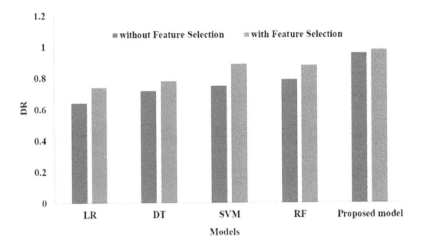

FIGURE 11.5 Accuracy validation

for a weight of XGBoost. When compared with all other models, the proposed model achieved better performance in accuracy analysis with 98%. In follow-up studies, we will investigate additional comparative factors, such as CPU use, latency, and detection, to assess how well the suggested model performs on a real-time IDS dataset. Parallel processing will also be used to evaluate big IDS data sets, speed up detection, and improve operational effectiveness.

REFERENCES

1. Khraisat, A., Gondal, I., Vamplew, P. and Kamruzzaman, J., 2019. Survey of intrusion detection systems: Techniques, datasets and challenges. *Cybersecurity*, 2(1), pp. 1–22.
2. Laqtib, S., El Yassini, K. and Hasnaoui, M.L., 2020. A technical review and comparative analysis of machine learning techniques for intrusion detection systems in MANET. *International Journal of Electrical and Computer Engineering*, 10(3), p. 2701.
3. Banerjee, S., Nandi, R., Dey, R. and Saha, H.N., 2015, October. A review on different intrusion detection systems for MANET and its vulnerabilities. In *2015 International Conference and Workshop on Computing and Communication (IEMCON)* (pp. 1–7). IEEE.
4. Soni, M., Ahirwa, M. and Agrawal, S., 2015, December. A survey on intrusion detection techniques in MANET. In *2015 International Conference on Computational Intelligence and Communication Networks (CICN)* (pp. 1027–1032). IEEE.
5. Almomani, O., 2020. A feature selection model for network intrusion detection system based on PSO, GWO, FFA and GA algorithms. *Symmetry*, 12(6), p. 1046.
6. Alsoufi, M.A., Razak, S., Siraj, M.M., Nafea, I., Ghaleb, F.A., Saeed, F. and Nasser, M., 2021. Anomaly-based intrusion detection systems in IoT using deep learning: A systematic literature review. *Applied Sciences*, 11(18), p. 8383.
7. Justin, V., Marathe, N. and Dongre, N., 2017, February. Hybrid IDS using SVM classifier for detecting DoS attack in MANET application. In *2017 International Conference on I-SMAC (IoT in Social, Mobile, Analytics and Cloud)(I-SMAC)* (pp. 775–778). IEEE.

8. Amouri, A., Alaparthy, V.T. and Morgera, S.D., 2018, April. Cross layer-based intrusion detection based on network behavior for IoT. In *2018 IEEE 19th Wireless and Microwave Technology Conference (WAMICON)* (pp. 1–4). IEEE.

9. Culpepper, B.J. and Tseng, H.C., 2004, October. Sinkhole intrusion indicators in DSR MANETs. In *First International Conference on Broadband Networks* (pp. 681–688). IEEE.

10. Saheed, Y.K., Abiodun, A.I., Misra, S., Holone, M.K. and Colomo-Palacios, R., 2022. A machine learning-based intrusion detection for detecting internet of things network attacks. *Alexandria Engineering Journal*, *61*(12), pp. 9395–9409.

11. Balyan, A.K., Ahuja, S., Lilhore, U.K., Sharma, S.K., Manoharan, P., Algarni, A.D., Elmannai, H. and Raahemifar, K., 2022. A hybrid intrusion detection model using egapso and improved random forest method. *Sensors*, *22*(16), p. 5986.

12. Ali, T.E., Chong, Y.W. and Manickam, S., 2023. Machine learning techniques to detect a DDoS attack in SDN: A systematic review. *Applied Sciences*, *13*(5), p. 3183.

13. Gopalan, S.S., Ravikumar, D., Linekar, D., Raza, A. and Hasib, M., 2021, March. Balancing approaches towards ML for IDS: A survey for the CSE-CIC IDS dataset. In *2020 International Conference on Communications, Signal Processing, and their Applications (ICCSPA)* (pp. 1–6). IEEE.

14. Ninu, S.B., 2023. An intrusion detection system using exponential henry gas solubility optimization based deep Neuro fuzzy network in MANET. *Engineering Applications of Artificial Intelligence*, *123*, p. 105969.

15. Vijayalakshmi, S., Bose, S., Logeswari, G. and Anitha, T., 2023. Hybrid defense mechanism against malicious packet dropping attack for MANET using game theory. *Cyber Security and Applications*, *1*, p. 100011.

16. Prasad, M., Tripathi, S. and Dahal, K., 2023. An intelligent intrusion detection and performance reliability evaluation mechanism in mobile ad-hoc networks. *Engineering Applications of Artificial Intelligence*, *119*, p. 105760.

17. Abbood, Z.A., Atilla, D.Ç. and Aydin, Ç., 2023. Intrusion detection system through deep learning in routing MANET networks. *Intelligent Automation and Soft Computing*, *37*(1), pp. 269–281.

18. Meddeb, R., Jemili, F., Triki, B. and Korbaa, O., 2023. A deep learning-based intrusion detection approach for mobile ad-hoc network. *Soft Computing*, 27, pp. 9425–9439. https://doi.org/10.1007/s00500-023-08324-4

19. Prashanth, S.K., Iqbal, H. and Illuri, B., 2023. An enhanced grey wolf optimisation–deterministic convolutional neural network (GWO–DCNN) model-based IDS in MANET. *Journal of Information and Knowledge Management*, *22*(4), p. 2350010.

20. Chen, Z., Jiang, F., Cheng, Y., Gu, X., Liu, W. and Peng, J., 2018. XGBoost classifier for DDoS attack detection and analysis in SDN-Based cloud. In *IEEE International Conference on Big Data and Smart Computing (BigComp)*. IEEE.

21. Murugan, P. and Durairaj, S., 2017. Regularization and optimization strategies in deep convolutional neural network. arXiv:1712.04711.

12 Artificial Intelligence and Automation in the Transport Industry
Envisioning the Future of Mobility

*K. Senthil, Almas Begum, G. Ayyappan,
and B. Sundaravadivazhagan*

12.1 INTRODUCTION

Technology is advancing quickly, especially in the field of artificial intelligence (AI), and this has had a profound impact on a number of industries, including transportation. The advent of AI-powered solutions as a result of this paradigm change is revolutionizing how to see, use, and optimize transportation networks. This chapter intends to examine the varied effects of AI-powered technologies in the transportation industry, with an emphasis on their implications for improved user experience, traffic management, safety, and energy efficiency [1]. The improvement of safety measures is one of AI's most important contributions to the transportation sector. AI-driven solutions that can analyze real-time data, foresee potential risks, and take preventive measures are supplementing and, in some circumstances, replacing traditional safety systems [2]. For instance, autonomous vehicles with cutting-edge AI systems can spot hazards, foresee crashes, and take snap judgments to prevent mishaps. These technologies have the potential to drastically cut down on human errors, which are a major factor in car accidents, and hence save many lives.

The integration of AI into traffic control systems has thoroughly transformed perspectives on urban mobility. In order to acquire insights into traffic patterns, congestion locations, and the best routes, AI-powered algorithms can evaluate enormous amounts of data from sensors, cameras, and connected devices. Intelligent traffic management systems can use this data to dynamically change traffic signals, redirect vehicles, and improve traffic flow in real-time. As a result, travel times are shortened, road infrastructure is used more effectively, and there is less idling, which lowers carbon emissions. Beyond traffic control and safety, AI has a significant impact on transportation that addresses important environmental issues. Vehicle energy

DOI: 10.1201/9781032642789-12

usage is being optimized using AI algorithms, furthering sustainability objectives. For instance, AI-driven algorithms that control energy distribution across multiple components, including the engine and battery, are advantageous for electric and hybrid vehicles [3]. By maximizing vehicle range and reducing energy waste, this optimization lowers greenhouse gas emissions. Predictive analytics powered by AI can also help forecast energy consumption, allowing for better planning of energy resources and lessening the load on power systems.

The total user experience in transit is improving as a result of AI-driven advances. AI algorithms are enhancing comfort, accessibility, and personalization across ride-sharing services and public transportation networks. Users may make well-informed choices about their travel routes, modes of transportation, and departure times thanks to real-time data analysis. Additionally, chatbots and virtual assistants powered by AI offer real-time information, respond to inquiries, and help users at every step of their trip [4]. This improved customer experience not only boosts satisfaction but also promotes the use of more environmentally friendly forms of transportation. Although there is no denying the advantages of AI-powered transportation advances, there are ethical issues that need to be taken into account. It is important to pay close attention to privacy issues surrounding data gathering and use as well as potential biases in AI systems. Additionally, establishing standards, rules, and frameworks that guarantee the responsible development and deployment of AI technologies requires a concerted effort from regulators, politicians, and industry stakeholders. This is necessary for the transition to an ecosystem for transportation powered by AI.

The application of AI in the transportation business is fundamentally changing the sector. AI-powered technologies are revolutionizing how to move and engage in urban environments, improving safety and traffic flow, boosting energy efficiency, and elevating user experience [5]. Navigating this era of revolution, it becomes essential to address ethical concerns, prioritize user privacy, and establish a collaborative framework. This framework should leverage AI to construct a transportation ecosystem characterized by enhanced safety, efficiency, and sustainability.

12.2   AI AND EFFECTIVE TRANSPORTATION TECHNOLOGIES

A new era of mobility has begun as a result of the fusion of AI and efficient transportation technology, which is characterized by better sustainability, decreased traffic, and improved user experience [6]. This section examines the mutually beneficial interaction between these technologies and the numerous advantages they offer contemporary transportation networks as shown in Figure 12.1.

12.2.1   EFFICIENT TRANSPORTATION TECHNOLOGIES

A wide range of technological advancements that attempt to improve the overall effectiveness of transportation networks and optimize resource utilization are included in the category of efficient transportation technology [7]. These innovations cover a range of transportation methods, from conventional cars to cutting-edge ones like electric vehicles (EVs), connected vehicles, high-speed rail, and autonomous systems [8].

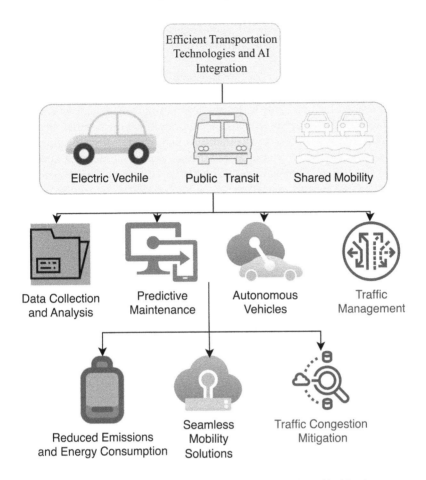

FIGURE 12.1 Integration of efficient transportation technologies with AI enhancement

For instance, the fight for environmentally friendly transportation is spearheaded by electric vehicles. With their help, pollution and reliance on fossil fuels might be greatly reduced. Similar to this, connected automobiles use communication technology to exchange real-time data with infrastructure, and other vehicles, providing better traffic management, navigation, and collision avoidance [9]. For medium-distance travel, high-speed rail networks offer a more environmentally friendly and time-efficient alternative to flying than commercial aircraft. AI-powered autonomous vehicles have the potential to revolutionize urban travel by streamlining traffic and enhancing safety with the help of cutting-edge sensor technology and predictive algorithms.

12.2.2 AI Synergies for Mobility Improvement

The fusion of AI with effective transport technology is catapulting the transport sector into a new era of increased mobility. The full potential of these transportation breakthroughs is made possible by AI technologies, which have the ability to process enormous datasets, identify trends, and make choices in real-time [10].

a. *Predictive Analytics and Traffic Management:* In order to forecast traffic congestion, examine previous patterns, and improve traffic flow, AI-powered traffic management systems can process data from sensors, cameras, and connected vehicles. AI can minimize travel times and traffic congestion by foreseeing bottlenecks and dynamically changing traffic signals. In order to create more efficient journeys, predictive analytics may also help in route planning that takes into account current conditions, weather, and events.

b. *Optimized Energy Consumption:* In energy-efficient transportation technology, AI algorithms are crucial for maximizing energy consumption. For instance, AI in electric vehicles may control battery use, adjust to road conditions, and choose the routes that use the least amount of energy. This increases the driving range of the car while simultaneously lowering greenhouse gas emissions.

c. *Improved Safety and Autonomous Driving:* Safety is greatly affected by the fusion of AI with effective transportation technologies. Modern vehicles, which offer functions like adaptive cruise control, lane-keeping assistance, and automatic emergency braking, are powered by AI algorithms. AI's capacity to comprehend complicated sensor data enables autonomous vehicles to navigate and interact with their surroundings, greatly lowering the chance of accidents brought on by human mistakes. The way people interact with transit systems is changing as a result of AI-driven personalization. Users can get personalized recommendations for routes, modes of transportation, and departure times through AI-enabled apps and platforms. AI-powered virtual assistants also improve user experience by offering real-time information, responding to inquiries, and resolving issues.

d. *Decision-Making Driven by Data:* Transportation agencies and service providers can now make data-driven decisions thanks to AI technologies. AI aids in the design of resource-efficient transportation networks, the allocation of resources, and the identification of areas for improvement by analyzing massive volumes of data, including traffic patterns, consumption trends, and infrastructure problems.

The fusion of AI and effective transportation technology signifies a fundamental change in the way to conceptualize, create, and experience mobility. Safer, more environmentally friendly, and more effective transportation systems are made possible by the mutual reinforcement between these advancements. The potential for additional synergies and beneficial consequences on society's mobility demands is enormous as AI develops and efficient transportation technologies expand, creating a bright future for the transportation industry.

12.3 AI FOR MOBILITY POWER CONSUMPTION OPTIMIZATION

A new age of effectiveness and innovation has begun as a result of the incorporation of AI into the field of mobility solutions. The increased need for computational power and the ensuing increase in power consumption are just two of the issues that come along with this revolutionary move toward AI-powered mobility [11]. This section examines the crucial role that power efficiency plays in AI mobility solutions and explores a number of strategies that can be used to reduce power consumption without compromising the viability and effectiveness of these solutions as shown in Figure 12.2.

12.3.1 POWER EFFICIENCY IN AI MOBILITY SOLUTIONS IS IMPORTANT

Predictive traffic management and autonomous driving are just two examples of the groundbreaking improvements that the convergence of AI and mobility solutions has enabled. However, these developments frequently involve computations that are resource-intensive and require a lot of electricity [12]. The resulting increase in power consumption has broad ramifications. These include increased operating expenses, a potential increase in carbon emissions, and a reduction in the battery life of electric vehicles [13]. Therefore, power efficiency is of utmost importance because

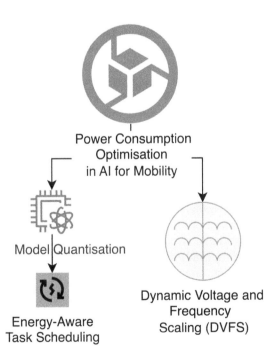

FIGURE 12.2 Power consumption optimization process in AI mobility solutions

it has a direct impact on environmental sustainability and the achievement of overall ecological goals in addition to having an economic impact on AI mobility solutions.

12.3.2 POWER CONSUMPTION OPTIMIZATION TECHNIQUES

Numerous tactics that try to achieve a harmonious balance between computing performance and energy usage are emerging in the quest to mitigate the problems caused by the power consumption in AI mobility solutions. Several of these methods consist of:

12.3.1.1 Model Quantization

The technique of model quantization entails reducing the accuracy of numerical values used to represent the parameters of AI models. This method frequently requires substituting lower-precision data types, such as 8-bit integers, for higher-precision floating-point values [14]. The result is a significant decrease in the computational complexity and memory requirements connected with AI models. As a result, inference processes proceed more quickly, and less energy is used. Model quantization fits well in contexts with limited resources, such as embedded systems seen in automobiles, where efficient energy use is crucial.

12.3.1.2 The DVFS, or Dynamic Voltage and Frequency Scaling

A method for orchestrating the change of the operating voltage and frequency for hardware elements like CPUs and GPUs is called dynamic voltage and frequency scaling (DVFS). This relates to changes being made in response to the demands of the on-going task. DVFS enables the lowering of both voltage and frequency during times when there is less demand for computing, which subsequently results in energy savings [15]. On the other hand, DVFS enables an increase in voltage and frequency to ensure optimal performance when faced with increasingly demanding activities. This adaptive strategy guarantees hardware effectiveness while also reducing energy consumption.

12.3.1.3 Energy-Conscious Task Scheduling

The goal of energy-aware task scheduling is to optimize the distribution of computing workloads among the available processing units in order to reduce energy usage. The computing requirements of the tasks, the power efficiency built into the processing units, and the time limits are all carefully taken into account. This thorough division of labor among the available tools guarantees a careful equilibrium between energy conservation and uncompromised performance [16].

12.3.3 A PARADIGM SHIFT IN THE DIRECTION OF SUSTAINABILITY IS NEEDED FOR THE EFFECTIVE USE OF POWER CONSUMPTION IN VEHICLES:

The way that power usage is monitored and optimized inside cars has undergone a profound transformation in recent years, according to the automotive industry. Predictive algorithms, data analysis, and the integration of modern technology have been the main drivers of this transition. The comprehensive approach to power consumption optimization is explored in this article along with its effects on vehicle sustainability, environmental impact, and efficiency.

Analyzing Data in Real-Time and Modifying the System: A new era of efficiency in vehicle power use has arrived with the development of AI. The time when power distribution in automobiles was primarily controlled by mechanical systems is long gone. Today, many systems are instantly adjusted by AI algorithms using real-time data gathered from a variety of sensors built into the car. This dynamic strategy guarantees optimal power distribution, hence reducing energy waste. The beneficial impact on fuel efficiency that real-time data analysis and adjustment have is one of the most important benefits. To make exact modifications, AI systems keep an eye on a variety of factors, including driving style, road conditions, and engine efficiency. This results in substantial environmental advantages in addition to improving the vehicle's overall performance. Lower fuel use directly correlates with less energy wasted, which lowers greenhouse gas emissions.

Improved Energy Distribution in Electric and Hybrid Vehicles: Vehicles that are electric or hybrid have taken the lead in the search for environmentally friendly transportation options. To get the most out of these cars, effective energy management is essential. Here AI-driven algorithms, which are crucial to maximizing energy distribution inside these vehicles. In an electric or hybrid car, the motor, battery, and other parts work together in harmony. To modify the flow of energy between these components, AI algorithms continuously monitor and assess their state. This orchestration makes sure that the electricity that is available is used as effectively as possible, resulting in increased vehicle range and fewer charge cycles. AI helps to make longer trips more convenient by maximizing energy use, which also eases the burden on power grids and charging infrastructure. The effects of improved energy distribution go beyond only the owners of individual vehicles. Energy grid stress during periods of high demand can be reduced using a fleet of electric vehicles that have been AI-optimized. Because of this, incorporating AI into energy management is consistent with the overarching objective of developing a more balanced and sustainable energy ecosystem.

Machine learning for Energy Demand Prediction: An element of prediction is added to power consumption optimization by machine learning, a branch of artificial intelligence. When discussing vehicle efficiency, this factor is quite useful. Machine-learning algorithms have the capacity to learn from past driving behaviors and contextual information, which enables them to properly predict energy usage [17]. These algorithms are able to anticipate power usage for various driving conditions by recognizing patterns and locating elements that affect energy requirements. This proactive strategy enables cars to adapt their energy consumption in advance, improving energy management and reducing the need for conventional fuel sources. The advantages of machine-learning-based energy anticipation go beyond specific vehicles. Data collected from a fleet of vehicles can help with infrastructure design, traffic control, and urban planning. Cities, for instance, can optimize the total transportation system by modifying traffic lights and road layouts depending on predicted energy demand.

The Future Path: A big step toward a sustainable future has been made with the optimization of vehicle power consumption with the use of AI and cutting-edge algorithms. It is clear that these technologies are redefining how power is distributed and consumed in traditional ways. Vehicle power usage is changing as a result of real-time data analysis, improved energy distribution, and machine-learning-based energy forecasting. The advantages of AI-driven power usage optimization are becoming more and more obvious as move to the future. A more sustainable transportation ecology is a result of less energy waste, better electric car range, and predictive energy management working together. In turn, this supports international initiatives to cut carbon emissions, slow down climate change, and shift to a cleaner, more effective energy paradigm. The use of power usage in automobiles has developed into a complex interaction of technology and data analysis, to sum up. The way power is distributed and consumed inside vehicles has been completely redesigned thanks to AI, real-time data, and machine learning. The combination of these technologies has produced real advantages in terms of increased vehicle range, improved fuel economy, and diminished environmental impact. The blending of innovation and sustainability promises to propel the automobile sector toward a more eco-aware and effective future as travels the future path.

12.3.4 Case Study: Optimization of Energy-Efficient Traffic Flow

The idea of energy-efficient traffic flow optimization is a useful case study that encompasses the promise of power consumption optimization within AI for mobility. Traffic management systems can process real-time data from various sources, including sensors, cameras, and connected vehicles, by using AI algorithms, which can streamline traffic signals and reduce congestion. These systems may smoothly combine accurate traffic predictions with low energy consumption by the strategic integration of power consumption optimization approaches, including model quantization and energy-aware task scheduling. In such a case, the AI models in charge of forecasting traffic patterns and improving traffic lights can be quantized, switching to representations with reduced precision. With this paradigm shift in computing complexity, energy usage is minimized. The methodical approach of energy-aware task scheduling also makes it easier to allocate computing resources based on the urgency and complexity of the tasks at hand, leading to the execution of computational operations that require a lot of power in the most resource-efficient way possible. Energy-efficient traffic flow optimization, which combines these various power consumption optimization techniques, exemplifies how AI mobility solutions can achieve their intended goals while judiciously lowering the environmental impact and operational costs linked to increased power consumption.

The integration of AI into the spectrum of mobility solutions brings about a number of fresh issues, one of which is increased power consumption. However, the power efficiency of AI mobility systems can be skillfully optimized by the strategic application of methods like model quantization, DVFS, and energy-aware job scheduling. In addition to extending the battery life of electric vehicles, this strategic

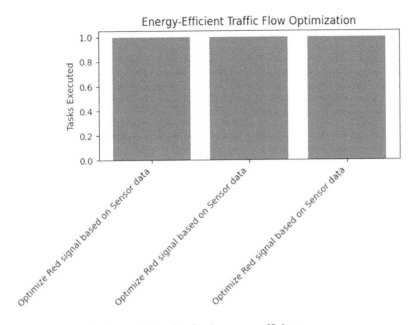

FIGURE 12.3 Traffic flow optimization for the energy-efficient

interaction also actively advances broader sustainability objectives and significantly reduces operational costs. The optimization of power usage is positioned to be a key player in creating a transportation ecosystem that is both operationally effective and ecologically responsible as the transportation industry taps into the promise of AI to nurture an era of increased mobility. Sample data has been collected and used for the Optimization of Energy-Efficient Traffic Flow the following results are shown in the ideal conditions and shown in Figure 12.3. The results based on real-time data may vary according to various conations.

Sample Analysis for the Case Study

Results
Sensor Data (Sensor): 99
Traffic Prediction (AIModel): 98.50223036496304
Optimized Signal (TrafficSignal): Green
Sensor Data (Sensor): 35
Traffic Prediction (AIModel): 39.92883230505423
Optimized Signal (TrafficSignal): Red
Sensor Data (Sensor): 83
Traffic Prediction (AIModel): 95.87922407683
Optimized Signal (TrafficSignal): Green
Energy-Aware Task Scheduling:
Executing task: Optimize Green signal based on Sensor data
Executing task: Optimize Red signal based on Sensor data

The presented findings shed light on a hypothetical situation for optimizing traffic flow while reducing energy consumption. Sensor readings are the first part of the data, and the first reading from the "Sensor" indicates a high traffic intensity of 99. Based on this information, the AI model ("AIModel") then forecasts traffic patterns, with a prediction score of roughly 98.50 indicating a continuation of high traffic intensity. As a result, the traffic signal optimization component ("Traffic Signal") reacts by flashing a "Green" light to indicate that traffic is moving without interruption. The following sensor readings show various traffic intensities, which cause the scenario to change. For example, a lower intensity of 35 causes a traffic prediction of roughly 39.93, which results in a "Red" signal that controls congestion. A restoration to a "Green" signal for better traffic flow is required for a sensor reading of 83, which generates a traffic projection of around 95.88. The energy optimizer executes actions that have been prioritized for reducing power usage to complete the procedure. The jobs entail specifically optimizing signals, switching between "Green" and "Red" according to sensor data. In order to achieve energy-efficient traffic management, this simulated scenario illustrates the dynamic interplay of sensor data, AI prediction, signal optimization, and power-aware task scheduling.

12.4 LIGHTWEIGHT MATERIALS INTEGRATION IN AI MODELS

The combination of AI models and lightweight materials marks a revolutionary development in the realms of technology and transportation [18]. This section explores how lightweight materials are revolutionizing transportation and how AI techniques like model distillation and pruning are improving the effectiveness and performance of lightweight AI models [19]. The integration of AI with the Lightweight materials flow is shown in Figure 12.4.

12.4.1 LIGHTWEIGHT MATERIALS FOR AI AND TRANSPORTATION

In particular, the transportation sector has undergone a revolution because of the introduction of lightweight materials. By improving fuel efficiency and lowering pollutants, these materials, which stand out for their excellent strength-to-weight ratio, have completely changed how vehicles are designed. This context's incorporation of AI models adds a new level of innovation [20]. These lightweight materials can be intelligently included thanks to AI, which also allows for efficient deployment of them. AI and lightweight materials interact in a variety of ways. Vehicles' physical characteristics are improved by lightweight materials, and decision-making that takes advantage of these characteristics is improved by AI models. A new era of technologically superior and energy-efficient transportation is being ushered in by smoothly merging these two fields.

12.4.2 MODEL DISTILLATION: BUILDING SMALL AI MODELS

Model distillation is a key technique for bridging the gap between AI models and lightweight materials. Model distillation essentially entails teaching a smaller,

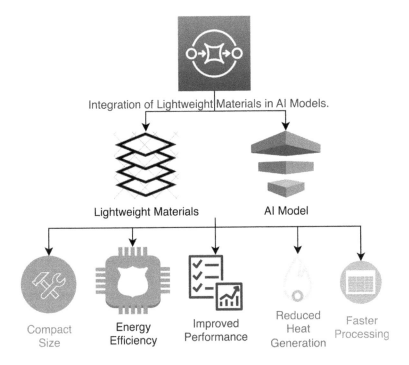

Integration of Lightweight Materials in AI Models.

Lightweight Materials   AI Model

Compact Size

Energy Efficiency

Improved Performance

Reduced Heat Generation

Faster Processing

FIGURE 12.4   Integration of lightweight materials in AI-enhanced models

simpler AI model to behave like a bigger, more sophisticated model. The huge model acts as the "teacher," passing on its knowledge to the small model acting as the "student." As a result, the AI model is more efficient and uses less memory and computing resources, which is completely consistent with the emphasis on efficiency placed on lightweight materials. Distillation makes it possible to integrate AI models into moving objects without taxing their computational capabilities. This method ensures that the scientific breakthroughs made possible by lightweight materials are seamlessly supplemented by the efficiency advantages of compact AI. It optimizes the symbiotic interaction between lightweight materials and AI models.

12.4.3   MODEL PRUNING: ELIMINATING DUPLICATION FOR EFFICIENCY

Another way to improve the integration of lightweight materials and AI models is through model pruning. It entails locating and eliminating unused or redundant parameters from an AI model. Model pruning reduces superfluous complexity in AI models, same as lightweight materials reduce excess weight in automobiles. As a result, models become leaner and use less processing power while yet performing as efficiently. Model pruning enhances the use of AI algorithms in resource-constrained situations, such as moving cars, in the context of transportation. AI models can be made more efficient to lower the computing requirements and facilitate easier integration with lightweight materials. Transportation solutions that are more flexible and energy-efficient are the outcome of the resulting synergy.

12.4.4 AI-Driven Simulations for Innovation in Lightweight Material Design

The use of AI in material design has become a revolutionary force in the constant pursuit of technological improvement. The development of lightweight materials, driven by AI-powered simulations, is one of the most promising fields of research. By rethinking the link between materials, performance, and sustainability, this combination has the potential to reinvent industries, particularly transportation. This essay explores how AI-driven simulations, and the use of lightweight materials are combined to create a more effective, environmentally friendly, and secure future [21].

The Influence of AI-Powered Simulations: AI and materials science working together has made previously thought-impossible possibilities possible. Researchers now have access to an unheard-of virtual laboratory where they can test out a variety of material compositions and structures thanks to AI-driven simulations. Traditional material testing, which frequently takes a long time and requires a lot of resources, is being revolutionized by simulations that quicken the learning curve. These simulations, which are based on complex algorithms, test the limitations of materials without compromising their structural integrity. This innovative method offers the path for the development of strong, lightweight materials that are also adaptable.

Applications for Improving Fuel Economy and Reducing Emissions: It is obvious how lightweight materials affect the transportation sector. Weight has a significant impact on vehicles, whether they are powered by internal combustion engines or electricity. Vehicles that are lighter require less energy to run, resulting in increased fuel efficiency. Additionally, lighter loads result in less emission, which is important in the fight against climate change. Lightweight materials created by artificial intelligence provide a multifaceted answer to these problems. Manufacturers may design cars that use less fuel and produce fewer pollutants by using the insights gained by AI simulations, helping to create a more sustainable form of transportation.

Optimizing Material Properties with Accuracy: The elegance of AI algorithms resides in their ability to precisely analyze large, complicated datasets. These algorithms are essential for optimizing material properties for particular applications in the context of material design. AI algorithms can choose the best material mix for different vehicle parts by looking at connections between material qualities, performance features, and environmental implications. This level of precision makes it possible to carefully include lightweight materials in vehicle design while maintaining performance standards. As a result, functional effectiveness and weight loss are harmoniously balanced.

Exploring the Potential for Innovation and Sustainability: AI-driven simulations and material design together represent more than just technological progress; they represent a paradigm leap in innovation and sustainability. Unprecedented levels of design inventiveness are possible thanks to how quickly innovative materials may be found and evaluated. This increase in innovation not only changes industries, but also shows how inventive people can be. The emphasis on lightweight materials is also consistent with the principles of sustainable development. Industries are well-positioned to lessen their environmental impact and contribute to a greener future by utilizing materials with small ecological footprints.

Problems and Prospects for the Future: Although the incorporation of AI into material design has tremendous promise, difficulties still exist. It is important to give serious thought to the ethical ramifications of automation, the veracity of data inputs, and the scalability of AI-driven simulations. Additionally, there may be challenges when moving from simulation to real-world application, needing on-going improvement and validation. The possibilities for the future are alluring. The blending of AI and material design may result in previously unheard-of materials with unconventional features. The possible uses span a variety of sectors, including consumer goods, healthcare, and aerospace, in addition to the transportation sector. A new era of innovation built on data-driven insights will emerge as AI algorithms become more sophisticated and better able to optimize materials for a variety of circumstances.

The fusion of lightweight material design and AI-driven simulations has the potential to redefine the parameters of innovation and reshape entire industries. The incorporation of AI algorithms ushers in a new era of efficiency, sustainability, and safety, from the field of transportation to broader applications. Although there are obstacles in the way of realizing this potential, the potential rewards are too great to pass up. The evolution of materials science is evidence of our capacity to use technology for the benefit of society as we advance into the age of artificial intelligence.

12.4.5 Case Study: On-Device Navigation Using Lightweight AI

The creation of lightweight AI for on-device navigation systems is a compelling case study that highlights the fusion of lightweight materials with AI models. In this case, using lightweight materials helps reduce vehicle weight and improve fuel economy. AI models are simultaneously charged with real-time navigation, a computationally taxing endeavor. The AI model in charge of on-device navigation can be reduced through the use of model distillation to a more manageable form that uses the least amount of computational resources and is optimized for real-time decision-making. In addition, model pruning helps by removing superfluous complexity, resulting in a navigation system that successfully directs the car while maximizing energy consumption. This case study highlights the potential for lightweight AI models to revolutionize on-device navigation, bringing about improvements in both efficiency and speed. It focuses on the synergistic effects that lightweight materials and AI models can have on the development of a transportation system that is both technologically and environmentally sustainable. The sample results are shown below and Figure 12.5, shows the performance comparison for the navigation using lightweight AI.

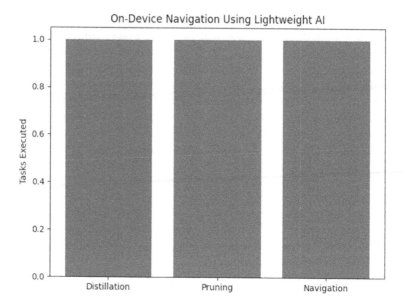

FIGURE 12.5 Navigation performance based on lightweight AI

Results

Model NavigationAI distilled to a lightweight form
Model NavigationAI pruned to remove complexity
Model NavigationAI making real-time navigation decision

The combination of AI models with lightweight materials creates a powerful synergy that has the potential to transform the transportation industry. The compatibility between AI and lightweight materials is optimized through the use of techniques like model distillation and pruning, resulting in efficient and effective solutions. The potential for innovation, sustainability, and improved mobility is increasing at an exponential rate as the transportation sector continues to embrace the opportunities given by lightweight materials and AI.

12.5 CONNECTED DEVICES USED TO OPTIMIZE REAL-TIME MOBILITY

The fundamental perception and utilization of the transportation system have undergone a significant change with the implementation of real-time mobility optimization and the incorporation of interconnected devices [22]. This section examines the transformative role of connected devices in improving mobility, the complexity of data collection and processing for real-time analysis, the power of AI-driven traffic management, and a case study demonstrating customized route recommendations made possible by connected data.

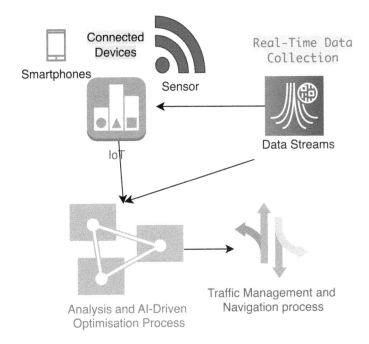

FIGURE 12.6 Utilizing connected devices for real-time mobility enhancement

12.5.1 THE FUNCTION OF CONNECTED DEVICES IN IMPROVING MOBILITY

In the area of improving mobility, connected gadgets have become crucial change agents. A vast and dynamic data ecosystem has been made possible by the widespread use of sensors, cellphones, vehicle telematics, and other associated devices [23], as shown in Figure 12.6. In addition to giving real-time information about traffic, road closures, weather patterns, and vehicle performance, these devices also create a framework for communication among various players in the transportation ecosystem [24].

A crucial transition from static data to dynamic, real-time information has been made with the integration of linked devices and mobility solutions. This change has significant effects on improving traffic control, navigation, and overall transportation effectiveness.

12.5.2 DATA PROCESSING AND COLLECTION FOR REAL-TIME ANALYSIS

The capacity of connected devices to gather a wealth of data from various sources in real time is their key competitive advantage. Due to the widespread use of smartphones and embedded sensors in infrastructure and vehicles, data is constantly being produced. The foundation of real-time analysis is this data, which enables transportation systems to anticipate changing circumstances. The processing and interpretation of this data is facilitated by the combination of linked devices and AI systems.

AI algorithms may find patterns, correlations, and anomalies in the data stream, turning unactionable data into insights that can be put to use. The basis for well-informed traffic management and navigation decisions is this real-time analysis.

12.5.3 TRAFFIC MANAGEMENT AND NAVIGATION POWERED BY AI

AI-driven traffic management and navigation become logical by-products of utilizing linked device capabilities. Real-time data can be used by traffic management systems to forecast congestion, spot bottlenecks, and dynamically change traffic signals. AI-driven navigation systems can provide real-time route suggestions that take into account the flow of traffic, road closures, and even individual driving styles. Traffic management has become a proactive process thanks to the union of AI and linked devices. These systems dynamically adjust to shifting circumstances to improve traffic flow, relieve congestion, and shorten travel times. Additionally, AI-enhanced navigation systems provide users with precise, real-time information, providing the best route options and improving overall travel experiences.

12.5.4 THE IMPACT OF AI-POWERED SENSORS AND CONNECTED DEVICES

Recent years have seen a seismic shift in the transport industry, driven by the quick development of connected devices and AI. This technological convergence has caused a paradigm shift that has altered how to view, use, and optimize transportation systems. The various effects of AI-powered sensors and connected devices on transportation are explored in this essay, along with the ways that real-time data enrichment, wise vehicle choices, and predictive insights are changing the world. In the transportation industry, the use of AI-powered sensors has ushered in a new era of real-time data collection and enrichment. These painstakingly planned and interconnected sensors serve as watchful sentinels, gathering a wealth of information about a variety of variables, including traffic flow, weather patterns, and road conditions. Vehicles and transport networks develop a thorough, real-time grasp of their environment by continuously updating this informational reservoir. A previously unachievable level of response is made possible by this dynamic awareness, opening the door for safer, more effective transportation. The intersection of AI and sensors has transformed the way that transportation is safe. Vehicles now have the capability to make judgments based on informed insights thanks to the influx of real-time data. This increased power results in a significant improvement in driving safety. The occurrences of AI-equipped vehicles receiving real-time data regarding accidents, road closures, and bad weather are dramatic illustrations of this phenomenon. These vehicles act as sentient organisms in a dynamic ecosystem by smoothly adapting their speeds, routes, and driving behaviors once they have this information. This adaptive decision-making reduces the likelihood of collisions and fosters a safer, more comfortable driving experience.

The incorporation of machine-learning algorithms that make use of the enormous datasets gathered from the maze of connected devices is essential to the evolution of transportation. These algorithms best represent the power of predictive insights since they can recognize complex patterns and trends. When AI-generated foresight is incorporated into the transportation equation, problems are approached head-on. Machine-learning systems forecast future occurrences like traffic jams or accidents on the basis of previous and real-time data. Armed with these forecasts, cars and traffic management systems adjust their routes and tactics in advance, maximizing the system's overall effectiveness. A turning point in the development of transportation may be seen in how AI-powered sensors, networked devices, and machine-learning techniques are coming together. This seamless integration not only protects people and things but also fosters synergy and synchrony within the transportation ecosystem. In the future when AI alters the very foundation of how we perceive and experience transport, the growing data reservoir supports this shift.

Looking ahead, the potential for AI to further transform transport is still really exciting. This trajectory is driven by the data's exponential growth, which is powered by the proliferation of connected devices. The depth of the data corpus grows day by day, giving AI systems access to tools and insights never before possible. This enhancement results in more accurate forecasts, flexible choices, and safer travel. The use of linked devices and AI in the transportation industry is not without its difficulties, though. Data security and privacy issues cast a shadow over this evolving environment. Concerns about security breaches are increased by the complex network of sensors gathering personal data and the crucial role AI plays in processing and analyzing this data. Strong data protection measures, strict privacy laws, and open data usage protocols are required to address these issues. As the transport industry moves farther into the AI space, finding the correct balance between innovation and protecting individual rights becomes more and more important. Additionally, players in the transportation industry face a high learning curve due to the deployment of AI and linked devices. It is crucial to make sure that all important actors, from legislators to manufacturers, are aware of the potential and constraints of AI-driven technologies. A smooth transition can be facilitated via training initiatives, cooperative projects, and multidisciplinary collaborations.

To sum up, the development of AI-powered sensors and linked devices has sparked a historic change in the transport industry. Our perspective on transportation networks has been completely transformed by the integration of real-time data enrichment, educated vehicle decisions, and predictive insights. This progress has brought about improved safety, more efficiency, and a more harmonious transportation ecosystem. The promise for a smarter, safer, and more responsive transportation scene is growing more and more exciting as AI continues to develop and connected devices proliferate. The difficulty is in realizing this promise while preserving moral principles, individual privacy rights, and comprehensive stakeholder participation.

12.5.5 CASE STUDY: USING CONNECTED DATA TO PROVIDE PERSONALIZED ROUTE RECOMMENDATIONS

The creation of personalized route recommendations is a compelling case study that demonstrates the possibility of using connected devices for mobility optimization.

AI algorithms can develop customized travel profiles for people by using data from connected sources like cell phones, car telematics, and other connected devices. These profiles consider past travel habits, preferences, and current traffic conditions. In reality, the AI-powered system analyses the available data to produce a customized route recommendation when a user starts a journey. This recommendation takes into account anticipated stops, preferred driving speeds, and scenic roads in addition to the fastest route. A personalized travel experience that optimizes route selection, reduces travel times, and raises user satisfaction is the end result. The revolutionary potential of linked devices and AI in influencing unique travel experiences is shown by this case study. It exemplifies how the combination of these technologies might bring about a time of individualized, effective, and data-driven mobility. The sample route recommendation system has been shown below and the comparison is shown in Figure 12.7.

Personalized Route Recommendation:

Recommended route for <__main__.User object at 0x79e71dcf5750>: Fastest route with scenic roads and preferred stops.

The new era of transportation is ushered in by the convergence of connected devices and real-time mobility optimization. These gadgets act as crucial data-collecting channels, allowing AI algorithms to power traffic management, navigation, and route suggestions. The potential for revolutionizing mobility, boosting efficiency, and providing personalized travel experiences becomes ever more evident as connected devices continue to proliferate and AI gets more advanced.

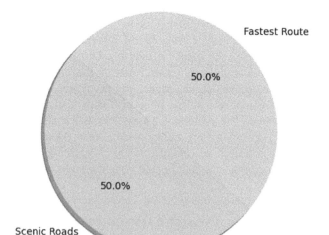

FIGURE 12.7   Route recommendation using the AI

12.6   ENABLING AUTONOMOUS MOBILITY SYSTEMS WITH AI

The evolution of autonomous mobility systems is a remarkable testament to the transformative power of AI [25]. This section delves into the profound impact of autonomous vehicles on mobility, the intricate AI technologies driving autonomous navigation, the imperative role of safety considerations in AI decision-making, and a case study that illuminates the potential of an AI-powered urban autonomous vehicle fleet. The following Figure 12.8, describes the components of autonomous mobility enabled by AI.

12.6.1   Autonomous Vehicles and Their Impact on Mobility

Autonomous vehicles have emerged as a groundbreaking innovation with the potential to revolutionize the concept of mobility, as shown in Figure 12.8. These vehicles, equipped with advanced sensors, AI algorithms, and real-time data processing capabilities, are redefining how people and goods move within urban environments [26]. The impact of autonomous vehicles extends beyond the realm of transportation—it influences urban planning, congestion reduction, and accessibility enhancement. The integration of AI into autonomous vehicles empowers them to navigate and make decisions independently. By eliminating the need for human drivers, autonomous vehicles hold the promise of safer, more efficient, and more accessible transportation

FIGURE 12.8   Components of autonomous mobility enabled by AI

options. This transformative potential is reshaping the future of mobility in ways that were once deemed futuristic.

12.6.2 AI Technologies for Autonomous Navigation

AI technologies form the bedrock of autonomous navigation, enabling vehicles to perceive, understand, and interact with their surroundings. Sensors such as LiDAR, cameras, and radar collect an abundance of real-time data, which is then processed and interpreted by AI algorithms. These algorithms enable vehicles to detect obstacles, interpret traffic signals, and make decisions based on complex environmental cues. Machine learning, a subset of AI, is particularly instrumental in training autonomous vehicles to navigate effectively. Through iterative learning processes, machine-learning algorithms enable vehicles to recognize patterns, anticipate behaviors, and adapt to dynamic situations. Reinforcement learning techniques empower autonomous vehicles to learn from trial and error, refining their decision-making abilities over time.

12.6.3 Safety Considerations and AI Decision-Making

The successful integration of AI in autonomous mobility systems hinges on ensuring safety and reliability. The complex task of making split-second decisions in unpredictable scenarios necessitates meticulous attention to safety considerations. AI algorithms must prioritize avoiding collisions, adhering to traffic rules, and interacting seamlessly with human-driven vehicles and pedestrians. The transparency and interpretability of AI decision-making processes are paramount. Explainable AI techniques are employed to render the decision-making rationale of AI algorithms comprehensible to human operators and regulators. This fosters accountability and builds trust in the capabilities of autonomous mobility systems.

12.6.4 Transforming Mobility with Cutting-Edge Technology

The rise of autonomous vehicles promise to revolutionize to view of mobility, safety, and accessibility on the roads, and as a result, the world of transportation is on the verge of a profound transformation. These cars, powered by highly developed AI systems, have the potential to completely transform the transportation industry. Along with altering how people move, the fusion of AI and autonomous vehicles is developing a symbiotic relationship between technology and transportation.

12.6.4.1 Navigation Powered by AI in Complex Environments

Transportation conventions are being steadily redefined as autonomous vehicles become more and more ingrained in our daily lives. AI-powered navigation, which enables vehicles to navigate through complex and dynamic situations with astounding precision, is the driving force behind this shift. These cars have an advanced set of sensors, cameras, and LiDAR systems that collaborate with AI algorithms to understand complicated road layouts, spot potential obstructions, and determine the best paths. The power of AI to process and analyze enormous volumes of real-time data is at the heart of this technology. The AI algorithms evaluate the data that the sensors collect about the environment around the car to make split-second decisions. This capacity enables autonomous vehicles to adjust to shifting traffic patterns, road conditions, and unforeseen impediments, delivering an unmatched level of precision and safety. The effects of AI-driven navigation are significant. Autonomous cars have the potential to greatly increase road safety by lowering the possibility of human error. Because AI algorithms are immune to the distractions, exhaustion, and emotional states that can impair human drivers, the chance of accidents brought on by these conditions is reduced. As a result, the technology has the ability to lower the number of accidents and fatalities on the road, making the road environment safer for all users.

12.6.4.2 Improved Communication to Optimize Traffic

The development of artificial intelligence in autonomous vehicles goes beyond each car's own capabilities. These cars are a component of a broader ecosystem in which interaction between moving objects and infrastructure along the route is crucial. Real-time information sharing between autonomous cars is made possible by the incorporation of AI-driven communication networks. Updates on traffic congestion, road closures, and other pertinent information that may affect the general traffic flow are shared in this information exchange. The seamless network of communication between infrastructure and autonomous vehicles paves the opportunity for coordinated operations that improve traffic flow. Vehicles can adapt collectively to changing conditions and make informed judgments that increase traffic efficiency when they can communicate and work together in real-time. This can improve commuters' overall transportation experiences by reducing traffic congestion and trip times, which has broad implications for urban mobility.

12.6.4.3 Reducing Human Error and Facilitating Access

The potential of autonomous vehicles to reduce accidents brought on by human mistakes is one of their most exciting features. Texting, being tired, and experiencing emotional discomfort are just a few of the countless distractions and limitations that human drivers are prone to, which can affect their ability to drive. As opposed to human operators, AI algorithms function without these flaws, increasing traffic safety. Autonomous vehicles have the potential to reduce the amount of collisions brought on by human error, saving lives and lowering injuries. These vehicles are more capable of anticipating and responding to possible threats as AI technology develops, making split-second judgments that put safety first. Additionally, the introduction of autonomous vehicles ushers in a new era of accessibility in the transportation industry. People who have trouble moving around, such as the elderly or people with impairments, frequently have trouble utilizing traditional transportation choices. This gap could be closed by autonomous vehicles by providing a kind of transportation that is suited to their need. A demographic group that has long been underserved by conventional transport systems can have their independence and quality of life improved by designing vehicles to fit different accessibility requirements.

The development of autonomous vehicles represents a critical turning point in the history of transportation. These cars are set to revolutionize how we move and interact on the roads thanks to the integration of AI-powered navigation, improved communication networks, and the potential to reduce human error. Everybody will have access to safer, more effective, and more accessible transportation solutions thanks to the interaction between AI and the transportation industry. The complex possibilities that lay ahead are brought to light as technology develops more. Along with upending preconceived concepts of transportation, the merging of AI and autonomous vehicles raises concerns about legal and ethical standards as well as potential societal repercussions. The advantages of AI-powered autonomous vehicles continue to be clear as stakeholders in the transportation ecosystem work through these difficulties. The fusion of transport and AI is transforming the world as we know it, opening the door to a new era of mobility that crosses boundaries and reimagines the future of transport. The future is full of opportunities, and as society begins to realize the potential of autonomous vehicles, the transition to safer, more effective, and more accessible transportation makes a significant stride forward.

12.6.5 Case Study: AI-Powered Urban Autonomous Vehicle Fleet

A compelling case study that epitomizes the potential of AI-enabled autonomous mobility is the development of an urban autonomous vehicle fleet. In this scenario, a fleet of AI-powered autonomous vehicles collaborates to optimize traffic flow, minimize congestion, and enhance overall urban mobility. These vehicles communicate with each other and with traffic management systems, sharing real-time data on road conditions, traffic patterns, and available parking spaces. Through AI algorithms, the fleet dynamically adjusts routes, coordinates traffic signals, and efficiently allocates parking spaces. The result is a harmonized transportation ecosystem that mitigates traffic congestion, reduces travel times, and enhances the overall quality of urban life. This case study underscores the transformative power of AI in creating interconnected and efficient autonomous mobility systems. Sample results are shown below in the graph in Figure 12.9.

Sample Result

Vehicle V1 Recommended Route: [1, 2, 3, 4]
Vehicle V2 Recommended Route: [1, 2, 3, 4]
Vehicle V3 Recommended Route: [1, 2, 3, 4]
Vehicle V4 Recommended Route: [1, 2, 3, 4]

The convergence of AI and autonomous mobility systems holds the promise of reshaping how we view transportation. As AI technologies power autonomous navigation, prioritize safety, and optimize decision-making, the potential for safer, more efficient, and more accessible transportation options becomes increasingly tangible. The case study exemplifies the real-world potential of AI-powered autonomous mobility systems in creating smart, interconnected urban environments. The journey

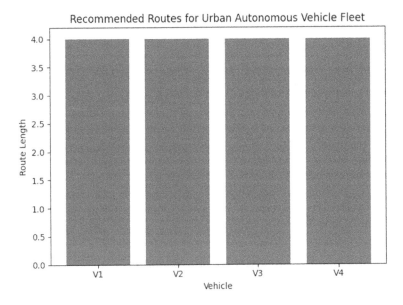

FIGURE 12.9   Autonomous vehicle fleet based on recommendation system

toward autonomous mobility is not just a technological evolution—it is a paradigm shift that redefines mobility and transportation.

12.7   ADJUSTING TO CHANGES IN PREFERENCES FOR MOBILITY

The dynamics of mobility choices are changing dramatically, and AI integration is becoming an essential tool for comprehending, anticipating, and adjusting to these changes [27]. The importance of understanding mobility behavior and preferences is explored in this section, along with the role data-driven prediction models play in forecasting shifts, the creation of adaptable mobility solutions informed by AI insights, and a case study showcasing the potential of predictive demand-responsive transportation.

12.7.1   Recognizing Mobile Attitudes and Preferences

As societies change, so do people's inclinations for movement. Changes in people's choice of where to go are influenced by a variety of factors, including urbanization, environmental concerns, technological development, and shifting socioeconomic dynamics [28]. It is essential to comprehend these intricate behavioral shifts in order to design transport systems that are in line with modern demands and ideals.

Analytics powered by AI provide a thorough insight into mobility behavior and preferences. AI systems find patterns, trends, and correlations by analyzing huge datasets from sources like cellphones, sensors, and social media. Understanding how people move, where they go, and what influences their mobility decisions is based on this data-driven insight.

12.7.2   MODELS FOR PREDICTING MOBILITY SHIFTS BASED ON DATA

The power of AI is best shown in its capacity to anticipate and adjust to new trends. Data-driven prediction models are essential for identifying trends in the mobility sector before they spread widely. These models estimate shifting mobility behaviors by combining historical information, socioeconomic variables, and outside factors. Data linkages that are concealed or cannot be seen by human observers are particularly well-suited for identification by machine-learning algorithms. These algorithms can spot early indications of mobility shifts by training on previous data. AI-driven prediction models provide crucial foresight to mobility planners and regulators, whether it be a spike in interest in electric scooters or a preference for shared rides.

12.7.3   AI-BASED SOLUTIONS FOR FLEXIBLE MOBILITY

The creation of flexible and adaptive mobility solutions is fueled by the insights gained from AI-driven analytics. Transport systems can proactively supply solutions that address changing needs by remaining aware of shifting preferences. For instance, a municipality might implement dynamic ride-sharing services, infrastructure for charging electric vehicles, or bike-sharing programs based on predictive AI insights. AI makes it easier to fine-tune transport services by enabling instantaneous changes. AI algorithms can quickly modify route design, vehicle allocation, and service offers when mobility preferences change. Transportation systems are kept current, effective, and user-responsive because of this adaptability.

12.7.4   EVOLUTION IN TRANSPORTATION PREFERENCES: THE IMPACT OF AI-POWERED MOBILITY SERVICES

The rise of mobility services powered by AI has had a significant impact on how the transportation scene is changing. Traditional norms have been upended by this paradigm change, which has led to the emergence of a fresh viewpoint on how people move around urban spaces. The fusion of artificial intelligence and transportation has created cutting-edge alternatives to traditional car ownership, fundamentally altering how people think about mobility. This essay explores the fundamental transformations brought about by AI-powered mobility services, looking at how they improve productivity, lessen traffic and pollution, and redefine urban mobility patterns.

12.7.4.1   AI-Powered Mobility Services for Change

A significant revolution in the transport industry has recently been brought about by the introduction of AI-powered mobility services. The expansion of services like ride-sharing and on-demand transportation has posed a threat to the conventional model of personal vehicle ownership. These services give people flexible alternatives to owning a car. They are made possible by advanced AI algorithms. The traditional transportation paradigm has been challenged by the convenience of booking rides at one's convenience and the seamless communication between drivers and passengers. With an emphasis on access rather than ownership, this change marks a divergence from the idea of personal automobile ownership.

12.7.4.2 Efficiency Through Route Matching and Optimization

Effective route planning and improved passenger–driver matching have both benefited from the incorporation of AI systems. These algorithms use real-time information on traffic conditions, destination locations, and available vehicles to design the best routes. AI-enhanced mobility services can make transportation more organized and time-effective by minimizing detours and cutting down on idle moments. These algorithms' operating efficiency has an impact on traffic congestion reduction on a larger scale than just personal convenience.

12.7.4.3 Shared Mobility Reduces Emissions and Traffic Jams

The development of shared mobility is a key aspect of this mobility revolution. Promoting carpooling and choosing public transport has two advantages. In the beginning, it results in a decrease in the total number of vehicles on the road. The burden on urban infrastructure is reduced as more individuals choose shared mobility, which reduces traffic congestion. Second, shared mobility contributes to sustainability objectives and environmental protection by lowering the number of private automobiles on the road, which reduces emissions and makes cities' air cleaner.

12.7.4.4 Accessibility and Socioeconomic Implications

Through AI-powered mobility services, transit is becoming more accessible than ever. The accessibility gap in cities could be filled by these services. These platforms offer an economical and practical form of transportation for people who might not be able to buy a car. This may have significant socioeconomic repercussions, allowing for greater mobility for a larger population and improving prospects for social contact, work, and education.

12.7.4.5 Technological Difficulties and Moral Issues

Although there is no denying the advantages of mobility services powered by AI, there are still difficulties in implementing such systems. The security and privacy of user data must be guaranteed. It is essential to safeguard this data against breaches and misuse because these platforms collect enormous volumes of information. To provide fair and equal access to these services, it is also essential to address algorithmic biases. To establish credibility and win public acceptance, it's critical to strike a balance between technological improvements and moral issues.

The adoption of mobility services powered by AI signifies a significant change in how society views and uses transportation. These services serve as a prime example of how AI has the power to radically alter urban mobility patterns while advancing efficiency, accessibility, and sustainability. The move away from traditional car ownership in favor of shared mobility denotes a paradigm change in favor of transportation options that are resource- and environmental-wise. Even though there are still issues, the development of AI-powered mobility services indicates a positive trend in the direction of a more integrated, effective, and fair urban transportation environment.

12.7.5   CASE STUDY: DEMAND-RESPONSIVE TRANSPORTATION

The creation of predictive demand-responsive transport is a compelling case study that illustrates the possibilities of AI-enabled flexible mobility solutions. In this case, real-time data, past travel patterns, demographic changes, and AI algorithms are used to estimate the demand for transit. By using this data to guide dynamic vehicle and service allocation, transportation resources are optimized to meet changing demand. For instance, a demand-responsive transport system powered by AI might foresee increasing demand during peak periods or special occasions. In order to handle the rush, it adds more trucks or modifies routes. This case study highlights AI's potential to not only predict changes in mobility but also dynamically modify transportation infrastructure to accommodate those changes. The sample results are shown below with a comparison in Figure 12.10 and Figure 12.11.

```
Enter time of day (Peak/Off-Peak): 2
Is it a special occasion? (Yes/No): Yes
Predicted Demand: 79
Vehicle Allocation:
Truck: 8
Van: 15
Car: 30
```

A disruptive approach to transport planning and service is provided by the integration of AI with understanding and accommodating shifts in mobility choices. The continued relevance and responsiveness of transport networks are ensured by data-driven prediction models and flexible solutions powered by AI insights. The case study demonstrates the ability to match transportation services with current demand, highlighting the potential of AI in predictive demand-responsive transportation. AI will be crucial in assisting in the development of transport options that suit the preferences of contemporary societies as the mobility landscape continues to change.

12.8   FUTURE PLANS AND RESEARCH POSSIBILITIES

AI is an emerging field that holds a lot of promise for innovation and discovery in the quest to improve mobility [29]. This chapter explores the fascinating world of future directions and research opportunities in the field of AI-driven mobility enhancement, including the emergence of new AI technologies, the framework's scalability to larger urban areas, the integration of explainable AI and ethical considerations, and the prospects of collaborative mobility ecosystems and cross-domain applications [30].

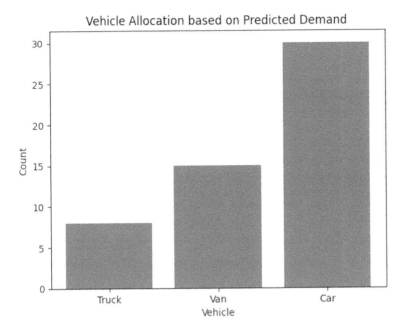

FIGURE 12.10   Vehicle allocation based on prediction with special occasion

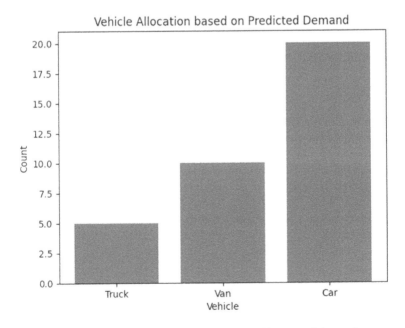

FIGURE 12.11   Vehicle allocation based on prediction without special occasion

12.8.1 New AI Technologies to Improve Mobility

The field of AI technology is constantly changing and offers a wealth of new opportunities for improving mobility. The combination of cutting-edge technologies like reinforcement learning, computer vision, and natural language processing offers enormous potential as AI algorithms get more complex. Natural language interfaces could help people and transport systems communicate easily, while computer vision could improve safety by improving object identification. Using reinforcement learning approaches, autonomous navigation and decision-making could be improved, leading to an overall improvement in mobility solutions. The combination of future technology and AI not only enhances current mobility services but also creates whole new opportunities. Innovative mobility experiences could result from the fusion of AI with Internet of Things (IoT) gadgets, 5G connection, and edge computing. In these scenarios, vehicles and infrastructure would be able to communicate in real time to create a more connected and efficient transportation environment.

12.8.2 The Framework's Scalability to Larger Urban Areas

Scaling AI-driven mobility frameworks to larger urban areas is one of the most urgent research issues. The success of these frameworks in vast metropolises with complicated traffic patterns and a variety of user behaviors is an issue that researchers are actively addressing, even if they have shown promise in controlled environments. In addition to technical factors, scalability also entails adaptable policy frameworks, urban planning techniques, and infrastructure development. While keeping the efficiency and efficacy shown in smaller-scale implementations, AI models must take into account the special characteristics of bigger urban regions.

12.8.3 Combining AI That Can Be Explained and Ethical Considerations

Transparency, accountability, and ethical considerations are becoming more and more crucial as AI gets more and more integrated into mobility solutions. A developing area of research called explainable AI (XAI) tries to make AI decision-making processes understandable to both professionals and non-experts. In safety-critical applications like driverless vehicles, where users and regulators must understand how AI systems make judgments, XAI is especially pertinent. For AI-enhanced mobility solutions to be beneficial to society as a whole, it is crucial to strike a balance between innovation and ethical considerations, including concerns about data privacy, bias reduction, and justice.

12.8.4 Cross-Domain Applications and Collaborative Mobility Ecosystems

Collaborative ecosystems that connect multiple areas and stakeholders hold the key to the future of mobility development. Researchers are investigating the seamless integration of shared mobility services, public transport, and urban infrastructure with AI-powered mobility solutions. These ecosystems have the ability to develop comprehensive and effective mobility solutions that meet a variety of user needs by encouraging cooperation across various types of transportation. Applications that span domains are a fascinating new area of study. AI-powered mobility insights can be used in emergency response systems, energy management, and urban planning. For example, using mobility data might help plan disaster recovery, arrange charging stations for electric cars, and time traffic lights more efficiently. There are many opportunities for AI-driven mobility enhancement in the future. Emerging AI technology, scalability to bigger urban areas, ethical considerations, and collaborative ecosystems are all potential hotspots for innovation and game-changing effects. The convergence of technology, society, and transportation promises a future where mobility is safer, more effective, and more accessible for all as academics and practitioners continue to push the limits of AI and mobility.

12.9 CONCLUSION

The fusion of mobility with AI has the potential to fundamentally alter how societies navigate their urban environments. Each aspect highlights the transformative potential of AI in transportation, from reducing power consumption in AI-driven mobility solutions to integrating lightweight materials in AI models, utilizing connected devices for real-time optimization, enabling autonomous mobility systems, and adapting to changes in mobility preferences. These innovations lead to a paradigm change toward more sustainable, open, and user cantered transportation experiences in addition to improved efficiency and safety. Looking ahead, there are several intriguing possibilities for AI-powered mobility. AI will continue to be at the forefront of improving mobility thanks to emerging AI technologies, which promise to further innovate and improve transportation solutions. The inclusion, transparency, and ethical soundness of the benefits of AI-driven mobility will depend on its scalability to wider urban areas and the combination of explainable AI and ethical considerations. A new era of interconnected urban systems, where AI insights go beyond transportation to influence urban planning, energy efficiency, and emergency response, is heralded by collaborative mobility ecosystems and cross-domain applications. The intersection of AI and mobility holds the potential for a more seamless, effective, and sustainable urban future as researchers, policymakers, and practitioners continue to investigate these future directions and research opportunities. The transformative potential of technology-driven mobility solutions illuminates the way forward by leveraging AI to adapt to changing preferences, optimize resources, and improve user experiences. The goal of a smarter, safer, and more accessible urban mobility landscape can be achieved for the benefit of societies everywhere via continual innovation and collaboration.

REFERENCES

1. Nikitas, A., Michalakopoulou, K., Njoya, E.T. and Karampatzakis, D., 2020. Artificial intelligence, transport and the smart city: Definitions and dimensions of a new mobility era. *Sustainability*, *12*(7), p. 2789.

2. Iyer, L.S., 2021. AI enabled applications towards intelligent transportation. *Transportation Engineering*, 5, p. 100083.
3. Saboor, A., Coene, S., Vinogradov, E., Tanghe, E., Joseph, W. and Pollin, S., 2021. Elevating the future of mobility: UAV-enabled intelligent transportation systems. arXiv Preprint ArXiv:2110.09934.
4. Shaheen, S., Totte, H. and Stocker, A., 2018. Future of mobility white paper.
5. Curtis, C., Stone, J., Legacy, C. and Ashmore, D., 2019. Governance of future urban mobility: A research agenda. *Urban Policy and Research*, 37(3), pp. 394–404.
6. Abduljabbar, R., Dia, H., Liyanage, S. and Bagloee, S.A., 2019. Applications of artificial intelligence in transport: An overview. *Sustainability*, 11(1), p. 189.
7. Kulkarni, P., 2021, July. Transformation of mobility industry by advanced digital technologies. *Journal of Physics: Conference Series*, 1964(4), p. 042020.
8. Alex David, S., Varsha, V., Ravali, Y. and Naga Amrutha Saranya, N., 2022. Comparative analysis of diabetes prediction using machine learning. In *Soft Computing for Security Applications: Proceedings of ICSCS* (pp. 155–163). Singapore: Springer Nature Singapore.
9. David, S.A., Mahesh, C., Kumar, V.D., Polat, K., Alhudhaif, A. and Nour, M., 2022. Retinal blood vessels and optic disc segmentation using U-net. *Mathematical Problems in Engineering*, 2022, pp. 1–11.
10. Jothi, C.S., Usha, V., David, S.A. and Mohammed, H., 2018. Abnormality classification of brain tumor in MRI images using multiclass SVM. *Research Journal of Pharmacy and Technology*, 11(3), pp. 851–856.
11. Ai, Q., Qiao, X., Liao, Y. and Yu, Q., 2021. Joint optimization of usvs communication and computation resource in irs-aided wireless inland ship mec networks. *IEEE Transactions on Green Communications and Networking*, 6(2), pp. 1023–1036.
12. Franki, V., Majnarić, D. and Višković, A., 2023. A comprehensive review of artificial intelligence (AI) companies in the power sector. *Energies*, 16(3), p. 1077.
13. Chon, Y., Talipov, E., Shin, H. and Cha, H., 2011, November. Mobility prediction-based smartphone energy optimization for everyday location monitoring. In *Proceedings of the 9th ACM Conference on Embedded Networked Sensor Systems* (pp. 82–95).
14. Ghorbani, E., Fluechter, T., Calvet, L., Ammouriova, M., Panadero, J. and Juan, A.A., 2023. Optimizing energy consumption in smart cities' mobility: Electric vehicles, algorithms, and collaborative economy. *Energies*, 16(3), p. 1268.
15. Thylashri, S., Femi, D., David, S.A. and Suresh, A., 2018. Vitality and peripatetic sustain cluster key management schemes in MANET. *International Journal of Engineering and Technology*, 7(2), pp. 43–46.
16. Maguire, J.F., Miller, M.A. and Venketesan, S., 1998. Processing of soft matter and composites: Integration of material sensors with process models and intelligent control algorithms. *Engineering Applications of Artificial Intelligence*, 11(5), pp. 605–618.
17. Sundberg, L.T. and Holmström, J., 2022. Towards 'lightweight' artificial intelligence: A typology of AI service platforms. *AMCIS 2022 Proceedings*. 13.16-21.
18. Xu, Y., Liu, X., Cao, X., Huang, C., Liu, E., Qian, S., Liu, X., Wu, Y., Dong, F., Qiu, C.W. and Qiu, J., 2021. Artificial intelligence: A powerful paradigm for scientific research. *Innovation*, 28(4), pp. 12–16.
19. Kumar, K.A., Ravikumar, S. and David, S.A., 2018. Compression and decompression of encrypted image using wavelet transform. *Journal of Computational and Theoretical Nanoscience*, 15(11–12), pp. 3528–3532.
20. Ravikumar, S., Kumar, K.A. and Koteeswaran, S., 2018. Dismemberment of metaphors with grid scratch via kernel k-means. *Journal of Computational and Theoretical Nanoscience*, 15(11–12), pp. 3533–3537.

21. Nah, F.F.H., Siau, K. and Sheng, H., 2005. The value of mobile applications: A utility company study. *Communications of the ACM, 48*(2), pp. 85–90.

22. Ravi, D., Wong, C., Lo, B. and Yang, G.Z., 2016. A deep learning approach to on-node sensor data analytics for mobile or wearable devices. *IEEE Journal of Biomedical and Health Informatics, 21*(1), pp. 56–64.

23. David, S.A., Ravikumar, S. and Begum, A., 2018. Handover authentication mechanism using ticket for IEEE 802.16 m. *Journal of Computational and Theoretical Nanoscience, 15*(11–12), pp. 3442–3445.

24. Fragapane, G., De Koster, R., Sgarbossa, F. and Strandhagen, J.O., 2021. Planning and control of autonomous mobile robots for intralogistics: Literature review and research agenda. *European Journal of Operational Research, 294*(2), pp. 405–426.

25. Dartmann, G., Schmeink, A., Lücken, V., Song, H., Ziefle, M. and Prestiflippo, G. eds., 2021. *Smart Transportation: AI Enabled Mobility and Autonomous Driving.* CRC Press.

26. Ahmed, S.T., Basha, S.M., Ramachandran, M., Daneshmand, M. and Gandomi, A.H., 2023. An edge-AI enabled autonomous connected ambulance route resource recommendation protocol (ACA-R3) for ehealth in Smart cities. *IEEE Internet of Things Journal, 19*(4), pp. 100–107.

27. Deane, G.D., 1990. Mobility and adjustments: Paths to the resolution of residential stress. *Demography, 27*(1), pp. 65–79.

28. Yang, Z., Chen, J., Hu, J., Shu, Y. and Cheng, P., 2019. Mobility modeling and data-driven closed-loop prediction in bike-sharing systems. *IEEE Transactions on Intelligent Transportation Systems, 20*(12), pp. 4488–4499.

29. Kozlov, I.P., 2022. Optimizing public transport services using AI to reduce congestion in metropolitan area. *International Journal of Intelligent Automation and Computing, 5*(2), pp. 1–14.

30. Mahor, V., Bijrothiya, S., Mishra, R., Rawat, R. and Soni, A., 2022. The smart city based on AI and infrastructure: A new mobility concepts and realities. *Autonomous Vehicles Volume 1: Using Machine Intelligence, 1*(4), pp. 277–295.

13 Leveraging Intelligent Systems and the AIoT/IIoT for Enhanced Waste Management and Recycling Efficiency

J. Vijay Arputharaj, Joanna Mariam Varkey, Rishi Vagadia, and Ramesh Kumar Ayyasamy

13.1 ADVANCING WASTE MANAGEMENT: SHIFTING PARADIGMS THROUGH INTELLIGENT SYSTEMS AND THE IIOT

The development of waste management is evidence of human ingenuity and adaptation. The evolution from primitive methods of garbage disposal used by ancient civilizations to the complex web of intelligent waste management systems used today is astounding. The problems with garbage disposal grew increasingly severe as populations increased and industrialization spread. However, difficulties also presented chances for invention.

This piece explores this evolution, following the path from outmoded practices to contemporary cutting-edge alternatives. The guiding lights of this change have emerged as Intelligent Systems and the Industrial Internet of Things (IIoT). By combining sensors, algorithms, and real-time information, they have transformed trash management into a data-driven ecosystem that optimizes every step of the waste journey [1].

Essentially, waste management has evolved from a critical issue to a hub of innovation. An image of efficiency, sustainability, and advancement has been painted on the canvas of waste management by Intelligent Systems and the IIoT.

The historical difficulty of waste management reverberates throughout eras, illustrating the tenuous balance between natural harmony and human advancement. Generations have been affected by the effects of poor disposal methods, which include pollution and health problems. However, this story has changed dramatically as a result of two forces at work: heightened societal awareness and the quickening rise of technological prowess [2].

DOI: 10.1201/9781032642789-13

A significant change happened as cultures became aware of the dangers of unrestrained waste. Growing environmental consciousness has highlighted the significance of ethical waste management. This change fostered a widespread commitment to protecting the environment by signaling a break from the "out of sight, out of mind" mentality. Technology, which is frequently seen as a source of difficulty, has simultaneously become a ray of optimism.

Waste management has undergone an alchemical transformation thanks to the integration of Intelligent Systems and the IIoT, going from a problem to a catalyst for change. Intelligent Systems introduced a level of precision that was previously unimaginable, empowered by artificial intelligence's (AI) brilliance. AI-powered sorting technology improved recycling while simultaneously reducing contamination, starting a sustainable loop

The IIoT is the crescendo of innovation. The IIoT is a network of linked sensors and gadgets that depicts real-time insights. Waste management is transformed into a symphony of efficiency and environmental awareness thanks to the IIoT's symposium of data, which includes waste bins that broadcast fill levels and processing centers that coordinate activities.

This chapter explains how the fusion of human will and technology prowess can recalibrate the trajectory of our ecological footprint. It is a journey into the heart of waste management's revolution. It reveals a future in which efficient, sustainable, and data-driven optimization coexist peacefully on a canvas, where waste management no longer represents degradation and its impact on various aspects of industrial operations are briefed along with the answers to the questions listed below:

- How is the technological and historical evolution of smart waste management involved in the transformation from Industry 4.0 to Industry 5.0?
- How does the role of Intelligent Systems and the IIoT in waste management contribute to Industry 5.0?
- What are the significance, impact, and challenges on the IIoT for waste management environment and recycling efficiency?

13.1.1 Technological and Historical Evolution

The history of waste management unfolds a narrative entwined with technological advancement and its effects on the environment. The problem of waste management grew from the earliest human settlements, where waste was placed in specific locations, to the thriving civilizations that came after. The emergence of crude landfills and incineration, symbolic of societies coping with the exponential rise in waste generation, was witnessed by the unrelenting march of time. Some of the important sustainable technologies in Industry 5.0 are shown in Figure 13.1

Waste management arose as a pressing concern as urbanization became the defining feature of modernity. These early trash disposal techniques emerged as a result of the emergence of densely populated cities, which demanded innovative solutions. A paradigm shift, however, began in the 20th century. A growing understanding of

Renewable Energy Sources   Smart Grid Technologies   Waste Management and   Water Conservation   Intelligent
and Mangement   Recycling   Technologies   Manufacturing Systems

FIGURE 13.1   Sustainable technologies in Industry 5.0

the effects on the environment compelled societies to reconsider their relationship with trash.

The turning point in trash management came during this era. Industrialization's aftereffects, such as pollution and ecological deterioration, prompted a shift in public opinion toward sustainable methods. Thus, the early steps toward a more responsible treatment of garbage were highlighted by the introduction of waste reduction methods and emerging recycling programs. The haphazard dumping tactics of the past were being replaced with improved landfill practices that were based on scientific knowledge.

Looking back, the development of waste management can be seen as a reflection of how humanity has progressed from crude disposal techniques to responsible policies that support the health of both society and the environment. This historical context serves as the foundation for contemporary waste management solutions, guiding us toward a future when trash is no longer a problem but instead presents an opportunity for growth.

Technology's incorporation into waste management heralds a paradigm change in which innovation melds with necessity. A new era of waste management has begun as a result of this modernization, which incorporates a variety of technical marvels like sensors, automation, and data analytics. This point reflects a fork in the road when sustainability meets efficiency and new possibilities open up.

Intelligent Systems, a symphony of artificial intelligence and machine learning, are at the center of this growth. These tools choreograph a data-driven revolution, making it possible to collect data in real-time that reveals the waste dynamics' rich tapestry. The predictive modeling canvas comes to life, revealing insights that take decision-making to a previously unheard-of level. What was formerly a space for educated guesses is now a space based on empirical accuracy.

With the development of IIoT applications [3], the story becomes more intense. The IIoT is an example of a network of linked equipment, sensors, and gadgets that come together to form a remote connection symphony. This connectivity brings an unanticipated dynamic to trash management, with sensors placed in waste bins transmitting fill-level data in real time, data analytics directing collection vehicles to the best routes, and processing centers utilizing findings for resource optimization [4].

With the fusion of these technologies, waste management is now an intelligent activity. It is an expression of human inventiveness supported by the skill of algorithms and the knowledge of real-time data. By combining these two concepts, waste management transcends its previous constraints and becomes an agile activity governed by the ideas of effectiveness, sustainability, and well-informed decision-making. Here's an overview of key technologies and year-wise advancements in waste management and recycling processes in advanced countries, specifically utilizing sensor technologies:

13.1.2 ROLE OF INTELLIGENT SYSTEMS

A role that resonates throughout every aspect of the waste journey is that of Intelligent Systems emerging as the architects of precision in waste management.

TABLE 13.1

Key Advancements in Waste Management and Recycling Processes in Advanced Countries

Country	Year	Remarkable advancement
United States	2000s	The adoption of RFID (Radio-Frequency Identification) technology [4] in waste bins to monitor fill levels and optimize collection routes began.
	2010s	Advanced sensors and GPS tracking integrated into waste collection vehicles [5] allowed for real-time route optimization and more efficient pickup schedules.
	2020s	Smart waste bins equipped with sensors for not only fill levels but also temperature, humidity, and even hazardous waste detection became more prevalent, enhancing waste management accuracy and safety [6].
Japan	2000s	Sensor technologies [7] were integrated into incineration plants for real-time monitoring of emissions and combustion processes, ensuring compliance with environmental regulations.
	2010s	Sensor-equipped waste bins capable of communicating fill levels allowed for optimized collection schedules and resource allocation [8].
	2020s	Enhanced data analytics and sensor technologies are integrated to monitor recycling rates and identify potential areas for improvement in the waste management process [9].
Netherlands	2000s	Smart waste bins with sensors for monitoring fill levels and integrated Wi-Fi connectivity were implemented for more efficient waste collection [10].
	2010s	Advanced sensor networks were utilized in waste-to-energy plants to monitor combustion processes, emissions, and energy production [11].
	2020s	Sensor-driven sorting systems and AI-based technologies have further improved waste recycling rates by accurately sorting different materials [12].
South Korea	2000s	RFID and barcode technologies were incorporated into waste collection to enable accurate waste-sorting at the source.
	2010s	Sensor-equipped bins were introduced to monitor waste generation patterns and optimize collection routes.
	2020s	Continued emphasis on sensor technologies for waste-sorting, combined with innovative waste-to-energy processes monitored by advanced sensors, has increased resource efficiency [12].

These technologies orchestrate a symphony of sustainability and efficiency in addition to sorting, and rewriting the history of trash management in the process.

Intelligent Systems shine as the accuracy-bearers in the sorting field. They decipher the complexities of trash streams, separating recyclables from the tangled web of mixed rubbish, using cutting-edge sensors and the wonders of AI. As a result, there has been a revolutionary leap that reduces contamination, increases recycling rates, and provides a lifeline to threatened ecosystems.

However, the effect of Intelligent Systems remains strong there. Their influence is felt right at the core of resource optimization, where their algorithms jive with the fundamentals of effectiveness. trash management goes beyond the conventional as a result of these systems' decoding of the best resource allocation, a symposium where trash reduction and sustainable resource usage become buddies.

Predictive maintenance algorithms [13] serve as efficiency saviors, demonstrating the need for Intelligent Systems. They are the masterminds behind optimization, assuring the continual efficiency of the equipment required for waste processing. As these algorithms predict the needs of the equipment, they orchestrate a ballet of smooth operations, reducing downtime and maintenance expenses to a bare fraction.

Intelligent Systems are essentially the lighthouses illuminating waste management's undiscovered oceans. They have made an enduring impression on everything from resource optimization's creativity to predictive maintenance's pragmatism. It's a distinction that elevates waste management to the level of a comprehensive display of effectiveness, sustainability, and foresight.

With the rise of the Industrial Internet of Things, waste management is given a fresh canvas where connectivity serves as the foundation for effectiveness and sustainability. In this age of connectivity, sensors can be found inside trash cans, on pickup trucks, and at processing plants. A linked ecosystem is born from the symphony of real-time data that follows, a web that leaves a trail of change in its wake.

Similar to the tune of an orchestra, the data contains insights that are just waiting to be revealed. This data transforms trash management into an art form through the power of analytics. Routes are no longer predetermined; instead, they are created through the analysis of data in real time, creating a tapestry of efficiency that reduces emissions and fuel consumption.

Waste bins become beacons of knowledge as a result of the dance of data that extends to fill levels. The system coordinates pickups that are both timely and effective as sensors convey fill levels. Overflowing trash cans and pointless trips become relics of the past, replaced by an orchestrated coordination of data-driven actions.

In this cutting-edge symposium, the IIoT is more than just a technological wonder; it's also the catalyst for a seamless waste management process. It has a cascading effect on operating efficiency, fuel conservation, and pollution reduction. Waste management occurs through a digital ballet of connectedness as a collaboration between technology and sustainability, not only as a method. The evolution of waste management paradigms: historical context and examples with reference to IIoT technology shown in Table 13.2.

Instead of only bringing efficiency, the integration of Intelligent Systems and the IIoT into waste management unleashes a wave of environmental advantages that extend far beyond the boundaries of the trash can. Here, the transformation story goes beyond merely operational improvement to become a story of stewardship.

A sign of this trend is the decline in landfill utilization. Intelligent Systems' accuracy ensures that garbage is divided, distributed, and recycled precisely. This reduces

TABLE 13.2

Evolution of Waste Management Paradigms: Historical Context and Examples

Era	Historical Context	Example
Pre-Industrial	Basic waste disposal, minimal environmental concern	Throwing waste into designated areas.
Industrialization	Urbanization, increased waste, rudimentary methods	Open dumping, basic incineration.
Environmental	Rise of environmental awareness, waste reduction	Introduction of recycling programs.
Information Age	Technology integration, data-driven insights	Smart waste bins for data-driven collection.
Intelligent Systems	AI and automation, waste-sorting optimization	AI-powered sorting facilities for recycling.
IIoT Integration	Networked devices, real-time monitoring	Sensors in bins for optimized collection routes.

the load on landfills, frees up space, and stops the flow of dangerous chemicals that pollute soil and water.

The shackles of mediocrity that long characterized waste management are being broken as recycling rates rise. These rates are accelerated by intelligent sorting, which saves recyclable materials from an unjust fate and redirects them to a new life cycle. It's a transformation that, on its own, reflects sustainability's beneficial cycle.

However, the reduction of greenhouse gas emissions continues to mark the most significant development. With the sophistication of data analytics, optimized collecting routes reduce the gasoline usage that formerly contaminated the environment. With this orchestration, waste management is portrayed as a tool for change toward a greener future, which is consistent with the larger goal of resource conservation.

Environmental advantages become more apparent as the crescendo in the symphony of Intelligent Systems and the IIoT. Resource conservation and emissions reduction are echoed by increased recycling rates, decreased landfill usage, and optimized collection routes. It is more than just a matter of improving operations; it represents a more accountable, environmentally conscious future.

13.1.3 SIGNIFICANCE, IMPACT, AND CHALLENGES OF THE IIoT FOR WASTE MANAGEMENT AND RECYCLING EFFICIENCY

The IIoT has the potential to bring about significant advancements in waste management and recycling efficiency, leading to improved sustainability, reduced environmental impact, and more streamlined operations. Here's a breakdown of the significance, impact, and challenges associated with applying IIoT in the waste management and recycling sector compared to Table 13.3.

TABLE 13.3

The IIoT in the Waste Management and Recycling Significance, Impact and Challenges

Significance and Impact	Challenges
Data-Driven Decision-Making: The IIoT enables the collection of real-time data from various sensors and devices deployed throughout the waste management and recycling processes.	Data Security and Privacy: The IIoT relies on data collection and transmission, which raises concerns about data security and privacy. Protecting sensitive data from breaches and unauthorized access is a critical challenge.
Remote Monitoring and Control: The IIoT allows waste management systems to be remotely monitored and controlled. This means that operators can manage waste collection, sorting, and recycling processes from a centralized location, reducing the need for on-site personnel and optimizing resource allocation.	Interoperability: Integrating various sensors, devices, and systems from different manufacturers can be complex due to compatibility issues. Ensuring seamless communication and interoperability is essential for a successful IIoT implementation.
Optimized Collection Routes: The IIoT can help optimize waste collection routes by analyzing real-time data on fill levels in waste bins. This leads to reduced fuel consumption, lower emissions, and minimized collection time.	Infrastructure and Connectivity: The IIoT requires robust and reliable connectivity to transmit real-time data. In some regions, especially remote or underserved areas, connectivity issues might hinder the deployment and effectiveness of IIoT solutions.
Predictive Maintenance: Sensors embedded in equipment can provide insights into the condition of machinery, predicting maintenance needs and preventing unplanned downtime. This leads to more efficient use of equipment and reduced maintenance costs.	Data Management and Analysis: Handling the large amounts of data generated by IIoT devices requires sophisticated data management and analysis tools. Extracting actionable insights from this data can be challenging without the right resources and expertise.
Environmental Benefits: By enabling better waste management and recycling practices, the IIoT can contribute to reducing the environmental impact of waste disposal and resource extraction, leading to a more sustainable approach.	Regulatory and Compliance Issues: Waste management and recycling are subject to various regulations and standards. Adapting IIoT systems to comply with these regulations can be a complex task.

The adoption of the IIoT in waste management and recycling can lead to more efficient, sustainable, and environmentally friendly practices. However, addressing challenges related to data security, interoperability, infrastructure, and data management is crucial to fully realize the potential benefits of the IIoT in this sector.

Data privacy is brought up as a vital factor. The dynamic sharing of real-time information necessitates the protection of personal information. To ensure that the advantages gained do not come at the expense of individual rights, the very data that drives efficiency must be covered in multiple levels of protection [14].

Another conundrum is the incorporation of technology. A variety of technologies must work in harmony to create the symphony of Intelligent Systems and the IIoT. System communication is seamless in this delicate ballet, and errors are not tolerated. A request for interoperability that goes beyond the domain is being made here.

The initial barrier to financial investment is frequently very high, despite it being a cornerstone of growth. A long-term perspective is required because the integration of Intelligent Systems and IIoT calls for resource allocation. Determining the return on investment, which includes both operational efficiency and the ecological benefits that subsequent generations will experience, is difficult [14].

In the future, efforts to overcome these obstacles are outlined in the innovation roadmaps. Intelligent Systems develop to more accurately understand subtleties as a result of the improvement of algorithms. The goal of improving interoperability is to create a seamless narrative by combining the knowledge of many technologies. The goal of raising public knowledge is what drives everything, after all.

The desire for a future that incorporates both technology marvels and the responsibility they involve grows as communities become more aware of the possibilities.

In short, the path of IIoT and Intelligent Systems in waste management is a monument to the harmony of innovation and difficulties. The goal of this journey is not simply operational excellence but also a comprehensive transformation that protects privacy, breaks down technical boundaries, and guarantees that the investments made today will have a positive impact on a better, greener future.

13.2 IIOT SOLUTIONS FOR SMARTER WASTE MANAGEMENT AND RECYCLING OPTIMIZATION

Incorporating real-time monitoring with the IIoT dashboards aligns seamlessly with Industry 5.0, elevating our waste management application. This integration enhances stakeholder engagement, fuels dynamic decision-making, and fosters sustainability. Interconnectivity: The IIoT connects devices, sensors, machines, and systems, enabling real-time data flow for better visibility and control.

IIoT solutions have the potential to revolutionize waste management and recycling by enabling smarter, more efficient processes. These solutions leverage sensors, data analytics, connectivity, and automation to optimize waste collection, sorting, recycling, and disposal operations.

13.2.1 Smarter Waste Management and Recycling Optimization

Here's how the IIoT can be applied to achieve smarter waste management and recycling optimization:

- *Smart Bin Monitoring:* IIoT-enabled sensors can be installed in waste bins and containers to monitor fill levels in real time. This data helps optimize waste collection routes by ensuring that collection trucks are dispatched only when bins are full, reducing unnecessary trips and saving fuel and operational costs. Enevo, a waste management company, utilizes sensors in trash bins to monitor fill levels. This data is then used to optimize collection routes, leading to cost savings and reduced environmental impact [15].

- *Route Optimization:* IIoT platforms can analyze data from sensors to optimize waste collection routes. By considering factors like real-time traffic conditions and bin fill levels, collection routes can be dynamically adjusted to minimize travel time and fuel consumption [16].
- *Predictive Maintenance:* Sensors can be deployed in waste collection vehicles and equipment to monitor their performance and detect potential issues. Predictive maintenance algorithms can use this data to identify maintenance needs before breakdowns occur, reducing downtime and increasing operational efficiency. FCC Environment, a waste management company, uses the IIoT to monitor the condition of its vehicle fleet. This approach has led to reduced downtime and improved operational efficiency [17].
- *Waste Tracking and Traceability:* The IIoT can provide end-to-end visibility into the waste management process, enabling better tracking, tracing, and reporting of waste materials. This supports compliance with regulations and enhances accountability. RecycleSmart Solutions offers a platform that uses IIoT sensors to track and trace waste materials in real time. This assists businesses in achieving their sustainability goals and complying with waste regulations [18].
- *Energy Management:* IIoT systems can optimize energy consumption in waste treatment and recycling facilities. By monitoring energy usage and analyzing data, operators can identify opportunities for energy efficiency improvements and cost savings. The City of London worked with Veolia to optimize energy usage in a waste transfer station using the IIoT. Sensors track energy consumption, helping to identify areas for efficiency improvements [19].
- *Supply Chain Visibility:* For recycling processes that involve multiple stages or facilities, IIoT can provide end-to-end visibility into the supply chain. This transparency helps optimize processes, track materials, and ensure compliance with regulations [20].
- *Data Analytics for Insights:* IIoT-generated data can be analyzed to gain insights into waste generation patterns, recycling rates, and operational efficiencies. This information can inform decision-making and guide strategies for waste reduction and resource optimization [21].
- *Remote Monitoring and Control:* IIoT platforms enable remote monitoring and control of waste management and recycling systems. Operators can manage processes, adjust settings, and address issues without the need for physical presence, improving operational agility [22].
- *Sustainability Reporting:* IIoT solutions can streamline the process of collecting and reporting sustainability metrics. Accurate data on waste reduction, recycling rates, and carbon footprint can be generated automatically for compliance and reporting purposes [23].

- *Public Engagement:* The IIoT can be used to engage the public in waste reduction efforts. Smart bins with displays can provide real-time feedback on waste disposal practices, encouraging responsible behavior and raising awareness [24].
- *Recycling Sorting Optimization:* IIoT technologies can enhance recycling processes by providing real-time data on the composition of incoming waste. This information helps optimize sorting processes, resulting in increased recycling rates and improved resource utilization. ZenRobotics employs robotic systems equipped with sensors and AI to sort recyclables from construction and demolition waste. The system identifies and separates different materials, boosting recycling efficiency [25].
- *Smart Waste-Sorting Facilities:* IIoT technology can be integrated into waste-sorting facilities to monitor equipment efficiency and optimize workflows. Real-time data helps operators make informed decisions to improve sorting accuracy and throughput. TITECH, a TOMRA company, provides waste-sorting solutions with IIoT capabilities. Their systems use sensors and data analytics to optimize waste-sorting processes, leading to increased recycling rates [26].

Implementing IIoT solutions for smarter waste management and recycling optimization requires careful planning, integration of hardware and software, and consideration of data security and privacy. Additionally, collaboration between municipalities, waste management companies, technology providers, and regulatory bodies is crucial to ensure successful implementation and achieve the desired environmental and operational benefits.

13.2.2 Significant Role of the AIoT in Revolutionizing Waste Management and Recycling Optimization

The convergence of AI and the Internet of Things (IoT), often referred to as the Artificial Intelligence of Things (AIoT), has a significant role in revolutionizing waste management and recycling optimization. The AIoT combines real-time data from IoT devices with AI-driven insights to enhance decision-making and operational efficiency. Here's how AIoT is shaping smarter waste management and recycling, along with recent examples:

- *Dynamic Route Optimization:* AIoT systems analyze real-time data from IoT sensors on waste bins to optimize collection routes. AI algorithms consider factors like fill levels, traffic conditions, and historical data to create the most efficient collection schedules. Ecube Labs' CleanCUBE uses the AIoT to optimize waste collection routes based on real-time data. This has led to a reduction in collection frequency and vehicle emissions [27].
- *Waste Composition Analysis:* AIoT-enabled sensors provide real-time information on the composition of waste streams. AI algorithms process

this data to identify recyclable materials, leading to improved sorting and resource recovery. AMP Robotics utilizes the AIoT to analyze waste composition and control robotic sorting systems. Their technology enhances recycling by accurately identifying and sorting different materials [28].

- *Predictive Maintenance and Equipment Optimization:* AIoT systems predict equipment failures by analyzing data from IoT sensors on machinery. This enables proactive maintenance, reducing downtime and improving operational efficiency. Suez, a waste management company, employs AIoT for predictive maintenance of its recycling machinery. This approach has led to significant cost savings and improved equipment uptime [29].

- *Energy Management and Efficiency:* AIoT platforms analyze energy usage data from IoT devices in waste management facilities. AI algorithms identify energy-saving opportunities and optimize energy consumption. GreenQ, an AIoT platform, optimizes energy consumption in waste management facilities. By analyzing data from sensors, it helps reduce energy costs and environmental impact [30].

- *Real-time Monitoring and Reporting:* AIoT solutions provide real-time monitoring of waste processes, enabling better decision-making and compliance reporting. AI-driven analytics offer insights into operations and help achieve sustainability goals. Bin-e's smart waste bin uses the AIoT to recognize and categorize waste as it's disposed of. This data provides insights into waste generation patterns and helps improve recycling initiatives [31].

- *Behavioral Analysis and Public Awareness:* AIoT systems analyze data from smart bins and public spaces to understand waste disposal behaviors. This information can be used to develop targeted awareness campaigns and encourage responsible waste disposal. The "Bigbelly" smart waste system uses AIoT to analyze waste disposal patterns. This data informs cities about peak usage times and helps in planning waste collection [32].

The role of the AIoT in waste management and recycling optimization continues to expand, driven by advancements in AI algorithms, sensor technologies, and data analytics. These solutions enable more efficient use of resources, reduced environmental impact, and better decision-making for waste management operations [33].

13.2.3 COMPARISON OF THE IIoT AND THE AIoT IN THE CONTEXT OF SMARTER WASTE MANAGEMENT AND RECYCLING OPTIMIZATION

Comparison of the IIoT and the AIoT in the context of smarter waste management and recycling optimization, along with recent real-time examples listed in Table 13.4.

The IIoT and the AIoT are complementary in the context of waste management and recycling optimization. The IIoT provides the data foundation through sensor connectivity, while the AIoT adds value by applying AI algorithms to derive insights, optimize complex processes, and make intelligent decisions [34]. The choice between

TABLE 13.4

The IIoT and the AIoT Comparison in the Context of Smarter Waste Management and Recycling Optimization

Comparison	IIoT	AIoT
Data Utilization	Emphasizes data collection and real-time monitoring from devices and sensors.	Focuses on data analysis and decision-making using AI algorithms on IoT data.
Optimization	Primarily optimizes operational processes, such as waste collection routes and machinery maintenance.	Optimizes complex tasks like waste-sorting, energy management, and predictive maintenance through AI-driven insights.
Complex Analysis	Offers data for analysis, but the complexity of analysis might be limited.	Applies advanced analytics, machine learning, and AI algorithms to process complex data patterns.
Decision-making	Supports informed decision-making based on real-time data.	Enables more intelligent and automated decision-making by deriving insights from IoT data through AI.
Application Scope	Primarily focuses on enhancing operational efficiency and resource management.	Broadens the scope to include AI-driven tasks like waste-sorting optimization, energy management, and behavioral analysis.
Example	Enevo's smart bin monitoring for optimized waste collection routes.	AMP Robotics' recycling sorting uses AI to identify and sort recyclables accurately.

these approaches depends on the specific goals and challenges of waste management operations.

13.3 OPTIMIZING RECYCLING PROCESSES WITH INTELLIGENT SYSTEMS AND IIOT

By using the AIoT, waste management organizations can improve efficiency, accuracy, cost-effectiveness, and environmental sustainability. Here is a simple analogy to help you understand the concept and detailed architecture of AIoT, the layers shown in Figure 13.2.

Consider an industrial waste collection vehicle integrated with advanced sensors under the realm of Industrial Internet of Things and Artificial Intelligence of Things advancements [35]. These sensors have the capability to accurately measure the fill level of each waste bin. The vehicle is interconnected with a central AI-driven computer system that not only monitors the real-time location of the vehicle but also precisely records the volume of waste accumulated. Leveraging these data points, the AIoT system orchestrates the optimization of collection routes in real time. This

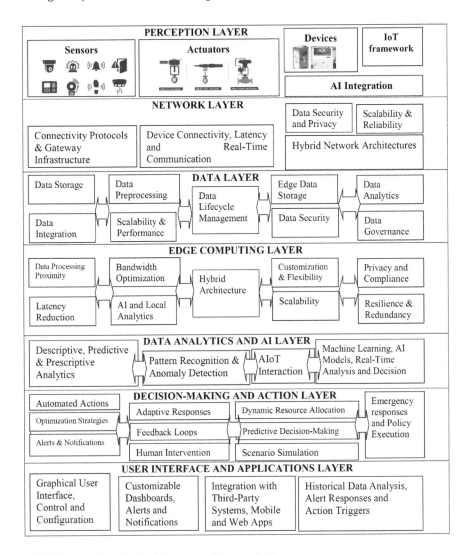

FIGURE 13.2 Detailed architecture and layers of AIoT

intelligent coordination ensures that the vehicle efficiently gathers the maximum waste within the minimum time span, thereby streamlining waste management operations.

13.3.1 Understanding AIoT and Real-Time Monitoring

- The AIoT can be used to collect and analyze data from smart bins, waste collection trucks, and other IoT devices. This data can be used to optimize waste collection routes, identify areas where waste is being generated, and prevent overflowing bins. AIoT can also be used to develop predictive models that can forecast future waste generation [36]. This information can be used to plan for future waste management needs and prevent waste from accumulating.

- *Predictive Maintenance and Resource Allocation:* Predictive maintenance can be used to predict when waste collection vehicles or other equipment are likely to need maintenance. This information can be used to schedule maintenance before problems occur, which can help to prevent breakdowns and reduce costs [37].

- *Resource Allocation:* Resource allocation can be used to optimize the allocation of resources, such as waste collection trucks and staff. This can help to ensure that resources are used efficiently and that waste is collected in a timely manner [37].

- *Customer Engagement for Sustainability:* Customers can be engaged in sustainability initiatives through a variety of channels, such as social media, email, and in-person events. Customers can be encouraged to reduce their waste generation, recycle and compost, and participate in other sustainability initiatives. Customers can also be provided with information about the waste management system and how they can help to improve its efficiency and sustainability [38].

- *Environmental Stewardship through the AIoT:* The AIoT can be used to monitor environmental conditions, such as air quality and water quality [39]. This information can be used to identify pollution sources and develop effective remediation strategies. AIoT can also be used to track the performance of waste management systems and identify areas where improvements can be made. This information can be used to improve the environmental sustainability of waste management.

- *The Path Forward:* Innovations and Collaborations: The field of the AIoT is rapidly evolving, and there are many new innovations and collaborations that are being developed. These innovations and collaborations have the potential to further improve the efficiency, sustainability, and effectiveness of waste management systems.

- *A Sustainable Future Powered by AIoT:* The AIoT, predictive maintenance, resource allocation, customer engagement, environmental stewardship, and innovations and collaborations are all important considerations for waste management systems. By incorporating these factors, we can create more efficient, sustainable, and effective waste management systems [38, 39].

13.3.2 Defining Objectives and Unveiling AIoT Applications for Sustainability

Envisioning a more environmentally sustainable future through the integration of Artificial Intelligence of Things (AIoT) requires a clear roadmap, and the journey begins with defining objectives that address key research questions. To chart our course, we must first determine what we aim to achieve—whether it involves curbing waste generation or enhancing efficiency. Simultaneously, we must consider strategies to safeguard the environment by minimizing waste output. Once our objectives are established, the groundwork for crafting effective strategies commences. The detailed flow chart and process of the AIoT/IIoT waste management system are shown in Figure 13.3.

The unveiling of AIoT applications for sustainability unveils a broad spectrum of possibilities. This innovative approach can significantly contribute to reducing waste generation by meticulously tracking waste levels and optimizing collection routes.

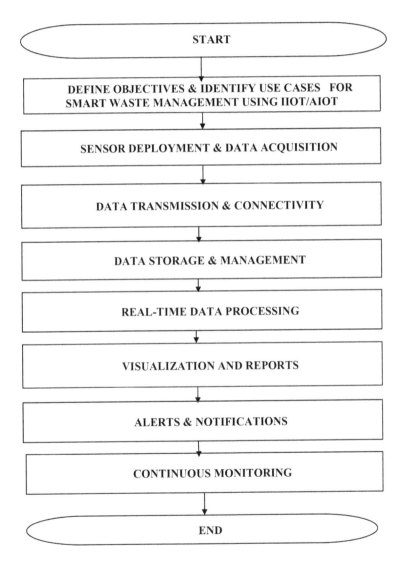

FIGURE 13.3 Flow chart and Process of AIoT/IIoT waste management system

Moreover, the potential to enhance operational efficiency is harnessed by predicting equipment malfunctions and proactively scheduling maintenance. Furthermore, environmental preservation is facilitated by continuously monitoring environmental parameters and swiftly identifying pollution sources.

In parallel, the engagement of customers plays an instrumental role in the success of sustainability initiatives. Effective channels such as social media, email communication, and interactive events can foster active participation. Customers can be encouraged to partake in practices that directly contribute to waste reduction, recycling, composting, and other sustainability endeavors.

By synergizing these pivotal elements within our waste management systems, we are poised to create a profound positive impact on both the environment and our communities. The journey toward a greener tomorrow, fueled by the potential of AIoT and IIoT technologies, becomes an attainable reality.

13.3.3 DEPLOYING SENSORS AND REAL-TIME DATA ACQUISITION FOR ENVIRONMENTAL INSIGHTS

- *Deploying Sensors:* The first step is to deploy sensors to collect data about the environment. These sensors can be used to measure a variety of factors, such as temperature, humidity, air quality, and noise levels [40].
- *Real-Time Data Acquisition:* The data collected by the sensors must be acquired in real time. This allows us to track changes in the environment and identify potential problems early on.
- *Environmental Insights:* The data acquired from the sensors can be used to gain insights into the environment [40]. This information can be used to improve environmental sustainability, such as reducing waste generation, improving energy efficiency, and protecting wildlife.

For example, in our waste management system, sensors can be used to measure the amount of waste in smart bins. This information can be used to optimize waste collection routes and prevent overflowing bins. The data can also be used to track the types of waste being generated, which can help to identify areas where waste reduction efforts can be focused.

By deploying sensors and acquiring real-time data, we can gain insights into the environment that can be used to improve environmental sustainability. Here are some additional benefits of deploying sensors and real-time data acquisition for environmental insights:

- Ultrasonic sensors are a type of sensor that uses sound waves to measure distance. They can be used to measure the amount of waste in smart bins, the distance between vehicles, and the level of noise pollution [41].

Here are some of the benefits of using ultrasonic sensors in waste management systems with real-time examples listed in Table 13.5.

TABLE 13.5
Benefits of Using Ultrasonic Sensors in Waste Management Systems with Real-Time Examples

Benefits of Ultrasonic sensors	Real-time examples
Accuracy and Reliability: Ultrasonic sensors are accurate and reliable, and they can be used to measure distances over a wide range.	In a smart waste management system, ultrasonic sensors are employed to accurately measure the fill level of waste bins. These sensors provide reliable data that enable waste collection vehicles to be dispatched only when bins are close to full capacity, optimizing collection routes and reducing unnecessary trips.
Cost-Effectiveness: Ultrasonic sensors are relatively inexpensive, which makes them a cost-effective option for waste management systems.	Municipalities seeking cost-effective waste monitoring solutions turn to ultrasonic sensors. By implementing these relatively inexpensive sensors across their waste bins, they can efficiently manage waste collection schedules, leading to reduced operational costs and optimized resource utilization.
Durability: Ultrasonic sensors are durable and can withstand harsh environmental conditions.	Waste-sorting facilities often operate in challenging environments with dust, debris, and varying weather conditions. Ultrasonic sensors, renowned for their durability, are adept at enduring these conditions, ensuring uninterrupted and reliable data collection for sorting processes.
Easy Installation Process: Ultrasonic sensors are easy to install, which makes them a convenient option for waste management systems.	A recycling company aiming to enhance its operational efficiency quickly integrates ultrasonic sensors into its bins. The simplicity of installation enables the company to deploy these sensors across multiple locations rapidly, facilitating real-time monitoring of fill levels without significant disruption.
Resource Optimization: Ultrasonic Sensors can be used to optimize the use of resources, such as water and energy. This can help to reduce environmental impact and save money.	A water treatment plant implements sensors to monitor water levels in reservoirs. By continuously tracking water levels and inflow rates, the plant optimizes its water distribution processes, reducing waste and ensuring a more efficient use of this precious resource.
Sustainable Development: Ultrasonic sensors can be used to track the progress of sustainable development initiatives which can be used to identify areas where improvements can be made and ensure that development is taking place in an environmentally responsible way.	A city embarks on sustainable development initiatives, including waste reduction and recycling programs. Sensors placed in key waste disposal areas track waste volumes and recycling rates over time. The data collected aids city planners in assessing the effectiveness of their initiatives and making informed decisions to drive further sustainable development efforts.

13.3.4 Seamless Connectivity in the AIoT/IIoT Ecosystem

Achieving seamless connectivity within the AIoT and IIoT ecosystem in smart waste management is essential for maximizing the efficiency, effectiveness, and responsiveness of waste management operations. This connectivity empowers stakeholders to harness the power of data, AI insights, and real-time communication to optimize resource allocation, reduce environmental impact, and transform waste management practices.

In the realm of smart waste management, achieving seamless connectivity within the AIoT and IIoT ecosystem is paramount. This connectivity fosters the efficient flow of data, insights, and actions, resulting in optimized waste management operations. Here's an exploration of how seamless connectivity is achieved in this context:

- *Real-time Data Exchange:* In a smart waste management system, sensors embedded in waste bins continuously gather data such as fill levels, temperature, and location. These sensors are seamlessly connected to the central AIoT/IIoT platform, enabling real-time data exchange. This instant flow of information empowers decision-making processes and ensures timely actions.
- *Interconnected Devices:* Various devices within the ecosystem, such as waste collection vehicles, sorting facilities, and central management systems, are interconnected through a network of communication protocols. This interconnectedness enables devices to communicate, collaborate, and share data effortlessly.
- *Edge-to-Cloud Connectivity:* Edge devices, like sensors and gateways, are equipped to perform localized data processing and analysis. They seamlessly communicate with cloud-based servers, where more extensive data processing, machine learning, and AI-powered insights occur. This synergy between edge and cloud ensures optimized performance and reduced latency.
- *Wireless Communication:* Wireless communication technologies, including Wi-Fi, cellular networks, and low-power communication protocols like LoRaWAN, enable devices to communicate without physical tethering. This wireless connectivity ensures flexibility and scalability within waste management operations.
- *Data Aggregation:* Gateways play a crucial role in aggregating data from multiple sensors or edge devices. This aggregated data is then transmitted to the cloud or central management system, ensuring that comprehensive insights are available for informed decision-making.
- *Seamless Handoff:* Devices, such as waste collection trucks, can seamlessly transition between different communication networks as they move through different areas. This handoff ensures uninterrupted connectivity and data transmission throughout the waste management process.
- *Remote Monitoring and Control:* Waste management personnel can remotely monitor and control connected devices and operations through intuitive user interfaces. This remote access streamlines operations, minimizes manual interventions, and ensures efficient resource allocation.

- *Data Security and Privacy:* While ensuring connectivity, robust security measures are implemented to protect sensitive data. Encryption, authentication, and access controls safeguard data as it traverses between devices and the cloud.
- *Scalability and Flexibility:* The AIoT/IIoT ecosystem is designed to be scalable, accommodating a growing number of devices and data streams. New sensors, devices, and functionalities can be seamlessly integrated into the existing ecosystem without disruption.

Here are some additional benefits of seamless connectivity in the AIoT ecosystem [42]:

- *Reduced Costs:* Seamless connectivity can help to reduce costs by eliminating the need for manual data entry and by improving the efficiency of operations.
- *Increased Efficiency:* Seamless connectivity can help to increase efficiency by providing real-time data and insights, and by automating tasks.
- *Improved Decision-Making:* Seamless connectivity can help to improve decision-making by providing timely and accurate data.
- *Enhanced Customer Experience:* Seamless connectivity can help to enhance the customer experience by providing a more convenient and efficient way to interact with the system.

13.4   STRATEGIES FOR EFFECTIVE DATA MANAGEMENT IN THE ERA OF AIOT/IIOT

Effective data management is crucial in the era of the AIoT and IIoT to ensure that the massive volumes of data generated by connected devices are organized, processed, and utilized efficiently. Here are strategies for effective data management in this context, along with examples shown in Table 13.6.

13.4.1   TRANSFORMING DATA STREAMS INTO ACTIONABLE INSIGHTS THROUGH REAL-TIME ANALYSIS

By incorporating transforming data streams into actionable insights through real-time analysis, you can improve the efficiency and effectiveness of your waste management system. This can lead to reduced costs, improved environmental sustainability, and improved public health. Some ways of implementing this are as follows:

- Use sensors to collect data from smart bins. The sensors can measure the weight and type of waste in the bins, as well as the temperature and humidity. This data can be collected in real time and used to track waste levels and identify potential problems [43].
- Use machine learning to analyze the data. Machine learning algorithms can be used to identify patterns in the data and make predictions about future

TABLE 13.6

Are Strategies for Effective Data Management with Examples

Strategy	Examples
Data Collection and Aggregation: Collect and aggregate data from various IoT devices and sensors to create a comprehensive dataset for analysis.	In a smart waste management system, data from smart waste bins, collection trucks, sorting facilities, and environmental sensors are aggregated to provide a holistic view of waste generation, collection efficiency, and environmental conditions.
Data Pre-processing and Cleaning: Clean and pre-process raw data to remove noise, outliers, and missing values, ensuring data accuracy and quality.	In an IIoT system for manufacturing, sensor data collected from machines is pre-processed to eliminate erroneous readings caused by sensor glitches or temporary malfunctions.
Data Storage and Archival: Choose appropriate storage solutions to securely store and archive collected data for future analysis and compliance.	A utility company uses a cloud-based storage system to retain historical data from smart energy meters. This data can be later analyzed to identify consumption patterns and make informed decisions.
Data Integration: Integrate data from diverse sources to gain a comprehensive view and discover correlations that might not be apparent from individual datasets.	In smart agriculture, data from soil moisture sensors, weather stations, and crop growth monitoring devices are integrated to optimize irrigation schedules and improve crop yields.
Real-time Data Streaming: Utilize real-time data streaming technologies to process and analyze data as it is generated, enabling timely decision-making.	A smart city traffic management system processes real-time data from vehicle sensors to dynamically adjust traffic signal timings and alleviate congestion.
Data Security and Privacy: Implement robust security measures, including encryption and access controls, to safeguard sensitive IoT data from unauthorized access.	A healthcare facility secures patient health data collected from wearable devices by encrypting the data during transmission and storage, ensuring compliance with privacy regulations.
Data Analytics and AI Integration: Leverage analytics and AI models to derive insights and predictions from collected data, enabling data-driven decision-making.	A smart retail system analyzes customer movement data from in-store beacons to optimize store layouts and product placements, enhancing customer engagement.

waste levels. This information can be used to optimize waste collection routes and avoid overflowing bins [44].

- Provide insights to waste collectors. The waste collectors can be given access to real-time data about waste levels and collection routes. This information can help them plan their routes more efficiently and ensure that they are collecting the right amount of waste [45].
- Provide feedback to customers. Customers can be given access to information about waste levels in their area. This information can help them to reduce their own waste production and make better recycling choices.

Here are some additional benefits of transforming data streams into actionable insights through real-time analysis:

- *Increased Visibility:* The system can provide real-time visibility into waste levels and collection activities. This can help to identify potential problems early on and take corrective action.
- *Improved Decision-Making:* The system can provide data-driven insights that can be used to make better decisions about waste management. This can lead to more efficient and effective waste management practices.
- *Enhanced Customer Service:* The system can provide customers with information about waste levels and collection schedules. This can help to improve customer satisfaction and reduce complaints.

13.4.2   Visualizing Sustainability: Impactful AIoT-Driven Insights

By incorporating visualizing sustainability: impactful AIoT-driven insights, you can make your waste management system more sustainable and help to educate others about the importance of environmental protection [46, 47].

- Use dashboards and visualizations to track progress toward sustainability goals. This could include tracking the amount of waste recycled, the number of trees planted, or the reduction in greenhouse gas emissions.
- Use predictive analytics to identify areas where sustainability improvements can be made. For example, you could use machine learning to predict which areas are most likely to experience flooding, so that you can take steps to mitigate the damage.
- Use social media to share sustainability stories and successes. This can help to raise awareness of sustainability issues and inspire others to take action.

13.5   PAVING THE WAY FOR SUSTAINABLE SOLUTIONS: ENVISIONING EFFICIENT WASTE MANAGEMENT WITH THE IIOT AND THE AIOT

In today's changing world the convergence of the IIoT and AIoT offers possibilities for transforming waste management practices. This opens up avenues for solutions that can reshape our environment's future. By integrating IIoT and AIoT technologies into waste management systems we can achieve efficiency, real-time monitoring and data-driven decision-making. These advancements lead to a conscious and resource-efficient approach.

The connectivity and sensor capabilities of the IIoT enable us to track and manage waste in time throughout the disposal cycle. Smart sensors in waste bins can monitor fill levels optimizing collection routes and schedules. As a result, we can reduce fuel consumption and carbon emissions. A prime example is Barcelona's waste management system, which successfully reduced collection truck routes by 25%. This demonstrates the impact of the IIoT on improving waste management efficiency [48, 49].

On the other hand, the AIoT's analytical capabilities contribute to maintenance and informed decision-making. Machine learning algorithms help predict equipment failures in advance allowing maintenance measures to prevent disruptions in waste processing plants. Veolia, a waste management company has successfully implemented AI-driven maintenance resulting in a 40% reduction in downtime and significant cost savings.

By leveraging these advancements in IIoT and AIoT technologies, within waste management systems we can revolutionize how we handle waste while prioritizing sustainability.

The merging of the IIoT and the AIoT also enables the implementation of sorting and recycling processes. Visual recognition systems powered by AI can effectively. Separate recyclable materials, from waste streams leading to recycling rates and reduced contamination. ZenRobotics, a company that specializes in robotic waste-sorting utilizes AI to detect and collect materials resulting in a significant enhancement, in recycling efficiency [49].

REFERENCES

1. Chander B, Pal S, De D, Buyya R. Artificial intelligence-based internet of things for industry 5.0. 2022. 10.1007/978-3-030-87059-1_1
2. Ferronato N, Torretta V. Waste mismanagement in developing countries: A review of global issues. *International Journal of Environmental Research and Public Health*. 2019 Mar 24;16(6):1060. doi: 10.3390/ijerph16061060. PMID: 30909625; PMCID: PMC6466021
3. Malik PK, Sharma R, Singh R, Gehlot A, Satapathy SC, Alnumay WS, Pelusi D, Ghosh U, Nayak J. Industrial internet of things and its applications in industry 4.0: state of the art. *Computer Communications*. 2021; 166:125–139. https://doi.org/10.1016/j.comcom .2020.11.016
4. Oke AE, Kineber AF, Akindele O, Ekundayo D. Determining the stationary barriers to the implementation of radio-frequency identification (RFID) technology in an emerging construction industry. *Journal of Engineering, Design and Technology*, Vol. ahead-of-print No. ahead-of-print. 2023. https://doi.org/10.1108/JEDT-07-2022-0348
5. Vishnu S, Ramson SRJ, Rukmini MSS, Abu-Mahfouz AM. Sensor-based solid waste handling systems: A survey. *Sensors (Basel)*. 2022 Mar 18;22(6):2340. https://doi.org /10.3390/s22062340. PMID: 35336511; PMCID: PMC8949905
6. Martikkala A, Mayanti B, Helo P, Lobov A, Ituarte IF. Smart textile waste collection system – Dynamic route optimization with IoT. *Journal of Environmental Management*. 2023; 335:117548. https://doi.org/10.1016/j.jenvman.2023.117548
7. Saha L, Kumar V, Tiwari J, Rawat S, Singh J, Bauddh K. Jiwan Singh, Kuldeep Bauddh, Electronic waste and their leachates impact on human health and environment: Global ecological threat and management. *Environmental Technology & Innovation*. 2021; 24:102049. https://doi.org/10.1016/j.eti.2021.102049
8. Vishnu S, Ramson SRJ, Rukmini MSS, Abu-Mahfouz AM. Sensor-based solid waste handling systems: A survey. *Sensors*. 2022; 22(6):2340. https://doi.org/10.3390/ s22062340

9. Ada E, Ilter HK, Sagnak M, Kazancoglu Y. Smart technologies for collection and classification of electronic waste. *International Journal of Quality & Reliability Management*, Vol. ahead-of-print No. ahead-of-print. 2023. https://doi.org/10.1108/IJQRM-08-2022-0259

10. Karthik M, Sreevidya L, Nithya Devi R, Thangaraj M, Hemalatha G, Yamini R. An efficient waste management technique with IoT based smart garbage system. *Materials Today: Proceedings*. 2023; 80(3):3140–3143. https://doi.org/10.1016/j.matpr.2021.07.179

11. Kumar NM, Mohammed MA, Abdulkareem KH, Damasevicius R, Mostafa SA, Maashi MS, Chopra SS. Artificial intelligence-based solution for sorting COVID-related medical waste streams and supporting data-driven decisions for smart circular economy practice. *Process Safety and Environmental Protection*. 2021; 152:482–494. https://doi.org/10.1016/j.psep.2021.06.026

12. Yang Y, Li H, Zhang H, Zuo Y, Liu W. A review of sustainable technologies in industry 4.0 and their application in industry 5.0. *Journal of Cleaner Production*. 2021; 318:128502.

13. Rojek I, Jasiulewicz-Kaczmarek M, Piechowski M, Mikołajewski D. An artificial intelligence approach for improving maintenance to supervise machine failures and support their repair. *Applied Sciences*. 2023; 13(8):4971. https://doi.org/10.3390/app13084971

14. Mousavi S, Hosseinzadeh A, Golzary A. Challenges, recent development, and opportunities of smart waste collection: A review. *Science of The Total Environment*. 2023; 886:163925. https://doi.org/10.1016/j.scitotenv.2023.163925

15. Omar MF, Termizi AA, Zainal D, Wahap NA, Ismail NM, Ahmad N. Implementation of spatial smart waste management system in Malaysia. *IOP Conference Series: Earth and Environmental Science*. 2016; 37:012059. 10.1088/1755-1315/37/1/012059

16. Lu X, Pu X, Han X. Sustainable smart waste classification and collection system: A bi-objective modeling and optimization approach. *Journal of Cleaner Production*. 2020; 276:124183.https://doi.org/10.1016/j.jclepro.2020.124183

17. Syed AS, Sierra-Sosa D, Kumar A, Elmaghraby A. IoT in smart cities: A survey of technologies, practices and challenges. *Smart Cities*. 2021; 4(2):429–475. https://doi.org/10.3390/smartcities4020024

18. Sozoniuk M, Park J, Lumby N. Investigating residents' acceptance of mobile apps for household recycling: A case study of New Jersey. *Sustainability*. 2022; 14(17):10874. https://doi.org/10.3390/su141710874

19. Oluwadipe S, Garelick H, McCarthy S, Purchase D. A critical review of household recycling barriers in the United Kingdom. *Waste Management & Research*. 2022 Jul;40(7):905–918. https://doi.org/10.1177/0734242X211060619. Epub 2021 Nov 20. PMID: 34802336; PMCID: PMC9109241

20. Qian C, Gao Y, Chen L. Green supply chain circular economy evaluation system based on industrial internet of things and blockchain technology under ESG concept. *Processes*. 2023; 11(7):1999. https://doi.org/10.3390/pr11071999

21. Farjana M, Fahad AB, Alam SE, Islam MM. An IoT- and cloud-based E-waste management system for resource reclamation with a data-driven decision-making process. *IoT*. 2023; 4(3):202–220. https://doi.org/10.3390/iot4030011

22. Mirani AA, Velasco-Hernandez G, Awasthi A, Walsh J. Key challenges and emerging technologies in industrial IoT architectures: A review. *Sensors*. 2022; 22(15):5836. https://doi.org/10.3390/s22155836

23. Javaid M, Haleem A, Singh RP, Suman R, Gonzalez ES. Understanding the adoption of industry 4.0 technologies in improving environmental sustainability. *Sustainable Operations and Computers*. 2022; 3:203–217. https://doi.org/10.1016/j.susoc.2022.01.008.

24. Khan R, Kumar S, Srivastava AK, Dhingra N, Gupta M, Bhati N, Kumari P. Machine learning and IoT-based waste management model. *Computational Intelligence and Neuroscience.* 2021, 11. Article ID 5942574. https://doi.org/10.1155/2021/5942574

25. Wilts H, Garcia BR, Garlito RG, Gómez LS, Prieto EG. Artificial intelligence in the sorting of municipal waste as an enabler of the circular economy. *Resources.* 2021; 10(4):28. https://doi.org/10.3390/resources10040028

26. Popova Y, Sproge I. Decision-making within smart city: Waste sorting. *Sustainability.* 2021; 13(19):10586. https://doi.org/10.3390/su131910586

27. Huh J-H, Choi J-H, Kyungryong S. smart trash bin model design and future for smart city. *Applied Sciences.* 2021; 11:4810. 10.3390/app11114810

28. Sarc R, Curtis A, Kandlbauer L, Khodier K, Lorber KE, Pomberger R. Digitalisation and intelligent robotics in value chain of circular economy oriented waste management – A review. *Waste Management.* 2019; 95:476–492. https://doi.org/10.1016/j.wasman.2019.06.035

29. Taha MF, ElMasry G, Gouda M, Zhou L, Liang N, Abdalla A, Rousseau D, Qiu Z. Recent advances of smart systems and Internet of Things (IoT) for aquaponics automation: a comprehensive overview. *Chemosensors.* 2022; 10(8):303. https://doi.org/10.3390/chemosensors10080303

30. Anh Khoa T, Phuc CH, Lam PD, Nhu LM, Trong NM, Phuong NT, Dung NV, Tan Y N, Nguyen HN, Duc DN. Waste management system using IoT-based machine learning in university. *Wireless Communications and Mobile Computing.* 2020:13. Article ID 6138637. https://doi.org/10.1155/2020/6138637

31. Bano A, Din IU, Al-Huqail AA. AIoT-based smart bin for real-time monitoring and management of solid waste. *Scientific Programming.* 2020:13. Article ID 6613263. https://doi.org/10.1155/2020/6613263

32. Ghahramani M, Zhou M, Molter A, Pilla F. (2021). IoT-based route recommendation for an intelligent waste management system. *IEEE Internet of Things Journal.* 1–1. 10.1109/JIOT.2021.3132126

33. Pardini K, Rodrigues JJPC, Diallo O, Das AK, de Albuquerque VHC, Kozlov SA. A smart waste management solution geared towards citizens. *Sensors.* 2020; 20(8):2380. https://doi.org/10.3390/s20082380

34. Chen CH, Liu CT. 3.5-tier container-based edge computing architecture. *Computers & Electrical Engineering.* 2021; 93:107227. https://doi.org/10.1016/j.compeleceng.2021.107227

35. Sasikumar A, Ravi L, Kotecha K, Saini JR, Varadarajan V, Subramaniyaswamy V. Sustainable smart industry: A secure and energy efficient consensus mechanism for artificial intelligence enabled industrial internet of things. *Computational Intelligence and Neuroscience.* 2022:12. Article ID 1419360. https://doi.org/10.1155/2022/1419360

36. Abuga D, Raghava NS. Real-time smart garbage bin mechanism for solid waste management in smart cities, *Sustainable Cities and Society.* 2021; 75:103347. https://doi.org/10.1016/j.scs.2021.103347

37. Fang B, Yu J, Chen Z, Osman AI, Farghali M, Ihara I, Hamza EH, Rooney DW, Yap PS. Artificial intelligence for waste management in smart cities: A review. *Environmental Chemistry Letters.* 2023 May 9:1–31. https://doi.org/10.1007/s10311-023-01604-3. Epub ahead of print. PMID: 37362015; PMCID: PMC10169138

38. Fiksel J, Sanjay P, Raman K. Steps toward a resilient circular economy in India. *Clean Technologies and Environmental Policy.* 2021; 23(1):203–218. https://doi.org/10.1007/s10098-020-01982-0. Epub 2020 Nov 11. PMID: 33199980; PMCID: PMC7655910

39. Asha P, Natrayan LB, Geetha BT, Beulah JR, Sumathy R, Varalakshmi G, Neelakandan S. IoT enabled environmental toxicology for air pollution monitoring using AI techniques. *Environmental Research.* 2021; 205. 112574. 10.1016/j.envres.2021.112574

40. Jo J, Jo B, Kim J, Kim S, Han W. Development of an IoT-Based indoor air quality monitoring platform. *Journal of Sensors*. 2020:14. Article ID 8749764. https://doi.org /10.1155/2020/8749764

41. Melakessou F, Kugener P, Alnaffakh N, Faye S, Khadraoui D. Heterogeneous sensing data analysis for commercial waste collection. *Sensors (Basel)*. 2020 Feb 12;20(4):978. https://doi.org/10.3390/s20040978. PMID: 32059411; PMCID: PMC7071114

42. Hou KM, Diao X, Shi H, Ding H, Zhou H, de Vaulx C. Trends and challenges in AIoT/IIoT/IoT implementation. *Sensors*. 2023; 23(11):5074. https://doi.org/10.3390/ s23115074

43. Lingaraju AK, Niranjanamurthy M, Bose P, Acharya B, Gerogiannis VC, Kanavos A, Manika S. IoT-based waste segregation with location tracking and air quality monitoring for smart cities. *Smart Cities*. 2023; 6(3):1507–1522. https://doi.org/10.3390/ smartcities6030071

44. Chen X. Machine learning approach for a circular economy with waste recycling in smart cities. *Energy Reports*. 2022; 8:3127–3140. https://doi.org/10.1016/j.egyr.2022.01 .193

45. Fang B, Yu J, Chen Z. et al. Artificial intelligence for waste management in smart cities: A review. *Environmental Chemistry Letters*. 21:1959–1989 (2023). https://doi.org /10.1007/s10311-023-01604-3

46. Abubakar IR, Maniruzzaman KM, Dano UL, AlShihri FS, AlShammari MS, Ahmed SMS, Al-Gehlani WAG, Alrawaf TI. Environmental sustainability impacts of solid waste management practices in the global south. *International Journal of Environmental Research and Public Health*. 2022 Oct 5;19(19):12717. https://doi.org /10.3390/ijerph191912717. PMID: 36232017; PMCID: PMC9566108

47. Acosta LA, Maharjan P, Peyriere HM, Mamiit RJ. Natural capital protection indicators: Measuring performance in achieving the sustainable development goals for green growth transition. *Environmental and Sustainability Indicators*. 2020; 8:100069. https://doi.org/10.1016/j.indic.2020.100069

48. Vishnu S, Ramson SRJ, Senith S, Anagnostopoulos T, Abu-Mahfouz AM, Fan X, Srinivasan S, Kirubaraj AA. IoT-enabled solid waste management in smart cities. *Smart Cities*. 2021; 4(3):1004–1017. https://doi.org/10.3390/smartcities4030053

49. Pardini K, Rodrigues JJPC, Diallo O, Das AK, de Albuquerque VHC, Kozlov SA. A smart waste management solution geared towards citizens. *Sensors*. 2020; 20(8):2380. https://doi.org/10.3390/s20082380

14 Solar Energy Forecasting
Enhancing Reliability and Precision

Rithika Badam, B. V. Ramana Murthy, Srinath Doss

14.1 INTRODUCTION

The emergence of solar energy marks the beginning of a fresh era in the worldwide pursuit of sustainable and environmentally friendly energy solutions. Its vast and renewable potential holds the promise of a cleaner and more sustainable future. Yet, harnessing the full potential of solar energy poses distinct challenges, particularly in forecasting energy production, optimizing maintenance procedures, and ensuring the reliability of solar power equipment. This chapter embarks on an ambitious journey into the realm of solar energy forecasting and optimization, forging a path guided by a fusion of statistical and machine-learning techniques. Our aim is to introduce a groundbreaking hybrid forecasting model, meticulously designed to yield highly precise predictions of solar energy production. This model takes into account various variables such as sensor data and weather conditions, time duration, season, geographical location, and solar energy data [1]. Its potential impact goes beyond merely predicting energy output; it holds the potential to optimize solar energy utilization and enhance overall energy efficiency.

Furthermore, this chapter delves into the critical domain of solar panel maintenance. By closely scrutinizing the performance and health of solar energy equipment—including solar panels, inverters, and batteries—through conditional monitoring, this work identifies potential issues, faults, or inefficiencies. Timely maintenance actions can then be initiated, reducing downtime and ensuring uninterrupted energy generation [21]. A pivotal theme throughout this chapter is the centrality of data-driven decision-making. We prioritize the thorough examination and presentation of gathered solar energy data, utilizing easily understandable visual representations like graphs, charts, and dashboards. These visual tools enable users to make well-informed decisions regarding energy usage and equipment upkeep, ultimately promoting more effective and environmentally sustainable energy management practices [3].

Moreover, we thoroughly explore the integration of solar energy into existing power grids. This endeavor encompasses the study of grid demand patterns, the effective management of excess energy, and the evaluation of solar energy's impact on

DOI: 10.1201/9781032642789-14

grid stability. It underscores the pivotal role that solar energy can play in the broader context of energy infrastructure. To provide a solid foundation for this multifaceted project, we propose a sophisticated system architecture. This architecture seamlessly integrates data acquisition, pre-processing, forecasting, maintenance optimization, equipment anomaly detection, and visualization/reporting components. It forms the cornerstone upon which this work's implementation and execution rest, ensuring the realization of its objectives.

This chapter represents a holistic endeavor with a focused mission to advance solar energy forecasting and optimization [11]. Our objectives are firmly focused on tackling the urgent issues of precise solar energy production forecasting and ensuring the dependability of equipment. Through harmonious blending of statistical and machine-learning techniques, our hybrid forecasting model aspires to revolutionize the precision of energy production predictions. Concurrently, our meticulous examination of panel maintenance practices and equipment monitoring seeks to detect anomalies and faults, guaranteeing uninterrupted energy generation while reducing operational costs [2]. The proposed system architecture serves as a guiding beacon, charting the course for data-driven progress in solar energy technology. Together, these initiatives significantly advance the larger goal of adopting cleaner and more sustainable energy options, laying the foundation for a future that is both environmentally friendly and economically viable.

14.2   LITERATURE REVIEW

In the domain of solar energy prediction and equipment supervision, various research initiatives and systems have arisen to address the challenges associated with precise prediction modeling and the detection of irregularities.

The study "Solar Energy Prediction with Decision Tree Regressor" (2021) makes a significant contribution by creating a predictive system for solar energy generation. This system relies on weather-related characteristics and employs a Decision Tree Regressor [9]. It is significant in the exploration of predictive modeling for solar energy generation. However, it falls short in discussing fault detection, which is a crucial aspect of solar energy systems. Nevertheless, it aligns with our research objectives, offering insights into predictive modeling techniques for solar energy, which we can incorporate into our hybrid model. Solar power generation prediction by using the K-Nearest Neighbor Method (2019) research adds to the field by comparing the K-Nearest Neighbor (KNN) method with Artificial Neural Networks (ANN) for predicting solar power generation [10]. While it predominantly focuses on prediction modeling and doesn't delve into equipment monitoring, it contributes to our understanding of predictive modeling techniques in the context of solar energy production. This knowledge can be integrated into our research aimed at developing a hybrid model for solar energy prediction.

The article "A Two-Step Approach to Solar Power Generation Prediction Based on Weather Data Using Machine Learning" (2019) introduces a two-step modeling process for solar energy generation prediction through machine-learning algorithms [1]. Although it introduces an innovative approach, it provides limited insights into equipment monitoring. Nevertheless, it enriches our understanding of predictive modeling techniques for solar energy production, which can complement our hybrid model development. The introductory review titled "Fault Detection and Diagnosis Approaches in Power Generation Plants—A Perspective on the Indian Power Generation Sector" (2018) provides a comprehensive summary of fault detection techniques applicable to power generation facilities, with a specific emphasis on the Indian power generation sector. While it does not specifically address solar energy systems, it provides valuable context and insights into fault detection methodologies that are pertinent to our study, particularly for monitoring solar energy equipment.

The study "An Effective Evaluation of Fault Detection in Solar Panels" (2021) conducts a comprehensive evaluation of fault detection techniques for solar panels [15]. Its emphasis on rigorous evaluation rather than predictive modeling is valuable. However, it has limited discussion of predictive modeling. Nonetheless, it significantly contributes to our research by shedding light on the critical aspect of fault detection in solar panels, which is essential for equipment monitoring. The article "Forecasting Solar Energy Production Using Machine Learning" (2022) focuses on forecasting solar energy production through machine-learning techniques [2]. While it doesn't extensively address equipment monitoring, it offers valuable insights into techniques like machine learning for solar power prediction, which can complement our hybrid model's predictive component.

The study "Analysis of Solar Power Generation Forecasting through Machine Learning Techniques" (2021) offers an in-depth examination of machine-learning methodologies for forecasting solar power generation [11]. While it predominantly concentrates on predictive modeling and does not delve into equipment monitoring, it contributes to our understanding by presenting a variety of machine-learning methods for predicting solar energy. Another research work, "Solar Power Prediction Using Machine Learning" (2023) is centered around the development of machine-learning models for forecasting solar power production [12]. While it doesn't extensively discuss equipment monitoring, it aligns with our research by exploring machine-learning-based approaches to predict solar power generation, which can be seamlessly integrated into our hybrid model.

The work "A Review of Data Mining and Solar Power Prediction" (2016) delves into data mining applied for forecasting solar energy, offering a broader perspective [13]. While it doesn't extensively discuss equipment monitoring, it provides valuable insights into data mining techniques relevant to our research, broadening our understanding of data-driven approaches in solar energy prediction. The study "Solar Power Prediction via Support Vector Machine and Random Forest" (2018) compares Support Vector Machine (SVM) and Random Forest models for solar power prediction, primarily focusing on predictive modeling [26]. Although it doesn't emphasize equipment monitoring, it contributes valuable insights into approaches for prediction, supporting the predictive component of our hybrid model.

In summary, the reviewed studies contribute various insights to the field of solar energy prediction, predictive modeling, equipment monitoring, and fault detection. Each study offers a unique perspective, and their collective findings can be leveraged to develop a comprehensive understanding and a robust hybrid model for solar energy prediction.

TABLE 14.1

An Overview of the Literature Review

Study Title	Main Focus	Key Contribution	Limitations	Relevance
Solar Energy Prediction using Decision Tree Regressor [9]	Energy prediction using Decision Tree Regressor	Developed a strong prediction system for solar energy generation based on weather attributes	Limited discussion of fault detection	Investigates predictive modeling for solar energy, similar to our hybrid model
Solar power generation prediction by using the K-Nearest Neighbor Method [10]	Solar power generation prediction using K-Nearest Neighbor Method	Comparison of KNN with ANN for solar power generation prediction	Focused on prediction modeling, not equipment monitoring	Explores predictive modeling for solar power generation, aligning with our objectives
An Effective Evaluation of Fault Detection in Solar Panels [15]	Evaluation of fault detection techniques for solar panels	Comprehensive evaluation of fault detection methods	Limited emphasis on predictive modeling	Addresses the essential aspect of fault detection in solar panels, aligning with our equipment monitoring component
Forecasting Solar Energy Production Using Machine Learning [2]	Solar energy production forecasting using machine-learning techniques	Utilization of machine-learning models for solar energy production prediction	Lacks extensive discussion on equipment monitoring	Provides insights into machine-learning techniques for solar energy prediction, aligning with our hybrid model
Analysis of solar power generation forecasting using machine-learning techniques [11]	Analysis of solar power generation forecasting using machine-learning techniques	Comprehensive analysis of machine-learning techniques for solar power generation forecasting	Limited focus on equipment monitoring	Offers a detailed exploration of machine-learning approaches for solar energy prediction, supporting our predictive model component

The literature review presented in Table 14.1 summarizes various authors' works, including an overview of their methods and the results they obtained.

14.3 METHODOLOGY

In this section, we explore the approach used to enhance solar energy prediction and equipment surveillance. This method encompasses several stages, starting from data gathering and pre-processing to model creation, analysis, and reporting. This

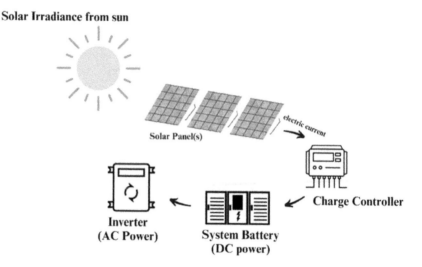

Solar Irradiance from sun

Solar Panel(s)

electric current

Charge Controller

Inverter
(AC Power)

System Battery
(DC power)

FIGURE 14.1 Data acquisition

systematic approach forms the foundation for achieving our work's objectives, contributing significantly to the advancement of solar energy technology. The proposed architecture encompasses the integration of various components and algorithms to achieve accurate solar energy production forecasting and equipment anomaly detection. The architecture consists of the following key elements:

a. *Data Acquisition:* The work begins with the acquisition of two derived datasets retrieved from Kaggle: one containing power generation readings and the other containing weather data, which are later merged together after working on time attributes [5]. Figure 14.1 represents the process of data acquisition, which includes using solar panels for utilizing solar energy and converting it into electrical energy that is stabilized using charge controllers that are sent to batteries and inverters as DC and AC power, respectively. These datasets, which include attributes such as DATE_TIME, SOURCE_KEY, DC_POWER, PLANT_ID, AC_POWER, TOTAL_YIELD, DAILY_YIELD, AMBIENT_TEMPERATURE, MODULE_TEMPERATURE, and IRRADIATION, serve as the foundation for the analysis and modeling stages.

b. *Data Pre-Processing:* The acquired datasets undergo a pre-processing stage to handle missing values, outliers, and data inconsistencies. This includes data cleaning, normalization, and feature engineering. The pre-processing step ensures the datasets are in a suitable format for subsequent analysis and modeling. Figure 14.2 represents the architecture of this proposed model depicting the following stages of machine-learning modeling and prediction [5].

c. *Hybrid Forecasting Model:* The core of the architecture involves the development of a hybrid forecasting model. This model combines statistical and

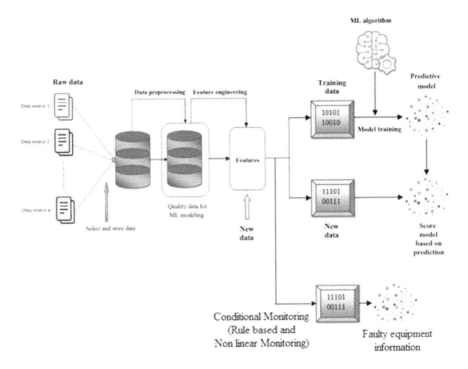

FIGURE 14.2 Model architecture of prediction of solar energy and fault detection in equipment

machine-learning techniques such as Random Forest, Decision Tree, KNN, and Linear Regression. By utilizing historical weather patterns and power generation readings, the hybrid model aims to provide accurate short-term solar energy production forecasts [1].

d. *Equipment Anomaly Detection and Monitoring:* Another crucial component of the architecture is the equipment anomaly detection and monitoring module. By leveraging sensor data and analyzing power generation patterns, the system identifies anomalies and detects equipment in need of immediate attention or replacement [19]. Proactive monitoring techniques are employed to minimize downtime, reduce maintenance costs, and ensure the reliability of solar power systems.

e. *Visualization and Reporting:* The final stage of the architecture involves visualizing and reporting the results obtained from the forecasting model, panel maintenance analysis, and equipment monitoring [17]. Visualizations, such as plots, charts, and dashboards, are generated to provide a clear understanding of the findings. A comprehensive report summarizes the outcomes, implications, and recommendations derived from the models.

The proposed architecture integrates data acquisition, pre-processing, a hybrid forecasting model, panel maintenance optimization, equipment anomaly detection, and visualization/reporting components. This architecture enables accurate solar energy production forecasting, optimized panel maintenance practices, and proactive equipment monitoring [5]. It forms the framework for the implementation and execution of the models, facilitating the achievement of the chapter's objectives.

The objective of this chapter is to introduce a forecasting model for solar energy generation. This model takes into account various factors including weather conditions, time of day, season, geographical location, and historical solar energy data to make accurate predictions [11]. This model could help optimize solar energy usage and improve energy efficiency (Figure 14.3). Implementing conditional monitoring involves overseeing the operational status and well-being of solar energy equipment, including solar panels, inverters, and batteries. This form of monitoring is instrumental in the detection of possible problems, malfunctions, or suboptimal performance, thus facilitating prompt maintenance and minimizing operational disruptions [22]. The examination of the amassed solar energy data and its presentation in a user-friendly format, such as through graphs, charts, or dashboards, equips users with the information they need to make knowledgeable choices regarding energy consumption and equipment upkeep. Exploring ways to integrate solar energy into existing power grids effectively. This could involve studying grid demand patterns, managing excess energy, and examining the impact of solar energy on grid stability.

The efficient conversion of solar energy into electricity is a crucial challenge in the widespread adoption of renewable energy sources. This chapter addresses this problem by developing an advanced hybrid forecasting model that combines statistical and machine-learning techniques to accurately predict future solar energy production. The primary objective is to overcome the limitations of traditional forecasting methods and provide reliable predictions for the next few days, taking into account historical weather pattern changes [1]. Furthermore, it also seeks to investigate the significance of panel cleaning and maintenance practices in optimizing solar energy

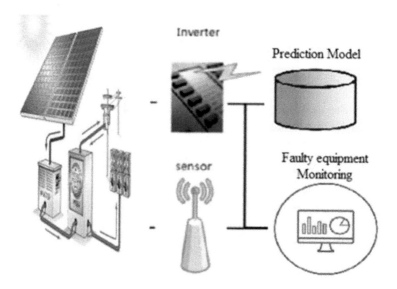

FIGURE 14.3   Solar power prediction and equipment monitoring

production. Proper care and cleaning of solar panels are essential for maintaining their efficiency and performance, but the optimal maintenance frequency and impact on energy generation need to be thoroughly understood.

In addition to forecasting and maintenance optimization, it designs an effective anomaly detection system using sensor data and power generation patterns. The system will be capable of identifying equipment anomalies and faulty components promptly, ensuring the smooth functioning of the solar power system and minimizing downtime. The project's problem statement revolves around three key challenges: accurate solar energy forecasting, optimization of solar panel maintenance practices, and the implementation of an efficient anomaly detection system. By tackling these challenges, it makes a valuable contribution to the progress of solar energy technology. This, in turn, enhances the dependability and effectiveness of solar power systems, and encourages the adoption of sustainable and eco-friendly energy solutions [13].

14.3.1 DATA STUDY

In this section there is an emphasis on the careful review of attributes and data considered for the study. The objective is to comprehend the dataset's intrinsic properties, including its distribution, structure, kind of data, and possible importance. This meticulous review not only strengthens the study's credibility but also establishes the groundwork for well-informed decision-making based on an in-depth knowledge of the data and its characteristics.

14.3.2 MODEL BUILDING

14.3.2.1 Linear Regression Model

Linear regression is a widely utilized and effective technique for forecasting AC power generation in solar power systems for several reasons. One key rationale is that linear regression presupposes a linear association between the independent variables (e.g., solar irradiance, temperature, etc.) and the dependent variable (AC power generation). While the relationship may not be strictly linear, linear regression can still capture the general trend and provide a reasonable approximation. These regression models are relatively simple and interpretable. The coefficients assigned to each independent variable in the model represent the magnitude and direction of their influence on AC power generation [27]. The models are computationally efficient and can handle large datasets and a high number of independent variables. Training and predicting with linear regression models typically require less computational resources compared to more complex algorithms, making them practical for real-time or large-scale applications.

The linear regression model makes predictions for AC power generation by leveraging the linear connection between independent variables and the dependent variable. The mathematical representation of this model can be expressed as follows:

$$AC\ Power\ Generation = \beta 0 + \beta 1 * X1 + \beta 2 * X2 + ... + \beta n * Xn + \varepsilon ...(1) \quad (14.1)$$

TABLE 14.2

Detailed Analysis of Attributes

Plant Generation Data		Weather Sensor Data	
Attribute	**Range**	**Attribute**	**Range**
DATE_TIME Each observation includes a date and time stamp, with data recorded at 15-minute intervals.	May 15, 2020, to June 18, 2020	DATE_TIME Each observation includes a date and time stamp, with data recorded at 15-minute intervals.	May 15, 2020, to June 18, 2020
SOURCE_KEY In this file, the source key corresponds to the identifier for the inverter, often referred to as the inverter ID.	unique values	SOURCE_KEY In this file, the source key corresponds to the identifier for the inverter, often referred to as the inverter ID.	unique values
DC_POWER The value in this context represents the amount of DC power generated by the inverter (identified by the source key) during each 15-minute interval.	0 to 14.5kv.	AMBIENT_TEMPERATURE This data point refers to the ambient temperature at the plant site.	20.4 to 35.3
AC_POWER The value provided here signifies the amount of AC power generated by the inverter, which is identified by the source key, during each 15-minute interval.	0 to 1.41kvi.	MODULE_TEMPERATURE The recorded temperature reading corresponds to the specific module, or solar panel, attached to the sensor panel.	18.1 to 65.5
DAILY_YIELD The "Daily Yield" represents the cumulative total of power generated up to a specific point in time on that particular day. It reflects the sum of power generated throughout the day until the given time.	0 to 9.16k	IRRADIATION The provided information represents the level of irradiation for the given 15-minute interval. Irradiation typically refers to the amount of solar energy or sunlight received at a specific location during that time period.	0 to 1.22
TOTAL_YIELD The given data refers to the total cumulative yield of the inverter up to the specific point in time. It reflects the sum of the yield or power generated by the inverter until that moment.	6.18 m to 7.85 m	PLANT_ID The "Plant ID" is a unique identifier that remains consistent throughout the entire file. It serves to designate the specific plant or facility associated with the data.	4.14 m to 4.14 m

In this equation:

- AC Power Generation represents the dependent variable that we aim to predict.
- $X1$, $X2$, and Xn are the independent variables used for prediction.
- $\beta\,0$, $\beta\,1$, $\beta\,2$, and βn are the coefficients that need to be estimated for each independent variable.
- ε symbolizes the error term, accounting for the variability that the model does not explain.

Linear regression provides numerous benefits that render it a valuable tool in the realm of data analysis. It provides a straightforward and easily interpretable model, making it accessible even to those without extensive statistical expertise. Secondly, linear regression is computationally efficient, particularly well-suited for handling large datasets, which is crucial in today's data-driven landscape [14]. Additionally, it offers valuable insights into the relationship between independent and dependent variables, helping us understand the impact of changes in one variable on another.

However, linear regression has its limitations. It presupposes a linear connection between variables, an assumption that might not be applicable in all real-world situations, possibly resulting in less precise predictions. Additionally, linear regression is susceptible to outliers and influential data points, which can have a notable impact on the model's accuracy. Furthermore, it has limitations in dealing with intricate non-linear relationships among variables [8]. In summary, linear regression is most suitable for datasets with a small number of independent variables and a clear linear relationship with the dependent variable. It is especially valuable when

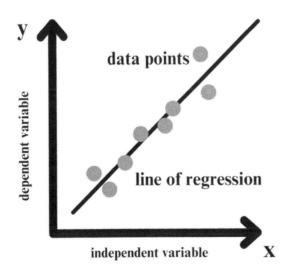

FIGURE 14.4 Linear regression plot

interpretability is a priority, but researchers should be cautious of its assumptions and limitations when applying it to their data analysis tasks.

14.3.2.2   K-Nearest Neighbor

K-Nearest Neighbor is a popular algorithm used for prediction tasks, including predicting AC power generation. Here are a few reasons why KNN can be a suitable choice for this prediction task. KNN is a non-parametric algorithm, which means it doesn't make strong assumptions about the functional form of the relationship between the independent variables and the dependent variable. In the context of predicting AC power generation, where the relationship between the predictors (such as solar irradiance, temperature, and time of day) and power generation may not be linear, KNN can be more flexible in capturing complex and non-linear patterns. KNN is based on the principle of localized learning. It assumes that similar data points tend to have similar target values [10]. In the case of predicting AC power generation, nearby data points with similar weather conditions (such as solar irradiance and temperature) are likely to have similar power generation. It is adaptable to changing patterns and relationships in the data. It does not require retraining the entire model when new data becomes available.

The KNN model predicts AC power generation considering the average of the K-nearest neighbors' values. Mathematical computation of the same can be summarized as follows:

$$AC\ Power\ Generation = \left(\frac{1}{K}\right) * \Sigma(y_i)...(2)$$
                                                                                              (14.2)

In this context:

- AC Power Generation signifies the value we are predicting.
- y_i represents the AC power generation of the ith nearest neighbor.

The K-Nearest Neighbor algorithm is a versatile machine-learning method that offers various advantages. First, it is a non-parametric model capable of capturing complex relationships within data. This flexibility allows it to adapt to various types of datasets without assuming a specific functional form of the relationship between variables. Furthermore, KNN has the capability to accommodate both numerical and categorical variables, rendering it well-suited for diverse data types. Nonetheless, KNN is accompanied by its share of limitations. Firstly, it can be computationally intensive when applied to sizable datasets, as it involves calculating distances between data points for every prediction. Second, the selection of the number of neighbors (K) holds great significance and requires thoughtful deliberation, as an ill-suited choice can result in suboptimal outcomes [10].

Furthermore, KNN is sensitive to the scale of the variables and the choice of distance metric, which can impact its performance and effectiveness. In terms of its scope, KNN is particularly well-suited for datasets with a moderate number of observations and variables. K-Nearest Neighbor excels in situations characterized by non-linear connections between independent and dependent variables, demonstrating its ability to effectively capture these complex patterns. Moreover, KNN finds its application in situations where local patterns or clusters in the data are crucial for making accurate predictions or classifications, emphasizing its utility in tasks where understanding localized relationships is essential.

14.3.2.3 Decision Tree Model

Decision trees are often the preferred method for predictive modeling due to their ease of understanding and effectiveness. The primary objective of a decision tree is to divide a dataset into smaller segments, ensuring a thorough examination of the outcomes of each branch while identifying nodes that may require further scrutiny. This property makes decision trees amenable to validation through statistical tests, establishing them as a transparent and accountable modeling approach [9]. The decision tree model forecasts AC power generation by iteratively dividing the data based on the values of independent variables. This process involves constructing a tree comprising decision and leaf nodes, with each node representing a criterion for splitting. Predictions are made by traversing the tree according to the values of independent variables.

Decision trees offer several advantages. First, they are non-parametric, capable of capturing complex relationships and interactions in data, rendering them versatile for diverse scenarios. Second, their interpretability allows users to visualize the decision-making process, gaining insights. Thirdly, they are robust to outliers and missing data, making them suitable for datasets with incomplete or noisy information. However, decision trees have drawbacks. They can overfit, particularly when the tree is deep and complex, hindering generalization to unseen data. They are sensitive to minor data changes, potentially leading to different tree structures and affecting model stability. Moreover, their ability to handle continuous variables and complex interactions is somewhat limited, necessitating more advanced modeling approaches.

Decision trees excel in datasets with a mix of numerical and categorical variables, making them versatile in terms of data types [9]. They shine in scenarios with non-linear relationships and interactions between independent and dependent variables, effectively capturing intricate patterns. Additionally, they are valuable when interpretability and the ability to visualize the decision-making process are crucial, making them valuable tools for scenarios requiring transparency and insight into model behavior.

14.3.2.4 Random Forest Model

Random Forest is a popular machine-learning algorithm that can be well-suited for predicting AC power generation in solar power systems. Here are some reasons why Random Forest is often considered a good choice for this type of prediction. Random Forest can effectively capture non-linear relationships between the independent variables (e.g., solar irradiance, ambient temperature, etc.) and the dependent variable (AC power generation) [26]. Solar power generation is influenced by various factors, and their interactions often exhibit complex, non-linear patterns. The capacity of Random Forest to model these non-linear relationships makes it well-suited for capturing the intricate dynamics of solar power generation. When dealing with datasets that encompass numerous independent variables or features, Random Forest can effectively manage high-dimensional data. It possesses the ability to handle a substantial number of features without succumbing to overfitting, rendering it suitable for datasets containing a broad spectrum of input variables.

Random Forest, as an ensemble learning method, amalgamates multiple decision trees to formulate predictions. This ensemble strategy enhances the model's stability and robustness, thereby reducing the risk of overfitting. Through the aggregation of predictions from multiple trees, Random Forest can furnish more precise and dependable forecasts for AC power generation. The Random Forest model forecasts AC power generation by consolidating the predictions from multiple decision trees. Each tree is trained on a distinct subset of the data and a randomly selected subset of the variables. The final prediction is derived by averaging the predictions of all the individual trees. Random Forest is a standard ensemble learning algorithm renowned for several significant advantages. First, as an ensemble model that integrates multiple decision trees, it effectively mitigates overfitting and enhances the model's resilience [28]. Second, Random Forest can handle high-dimensional data and a large number of variables, making it suitable for complex datasets with many features. Thirdly, it provides feature importance measures, allowing users to gain insights into the importance of different variables in making predictions.

However, Random Forest also comes with certain disadvantages. It can be computationally expensive, particularly when using a large number of trees in the ensemble, which may require significant computational resources. Additionally, Random Forest lacks the interpretability of a single decision tree, as it can be challenging to understand the combined decision-making process of multiple trees. Moreover, it may not perform well with sparse or highly imbalanced datasets, as the majority class can dominate the learning process. In terms of its scope, Random Forest is well-suited for datasets with a large number of observations and variables, making it suitable for complex and high-dimensional data. It excels in situations where there are complex non-linear relationships and interactions between independent and dependent variables, allowing it to capture intricate patterns effectively. Furthermore, Random Forest is applicable when robustness and generalization performance are crucial, as it mitigates over fitting and enhances the model's ability to make accurate predictions on unseen data.

Why is Random Forest the best model for this dataset?

i. *Accuracy:* Random Forest has the potential to provide high prediction accuracy. By aggregating predictions from multiple decision trees, it can capture complex relationships between independent variables and AC power generation, leading to accurate predictions. Nonetheless, the model's actual accuracy hinges on various factors, including data quality, feature selection, hyperparameter tuning, and several other critical considerations.

ii. *Robustness:* Random Forest is robust to outliers and missing data. It can handle noisy or incomplete datasets without significantly affecting its performance. This robustness makes Random Forest suitable for real-world datasets where data quality and completeness can be a concern.

iii. *Non-Linearity:* Random Forest exhibits the capacity to capture non-linear associations between independent variables and AC power generation [29]. Given that solar power generation is affected by numerous factors, many of which involve non-linear relationships, Random Forest's proficiency in modeling such connections renders it a well-suited choice for this prediction task.

iv. *Ensemble Learning:* Random Forest operates as an ensemble learning technique, amalgamating multiple decision trees [29]. This ensemble strategy serves to mitigate the risk of overfitting and enhances the model's ability to generalize from the data. By aggregating predictions from multiple trees, Random Forest can provide more stable and reliable predictions.

14.3.3 Mechanism

In this chapter, several crucial mechanisms for managing and analyzing solar power plant data are outlined. The process begins with data collection and pre-processing, where information from two solar power plants in India is gathered, encompassing power generation data and sensor readings [2]. To ensure data quality, pre-processing steps are applied, addressing missing values, outliers, and inconsistencies within the raw data. The core of the study revolves around a hybrid forecasting model, which is developed using a combination of statistical and machine-learning techniques. Historical weather patterns and solar energy production data serve as the foundation for training the model. This process empowers the model to grasp intricate relationships between changes in weather conditions and the generation of solar energy [1]. Once adequately trained, the model gains the capability to predict solar energy production for upcoming days, which can be invaluable for efficient energy management.

Simultaneously, a panel maintenance study is conducted to analyze panel efficiency, performance data, and maintenance practices. Through this analysis, correlations between maintenance activities and energy output are identified, shedding light on the impact of regular panel cleaning and maintenance on energy production. This study emphasizes the importance of proactive care for maintaining optimal energy generation from solar panels. Furthermore, an anomaly detection system is introduced, utilizing sensor data and historical power generation patterns [13]. Machine-learning algorithms are employed, taking into account the imbalanced nature of anomaly data. The system establishes criteria for identifying anomalies and faulty equipment, enabling swift detection and intervention, which is vital for minimizing downtime and ensuring the reliability of the solar power infrastructure.

To validate the effectiveness of these mechanisms, a comprehensive results and analysis phase is executed. The forecasting model is rigorously validated using appropriate metrics to assess its accuracy in predicting solar energy production.

The findings from the panel maintenance study are presented, highlighting the significance of regular cleaning and care practices in maintaining and optimizing energy output. Additionally, the anomaly detection system's performance is evaluated, measuring its effectiveness in promptly identifying equipment anomalies and contributing to the overall reliability and efficiency of the solar power plants [23]. The mechanism it involves a systematic approach, initially data collection and pre-processing to model development, through analysis, and then reporting. It integrates various tools and techniques to address the challenges of solar energy forecasting, maintenance optimization, and anomaly detection, contributing to the advancement of solar energy technology and promoting sustainable energy solutions.

The model-building section is integral to our research work, contributing significantly to the advancement of solar energy technology. By developing a significant hybrid forecasting model, we can accurately predict solar energy production, enabling better energy planning and grid integration [25]. Furthermore, our panel maintenance study sheds light on the importance of regular care, maximizing solar panel efficiency and performance. The implementation of an effective anomaly detection system ensures quick identification of equipment issues, minimizing downtime and enhancing system reliability. This comprehensive approach to model building empowers us to achieve our work's objectives, ultimately promoting the reliability, efficiency, and sustainability of solar power systems.

14.4 IMPLEMENTATION, RESULTS, AND DISCUSSION

The implementation of the project involves the practical steps and procedures to execute the proposed architecture and achieve the desired outcomes. It's important to adapt the implementation steps to the specific requirements and constraints of your project, such as the available tools, programming languages, and datasets. Regular testing, validation, and iteration are essential throughout the implementation process to ensure the accuracy and reliability of the results.

14.4.1 PREDICTIVE MODELING: FORECASTING SOLAR POWER GENERATION

The flow of implementation of this section of project is as follows as depicted in Figure 14.5. The data is collected from static or dynamic sources like Kaggle, GitHub, Open websites like government sites or public sources or through dynamic ways like surveys. After data is collected the data is pre-processed as follows:

i. *Data Cleaning:* remove null values, and redundant and inconsistent data.
ii. *Data Merging:* Integrate and combine the two datasets, i.e., power generation and weather generation data.
iii. *Feature Scaling and Feature Extraction:* Scale the data and extract the significant features etc.
iv. *Perform EDA:* EDA stands for Exploratory Data Analysis which is used for summarizing data and extracting values like mean, sum, average and many more from the attributes. Figure 14.6 represents the correlation between different attributes of the dataset [24].

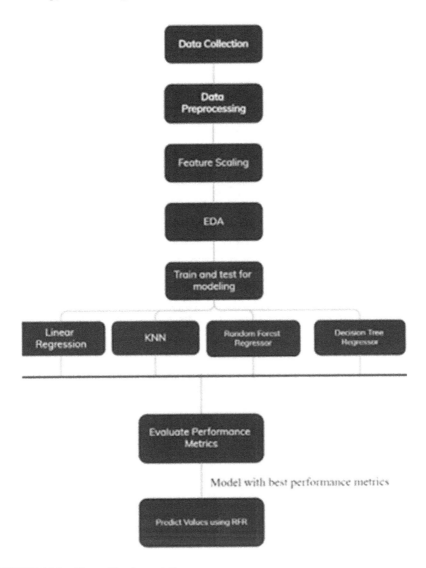

FIGURE 14.5   Flow of implementation

Data Collection and Pre-Processing: Collect the power generation readings and weather data from the two solar power plants in India. Clean the datasets by handling missing values, outliers, and inconsistencies [13]. Normalize the data and performing feature engineering to prepare it for further analysis.

Visualization and Reporting: Generate visualizations, such as plots, charts, or dashboards, to present the results of the forecasting model, panel maintenance analysis, and equipment monitoring. Create a comprehensive report summarizing the findings, implications, and recommendations [23]. Communicate the results effectively, highlighting the accuracy of the forecasts, the significance of panel maintenance,

	Unnamed: 0	DC_POWER	AC_POWER	DAILY_YIELD	TOTAL_YIELD	AMBIENT_TEMPERATURE	MODULE_TEMPERATURE	IRRADIATION
Unnamed: 0	1.000000	-0.016338	-0.016333	0.035585	0.179783	-0.170281	-0.064143	-0.020969
DC_POWER	-0.016338	1.000000	0.999996	0.076710	0.004055	0.703796	0.954692	0.991305
AC_POWER	-0.016333	0.999996	1.000000	0.076626	0.004043	0.704035	0.954810	0.991260
DAILY_YIELD	0.035585	0.076710	0.076626	1.000000	0.007277	0.489709	0.203702	0.071937
TOTAL_YIELD	0.179783	0.004055	0.004043	0.007277	1.000000	-0.036532	-0.014713	-0.004981
AMBIENT_TEMPERATURE	-0.170281	0.703796	0.704035	0.489709	-0.036532	1.000000	0.843456	0.702218
MODULE_TEMPERATURE	-0.064143	0.954692	0.954810	0.203702	-0.014713	0.843456	1.000000	0.959346
IRRADIATION	-0.020969	0.991305	0.991260	0.071937	-0.004981	0.702218	0.959346	1.000000

FIGURE 14.6 Correlation of the attributes of the dataset

and the importance of proactive equipment monitoring. For instance, Figures 14.7 and 14.8 show the DC power generated and irradiation for the data recorded [16].

Prediction: Hybrid Forecasting Model Implementation: Split the pre-processed dataset into training and testing sets. Implement the selected algorithms (Random Forest, Decision Tree, KNN, and Linear Regression) to develop the hybrid forecasting

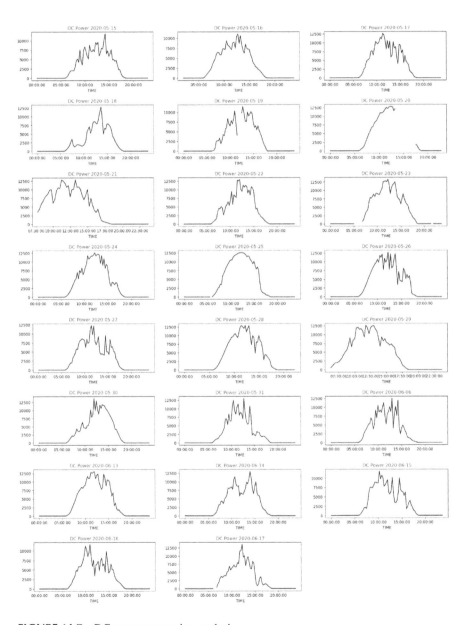

FIGURE 14.7 DC power generation analysis

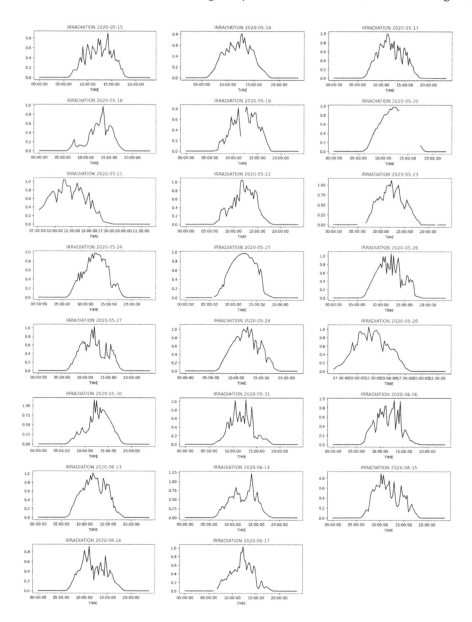

FIGURE 14.8 Irradiation analysis plots during the day

model. Train the model using the training data, considering the historical weather patterns and power generation readings [7]. Fine-tune the model parameters and evaluate its performance using appropriate evaluation metrics. Generate solar energy production forecasts for the upcoming days using the trained model.

Performance Evaluation: In the context of predicting solar power generation, these evaluation metrics can be used to assess the accuracy and performance of the models. Lower values of MAE, MSE, and RMSE indicate better accuracy, while a higher value of R-squared suggests a better fit of the model to the data [23]. Additionally, the Confusion Matrix is not directly applicable to regression tasks as it is primarily used for classification tasks where the prediction involves assigning samples to specific classes. In regression, the focus is on the continuous prediction of the target variable rather than class labels.

14.4.2 EQUIPMENT MONITORING: FAULT DETECTION IN EQUIPMENT

Equipment Anomaly Detection and Monitoring: Utilize sensor data and power generation patterns to detect anomalies and identify equipment in need of attention. Implement anomaly detection algorithms or techniques to identify deviations from normal operating conditions. This metric reflects the efficiency of our photovoltaic panel lines in converting sunlight into DC power [5]. Any anomalies in this conversion process signify potential issues with the functioning of our photovoltaic panel lines. Our dataset evidently displays instances where certain inverters received no DC power despite ample sunlight for power generation. It's apparent that there are equipment malfunctions present in our data.

A. Rule-Based Fault Detection

Throughout the data exploration process, we have identified a simple technique for identifying faulty equipment: When no power is recorded at the inverter during typical daylight hours, we can make an inference or identify equipment malfunctions [18]. To facilitate this identification, we introduce a new column labeled "STATUS." As illustrated in Figure 14.9, this column displays equipment performing adequately in blue and malfunctioning equipment in red, thereby highlighting irregularities in

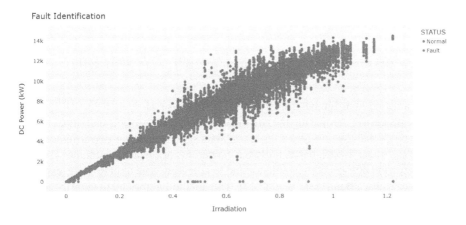

FIGURE 14.9   Fault Identification using "STATUS"

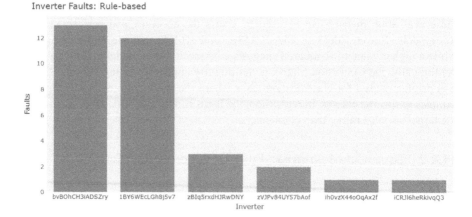

FIGURE 14.10   Faults in the inverters identified through a rule-based technique

the conversion of solar energy to electricity, particularly indicating issues with photovoltaic panel lines [17]. In Figure 14.10, we further illustrate faults in the inverters.
Our data unequivocally reveals instances where certain inverters did not receive
DC power even when ample sunlight was available for power generation, signaling
apparent equipment malfunctions within our dataset.

    B.   Fault Detection with Regression Models
      i.   Linear Model: A first attempt at predicting DC power from irradiance
         by assuming a linear relationship

$$P(t) = a + b \cdot E(t)$$

With the generated DC power $P(t)$, irradiance $E(t)$, and coefficients a, b.

      ii. *Non-Linear Model:* As per Hooda et al. (2018), the generated power of a
         photovoltaic cell can be described using a non-linear equation.

$$P(t) = lE(t)\left(1 - m\left(T(t) + \frac{E(t)}{800} * (n - 20) - 25\right) - oln\big(E(t)\big)\right)$$

With irradiance $E(t)$, Temperature $T(t)$ and coefficients l, m, n, o.

    In the process of comparing the two models, we can assess their individual residu-
als. It appears that the non-linear model exhibits slightly superior performance compared to the linear model, particularly during periods of elevated irradiance [19]. NL
Fault Detection utilizes both irradiance and temperature data to predict the expected
DC power using a non-linear model [15]. This method allows us to identify further
deviations by comparing the actual DC power with the predicted values. These additional anomalies serve as indications of equipment functioning below expectations
or requiring maintenance.

14.5 CONCLUSION AND FUTURE SCOPE

This chapter tackles essential issues related to the prediction and optimization of solar energy, with a primary emphasis on improving the reliable incorporation of renewable energy sources into the global energy framework. The shift toward renewable energy, especially solar power, is vital to combat the adverse impacts of climate change and decrease our dependence on finite fossil fuels [4]. The outcomes and insights obtained from this research endeavor make a substantial contribution to the progression of solar energy technology and lay the groundwork for a more environmentally friendly and sustainable future. The driving force behind this chapter originates from the pressing necessity to address limitations in solar energy prediction and optimization, ensuring its smooth integration into the existing energy infrastructure [11]. Precise solar energy prediction holds paramount importance for effective energy planning and seamless grid integration. The developed hybrid forecasting model, which combines statistical and machine-learning techniques, demonstrated promising results in accurately predicting solar energy production. By leveraging historical weather patterns and power generation data, the model achieved improved precision in short-term solar energy production predictions, enabling better resource allocation and decision-making processes [6]. Furthermore, the investigation into the significance of panel maintenance and equipment monitoring was instrumental in optimizing solar energy generation. Proactive monitoring techniques allowed for the early detection of anomalies and faulty equipment, leading to reduced downtime, minimized maintenance costs, and improved system reliability. The study emphasizes the importance of regular cleaning and maintenance to ensure the long-term sustainability and economic viability of solar power systems [29]. The chapter opens up several avenues for future research and development. These include the integration of advanced machine-learning techniques, deep learning techniques incorporation of real-time data, development of smart monitoring systems, optimization of maintenance schedules, validation and generalization of models, integration of external factors, and long-term performance analysis of solar power systems [3]. By exploring these areas of future scope, this chapter can continue to contribute to the advancement of solar energy technology, enhance forecasting accuracy, optimize maintenance practices, and facilitate the adoption of clean and sustainable energy solutions [20]. This journey toward a more sustainable future is driven by innovation and research, and this chapter represents a meaningful step in that direction.

REFERENCES

1. Kim, S.-G., Jung, J.-Y., & Sim, M. K., "A two-step approach to solar power generation prediction based on weather data using machine learning," *Sustainability*, vol. 11, no. 5, p. 1501, 2019.
2. Mohanavel, V., Vennila, C., Titus, A., Sudha, T. S., Sreenivasulu, U., Reddy, N. P. R., Jamal, K., Lakshmaiah, D., Jagadeesh, P., & Belay, A., Forecasting solar energy production using machine learning, *International Journal of Photoenergy*, pp. 1–7, 2022.
3. Alharkan, H., Habib, S., & Islam, M., "Solar power prediction using dual stream CNN-LSTM architecture," *Sensors*, vol. 23, no. 2, p. 945, 2023.

4. Kim, E., Akhtar, M. S., & Yang, O. B., "Designing solar power generation output forecasting methods using time series algorithms," *Electric Power Systems Research*, vol. 216, p. 109073, 2023.

5. Zhu, H., Zhang, B., Song, W., Dai, J., Lan, X., & Chang, X., "Power-weighted prediction of photovoltaic power generation in the context of structural equation modeling," *Sustainability*, vol. 15, no. 14, p. 10808, 2023.

6. Kaur, D., Islam, S. N., Mahmud, M. A., Haque, M. E., & Anwar, A., "A VAE-Bayesian deep learning scheme for solar power generation forecasting based on dimensionality reduction," *Energy and Ai*, 14, p. 100279, 2023.

7. Zheng, J., Du, J., Wang, B., Klemeš, J. J., Liao, Q., & Liang, Y., "A hybrid framework for forecasting power generation of multiple renewable energy sources," *Renewable and Sustainable Energy Reviews*, vol. 172, p. 113046, 2023.

8. Han, G., Tan, S., & Zhang, Z., "Load regulation application of university campus based on solar power generation forecasting," *Archives of Electrical Engineering*, pp. 429–441, 2023.

9. Rahul, A., Gupta, A., Bansal, A., & Roy, K., "Solar energy prediction using decision tree regressor," in *2021 5th International Conference on Intelligent Computing and Control Systems (ICICCS)*, pp. 489–495, Madurai, 2021, doi: 10.1109/ICICCS51141.2021.9432322.

10. Ramli, N. A., Abdul Hamid, M. F., & Azhan, N. H., "Solar power generation prediction by using k-nearest neighbor method," *AIP Conference Proceedings*, vol. 2129, 2019, doi: 10.1063/1.5118124.

11. Anuradha, K., Deekshitha Erlapally, G., Karuna, V., Srilakshmi, V., & Adilakshmi, K., "Analysis of solar power generation forecasting using machine learning techniques," in *E3S Web of Conferences*, vol. 309, p. 01163, EDP Sciences, 2021.

12. Subramanian, E., Karthik, M. M., Krishna, G. P., Prasath, D. V., & Kumar, V. S., "Solar power prediction using Machine learning," arXiv Preprint ArXiv:2303.07875, 2023.

13. Yesilbudak, M., Çolak, M., & Bayindir, R., "A review of data mining and solar power prediction," in *IEEE International Conference on Renewable Energy Research and Applications (ICRERA)*, pp. 1117–1121, IEEE, 2016.

14. Long, H., Zhang, Z., & Su, Y., "Analysis of daily solar power prediction with data-driven approaches," *Applied Energy*, vol. 126, pp. 29–37, 2014.

15. Dhanraj, J. A., Mostafaeipour, A., Velmurugan, K., Techato, K., Chaurasiya, P. K., Solomon, J. M., Gopalan, A., & Phoungthong, K., "An effective evaluation on fault detection in solar panels," *Energies*, vol. 14, no. 22, p. 7770, 2021.

16. Loschi, H. J., Iano, Y., León, J., Moretti, A., Conte, F. D., & Braga, H., "A review on photovoltaic systems: Mechanisms and methods for irradiation tracking and prediction," *Smart Grid and Renewable Energy*, vol. 6, no. 7, p. 187, 2015.

17. Haba, C.-G., "Monitoring solar panels using machine learning techniques," in *8th International Conference on Modern Power Systems (MPS)*, pp. 1–6, IEEE.

18. Zahraoui, Y., Alhamrouni, I., Hayes, B. P., Mekhilef, S., & Korõtko, T., "System-level condition monitoring approach for fault detection in photovoltaic systems," in *Fault Analysis and its Impact on Grid-Connected Photovoltaic Systems Performance*, pp. 215–254, 2022.

19. Triki-Lahiani, A., Bennani-Ben Abdelghani, A., & Slama-Belkhodja, I., "Fault detection and monitoring systems for photovoltaic installations: A review," *Renewable and Sustainable Energy Reviews*, vol. 82, pp. 2680–2692, 2018.

20. Luk, P. C. K., Lai, L. L., & Tong, T. L., "GA optimisation of rule base in a fuzzy logic control of a solar power plant," in *DRPT2000. International Conference on Electric Utility Deregulation and Restructuring and Power Technologies. Proceedings (Cat. No. 00EX382)*, pp. 221–225, IEEE.

21. Prema, V., & Rao, K. U., "Development of statistical time series models for solar power prediction," *Renewable Energy*, vol. 83, pp. 100–109, 2015.
22. Asrari, A., Wu, T. X., & Ramos, B., "A hybrid algorithm for short-term solar power prediction—Sunshine state case study," *IEEE Transactions on Sustainable Energy*, vol. 8, no. 2, pp. 582–591, 2016.
23. Gutiérrez, L., Patiño, J., & Duque-Grisales, E., "A comparison of the performance of supervised learning algorithms for solar power prediction," *Energies*, vol. 14, no. 15, p. 4424, 2021.
24. Hossain, M. R., Oo, A. M. T., & Ali, A. B. M. S., "The combined effect of applying feature selection and parameter optimization on machine learning techniques for solar power prediction," *American Journal of Energy Research*, vol. 1, no. 1, pp. 7–16, 2013.
25. Mishra, S., Tripathy, L., Satapathy, P., Dash, P. K., & Sahani, N., "An efficient machine learning approach for accurate short term solar power prediction," in *International Conference on Computational Intelligence for Smart Power System and Sustainable Energy (CISPSSE)*, pp. 1–6, IEEE, 2020.
26. Yen, C.-F., Hsieh, H.-Y., Su, K.-W., Yu, M.-C., & Leu, J.-S., "Solar power prediction via support vector machine and random forest," in *E3S Web of Conferences*, vol. 69, p. 01004, 2018.
27. Tsai, W. C., Tu, C. S., Hong, C. M., & Lin, W. M., "A review of state-of-the-art and short-term forecasting models for solar PV power generation," 2023. doi: 10.20944/preprints202305.1534.v1
28. Alamaniotis, M., & Karagiannis, G., "Toward smart energy systems: The case of relevance vector regression models in hourly solar power forecasting," in *Fusion of Machine Learning Paradigms: Theory and Applications*, pp. 119–127, Cham: Springer International Publishing, 2023.
29. Solano, E. S., & Affonso, C. M., "Solar irradiation forecasting using ensemble voting based on machine learning algorithms," *Sustainability*, vol. 15, no. 10, p. 7943, 2023.

Index

Milton Keynes UK
Ingram Content Group UK Ltd.
UKHW031128141024
449569UK00006B/359